DISABILITY AND
THE FAMILY LIFE CYCLE

DISABILITY
AND THE
FAMILY LIFE CYCLE

LAURA E. MARSHAK
MILTON SELIGMAN
FRAN PREZANT

BASIC
BOOKS

A Member of the Perseus Books Group

Published by Basic Books,
A Member of the Perseus Books Group

A CIP catalog record for this book is available from the Library of Congress.
ISBN 0-465-01632-4

00 01 02 03 ❖/RRD 10 9 8 7 6 5 4 3 2

This book is dedicated with great love and gratitude
to Ed, Nathaniel, Reuben, and Eli
—L.M.

This book is affectionately dedicated
to my mother, Irma Seligman
—M.S.

To Jennifer, Jason, and Bob—
my constant reminders that strong families are maintained
and nourished by love, commitment, hard work,
and a good sense of humor—
and to my parents for their love
—F.P.

Contents

Preface

If we draw a line as to how much of a life we can live, we all lose.
—Leigh Campbell-Earl in Disability Rag ReSource, 1993, p. 10

Quality of life has been described as "the degree to which the person enjoys the important possibilities of his or her life" (Woodwill, Renwick, Brown, & Phahael, 1994, p. 67). This book provides an understanding of the psychological issues and practical problems faced by children with disabilities and their families throughout different stages of the life cycle. In this context, we are concerned with issues that affect the quality of life of the family unit as well as individual family members. Too often family members are viewed as "resources" for persons with disabilities rather than as having individual needs as they progress through life stages (Slater & Wilker, 1986, as cited in Smith, Fullmer, & Tobin, 1994, p. 34).

It is important to understand disability experiences from a developmental perspective. First, many of the problems experienced by families and individuals with disabilities stem from a clash between developmental needs and access to necessary opportunities and resources. Persons with disabilities are often regarded as children far beyond the end of childhood itself (even after entering adulthood). Consequently, needs that naturally arise after childhood are often not addressed in a time-appropriate manner. This period of extended childhood often segues into a premature "retirement" phase during which men and women with disabilities are often regarded as having few new options left in life. Developmental timelines may be skewed by virtue of the disability itself, but much of the asynchronicity between developmental needs and lifestyle is due to a failure to provide opportunities to develop capabilities throughout all phases of the life cycle. This is apparent in areas of life such as sexuality, marriage, career, and preparing for retirement. As discussed by Seltzer (1993), some persons with disabilities do not experience growth throughout the life cycle because they do not have access to age-differentiating experiences. Similarly, others assert that greater attention needs to be paid to emphasizing increased age differentiation by diversifying the types of activities people are exposed to based on their ages (Lipe-Goodson & Goebel, 1983; Thurman, 1986).

Second, the abilities of children and adults with disabilities to progress developmentally is affected by the abilities of their family members to progress with their own age-related tasks of maturation. Erikson (1994) expressed this synergistic relationship, which begins in infancy but often continues throughout life:

> A baby's presence exerts a consistent and persistent domination over the outer and inner lives of every member of a household. Because these members must reorient themselves to accommodate his presence, they must also grow as individuals and as a group. It is as true to say that babies control and bring up their families as it is to say the converse. A family can bring up a baby only by being brought up by him. His growth consists of a series of challenges to them to serve his newly developing potentialities for social interaction. (p. 57)

The interrelatedness of parental and child development is also evident in adolescence. The teenager's ability to progress with developmental tasks of individuation and separation is interwoven by the parents' abilities to "let go" in many respects.

Third, a developmental perspective on disability is necessary because many of the problems experienced by the families and individuals with disabilities have to do with disparities between traditional expectations and the timing (and sometimes absence) of particular developmental milestones. For those milestones that do occur, many events occur either too early or too late according to individual and social expectations (Mallory, 1986). Developmental delays may result from impaired cognition, prolonged physical dependency on family members, or restricted opportunities (Mallory, 1986). Siblings of children with disabilities may experience developmental timelines that are skewed in the opposite direction. They are often faced with "an acceleration of social development and premature initiation into adult roles" (p. 324). The lifestyle of parents also often differs from the more typical life cycle. As described by Mallory (1986), they are often "required to provide continued physical, emotional, and financial supports as they enter the later stages of their careers and anticipate retirement and their own increased dependency on social services" (p. 324).

Finally, a developmental framework enables an understanding of transitions that can threaten to exceed a family's coping abilities and result in crises. Erikson (1994) wrote of the "normal crises" that arise as the individual's perspective changes as part of growth itself. Additional crisis points commonly occur by virtue of coping with certain disabilities. Colwell (1984) referred to Wikler, Wasow, and Hatfield (1981) while discussing periodic increases in feelings of sadness, guilt, and distress associated with parenting a child with mental retardation:

> These recurrences often happen at times of stress and are frequently precipitated by the child's deviance from normal developmental patterns at specific crisis points. For adolescents, these developmental crisis points include the onset of puberty, the retarded child's 21st birthday, discussion about placement outside the home, and arrangement of guardianship and care after the parents die. (p. 336)

An understanding of "predictable" crises throughout the life cycle can enable parents and professionals to be better prepared to meet the related demands for family reorganization, role changes, and acquisition of new resources and coping strategies.

Diverse disabilities are used for illustrations in this book, ranging from psychiatric (neurobiological brain disorders) disabilities to ones that primarily affect one's physical functioning. Despite the clear-cut differences between disabilities, we find there are often overriding commonalities. Two of the most striking are stigmatization and deviation from the norm. Stigmatization can be viewed as the heart of disability-related problems. Meyerson (1963) regarded disability as a "social value judgment" rather than as an objective personal characteristic. Although this is an extreme position, it underscores the fact that many of the most distressing aspects of raising a child with a disability are related to societal reactions, such as restrictions to equal opportunities in the life domains of education, socialization, and vocation. Friedson (1965) similarly underscored the impact of stigmatization and connected it to deviation from the norm:

> What is a handicap in social terms? It is an imputation of difference from others: more particularly, imputation of an *undesirable* difference. By definition, then, a person said to be handicapped is so defined because he deviates from what he himself or others believe to be normal and appropriate. (p. 72)

Coping with differences and social stigma in a society that emphasizes conformity is a problem that cuts across disabilities despite their differing particulars. Similarly, coping with lack of resources, economic pressures, unusually high parenting demands, and initial or recurrent feelings of sorrow or frustration are not restricted to any particular disabilities.

We have also chosen a cross-disability perspective because there is so much diversity within disability categories that the type of disability per se does not adequately describe the different ways in which the person and family may be affected. For example, there is no "typical" child with cerebral palsy, just as there is no "typical" impact on a family of raising a child with a seizure disorder.

This book is the product of a collaboration that draws on an integration of research and the professional and life experiences of the three authors. As a result, it includes knowledge from the domains of education, parent advocacy, family therapy, sociology, legislation, and psychology.

The book includes many quotations from parents; these have been obtained from interviews and from responses to a survey that was completed by 125 families of sons and daughters with disabilities. The offspring ranged in age from infancy through adulthood. We have chosen to preserve the anonymity of all parents and children quoted in the book; for the same reason, we have often changed the demographic characteristics of case examples.

Chapter 1 provides a theoretical framework for the chapters that follow. It includes key family systems concepts such as interdependence and family structure and functions. Because families live in a broad societal context, this chapter also addresses ecological concepts such as stress, social support, and theories of adjustment to disability.

Chapter 2 explores periods of family adjustment to early information about a child's disability. Theories of family response to infant and childhood disability, as well as common stresses and challenges, are discussed. Information is provided about the specific challenges of fathers, siblings, and grandparents.

Chapter 3 addresses challenges of the school-age years with particular attention to the child's increasing interactions with people outside of the family. Entrance to school, socialization with peers, and legal rights to an appropriate education are discussed. The ongoing and cumulative stressors associated with disability in childhood, social isolation of families, and needed supports and advocacy are covered in the context of the family constellation.

Chapter 4 focuses on the developmental tasks that face adolescents with disabilities as well as their family members. The difficulties of individuation and separation are discussed in the context of the complexities introduced by virtue of the presence of disabilities. This chapter includes topics such as healthy incorporation of disability into one's self-image, easing social relationships with peers, and sexuality.

Chapter 5 is devoted to the transitional period between adolescence and adulthood. The historical and legal foundations explaining educational and adult service system differences are discussed in the context of obstacles faced by youth during this period. Self-determination, choice making, and preparedness to work are explored in terms of the individual and the family.

Chapter 6 focuses on the developmental needs of various members of families with adult sons and daughters with disabilities. Equal access to opportunities to enhance the quality of life is the focal point. This includes discussion of future planning for life after parents are unable to continue active caretaking, love relationships and marriage for adults with disabilities, and the needs of adult siblings.

Chapter 7 provides a discussion of the lives of persons with disabilities who have grown elderly. Developmental tasks of adaptation to old age are discussed, including issues such as attaining a greater degree of psychological peace as one faces the end of life. In addition, critical and practical matters such as access to quality health care and residences are discussed as part of the larger issues of life satisfaction.

Approaches that strengthen a family's ability to cope are discussed throughout the entire book in the context of discussing developmental needs and obstacles. The final chapter focuses exclusively on a more in-depth discussion of various approaches professionals can employ in their work with families of children with disabilities. Individual, family, and group approaches are explored. In terms of intervention efforts, we believe that most families can cope admirably with their circumstances. But during periods of increased stress, a variety of interventions should be available for families that seek professional or peer help.

We wish to acknowledge the many people whose contributions have helped in the development of this book. First, we sincerely thank the many families and individuals who have willingly shared with us their experiences and feelings. We also acknowledge Dr. Ginger Brown of Indiana University of Pennsylvania, who obtained financial assistance for the completion of our family survey; Jean Serio for support in survey preparation; and Paula Cerrone for her analysis of the survey data. We are also appreciative of the assistance by Alicia Montedoro and Rebecca Harlan. We thank Elizabeth Lasher for her help in interviewing young adults with spinal cord injuries and their parents and Laurie Filitske for her encouragement and support. Barbara Telthorster and Deb and Dick Dale need to be recognized for their ongoing support of Parent Information Project efforts, which made possible much of the anecdotal information in this book. We also acknowledge the Developmental Disabilities Planning Council of Pennsylvania for its help in funding the Parent Information Project. Karen Seligman is greatly appreciated for her keen insight into family dynamics and her continuing support.

CHAPTER 1

Families Coping
with Disability

Foundational and Conceptual Issues

T he concept of systems, long a focus of sociologists, has increasingly
become an important perspective in psychology and in such practice
fields as nursing, social work, and counseling (Seligman & Darling,
1997). In the realm of family functioning, the fields have come to share a systems approach. We believe that knowledge of family systems theory contributes to an understanding of the reciprocal effects a family member with
a disability and other family members have on one another. A richer and
more complete portrait of persons with disabilities is achieved within the
context of that person's more immediate ecological reality, namely, the family. Therefore, we first review some of the key concepts of family systems
theory and consider some of the factors and events outside of the family's
boundaries that can affect interaction within the family unit.

BUILDING BLOCKS OF FAMILY SYSTEMS THEORY

It is only in relatively recent years that theories of general systems (Von Bertalanffy, 1968) and family systems (Gurman & Kniskern, 1981) have emerged. In
contrast to earlier theories, a family systems approach differs from the view
that linear relationships characterize family life and that the only important
relationship is that between a mother and her child (Bowlby, 1951). Instead,

families are viewed as interactive, interdependent, and reactive; that is, if something occurs to one member in the family, all members in the system are affected. As one family therapist noted, families can be likened to a baby's mobile that hangs over a crib (Elman, 1991). When one of the objects on the mobile is touched, all of the other objects are disturbed. As noted by McGoldrick and Gerson (1985), "The physical, social and emotional functioning of family members is profoundly interdependent, with changes in one part of the system reverberating in other parts of the system"(p. 5).

General systems theory holds that each variable in any system interacts with the other variables so thoroughly that cause and effect cannot be separated. Regarding deafness in the family, Luterman (1984) wrote, "This notion implies that when a deaf child is born into a family, to some extent, everybody is 'deaf'"(p. 2).

As early as 1937, Nathan Ackerman, one of the pioneers in the family therapy field, wrote about the context in which humans are born:

> None of us live our lives utterly alone. Those who try are doomed to a miserable existence. It can fairly be said that some aspects of life experience are more individual than social, and others more social than individual. Nevertheless, principally we live with others, and in early years almost exclusively with members of our own family. (quoted in Guerin, 1976, p. 4)

In support of Ackerman's view, McGoldrick and Gerson (1985) were unequivocal in their belief that the family is the primary and the most powerful system to which a person ever belongs. Although Ackerman wrote about the family in the 1930s, the conceptual and treatment bases of family interventions in health care did not begin to develop systematically until family systems theory and family therapy emerged in the 1950s (Doherty, 1985). Today, family systems theory is flourishing, as it is considered a particularly useful conceptual model for understanding human behavior.

THE FAMILY AND INTERDEPENDENCE

The fact that all members in a family are affected by the actions of any one member is the central and perhaps most important feature of family systems theory. For example, the physical incapacitation of a wife (and mother) has direct implications for the husband (and father), the children, and the extended family. Also, the reaction of the husband in response to an incapacitated spouse further affects the family. And of course, childhood disability has implications for both the nuclear and extended family. For the family to successfully cope with such situations, new roles need to be negotiated. In addition, the family needs to come to grips with the disability and the subsequent changes in communications and relationships and how a major disruptive event, such as a chronic disability, will influence and perhaps alter the family's lifestyle and future goals. Before we explore such family interactions further, we first examine more static aspects of the family structure, such as membership characteristics, cultural factors, and ideological style.

FAMILY STRUCTURE

Family structure refers to the membership characteristics that serve to make each family unique. This relatively stable factor includes membership characteristics, cultural style, and ideological style.

Membership Characteristics

Families differ with regard to membership characteristics such as families with varying numbers of children; families with extended family members who may or may not reside in the household; single-parent families; families with an unemployed member; or families in which there is a major psychological disorder, chronic illness, or disability. Membership characteristics change over time. For example, the "leaving" of a family member (e.g., an 18-year-old daughter who leaves for college) will precipitate different communication and relationship patterns that were not evident earlier. Other examples are the inclusion in the household of a grandparent who may be elderly and frail or the death of a family member. These changes in family structure have important implications for family interaction. For example, the absence of the 18-year-old daughter may mean that the family's 15-year-old son will be the oldest or only child in the family. This simple structural change will most likely affect family communications between the son and his sister and the son and his parents.

Cultural Factors

A family's cultural beliefs shape its values and outlook on life, as well as its interactional patterns and functional priorities. Cultural style may be influenced by ethnic, racial, or religious factors or by socioeconomic status. Cultural beliefs can affect the manner in which families adapt to each other and to a member with a disability and can influence the utilization of and trust in caregivers and caregiving institutions (Schorr-Ribera, 1987). The powerful impact that culture has is reflected in the following observation by McGoldrick (1993):

> What you think, how you act, even your language, are all transmitted through the family from the wider cultural context. This context includes the culture in

which you live, and those from which your ancestors have come. This context is influenced not only by the class, religion, and geographic background of your family, but also by its ethnicity and by the cultural experiences its members have had. No two families share exactly the same cultural roots. Understanding a family's cultural roots is essential to understanding its members' lives, and the development of the particular individual as well. (pp. 331–332)

Historically, societal response to disability has been guided by philosophies of utilitarianism, humanitarianism, and human rights (Newman, 1991). These concepts provided the background and impetus for both positive and destructive action against those with disabilities. In terms of reactions from people from different cultures, Seligman and Darling (1997) noted that there are vastly different reactions to disability. For example, obesity in women is admired in most African tribes, yet stigmatized in the American middle class. The term "saint" is applied to persons with mental retardation among Middle Eastern Muslims, and these persons are afforded benevolent and protective treatment. Children with deformities are buried alive at birth among the Wogeo, a New Guinea tribe, but children who become disabled in later life are provided with loving care. Also, among the Palaung, one is considered fortunate to be born with extra fingers and toes and extremely lucky to be born with a cleft palate.

Ideological Style

Ideological style is based on a family's beliefs, values, and coping behaviors and is also influenced by culture. For example, some Jewish families have been found to place a great deal of importance on intellectual achievement, whereas some Italian families emphasize family closeness and affection (McGoldrick, Pearce, & Giordano, 1982). Other beliefs and values may be handed down from generation to generation and influence how family members interact with one another and with other systems (such as schools, social service, and governmental agencies). But it is important to keep in mind that families from the same culture differ.

Although a family's response to a member with a disability may be influenced by ideological style, it is also true that disability can influence a family's values. Nicholas Kappes (1995), the father of a son with Down syndrome reflected on how his son has altered his views of others with disabilities:

This was the perfect karmic kickback for an arrogant man who had always seen the retarded as the butts of a lifetime of MR jokes—Simply conquering prejudice about citizens suffering with mental disability represents a complete about-face for me. I have been indelibly sensitized to the misfortunate in our society. I have developed a far greater compassion. (pp. 14–15)

Confronting Disability

When first confronting a disability, the family not only responds to the event itself but also must confront its beliefs about people who have disabilities. In addition to coping with what the disability means to the family functionally and psychologically, the family also must come to terms with prejudicial and stereotypic attitudes that members may have held toward persons with disabilities. As noted by Kappes (1995), in the wake of disability it is not unusual for family members who hold dogmatic attitudes toward "the handicapped" to gradually emerge as spokespersons and advocates for this same population. Darling (1991) referred to a pattern of advocacy as a "crusadership role" as one possible response to disability in the family.

As family members confront chronic disability, they must also cope with their beliefs about what and who can influence the course of events (Rolland, 1994). It is helpful to know if the family believes the control of the disability is in its hands, God's hands, in the hands of others, or left purely to chance. These views influence how family members interpret events related to the disability, their help-seeking behavior, and their approach to caregiving. Rolland (1994) believed that professionals should assess the family's views about what caused a disability or illness and what might influence the outcome. A strongly held opinion that someone is to blame or powerful feelings of shame or guilt may negatively influence the family's ability to come to grips with chronic illness or disability.

FAMILY INTERACTION

There are four main components of the family system: subsystems, cohesion, adaptability, and communication (Turnbull, Summers, & Brotherson, 1986).

Subsystems

There are four subsystems in a family:

1. Marital—husband and wife
2. Parental—parent and child
3. Sibling—child and child
4. Extrafamilial—extended family, friends, professionals, and so on

Subsystems are affected by the structural characteristics of families (e.g., single mother or father, number of children) and by the current life cycle stage (e.g., school age, postparental). For example, a single mother in her 20s with a child with a disability must negotiate the tasks typical of her life stage, which differ from those of a mother in her 40s or 50s residing with an adult who has a disability. A single 25-year-old parent caring for a child with a chronic illness may have fewer supports than a parent in an intact nuclear family with an available extended family. From a systems perspective, professionals must be cautious about intervening in a subsystem. For example, an intervention designed to strengthen the bond between a mother and her child with a disability may have implications for the mother's relationship with her husband and other children. Thus, the resolution of one problem can bring about the emergence of others. Professionals need to be sensitive to this aspect of family systems interventions.

Cohesion

Cohesion can be illustrated by the concepts of enmeshment and disengagement. Highly enmeshed families have weak boundaries between subsystems and therefore can be characterized as overinvolved and overprotective (Minuchin, 1974). Overinvolved families find it difficult to allow for individuality and therefore tend to have a deleterious effect on a member's desire to be more independent.

On the other hand, disengaged families have rigid subsystem boundaries (Minuchin, 1974). Interactions in these families tend to be designed to avoid anxiety. Therefore, a person with a disability may feel free to initiate independent activity but rarely feel supported or loved in this endeavor. In the case of a 12-year-old with spina bifida, the parents may provide fragmented instead of coordinated care, primarily due to the parents' inability to communicate and collaborate on important caretaking issues. By communicating and being more cooperative, the parents must inevitably deal with the anxieties surrounding their child, and dealing with this issue is anathema to their typical style of avoidance of uncomfortable emotions.

A balance between enmeshment and disengagement characterizes well-functioning families. Boundaries between subsystems are clearly defined and family members feel both a close bonding and a sense of autonomy.

Adaptability

Adaptability is the family's ability to change in response to a stressful event (Olson, Sprenkle, & Russell, 1980). Chaotic families are characterized by instability and inconsistent change, and rigid families do not change in response to stress. A rigid family would have difficulty adjusting to the demands of caring for a family member with a disability. A father's rigid "breadwinner" role, for example, would not allow him to help with domestic chores or perhaps to assist his spouse who is ill or has a severe disability because he would view such tasks as "woman's work." If there is a child or adolescent with a disability in the family, this type of rigid stance can place an inordinate burden on the mother, who must put all of her energies into caretaking responsibilities. This, in turn, may leave the mother little time for her other children or for friendships and other activities. Indeed, for some mothers who work or want to work, a rigid family structure could create considerable family tension.

Another example is where the mother (wife) has a permanent disability that would necessitate role changes on the part of the husband and the children. The extent to which family members are unwilling to be flexible in their roles determines in part the amount of problems families will face.

Chaotic families have few rules to live by, and those rules that do exist are changed frequently. There is often no family leader in a chaotic family and there may be endless negotiations and frequent role changes (Turnbull & Turnbull, 1990). Chaotic families can move quickly from enmeshment to disengagement, whereas well-functioning families maintain a balance between emotional unity and autonomy.

In families where roles are confusing or ambiguous or rigid, the clinician, after a careful assessment of the family's ability to adapt, needs to sensitively communicate that the family's rigid, uncompromising position may be creating excessive stress and tension. One can point out who in the family is particularly burdened by this inflexibility and how it will eventually create problems for all family members. On their own, some families will negotiate productive changes, whereas others will ask for guidance. In the latter case, the clinician can point out how role changes and expectations can alter behavior in a positive direction. Of course, some families will elect to continue to function as they have in the past.

Communication

Family systems theory holds that communication breakdowns reflect a problematic system rather than faulty people. Breakdowns in communication reside in interactions between people, not within people (Turnbull & Turnbull, 1990). In working with families, the focus is on changing patterns of interaction and not on changing individuals. Professionals should avoid placing blame on a particular family member and instead make an effort to explore factors that contribute to problematic communication patterns. In practice, families often believe that a particular family member is responsible for the problems they are experiencing, but with professional help they can discover that difficulties often reside in faulty communication and that, in most cases, everyone plays a part in the conflict and in its resolution. For some, blaming someone else is less anxiety provoking than examining dysfunctional communication patterns for which all family members have a responsibility.

An illustration of falsely identifying a cause for family problems is when a family member with a disability is blamed for the problems. Simple cause-and-effect explanations such as this can be a "red herring" issue as the family finds a scapegoat for its woes that most likely are rooted in faulty interactional and communication patterns that existed before the disability. It is less anxiety provoking to single out the member with a disability or the disability itself than to look at family patterns for the origin and continuation of the problem. This is not to say that a disability in the family cannot exacerbate existing tensions or bring them to awareness. But by blaming the disability on a family member, the real problem may be masked and a solution delayed. For example, by accusing the person with the disability, the family might fail to recognize that rigid role taking had caused problems earlier or that there was a tendency for family members to disengage when changes occurred, tension increased, or the family was confronted with a challenge.

FAMILY FUNCTIONS

A disability in the family has implications for the functions family members assume. Considerable interdependence within the family and its extrafamilial network is required so that necessary functions are performed for survival. In this context one needs to keep in mind that families differ in regard to the priorities attached to different functions and in regard to who is expected to carry out certain functions and roles.

The following are typical family functions and roles.

1. Economic (generating income, paying bills, and banking)
2. Domestic/health care (transportation, purchasing and preparing food, medical visits)
3. Recreation (hobbies, family and individual activities)
4. Socialization (interpersonal relationships, friends, neighbors, and colleagues)
5. Self-identity (sense of belonging, recognizing strengths and weaknesses)
6. Affection
7. Educational/vocational (career choice, development of work ethic, homework) (Turnbull & Turnbull, 1990)

In terms of the effects a disability may have on family activity and functions, it is conceivable that the family's self-identity will change, its earning capacity may be reduced, its recreational and social activities may be restricted, and career decisions may be affected. The task of professionals and the social service agencies that serve these families is to help minimize the negative effects of disability by providing respite care, counseling, recreational outlets, and the like. Society, social service agencies, and the professionals who populate them play a key role in establishing funding priorities that can either facilitate adjustment or create insurmountable barriers.

Professionals in health and educational systems can alleviate stress but they can also contribute to it. In this regard, Imber-Black (1988) observed that professionals "must appreciate the requirement for ongoing interaction with larger systems, the stress generated thereby, and the need to intervene in ways that promote autonomy, enhance family resources, and facilitate empowerment of the family on behalf of their handicapped member" (p. 105).

SOCIAL ECOLOGY AND THE FAMILY

In the early literature on families with a member who has a disability, researchers defined the unit of study or intervention in very specific terms, focusing on the family member with the disability and ignoring the family as a legitimate focus. In the field of disability, the first studies reported on the interaction between the mother and her child. Later, siblings, fathers, and grandparents were included as family members who are affected by a member with a disability. The consideration of the family as a dynamic, interdependent unit was a profound step forward, yet there continued to be something missing. We know that children and adults with disabilities do not live in isolation—they reside within a family context. Similarly, the family lives in a broader context. The conceptualization of the family in a social ecology framework has been discussed extensively by Bronfenbrenner (1979) and has been the focus of social scientists concerned with the family.

Similarly to boundary concerns between subsystems in the family systems model, concerns over the permeability of the family when it interacts with environmental systems are of importance in the social ecology model. For example, is a family with a member with a disability open to the supportive influences of other similarly situated families (e.g., support groups) or amenable to assistance from social service agencies or other sources of help? The permeability of the family vis-à-vis the environment may influence the amount of isolation, support, and stress it experiences. Contrast, for example, a family that cooperatively works with medical professionals or the social service system, becomes involved in support groups with other families, and utilizes available respite care services to a family that feels that its members should "take care of their own," resists medical advice, isolates itself from others in similar circumstances, and refuses social services. Possibly due to the family's personal philosophy, determined by its families of origin and religious and cultural values, the second family will not feel supported by and connected to others and may be suspicious of offers of help. By the same token, there are some families with a richness of resources within that allows them to cope with minimal outside support. Others have broad kinship networks that provide concrete help and emotional support.

The social ecology point of view asserts that a family can be affected by remote events. For example, political and economic factors bear a direct relationship to the funds available for services for persons with disabilities. International conflicts can mobilize sentiment that supports arms buildup rather than educational and social service endeavors. Thus, the dynamics of a family with a member with a disability can be influenced by a variety of external and remote events. In light of this reality, a broad conceptualization of the forces that impinge on family life provides additional meaning to an understanding of the family.

Bronfenbrenner's (1979) social ecology model includes the microsystem, mesosystem, ecosystem, and macrosystem, with each system reflecting activity increasingly removed from the family but nevertheless influencing it. This model is easily applied to families with members of any age who have disabilities.

The *microsystem* constitutes the pattern of activities, roles, and interpersonal relations experienced by the family. In it, one finds the following components: parents and children. The microsystem functions in a *mesosystem* comprising a wide range of settings in which a family actively participates. The following combine to make up the mesosystem: medical and health care workers, the extended family, friends and neighbors, work associates, other parents, and other local community factors. In the *ecosystem*, there are more remote settings that the family is not actively involved in yet can be affected by, such as mass media, health care systems, social welfare agencies, and educational systems. Finally, there is the *macrosystem*, the ideological or belief system inherent in the social institutions of society. It includes ethnic, cultural, religious, socioeconomic, and political elements.

To understand a family, it is not sufficient to study only certain family members. It is becoming increasingly important to examine the family in the context of larger social, economic, and political realities. When social factors are responsible for a client's distress, the professional's role may be to help him or her to successfully negotiate the system rather than to change the individual.

SOCIAL SUPPORT

Social support is often viewed as a mediating or buffering factor in meeting the demands of a stressful event (Cobb, 1976; Crnic, Greenberg, Ragozin,

Robinson, & Basham, 1983). The presence in the family of a child, adolescent, or adult with a disability is considered a stressful event (Crnic et al., 1983) and one that is considered chronic in nature (Olshansky, 1962). Social support is an external coping strategy that has been shown to reduce family stress (Beckman & Porkorni, 1988).

The concept of social support has been studied in terms of three levels: (a) intimate relationships (e.g., spousal); (b) friendships, and (c) neighborhood and community support. For example, in a study designed to assess the relationship of maternal stress and social support, it was found that mothers with greater social support were more positive in their behavior and attitudes toward their infants (Crnic et al., 1983). Intimate (spousal) support proved to have the most positive effects.

A member's disability can have an isolating effect on families. For example, Marsh (1993) observed that a diagnosis of mental retardation can develop into a familial membrane that removes the family from mainstream society. Some of the reasons for this isolation are the emotional and physical exhaustion of families, the stigma experienced by some families, social exclusion derived from a lack of acceptance and understanding, and the specialized needs of persons with disabilities (Marsh, 1993; Parke, 1981). It is the availability of social support that helps to buffer some of the more arduous effects of disability.

Both formal (e.g., social service agencies) and informal (e.g., family, friends) support can contribute to coping and adaptation. By the same token, typical contributors of support can add stress to the family. Rejecting extended family (informal) and cold, distant, uncommunicative professionals (formal) can burden the family with their lack of support and unsympathetic attitudes. Generally speaking, social support reduces the subjective distress of families (Floyd & Zmich, 1989); encourages positive personal, family, and child functioning (Dunst, Trivette, & Cross, 1986); and enables family members to maintain a sense of normality and coping effectiveness (Schilling, Gilchrist, & Schinker, 1984). Also, a powerful resource for family members is professional or peer-led self-help groups (Seligman, 1993). These groups provide a forum for catharsis, education, mutual aid, and advocacy. The reader is referred to Chapter 8 for a more detailed discussion of group interventions.

As noted previously, the existence of social support appears to be a prerequisite for good family functioning, especially during difficult times. Professionals need to be cognizant of the family's need for help both within and external to the family. But they also need to be aware of circumstances where social support may be available in forms that vary from ones usually experienced. For example, in rural communities and in small towns extended family members tend to live in close proximity and serve as sources of support for one another (Darling, 1991). Darling notes that among families living in the

Blue Ridge Mountains of Virginia, the identities of nuclear and extended families were fused. The major source of support was kin, and involvement with relatives was obligatory. On the other hand, urban middle-American families are not as obliged to have such close relationships with kin.

STRESS AND COPING

Stress is a factor in relation to life cycle changes and is also implicated in events occurring in the family's immediate environment. Hill (1949) developed a model of stress that is often cited in the family literature (McCubbin & Patterson, 1983; Wikler, 1981) and has been designated the ABCX family crises model:

> A (the stressor event) interacting with B (the family's crisis-meeting resources) interacting with C (the definition the family makes of the event) produces X (the crisis).

The A factor (the stressor) is a life event or transition impacting the family that can produce change in the family system. The family's boundaries, goals, patterns of interaction, roles, or values may be threatened by change caused by a stressor (McCubbin & Patterson, 1983). A stressor event, for example, may be the family's need to generate more income as a result of the economic burdens brought on by the realities of a disability. This hardship can place demands on the roles and functions of family members, alter their collective goals, and affect the family's interaction.

The B factor (family resources) has been described as the family's ability to prevent an event or change in the family from causing a crisis (McCubbin & Patterson, 1983). The B factor is the family's capacity to meet obstacles and shift its course of action. This factor relates directly to the notion that the family's flexibility and quality of relationship prior to the presence of a disability or chronic illness may be an important predictor of its ability to adapt. Resources can also be acquired outside of the family through community services.

The C factor is the definition the family makes of the seriousness of the experienced stressor. The C factor reflects the family's values and its previous experience in dealing with change and meeting crises. This factor resembles a key component of Ellis's (1958) theory of neurosis. He asserted that it is not the event itself that is disturbing to an individual but the meaning attributed to the event that constitutes the source of problematic thinking and behavior. Recent literature has explored cognitive coping strategies that contribute to adaptive responses to family problems (Singer & Powers, 1993; Turnbull et al., 1993).

Taken together, the three factors all influence the family's ability to prevent the stressor event from creating a crisis (the X factor). A crisis reflects the family's inability to restore balance and stability. It is important to note that stress may never become a crisis if the family is able to use existing resources and defines the situation as a manageable event. In the same theme, Patterson (1988) described the Family Adjustment and Adaptation Response Model (FAAR). FAAR asserts that families attempt to maintain balanced functioning by using their *capacities* to meet the *demands* made on them. A critical factor is the *meaning* (similar to the C factor in Hill's, 1949, model) the family gives to a situation (demands) and how the family copes with the situation (capabilities). A crisis happens when demands exceed existing capabilities and an imbalance occurs. Balance can be restored by (a) acquiring new resources or learning new coping behaviors, (b) reducing the demands that confront the family, (c) changing the way the situation is viewed, or (d) a combination of these factors.

An illustration of a potentially dysfunctional coping strategy comes from a study that revealed that fathers of adolescents who have mental retardation, compared to a matched control group of fathers with nondisabled adolescents, employed significantly more withdrawal and avoidance behaviors to cope with their anxiety (Houser, 1987).

COPING STYLES

Coping styles can be classified into internal and external strategies: *Internal* strategies include passive appraisal (problems will resolve themselves over time) and reframing (making attitudinal or cognitive adjustments to live with the situation constructively), whereas *external* strategies include social support (ability to use family and extrafamilial resources), spiritual support (use of spiritual interpretations, advice from clergy), and formal support (use of community and professional resources) (McCubbin & Patterson, 1981). In a book on cognitive coping for families, Turnbull et al. (1993) described a family member with a disability as a source of happiness, a source of love, a source of learning life's lessons, a source of fulfillment, a source of pride, and a source of strength. The thrust in this book was in response to the negative and pathological views of persons with disabilities that characterize some of the literature.

RESOURCES TO HELP FAMILIES COPE

Patterson (1988) identified three categories of resources for families: personal resources, family system resources, and community resources.

Personal Resources

Personal resources include individual personality characteristics derived primarily from early social interaction. For example, self-esteem is a pervasive human characteristic that mediates one's response to life events. Self-esteem contributes to a sense of mastery and self-efficacy. For example, high self-esteem is associated with better adherence to treatment regimens and control of disease by children with diabetes. Also, high parental self-esteem contributed to the well-being of a chronically ill child. In families with a diabetic child, parental self-esteem was a key factor in predicting better functioning and child self-esteem (Patterson, 1988).

Mental health professionals can contribute to the self-esteem of a person with a disability by focusing on strengths and by treating the person with dignity and respect. For example, by focusing on a person's abilities, professionals can help increase the person's feelings of efficacy, control, and worthiness. Particularly important is the underlying prizing attitude conveyed by the professional to the family and the family member with a disability. Uncaring attitudes surely result in a lowering of a person's sense of worthiness. Others with disabilities and their families look to professionals for a confirmation of their healthy view of themselves. When it is not forthcoming, self-esteem may suffer. Professionals must not contribute negatively to stressful family situations that challenge a person's sense of dignity, worthiness, and efficacy. Some years ago, Ross (1964) expressed his beliefs regarding professionals who work with families:

> No amount of exhortation can make a rejecting person accepting, a frigid person warm, or a narrow-minded person understanding. Those charged with the selection, education, and training of new members of the helping professions will need to keep in mind that the presence of certain personality characteristics make the difference between a truly helpful professional and one who leaves a tract of misery and confusion in the wake of his activities. (pp. 75–76)

Some of the behaviors mental health professionals practice that contribute to negative self-evaluation and negative attitudes toward professionals are abruptness, inattentiveness, misinformation or lack of information, and an attitude of coldness or aloofness. Some family members conclude that professionals do not want to become involved with families in which there is a disability. With regard to information sharing, professionals should communicate what can reasonably be expected of the family member who has a disability. Professionals should be well informed about community services. Some families complain about the lack of a central coordinator. It is often difficult to know how to integrate and make sense of the information received from several professionals.

Furthermore, family members are puzzled by inept, inaccurate, and ill-timed professional advice and by the communication of essential information in professional jargon. In addition, family members who are trying to help find it discouraging when professionals ignore them and only relate to the family member who has a disability. Professionals who engage in this behavior do not understand the systemwide impact a disability can have on families.

Family System Resources

There are studies and reports in support of the claim that the family can supply many of the resources needed to cope with disability (Patterson, 1988). In particular, family organization seems to be a crucial variable and includes such elements as clarity of rules and expectations, family routines, and clear role allocation. Clear generational boundaries with a parental hierarchy that cooperatively works to make decisions and establish and maintain discipline of children are also essential organizational attributes (Elman, 1991).

Due to changes in circumstances and needs, the family organization needs to be sufficiently flexible to meet these changes. In the case of chronic illness or disability, a person's condition may worsen, improve, or remain the same (Rolland, 1993). Family flexibility is important whether the change is positive or negative. In conditions that are cyclical in nature (e.g., multiple sclerosis), family members may need to change their roles depending on whether the condition allows for a full range of activities, whether there are some restrictions, and whether hospitalization is required.

Other family resources include an active family recreation orientation in which an atmosphere of normalcy is maintained and cohesion increases as the family learns to cope with the demands of the disability (Patterson, 1988; Wallinga, Paquio, & Skeen, 1987). In the case of childhood disability, the father's support tends to set the tone for the family (Lamb & Meyer, 1991). The father's acceptance or rejection of the disability appears to affect the perception of other family members and his psychological and instrumental support helps to lessen the family's burden. Lillie (1993) reported that in some cases fathers avoid certain family responsibilities because of the masculine injunction that certain activities are not manly. On the other hand, some fathers are actively discouraged from assuming a more active role in the family, especially a nurturing one, because of the mother's opposition. In such cases, Lillie (1993) asserted, it is the mother's invitation that allows fathers a more nurturing family role.

As noted earlier, families are resources when they can achieve a balance between enmeshment and cohesion (Olson, Russell, & Sprenkle, 1979). Family members that are too close are overly reactive to each other and suffocate attempts at independence. They do not provide the emotional support that results in security and self-efficacy.

Marital relationships characterized by mutual support, intimacy, and shared goals are an important resource in effective family functioning (Patterson, 1988). It is essential for all family members to maintain a balanced life by finding time for themselves, even in the face of severe disability. Respite from caretaking and the pursuit of hobbies and other personal or collective interests provides balance for family members who must devote considerable energy to help manage and support the family member who has a disability. Mental health professionals should encourage family members to develop or resume activities that enhance their growth and pleasure. Some persons, however, may experience guilt in pursuing personal interests and goals. Professionals can give family members "permission" to engage in such activities by noting that they can increase satisfying family relationships.

In families where there are multiple, competing demands, it is useful to have good problem-solving abilities and conflict resolution skills (Patterson, 1988). These skills help lower the level of conflict and stress for the family. Such skills can be learned in consultation with a competent professional. Finally, a communication style that encourages the expressions of emotions is particularly adaptive for families who experience conflicting and powerful emotions. Here again the mental health professional can help by pointing out that both positive and negative emotions are inevitable and normal. Furthermore, the expression of such feelings, if it is done in a caring and compassionate manner, will deepen relationships and prevent smoldering emotions from building and causing harm to the family.

Community Resources

The final type of help for families is community resources (Patterson, 1988). Although not really a community resource per se, the extended family can provide emotional support and practical help (Seligman, 1991). For example, in childhood disability, grandparents have provided help by baby-sitting, shopping for the family, taking the child for medical appointments, helping with domestic chores, and even helping financially (Seligman & Darling, 1997). Another resource for families is respite care (Upshur, 1991). While a trained respite care worker remains with the family member who has a disability, other members can go shopping; enjoy dinner out or go to a movie; and, in some instances, take a vacation. Not only is respite care beneficial for caretakers but it is also healthy for the person with the disability. For periods of time, this family member is relieved of the burden of being constantly reliant and dependent on parents, siblings, or spouses. This can contribute to more self-reliance, greater feelings of self-efficacy—and reduced guilt. Many communities now have respite care services available and professionals should be able to direct families to them. Many families are able to cope better when financial resources are available, such as Social Security Income (SSI). Legislation can help in establishing programs and policies that improve the lives of persons with disabilities (e.g., the Americans With Disabilities Act of 1990 [ADA], which went into effect in 1992 [Meyen, 1992]). In regard to the ADA, Turnbull (1993) noted that this legislation

> extends its civil rights nondiscrimination protection to the following sectors of American life: employment in the private sector; privately-owned public accommodations (for example, theaters, hotels, restaurants, shopping centers, and grocery stories); services provided by state and local governments, including public and private transportation services; and telephone communications services (for people with hearing or visual impairments). (p. 24)

Patterson (1988) echoed Ross's (1964) concern that professionals should be sensitive to the emotional reactions of the family and provide information and offer support when indicated. Professionals who are attuned to their own emotional reactions are better able to help families become aware of their feelings (Zucman, 1982). Zucman challenged health care providers to empower families to care for themselves instead of making them overly dependent on community services. In this regard, Laborde and Seligman (1991) discussed *personal advocacy counseling,* which refers to the process of assisting families to actively and purposively work for their own welfare by obtaining the support and services necessary. This approach helps families become their own case managers. The goal is to assist families to experience a sense of control over events in their lives. This goal is important because through chronic disability or illness, a person's experience of mastery and control over life events can become compromised (Brinthaupt, 1991). Advocacy will be covered in more depth in Chapter 8.

A final source of community support is from others who are coping with the same or similar disability, namely, peer self-help or support groups (Hornby, 1994; Lieberman, 1990; Seligman, 1993). Support groups represent a powerful medium of emotional support and practical help. The quick identification of persons in similar circumstances helps family members feel less alone in their struggles and provides a network of friends who understand and who can provide instrumental assistance. Here again, professionals can direct families to appropriate support groups. More will be said about group interventions in Chapter 8.

Before we begin a discussion of atypical families and multicultural issues, we want to review Rolland's (1993) conceptualization of family adjustment to disability, which emphasizes intersecting life and illness cycle events.

ROLLAND'S MODEL OF FAMILY ADJUSTMENT TO CHRONIC ILLNESS

Rolland's (1993) model of family adaptation to chronic illness relies on an understanding of a series of life cycle- and illness-related variables. Pollin (1995) also supported the view that there are phases, or "crisis points," when some type of intervention may be indicated. Writing about chronic illness, Pollin asserted that there are three key crisis points: diagnosis, release from hospitalization, and illness exacerbation. She also believed that the family is vulnerable during certain life transitions such as a child leaving for college, marriage, moving, or job loss. Although Pollin acknowledged family factors, her primary focus was on the ill individual. In contrast, Rolland (1993) embraced a more comprehensive view of family—person interactions. He believed that it is helpful for professionals to be knowledgeable about the characteristic and general patterns of an illness or disability over the course of the condition. As an illustration, an illness can have an acute or gradual *onset*. For acute-onset problems (e.g., stroke, accident), families are forced to cope with the situation in a short period of time. Family members need to mobilize their resources quickly to cope with the situation, whereas a gradual-onset illness may develop more slowly and require patience and a tolerance for ambiguity as symptoms unfold. For gradual-onset illness, the patient and the family may have to endure rounds of medical tests and examinations before a diagnosis is known.

The *course* of an illness is another disease variable that should be considered. For example, illnesses can be progressive, constant, relapsing or episodic. In a constant-course illness, family members face a fairly stable and predictable situation, whereas in an episodic-course illness, family members may find it stressful to cope with the transitions between crisis and noncrisis and the uncertainty of when an episode will occur.

Two additional illness factors are *outcome* and *incapacitation*. In terms of outcome, a condition can be fatal (e.g., AIDS) or chronic and nonfatal (e.g., arthritis). The key difference between these outcomes is the degree to which family members anticipate loss (Rolland, 1993). In terms of incapacitation, an illness or disability can affect cognitive abilities (e.g., mental retardation), mobility (e.g., spina bifida, stroke, auto accident), sensation (e.g., blindness), stigma (e.g., AIDS), and disfigurement (e.g., burns). According to Rolland, the timing, extent, and type of incapacitation imply differences in the degree of family stress.

Illnesses also have *time phases,* such as crisis, chronic, and terminal. During periods of *crisis,* families are particularly vulnerable. Professionals have enormous influence over a family's sense of competence during this phase. Rolland (1993) viewed the initial meetings with professionals (diagnosis and advice) as a "framing event." He advised professionals to be very sensitive in their interactions with family members at this stage. For example, who is included during these early meetings can influence family communication patterns about the illness.

The *chronic* phase may be marked by constancy or by periods of episodic change or even death. The chronic phase challenges the family to maintain a semblance of a normal life while living with uncertainty. Chronic illnesses can strain family relations as expectations and personal life or career goals may need to be altered.

Families that adapt well to the *terminal* phase are those that are able to shift from trying to control the illness to "letting go" (Rolland, 1993). Being open to emotions and dealing with the numerous practical tasks that need to be done characterize a family that is coping well.

A key component of Rolland's (1993) model of family adaptation to chronic illness is the concept of centripetal versus centrifugal family styles and phases in the family life cycle. These concepts describe typical and normative periods of family closeness (centripetal) and periods of family disengagement (centrifugal). Centripetal periods are characterized by an emphasis on internal family life. During centrifugal periods, the family accommodates the family members' interactions with the extrafamilial environment. In the concept of the family life cycle, the family is seen at its centripetal best after the arrival of a newborn. A generally acknowledged centrifugal period is after the family's children are launched, when both children and parents pursue interests outside of the nuclear family. The implications of centripetal and centrifugal phases on family dynamics is illustrated in the following passage:

> If a young adult becomes ill, he or she may need to return to his or her family of origin for disease-related caretaking. Each family member's outside-the-family autonomy and individuation are at risk. The young adult's initial life structure away from home is threatened either temporarily or permanently. Both parents may have to relinquish budding interests outside the family. Family dynamics, as well as disease severity, will influence whether the family's reversion to a centripetal life structure is a temporary detour within their general outward movement or a permanent, involutional shift. A parent's fused or enmeshed family

frequently faces the transition to a more autonomous period with trepidation. A chronic illness provides a sanctioned reason to return to the "safety" of the prior centripetal period. For some family members, the giving up of the building of a new life structure that is already in progress can be more devastating than when the family is still in a more centripetal period in which future plans may be at a more preliminary stage, less formulated, or less clearly decided upon. An analogy would be the difference between a couple discovering that they do not have enough money to build a house versus being forced to abandon their building project with the foundation already completed. (Rolland, 1993, p. 448)

In his writing, Rolland (1993) discussed other implications of disease on-set, course, incapacitation, and so forth as they interact with individual and family life cycle phases. In the face of chronic disease, one needs to be mindful that the demands presented by an illness can seriously interfere with the personal life goals of family members. A balance, if possible, between meeting the requirements of the disease and achieving dreamed-of personal goals would be an optimal situation. To help achieve such a balance, Rolland (1993) suggested,

It is vital to ask what life plans the family or individual members had to cancel, postpone, or alter as a result of the diagnosis. It is useful to know whose plans are most and least affected. By asking a family where and under what conditions they will resume plans put on hold or address future developmental tasks, a clinician can anticipate developmental crises related to "independence from" versus "subjugation to" the chronic illness. (p. 454)

MEDICAL CRISIS COUNSELING MODEL

There is another theoretical lens and practical approach to adjustment to disability or medical illness. Pollin (1995) and Shapiro and Koocher (1996) elaborated on the Medical Crisis Counseling (MCC) model used to understand a person's response to chronic illness or disability. Some of the tenets of MCC have implications for the member with an illness or disability and the family. In MCC, the therapeutic goal of restoring a person's life to a precrisis stage is viewed as unrealistic: "The landscapes of most lives are permanently altered by illness, even in positive ways, and that returning to an old way of life is simply not possible" (Shapiro & Koocher, 1996, p. 110). Although a person's or family's life is altered following illness or disability, the ability to construct some sense of normalcy is within the individual's or family's reach. The goal of MCC is to help the client (and family) optimize functioning within the constraints of the illness or disability. When working in this model, Shapiro and Koocher (1996) asserted that there are four primary clinical assumptions.

CLINICAL ASSUMPTIONS

The first assumption is that responses to illness or disability rarely represent psychopathology. Shapiro and Koocher (1996) note that some people may exhibit a variety of symptoms (e.g., depression, denial, dissociation, anxiety) in response to an illness or disability; these responses do not warrant the same treatment as for persons having the same symptoms independent of a medical crisis, however.

Second, Shapiro and Koocher assumed that there is a continuum of vocational, social, and biomedical functioning. By this they meant that the coping response of two persons, essentially similar on a variety of characteristics, may be vastly different.

The third assumption, one that has been discussed earlier and forms the foundation for this volume, is that responses to illness or disability can not be understood in a vacuum. A person's relationships at school, at work, and at home are often affected by the event.

The fourth assumption, also suggested by Rolland's (1994) model discussed earlier, is that a given crisis will vary according to the disease and the person. Given the person and illness variables, there are an infinite number of permutations.

IMPEDIMENTS TO OPTIONAL FUNCTIONING

For some persons who have chronic illnesses or disabilities, emotional and interpersonal isolation is the norm (Shapiro & Koocher, 1996). Some avoid talking to family and friends for fear of burdening others. "As a result of this silence, patients often feel emotionally starved at a virtual banquet of social support" (Shapiro & Koocher, 1996, p. 110). Other factors that contribute to the prevalence of avoidance include embarrassment over one's appearance, fatigue and changes in sexual functioning, and dependence on medication routines (which can limit a patient's security in leaving a familiar place). Another factor that can contribute to isolation is differences in coping styles: "For example, a husband adopts a cheerful optimism, whereas his wife prefers to prepare for the worst case scenario. These differences in coping styles can be problematic" (Shapiro & Koocher, 1996, p. 111).

Loss and dependency are by-products of illness and disability (Marshak & Seligman, 1993). Clients' appearance can change; freedom of movement may be curtailed; strength and sensory and mental acuity can be impaired. Losses of independence, occupational identity, financial security, family roles—and even dreams, hobbies, and a sense of personal meaning—are often grieved for.

According to Shapiro and Koocher (1996), the media have desensitized us to sudden death, but less violent death continues to be a mystery: "Our culture has no social rules or rituals for families and individuals facing death before it happens" (p. 111). There are rituals for a host of occasions, but there are no rituals or social rules for communicating with the dying.

Another impediment to optional functioning is the fear of death. This fear coaxes one to engage in behaviors that can be problematic. Alluding to death anxiety, Yalom (1980) observed, "Death whirs continuously beneath the membrane of life and exerts a vast influence upon experience and conduct. Death is a primordial source of anxiety and, as such, is the primary fount of psychopathology" (p. 29).

Shapiro and Koocher (1996) reported that professionals often respond poorly to impending death. They claimed that physicians and mental health workers do not respond well to the final stage of life, even though they share the experiences of death with their patients. In regard to psychotherapists, Yalom (1980) noted,

> Some therapists state that death concerns are simply not voiced by their pa-
> tients. I believe, however, that the real issue is that the therapist is not prepared
> to hear them. A therapist who is receptive, who inquires deeply in to a patient's
> concerns will encounter death continuously in his or her everyday work. (p. 57)

Care providers and others often feel that by asking questions they are being intrusive, when more likely they avoid the topic in fear of raising questions about their own mortality. Given these negative responses, it is no surprise that people facing death often have few opportunities to explore their thoughts and feelings with family members, friends, and professionals. Shapiro and Koocher (1996) believed that medical crisis professionals should be well situated to provide the patient with an opportunity to discuss death by gently asking such questions as, "Have you been thinking about dying?" The approach should be open, nonjudgmental, and combined with sensitive questions giving the patient an opportunity to talk about death or to feel free to decline to do so.

Another impediment to full functioning is what Shapiro and Koocher (1996) called the "vague confines of illness." Professionals often tell clients that where they will fall in the potential range of functioning is impossible to predict, which results in a situation of intense ambiguity and anxiety. Such statements put patients in a state of continuous vigilance and uncertainty about their future. According to Shapiro and Koocher (1996), the professionals' task is to assist patients in conceiving ways of testing the limits of their capacities to help minimize unnecessary self-imposed limitations.

Lack of familiarity with medical environments constitutes a final impediment to functioning. Patients face two common problems in medical settings.

First, because they have difficulties communicating with the medical staff, they often feel left out, unaware of their current medical status, and uncared-for as individuals. The second impediment concerns the level of vulnerability, dehumanization, and powerlessness they feel in medical settings. In such settings, patients need survival lessons to help them have realistic expectations of their medical milieu and to be provided with some strategies to help them cope in this alien and often exasperating and frightening environment.

ATYPICAL FAMILIES

The concept of the "normal" family as two parents and two children is an illusion in society today. The composition of the contemporary family bears no resemblance to earlier notions. Presently, families may contain two parents or one; single, divorced, or same-sex partners; step, blended, adoptive, and foster members; and grandparents. What is a family? Certainly the middle-class ideal, nuclear family of a married man and woman and their unmarried children is not universal in society today (Seligman & Darling, 1997). Sixty-seven percent of the children born in the United States today will be raised by a single parent for part of their lives and around 75% of all children under the age of six will be in day care while their parents work (Vincent & Salisbury, 1988). Contemporary families are more diverse than at any time in history, which can be attributed to both cultural and structural factors (Zinn & Eitzen, 1993). Structural factors are rooted in economic changes that have affected the labor market and cultural factors are now more important as the United States has acknowledged its diversity (Seligman & Darling, 1997). The diversity among families encompasses significant variations in parent characteristics. There are more teen pregnancies now than in the past and other parents delay having children until they are in their 30s or 40s. Sometimes grandparents become involved in raising their teenage children's children. Adding to family diversity, educational levels in some communities are vastly different. In some communities, few complete high school, and in others, most are college graduates. Also, there are some parents who have mental illnesses, are mentally retarded, or have physical disabilities. Professionals who provide services to families need to take this enormous diversity in structure, education, and values into account.

Multicultural Issues

Although not atypical, minority group families and families from other cultures may have values regarding who is or is not included in the family group. For example, African American families consider good friends to be kin and gain support from these "extended" family members. In Western cultures human development is perceived as growth in one's capacity for differentiation, whereas African Americans' sense of identity is more communal (McGoldrick, 1993). There are pronounced differences in communication proclivities across race and cultural lines. To illustrate, people who are Jewish typically value articulating their experiences, whereas in the WASP culture, words typically are valued primarily for their utilitarian, pragmatic value. As McGoldrick (1993) observed, "Attitudes toward verbalizing one's feelings is reflected in the movie, *Ordinary People*, where in regard to his brother's death, a son declares, 'What's the point of talking about it. It doesn't change anything'" (p. 336).

In the Irish culture, words are often used to soften the harshness of experience. The Irish use humor and poetry to make reality more tolerable. McGoldrick (1993) noted, "The Irish have raised poetry, mystification, double meanings, humorous indirection, and ambiguity to a science, in part, perhaps, because their history of oppression led them to realize that telling the truth could be dangerous to their lives" (p. 336). Eschewing the American way of what some might say is brutal honesty, the Chinese may communicate important issues through food, similar to Italians, although the Italians often use language to convey emotional intensity primarily for drama. Attitudes toward spirituality vary across cultures as well. For example, WASP and Jewish cultures consider their spiritual values to be practical and reality oriented. In the Hispanic culture, however, spirituality travels between dreams and the everyday world (McGoldrick, 1993).

Differences in history and values are also reflected in views toward disability. In cultures where responsibility and blame for perceived misfortune are high, one may see higher rates of guilt, shame, depression, and isolation than in cultures that harbor more benign attitudes. (See McGoldrick, 1993; Seligman & Darling, 1997 for a more extensive examination of culture and disability.)

CLINICAL SENSITIVITY TOWARD ATYPICAL FAMILIES

Families, then, are different from a number of perspectives, including cultural variability, lifestyles, and family composition. It is essential that professionals take these differences into account when they provide services to families whose attitudes and values differ from their own. Knowledge about cultural diversity helps professionals to comprehend attitudes and behavior more accurately. It may seem paradoxical to the professional for a family to present for services and yet be unwilling to fully disclose the problems it is facing. For such families, empathic, patient listening while gently asking relevant questions should eventually bear fruit. For some families from different cultures, the use of indirect questions yields more information than direct ones.

It is important for service providers to understand the extraordinary stresses that a single or gay parent or parents in the throes of poverty may face. It is sometimes a challenge for professionals who come from middle-class backgrounds to empathize with persons who differ from them culturally, ethnically, and socioeconomically. It is for this reason that a major current training emphasis in medicine, education, and the social sciences is cross-cultural sensitivity (Weinrach & Thomas, 1996). Graduate training programs need to be cognizant of students who exhibit insensitivity to family values or structures that differ from their own. At minimum, graduate students should be exposed to literature on cultural and family diversity, engage in open discussions on this topic, and explore their own biases. In the final analysis, professionals must be knowledgeable about diversity so that they are aware of cultural and intracultural differences and how their cultural values can affect their work with others.

THE ENDLESS BURDEN

The chronicity of care that families with a child or adult with a disability anticipate constitutes a major feature that distinguishes them from families confronting more acute crises. For some families, the care is necessary 24 hours a day, 7 days a week, for many years. The stress can be relentless, draining the family physically and psychologically. Add to this the financial worries that may exist, and the family has the potential for being at risk. The degree to which the family has problems may depend on how it conceptualizes its life circumstance, how supportive family members are of one another, the availability of social support outside the family, and the existence of financial concerns or other family problems.

The burden of care is not only chronic; it can be experienced as a dark cloud that will continue to engulf the family for years to come. Family members may see little relief when they look to the future. Instead of independence, growth, and differentiation, a family may see only despair, dependence, and social isolation. In regard to childhood disability, "The mental health needs of exceptional parents may be cumulative. That is, living with a handicapped child over many years can take its toll psychologically, physically and financially" (Seligman & Meyerson, 1982, p. 103).

In facing the future, family members must decide how they plan to negotiate their special life circumstance. As noted earlier, flexibility and adaptability are important contributions to successful family living. For example, children may need to help with caretaking more than they otherwise would and adults may need to assist instrumentally and also be psychologically supportive of each other. In the case of childhood disability, mothers need to learn to facilitate, without undue guilt, as much growth and independence as their child is capable of achieving. All in all, over the family's life span, members need to adapt, negotiate, and communicate. This is sound advice for all families, but it has special relevance to families in which there is a disability.

As noted earlier, in addition to providing help within the family, the family system needs to be permeable enough to allow for outside help, such as respite care, when such help is needed and available. Wikler (1981) reported that respite care leads to a decrease in negative maternal attitudes toward children and increased positive family interaction. Upshur (1991) stressed the importance of respite care services and advocated a spectrum of types of respite care to meet different family needs. Again, receptiveness to outside help is important in enabling the family to cope with a chronic and stressful situation, although some families prefer and cope well with the help of nuclear and extended family. And it is in this context that professional psychologists, counselors, social workers, and physicians need to facilitate the family's adaptation to its situation. They may also have to help families create resources where these do not exist.

This discussion may appear unnecessarily pessimistic. We believe that fewer families fall into adverse circumstances than become well adjusted to the disability or even thrive beyond expectations. We acknowledge that the preponderance of research evidence supports the contention that families incorporate their special circumstances with minimal distress. Also, parents have authored accounts that bear testimony to their ability to manage well. There are, however, other accounts and research studies that report on the difficulties some families have in adjusting to a disability. It is essential for the professional to learn that there is a full spectrum of reactions to a chronic illness or disability.

STIGMA

Persons who have physical or mental disabilities—or both—are often victims of stigmatization. To the extent that individuals deviate from the societal norm of physical and mental perfection, they are likely to be shunned, ridiculed, avoided, or ostracized. Apropos to this discussion is the observation once made by Mark Twain:

> There is something that he [man] loves more than he loves peace—the approval of his neighbors and the public. And perhaps there is something which he

dreads more than he dreads pain—the disapproval of his neighbors and the public. (Neider, 1963, p. 344)

The conditions of stigmatization vary for different disabilities. Goffman (1963) observed that some disabilities are "discredited," whereas others are "discreditable." A discreditable condition is one that is not readily apparent. A person with a disfigurement hidden by clothing, an adult with cancer, or a child with a disease such as cystic fibrosis might be able to pass as normal in many situations and thus avoid stares and unwanted questions. On the other hand, a child with a more visible defect, such as Down syndrome or spina bifida, or an adult with hemiplegia would be discredited immediately.

Individuals with discreditable disabilities and their families sometimes engage in what Goffman (1963) called "impression management" to appear "normal." Even if a person is not intentionally trying to pass, encounters with strangers may be stressful because people generally assume that others do not have a disability. The person must then decide whether to play along with the assumption of normality.

In the case of discredited conditions, which are immediately obvious to strangers, the problems of impression management are different. Passing as one without a disability is not possible in these cases. Davis (1961) suggested that when those with visible disabilities come into contact with nondisabled persons a kind of mutual pretense takes place. Both the stigmatized person and the person without a disability act as though the disability does not exist. Davis called this mode of interaction "fictional acceptance" because the nondisabled person does not really accept the person with a disability as a moral equal.

Typically, interaction between persons with and without disabilities never moves beyond a superficial level. Some people may be hesitant to become close to a stigmatized person because they, in turn, might be stigmatized. Goffman (1963) suggested that close associates of persons with disabilities come to bear a "courtesy stigma" and may suffer similar reactions of avoidance, rejection, or ridicule. For this reason stigmatized individuals and their families may choose their friends from what Goffman (1963) called "their own"—others who already share a similar stigma.

Anspach (1979) delineated four potential responses to stigmatization: (a) normalization, (b) disassociation, (c) retreatism, and (4) political activism. The person who chooses *normalization* is committed to cultural notions of normalcy. For the normalizer,

> The typical existential stance—is that s/he is "superficially different but basically the same as everyone else" or that ultimately "differences don't matter."

Generally, the normalizer attempts, insofar as possible, to participate in the round of activities available to "normals" and to aspire to "normal" attainments. (Anspach, 1979, p. 768)

Disassociation also revolves around sustaining an attachment to the values of the larger society, yet the individuals view themselves as disqualified from ever achieving social acceptance and are therefore unwilling to make efforts to attain acceptance. Persons engaging in disassociation practice self-exclusion so they can avoid the pain of rejection. Those engaged in *retreatism* are persons who do not aspire to societal values and withdraw from the majority world of the nondisabled. Dramatically different from the retreater, those engaged in *political activism* repudiate the values society places on physical perfection, competition, and similar values. Political activists are more concerned with influencing the behavior of groups, organizations, and institutions than they are with changing their own values and behavior.

Depending on an individual's response to stigmatization, the family will also respond in some way. For example, the decision of a person with a disability to retreat, as defined by Anspach (1979), carries implications for the values of family members who may either oppose or support such a position. There may be conflict if the person with a disability and the other family members hold differing views. Whether there is conflict depends on how well family members are able to respect each others' views.

Studies have consistently shown that persons with disabilities are viewed negatively by the general public (Resnick, 1984). Research has also demonstrated that certain disabling conditions are more acceptable than others and, furthermore, that even professionals hold attitudes that are negative (Darling, 1979; Resnick, 1984). Based on his literature review, Resnick (1984) reported on the negative attitudes held by teachers, counselors, social workers, and physicians. Furthermore, negative attitudes toward persons with disabilities are reinforced by training in medical schools and other professional training programs, which may account in part for the negative attitudes professionals hold (Darling & Darling, 1982).

Goffman (1963) stated that the predominant social attitude toward those who are different is one of stigma and that stigmatized persons are regarded as morally inferior to those who are "normal." As Newman (1991) pointed out, "In early societies, illness and disability were seen as the work of evil demons and supernatural forces—disease and disability [were seen] as the scourge of God, as punishment for sin" (p. 9). As suggested above, persons with disabilities are stigmatized, but family members suffer from a "courtesy stigma" because of their association with the person who happens to have a disability. Wikler (1981) believed that families must develop competence in managing uncomfortable social situations. She went on to comment that they "face hostile stares, judgmental comments, murmurs of pity, and intrusive requests for personal information whenever they accompany their child to the grocery store, on the bus, or to the park" (p. 282).

It seems that the positive portrayals of persons with disabilities in the media have positively affected attitudes. Nevertheless, our present state of knowledge regarding public and professional sentiment regarding persons with disabilities informs us that attitudes continue to be negative. Thus, stigma must be added to the other burdens families must endure. We now turn to a discussion of resilience, a characteristic that helps to combat the effects of stigma and other stresses associated with illness and disability.

RESILIENCE

The notion of resilience in children is critical to understanding why some are challenged by a major life event, such as illness or disability, and others succumb to it. Resilience can be defined as an ability to return to the original form or the ability to recover from illness or other types of adversity. It is a capacity to avoid negative outcomes such as delinquency, drug abuse, depression, excessive dependence, and the like (Rak & Patterson, 1996). One of the factors implicated in resilience is the child's immediate environment, namely, the family. We will discuss family factors after an examination of other elements that contribute to resilience, or hardiness.

One of the more ambitious studies of resilience is that conducted by Werner and Smith (1982, 1992). These researchers followed the progress of over 200 high-risk children in Hawaii for a period of 32 years. A multifaceted assessment procedure was employed in the studies to determine how the children adjusted to emotional and work-related aspects of living.

Other major studies include those of Garmezy and his associates (Garmezy, Masten, & Tellegen, 1984), who studied about 200 children from urban environments in mainland United States, and Rutter (1979), who studied children from the Isle of Wight (Great Britain) and in the city of London. These studies identified factors in the histories of the children that seem to have buffered the impact of their high-risk early life.

For example, personal factors that contributed to a child's ability to overcome adversity included an active problem-solving approach, an ability to gain others' positive attention, and an optimistic view of life in spite of untoward experiences. Other personal factors included an ability to be autonomous, a tendency to seek novel experiences, and a proactive perspective.

A significantly higher proportion of resilient children were firstborn, were remembered by their mothers as having been good-natured and active infants, and evidenced a tendency to recover more quickly from childhood illnesses than their peers (Werner, 1986). Self-concept factors included a capacity to understand oneself and one's boundaries in relation to long-term family stressors (Beardslee & Podorefsky, 1988). According to Rak and Patterson (1996), "It appears that when stressful events do not overwhelm the ability to cope, the victory over adversity enhances a sense of self-competence" (p. 370).

In terms of social support, role models such as teachers, school counselors, coaches, neighbors, and clergy were identified as potential buffers for vulnerable children (Beardslee & Podorefsky, 1988; Garmezy et al., 1984; Werner, 1984, 1986). Children who were resilient often had a number of role models (mentors) outside the family throughout their development.

In their review of the literature on resilient children, Rak and Patterson (1996) described several family factors that help buffer the effects of early high-risk environments. Some of these factors included age of the opposite-sex parent (younger mothers for resilient males, older fathers for resilient females); four or fewer children in the family, spaced more than 2 years apart; nurturing from the primary caregiver during the first year of life and little prolonged separation from that person; availability of alternate caregivers when parents were not consistently present; presence of kin and sibling caretakers; and structure and rules in the household during adolescence despite poverty and other stressors.

Family disorganization, disruption in the family, and poverty are key risk factors experienced by young children, some of whom may additionally have disabilities. Some parents have few parenting skills, but even for those who do have some knowledge of proper parenting, work stress, financial worries, health problems, and marital discord can contribute to neglect and abuse of children. Furthermore, for some children there will be changes in the nuclear family. About half of the children born in the past 10 years will spend some time in a single-parent home (Hetherington, Stanley-Hagan, & Anderson, 1989).

Parent education and counseling can help children and families at risk. It is helpful for parents to be reminded that children do well in environments where they are loved and where there are clear expectations for behavior (Smith, 1991). Parents can profit from courses and workshops designed to enhance their skills as effective parents. Professionals should recommend such experiences for parents who are struggling to provide a proper, emotionally consistent environment for their children. Professionals also need to be aware of the family changes and stressors when childhood or adult disability is present in the family. And for families who are open to counseling, referrals to competent mental health professionals should be considered.

The concept of resilience applies to families as well as individuals (Singer & Powers, 1993). As with children, one way to look at family resilience is to explore the characteristics of successful families. Patterson (1991b), who reviewed the literature on families of children with chronic illness, reported that well-functioning families faced with a chronic health challenge coped well by doing the things successful families accomplish. She described resilient families confronted by childhood illness as exhibiting the following characteristics:

1. Maintaining family boundaries—Families maintain boundaries in spite of the intrusive involvement by a variety of professionals. They have a clear perception of family member needs and take appropriate assertive action when necessary.
2. Developing communicative competence—There is some evidence that families in which members openly express feelings to one another are more likely to succeed in caring for their chronically ill child, even in the face of internal pressure to protect others by keeping emotions inside.
3. Attributing positive meaning to the situation—Families find positive meanings in challenging situations.
4. Maintaining family flexibility—Families can exchange roles and tasks when necessary within the family.
5. Maintaining a commitment to the family unit—Teamwork and cooperation facilitate resilience. There is a basic commitment to the needs of family members, regardless of disability.
6. Engaging in active coping efforts—Resilient families rarely approach challenges with an attitude of passive resignation. These families actively seek out and utilize existing resources.
7. Maintaining social integration—Families stay involved in positive social networks instead of becoming isolated. Despite family challenges, resilient families manage to maintain important social links.
8. Developing collaborative relationships with professionals—It is important to engage in collaborative and mutually respectful relationships with professionals. Poor relationships can lead to added stress for the family and withdrawal from needed social, educational, and medical services.

DEVELOPMENTAL TRANSITIONS

Depending on the nature and severity of a child's disability and the family's response to it, families of children who have disabilities must concern themselves with a series of stages, a sense of chronic sorrow, or both that, at least to some extent, are unique to them. For some families it is not possible to apply any type of developmental or stage theory model because of new major events that continue. This may be true, for example, in a family with a hemophilic child where periodic "bleeds" can cause considerable ongoing stress. Such events trigger a new cycle of upset, changing demands, and new adaptations.

Children with disabilities will be slower accomplishing certain life cycle or developmental milestones and some may never achieve them (Farber, 1975; Fewell, 1986). As the child approaches critical periods, parents may experience renewed anxiety or sadness. Fewell (1986) described six periods that are particularly stressful to parents of children with disabilities:

1. Encountering the disability
2. Early childhood
3. School entry
4. Adolescence
5. Beginning adult life
6. Maintaining adult life

ENCOUNTERING THE DISABILITY

The nature of a child's disability generally determines when the parents learn about it. Genetic disabilities, such as Down syndrome, are apparent soon after birth; therefore parents become aware of their child's condition early. Conditions such as deafness and language and learning disabilities may not be discovered until the child is older. The confirmation of a serious and chronic problem often precipitates a crisis and affects the entire family. Immediate reactions may be those of shock, great disappointment, anxiety, and depression (Hornby, 1994). As noted earlier, the loss of the expected child may precipitate a mourning period much like the death of a family member. Contact with physicians and health care workers is particularly intense at this stage. It is also during this time of considerable stress that the family needs to inform other family members, friends, and work acquaintances of its situation. The awkwardness some family members feel can lead to withdrawal or isolation during a stressful period when social support would be very helpful. A father who found out that his daughter had Down syndrome wrote,

> I didn't want to see my friends. We became very isolated as a result of it. We drifted away from a lot of the friends we had—I found that I couldn't talk to friends. I couldn't face them—I think this is a little bit sad in the sense that I was very close to quite a few guys who had played soccer with me since I was very

young—after Sally was born they just completely faded out of existence. (quoted in Hornby, 1994, p. 57)

Related to the initial encounter is the notion that a child's disability is an unanticipated event. Generally speaking, adults have expectations of the normal expectable life cycle events. Adults "internalize expectations of the consensually validated sequences of major life events—not only what these events should be but when they should occur" (Neugarten, 1976, p. 18). It is the unanticipated life event (birth of a child with a disability; early onset dimentia) that is likely to be experienced as a traumatic event. Major stressors tend to be caused by "off–time" events that fall outside of the family's expectations (Marsh, 1992).

EARLY CHILDHOOD

The early childhood years can be difficult ones for family members as they anxiously watch for their child to achieve certain developmental milestones. The chronicity of a child's disabilities and what it means to the family is a major part of the early childhood years. The nature and severity of the disability may play a key role in the family's perception and behavior (Fewell, 1991; Lyon & Lyon, 1991). In regard to a child's developmental delay, Fewell (1986) observed,

> The task of diapering a three-year-old is simply not as easy as it was when the child was one year old. The larger and heavier child requires more energy to lift and carry. The emotional burden is also great: parents anticipate the end of diapers and two o'clock bottles, and when these things don't end, it can shatter dreams and invite questions about the future. (pp. 16–17)

Concerns about what the future holds for the child and family begin to emerge during early childhood; for some, as early as infancy. A parent's concern about the future was vividly portrayed by the educator and parent Helen Featherstone (1980):

> I remember, during the early months of Jody's life, the anguish with which I contemplated the distant future. Jody cried constantly, not irritable, hungry cries, but heartrending shrieks of pain. Vain efforts to comfort him filled my nights and days. One evening when nothing seemed to help, I went outside, intending to escape his misery for a moment, hoping that without me he might finally fall asleep. Walking in summer darkness, I imagined myself at seventy, bent and wrinkled, hobbling up the stairs to minister to Jody, now over forty, but still crying and helpless. (p. 19)

Although early intervention programs are generally applauded, Fewell (1986) noted that a crisis may develop when a child enters an early intervention program, because

1. families see older children with a similar condition and wonder whether their child will resemble them as he or she develops;
2. families who share their experiences with other families realize that they may need to "fight" for the services their child needs, further draining the family's resources; and
3. families learn that they are often expected to be their child's primary caregivers and teachers.

In this regard, Turnbull and Turnbull (1990) quoted a mother who said,

I found the infant stimulation program to be very helpful in providing an opportunity to learn parenting skills. (Peter was our first child.) It also helped our morale in that it gave us specific things to teach Peter, so we could see steady progress in his development. This created strong feelings of guilt in me because I felt that if I wasn't working with him at every opportunity, then I wasn't doing enough. If his progress was slow, I felt it was my fault. (p. 51)

During this phase, parents come into increasingly more contact with professionals who may treat the parents as patients who need treatment rather than as experts as parents and caregivers (Alper, Schloss, & Schloss, 1994; Seligman & Seligman, 1980). For some, what can be disheartening at this stage is the realization of the chronic burden a child might be for parents and siblings as they view the future with some degree of uncertainty and anxiety. But early intervention programs help to prepare the family for the marathon ahead.

SCHOOL ENTRY

Parents may experience another setback or period of adjustment when they realize that their child fails to fit into the mainstream of the traditional educational system. A child may require special education classes and a separate transportation system. Siblings may find this a particularly difficult period, as more of their schoolmates learn that they have a disabled brother or sister. This stage can be characterized as the period when the family "goes public" as members venture beyond the boundaries of the family. And finally, parents, if they have not done so already, must adjust the educational and vocational goals they had envisioned for their child. Parents should be reassured, however, that as some doors may be closed to their children, others will open.

It is important to note that the difficulties parents experience depend on the nature of the child's disability (e.g., there may be relatively few adjustments if the child is only moderately physically disabled) and the preparedness of the school system to provide adequate educational and adjunct services for special needs children. Also, during this period, parents may debate the merits of a segregated versus inclusive educational setting for their child. We discuss the educational system and families in more detail in Chapter 3.

ADOLESCENCE

Adolescence marks the period when children begin to separate from their parents. This period also is the time when children experience considerable change, turmoil, and ambivalence (Marshak, 1982). For families with children with disabilities, this stage can be a painful reminder of their children's failure to successfully traverse this life cycle stage as they continue to remain dependent.

Peer acceptance or the lack of it may be particularly painful for the entire family during the adolescent years. Peer acceptance may determine the extent to which the child may feel rejected and isolated, which in turn may contribute to the stress parents and siblings experience. Because of their disabilities, adolescents deviate from their nondisabled peers. One of us expressed his concerns about his children's experience of rejection thus:

> As Lori grew to pre-adolescence and adolescence her deficiencies became more obvious and the adulation she basked in earlier was replaced by a certain amount of scorn and rejection. The kids congregating in the neighborhood cul-de-sac played with her only if others were unavailable. Although a few of the neighborhood children seemed to be fond of her, I was aware that some children chronically taunted her and referred to her as "slow" and a "retard."
>
> As Lori's sib, Lisa had to make instantaneous decisions about whether she was going to side with her sister or the neighborhood kids. If she sided with her sister, Lisa jeopardized her friendship with the other kids and, if she supported Lori, I wondered whether she was angry at her pals and angry toward Lori for being different and threatening her friendships. This must have been an insufferable bind.
>
> I often observed the kids interacting from our living room window. My heart ached to see either Lisa or Lori hurt. I felt impotent to help either one avoid the pain. (Seligman, 1995, pp. 175–176)

Because of their disabilities, adolescents deviate from their nondisabled peers. The issues of deviance and conformity are particularly salient during the adolescent years.

> Adolescence is a particularly difficult phase of life for many with disabilities. The value placed on conformity during adolescence typically causes considerable distress because of the difference inherent in having a disability. Differentness becomes bad. An additional source of distress is the heightened importance placed on attracting a member of the opposite sex. Issues of independence and emancipation also become pronounced and a source of considerable turmoil. (Marshak & Seligman, 1993, p. 15)

Beginning Adult Life

Public education offers both children and parents several benefits. It helps the child gain important educational and vocational skills and independence and provides respite for the parents. But as a child's education draws to an end, parents must make some difficult choices. Because of limited vocational possibilities and inadequate community living arrangements, some families may be left with few choices. This is a stressful period in that the specter of the child's future looms and can cause considerable concern and anxiety.

Maintaining Adult Life

Where an adult with a disability will live and the level of care the person requires characterize the family's concerns at this stage. A major concern is the future care of their adult child as parents worry about the ensuing years when they may not be able to be active overseers or when they are deceased. One of us wrote about his fears regarding his young adult daughter when he is no longer alive:

> Tears come to my eyes when I think of Lori without her parents. She is so accustomed to having them around. I try to suppress the apprehension that wells up in me when thoughts of Lori's future come to mind. But I can't deny the reality that anxieties about Lori's future are relentless. (Seligman, 1995, p. 182)

Mental health professionals are particularly important at this stage to help families plan for their child's future in terms of vocational and leisure time activities and in terms of living arrangements. Adult siblings as well as other extended family members may be a useful resource and should be explored as potential helpers during this period. Although community support services are always needed, their availability and accessibility become particularly acute here.

In a fitting conclusion to her discussion of these six stages, Fewell (1986) noted,

> When a family has a disabled child, all the actors in this support network must adapt to the extended needs of the disabled member. The adaptations family members make are often significant, and individual destinies may be determined by the experience. Family adaptations change as the child matures; the stress at various periods may affect family members differently, for much depends on the familial and environmental contributions to the dynamic interactions of adaptation at a given point in time. (p. 19)

CONCLUSION

In this chapter we have attempted to provide the reader with a number of concepts related to the challenge of coping with disability in the family. We feel that these concepts represent important conceptual lenses and foundational material that should prove useful in the following chapters.

In terms of developmental and life cycle issues, this section represents a truncated version of the remainder of this book. The chapters that follow reflect the issues families must concern themselves with when they first encounter disability and as their child matures and grows into adolescence, adulthood, and beyond.

CHAPTER 2

Infancy and
Early Childhood

Two major theories pertain to how family members respond to the birth of an infant with a disability. Stage theory holds that family members negotiate a series of stages, or phases, that begins with shock or disbelief and culminates in acceptance. The other prominent theory suggests that parents experience lifelong sadness, or chronic sorrow. A third model might suggest that some families experience a combination of the two.

Since the birth of a child with a disability is experienced as a traumatic and life-altering event, there has been considerable interest in the initial and subsequent responses of family members to this occurrence. A number of efforts have been made to chart the phases or stages parents experience after they have been informed of their child's disability. Blacher (1984) listed 24 studies that present some variant of stage theory. Before we explore these reactions to the birth of a child with a disability, however, it is essential to acknowledge that before childbirth, most parents have a limited experience with disability.

THE PRENATAL PERIOD

Most parents have had limited personal experiences with persons who have disabilities prior to their child's birth. Although there is exposure to disability issues on television and in human interest stories in newspapers, many people hold stereotypes, stigmatizing attitudes, and misinformation about persons with disabilities.

As a result, during the prenatal period, most parents dread the possibility of giving birth to a child with a disability. As one mother of a Down syndrome child said, "I remember thinking, before I got married, it would be the worst thing that could ever happen to me" (Darling, 1979, p. 124). Parents' concern is heightened when they know of other families who have children with disabilities.

Some parents claim to have had premonitions that something was wrong with their baby (Seligman & Darling, 1997). Their concerns seem to be based on personal experience, as their expectations of what pregnancy should be like did not fit their actual experience of pregnancy.

> I felt strongly that she was deformed—she didn't kick as much as I thought she should.

> I thought something might be wrong because I was sick all the time and I wasn't sick at all during my first pregnancy. (Darling, 1979, pp. 125)

On the other hand, parents' fears about their unborn newborn are generally neutralized by family and friends, so that in the end anxieties about giving birth to a child with a disability is reduced.

Childbirth classes help parents to expect a healthy infant:

> Although these classes typically cover the possibility of unexpected events during labor and delivery, the end product of the birth process that is presented to prospective parents is generally a normal, healthy baby. The possibility of birth defects is usually not mentioned at all. (Seligman & Darling, 1997, p. 32)

Due to supportive comments by family and friends, which can contribute to denial, and because of the failure of childbirth classes to inform parents about the possibility of childhood illness or disability, most parents are not prepared for the birth of a child with a medical problem. Modern technology makes it possible for some childhood disabilities to be diagnosed prenatally, however, through such techniques as amniocentesis, ultrasound, and maternal serum testing. In situations where a disability is diagnosed prenatally, anticipatory grieving may be tempered by the hope that the diagnosis was a mistake.

The birth situation, then, is embraced with a particular set of knowledge, attitudes, anxieties, expectations, and hopes. Parents possess varying degrees of knowledge about disabilities and hold various attitudes toward people with disabilities as well as differing expectations about the birth situation, parenthood, and the unique attributes of their unborn child.

Concerns about a baby are sometimes not revealed directly to parents in the delivery room, yet they may become suspicious because of unintentional clues given by physicians and nurses:

> When Billy was born I heard the nurse say, "Is it a boy or girl?" and I knew right away something was wrong. . . . They wrapped him up so I could just see his head and they said, "We're going to bring him to the nursery now." I let him go because I knew something was wrong and I wanted him to be taken where he would get attention. (Darling, 1979, p. 132)

> I remember very vividly. The doctor did not say anything at all when the baby was born. Then he said, "It's a boy," and the way he hesitated, I immediately said, "Is he all right?" And he said, "He has ten fingers and ten toes," so in the back of my mind I knew there was something wrong. (Darling, 1979, p. 129)

After the birth, parents want to know if there is a problem with their infant. At times, physicians can contribute to the parents' feelings of anomie (meaninglessness, powerlessness) by withholding information (Seligman & Darling, 1997). Although physicians may believe that they are protecting the parents by withholding information, they unwittingly contribute to the parents' suspicions, uncertainty, and anxiety. Examples such as those cited previously continue to occur in delivery rooms, but much less commonly now than in the past. Withholding untoward information from family members seems to be discouraged by medical professionals, but such information must be communicated with gentle honesty, compassion, and empathy. Yet sometimes information is not forthcoming because of the uncertain nature of the newborn's disability.

> Any definitive prognostic implications of her condition could not be made due to her young age and because of her "borderline" diagnosis. Looking back I am very appreciative of the fact that the professionals did not offer a prognosis in the face of her ambiguous diagnoses. I know from other parents that they were not so lucky. In some cases their child's disability was pronounced to be severe and unchangeable and they were encouraged to institutionalize their child. I have often felt that professionals sometimes advise parents according to their own attitudes, prejudices, and values and not what is best for the child and the family. (Seligman, 1995, p. 173)

In addition, birth generally takes place in medically controlled settings, placing parents in a state of submission to professional authority, which leads to powerlessness and anxiety when events fail to follow expectations.

THE POSTPARTUM PERIOD

Understandably, the parents' initial response to the news that their child has a disability generally tends to be negative and it is not uncommon for the parents to reject their baby during the early postpartum period.

> I was kind of turned off. I didn't want to go near her. It was like she had a disease or something, and I didn't want to catch it. I didn't want to touch her. (Mother of a child with Down syndrome)

> I saw her for the first time when she was 10 days old. . . . She was much more deformed than I had been told. At the time I thought, "Oh my God, what have I done?" (Mother of a child with spina bifida) (Darling, 1979, pp. 135–136)

During this period, parents may be more susceptible to a professional's suggestion that their child be institutionalized or not be treated. Physicians need to be cautious to not urge parents to make decisions during this early and vulnerable period. It would be more appropriate to inform parents about their child's disability and to make necessary treatment recommendations instead of encouraging them to take some action that they may regret the rest of their lives. One example can be found in the comments of one parent who was involved in our survey research. She wrote, "When he was in prenatal care in the hospital, the social worker kept leaving adoption pamphlets on his incubator for me."

Most important, professionals need to be sensitive to their early interaction with parents:

> I believe that parents of children with disabilities recall early events (especially around diagnostic information) with searingly vivid memories—some good and some bad. These recollections should inform professionals who provide services to family members that they must be on their very best behavior so that their memories of interactions with professionals are positive. Furthermore, I believe that a professional's response and attitude toward children with disabilities plays some role in how parents perceive their own children. Contrast a professional's cold and distant demeanor with one who is warm and accepting of the child and parents and is realistically optimistic and encouraging about the future. (Seligman, 1995, pp. 171–172)

There is some speculation that parents of newborns do not automatically develop an attachment relationship to their child, even when the infant has no disability (Eyer, 1992). Attachment occurs out of the process of parent-child interactions. It is enhanced when babies begin smiling and making sounds in response to parental gestures. But the existence of certain characteristics that may be more common with babies who have disabilities does tend to impede the formation of parent-child attachment (Bailey & Wolery, 1984; Blacher, 1984; Collins-Moore, 1984). Such characteristics as the following can lead to delayed attachment: unpleasant crying, lack of responsiveness, feeding difficulties, inability to vocalize or maintain eye contact, prolonged hospitalization (and consequent separation), and the like.

Atypical infant responses, then, can lead to parental withdrawal. Furthermore, child abuse is disproportionately high in the instance of infants who have disabilities (Frodi, 1981). By the same token, parents have a tremendous adaptive capacity to overcome initial obstacles and eventually form positive attachments to their infants with disabilities.

> In general, all but the children with the most severe disabilities are able to respond to their parents to some extent—by sound, gesture, or other indication of recognition. In addition, attachment is usually encouraged by supportive interactions with other people. (Seligman & Darling, 1997)

As noted earlier, in some instances a child's disabilities may be elusive, not because medical professionals withhold diagnostic information but because the symptoms do not readily lend themselves to a definitive diagnosis. In such instances, anomie-related stress can become protracted:

> Sometimes I wish my son had cerebral palsy or Down syndrome—something definite and preferably a little visible. . . . It is . . . the elusiveness of our son's problems that causes so much pain. So, as awful as it sounds, I have thought of what it might be like to have a child with a defined disability. (Gundry, 1989, pp. 22–24)

After the early period of "first information," the ability of family members to cope depends on how they define the situation (i.e., as a catastrophic experience or as a challenging yet manageable event). Because the birth of a child with a disability is an unanticipated occurrence, families must rely, in part, on other people to establish a perceptual lens for them. Because of this, professionals play a key role by providing diagnostic, prognostic, and treatment information that helps to reduce feelings of helplessness. Furthermore, the extent to which families can restore a "normalized" lifestyle after the infancy period will vary according to the child's disability, the parents' personal resources, and the availability of social supports.

THE STAGES OF MOURNING

The stages noted next have been used in reference to families of children with special needs in response to the observation that the birth of an infant with disabilities is a traumatic loss often experienced by the parents as the death of the expected normal, healthy child (Solnit & Stark, 1961). Duncan (1977) adapted Kübler-Ross's (1969) stages, which characterize reactions to impending death, to infant disability. The stages should be viewed flexibly because of the complexity of the adjustment process and the variability of individual responses. The stages include

1. Shock and denial
2. Bargaining
3. Anger
4. Depression
5. Acceptance

SHOCK AND DENIAL

Shock and denial (denial often follows shock) are a parent's initial response to diagnostic information. Denial appears to operate on an unconscious level to ward off unbearable anxiety in the face of a life-altering event. Denial can serve a useful, buffering purpose early on but can cause difficulties if it persists. If, over time and in the face of clear evidence, parents continue to deny the existence of their child's disability, professionals in early contact with the parents need to be cautious that

*   the children are not pushed beyond their capabilities;
*   the parents do not make endless and pointless visits to doctors or other professionals to get an acceptable diagnosis; and
*   the parents do not fail to utilize social services designed to help them cope and to help the child achieve attainable levels of potential.

When parents are in shock they report feeling confusion, numbness, disorganization, and helplessness. Some parents are unable to hear much of what they are told when the child's diagnosis is communicated:

One mother told me that when the pediatrician told her that her 18-month-old son had cerebral palsy she "burst into tears" and didn't hear anything else. Another mother recalled how she had listened very calmly as the neurologist explained the extent of the brain damage her 14-year-old daughter had sustained as the result of a car accident. Then she got in her car and began to drive home, but after a few hundred yards, as she was crossing a bridge, she felt sick and her legs felt like they'd turned to jelly, so she got out of the car and leaned over the side of the bridge to get some air. (Hornby, 1994, p. 16)

It is important for professionals to realize that after receiving a diagnosis parents may not be in an emotional state to hear about the details of the disability. Explanations about etiology, course, and prognosis may not be heard, often necessitating a follow-up meeting. Professionals need to deliver the diagnosis honestly and with compassion and respond to any questions the parents may have.

BARGAINING

The bargaining phase is characterized by a type of magical or fantasy thinking. The underlying theme is that if the parent works extra hard, the child will improve. A child's improved condition is compensation for hard work, being useful to others, or contributing to a worthy cause. For example, during bargaining, parents may join local groups in activities that benefit a particular cause. Another manifestation of the bargaining phase is that parents may turn to religion or look for a miracle.

ANGER

As parents realize that their child will not improve significantly, anger develops. There may be anger at God ("Why me?") or at oneself or one's spouse for having produced the child or for not helping care for the child. Indeed, poor outcomes are expected when a family member is blamed or held responsible for a child's disability (Garwick, Kohrman, Titus, Wolman, & Blum, 1997). Anger also is frequently projected onto professionals for not healing the child (doctors) or for not helping the child make significant learning gains (teachers). Anger can be related to an unsympathetic community, insensitive professionals, inadequate services, fatigue due to long hospital stays, and the like. Guilt can turn anger inward where parents (in particular, mothers) blame themselves for the disability.

DEPRESSION

Expressing anger is often cathartic and cleansing and can reduce the negative effect of powerful emotions, but when parents realize that their anger does not change their child's condition and when they accept the chronic nature of the disability and its implications for the family, a sense of depression may set in. For many parents, depression (or having the blues) is temporary or episodic and is generally considered a normal reaction to a traumatic event.

Hornby (1994) believed that detachment sometimes follows anger when parents report feeling empty and nothing seems to matter. Life has lost its meaning. This reaction is thought to indicate that the parent is reluctantly beginning to accept the reality of the disability. This, then, for some is a turning point in the adaptation process.

Acceptance

Acceptance is achieved when parents demonstrate some of the following characteristics:

1. They are able to discuss their child's shortcomings with relative ease.
2. They evidence a balance between encouraging independence and showing love.
3. They are able to collaborate with professionals to make realistic short- and long-term plans.
4. They pursue personal interests unrelated to their child.
5. They can discipline their child appropriately without undue guilt.
6. They can abandon overprotective or unduly harsh behavioral patterns toward their child.

Drotar, Baskiewicz, Irvin, Kenell, and Klaus (1975) referred to this final stage as "reorganization," when positive, long-term acceptance has developed and guilt is lessened.

Differences in Coping with Stages of Mourning

In applying these stages one needs to be mindful that families are not homogeneous and that these stages may not be a good fit for some families. For some, these stages are cyclical and recur as new developmental milestones are achieved or when a crisis occurs (e.g., a child's condition worsens). For others, although a particular reaction may be the most dominant one, other reactions may also be present (Hornby, 1994). For example, when parents' predominant emotion is one of anger they may also be experiencing some denial and sadness at the same time. Other factors that affect the manifestation of these stages include whether manifestation is determined in part by the parents' culture, whether social support is available, and the like (Goodheart & Lansing, 1997; Thompson & Gustafson, 1996). Another factor to consider is whether all family members experience the same stage at the same time and how long a particular stage lasts. According to Hornby (1994),

> Some parents appear to work the process in a few days, whereas others seem to take years to reach a reasonable level of adaptation. Just as for any major loss it is considered that most people will take around two years to come to terms with the disability. However, some parents seem to take longer and a few possibly never fully adjust to the situation. (p. 20)

OPIRHORY AND PETERS MODEL

Employing a stage model, Opirhory and Peters (1982) provided a useful guide to interventions with parents of newborns with disabilities. As noted earlier, stage theory holds that parents generally follow predictable series of feelings and actions after a child's diagnosis has been communicated. Opirhory and Peters (1982) believed that these stages, or phases, are useful general benchmarks for considering appropriate interventions.

During the denial stage, professionals should gently provide an honest evaluation of the situation the parents are confronting. They should simply describe the child objectively and indicate the care that is needed. They should not remove the parents' hope or interfere with their coping style unless it is inappropriate or dysfunctional to the family.

During the anger stage, professionals must create an open and permissive atmosphere so that parents can vent their anger and pain without fear of ridicule or rejection. They must be accepting of the parents' criticism, even if it is directed toward them, without personalizing the parents' remarks or defending other professionals or themselves. It is important to keep in mind that projected anger reflects the parents' own anxiety in the face of a situation that will significantly change their lives. Clinicians should be mindful, too, that some parents have been treated so atrociously by other professionals that their anger and frustration derive from thoroughly objective circumstances.

Opirhory and Peters (1982) recommended that professionals discourage parents from dwelling on a review of the pregnancy during the bargaining stage. During this phase, parents feel that they can reverse their child's condition by engaging in certain redemptive activities. The authors advise the professional to point out the child's positive characteristics, encourage involvement, and remain optimistic without giving any guarantees about the child's potential progress. It is also essential that while parents continue to establish a warm and loving relationship with their child who has a disability, they are encouraged to nonetheless balance their lives with personally fulfilling goals and activities. Professionals need to be wary of parents who either fill their lives with a variety of outside activities at the expense of their child or are so involved with the child that their lives become severely restricted and they begin to withdraw from others.

The depression stage can be characterized by mild or severe mood swings. Again, the professional needs to be able to distinguish between clinical depression and milder forms of dysphoria. Mild, situational, and time-limited depression is common and liable to emerge at various points in the child's development. Parents need to be reassured that what they are experiencing is normal and not be overpathologized or criticized for their emotions. Opirhory and Peters (1982) believed that one needs to be especially alert to signs of regression to earlier stages, although we do not necessarily view this with alarm. Anger and mild denial, for example, can resurface and should be considered normal unless these feelings become chronic, excessive, and rigidly held.

During the acceptance stage, the professional should continue to reinforce the positive aspects of the parent-child relationship. Because a realistic adjustment to the infant or child is achieved during this stage, it is typically characterized by fulfilling family relationships. Therefore, the need for professional help and support is unlikely to be crucial, although, as mentioned, problems may emerge when the child reaches certain developmental milestones.

CHRONIC SORROW

The second major theoretical view of family adjustment to infant childhood disability is the position developed by Olshansky (1962) and later embraced by others (Damrosch & Perry, 1989; Wikler et al., 1981). Olshansky coined the term "chronic sorrow" to connote a longer, perhaps even lifelong sadness, brought about by changes in the child and external events, such as school entry. In regard to chronic sorrow, Marsh (1992) wrote,

> Stage theories generally reflect an assumption of movement toward a final state of closure characterized by acceptance and adjustment. Increasingly, that view has been challenged by clinicians and researchers who have emphasized the continuing emotional upheavals of families, as well as the absence of time-limited sequential movement through a series of stages. (pp. 121–122)

The intensity of the experience of chronic sorrow is seen as varying over time and can be influenced by the degree of changes in the disability or by life events as suggested previously, but also by the parents' personality, ethnic group identification, religion, and social class. Max (1985) suggested that reactions such as anger, sadness, and denial are not resolved but become an integral part of the parents' emotional life. As will be illustrated in subsequent chapters, this reoccurrence of parental reactions tends to emerge at various transition points in the child's development, such as school entry, the onset of puberty, leaving school, or leaving home (Hornby, 1995). It can also occur when parents are informed about an additional disability at some time subsequent to the initial diagnosis. One parent recounts how having apparently come to terms with her child being blind, she was devastated when mental retardation was later diagnosed (Featherstone, 1981). Firestein (1989) discussed the dreams that can be destroyed by childhood illness or disability. He asserted that the sense of lost dreams is chronic and grief is experienced in some measure over many years.

Olshansky (1962) believed that chronic sorrow is a natural response to infant disability, because unlike families of children without disabilities, some of these families will not see their children ultimately become self-sufficient adults. In this view, a parent who experiences sadness about a child's disability can still be competent and caring. Too often, professionals have been quick to label parents as unaccepting or poorly adjusted when they are, in fact, reacting normally to their continuing burden.

From their research, Wikler et al. (1981) reported that parental sorrow appeared to be periodic rather than continuous, with the level of intensity related to some of the developmental junctures noted earlier and to the coping abilities of the parents. In another study, mothers and fathers of children with Down syndrome reported that the majority of mothers (68%) experienced peaks and valleys, as well as periodic crises (Damrosch & Perry, 1989). A majority of fathers (83%), however, depicted their adjustment in terms of steady, gradual recovery. This study suggested that there may be a gender difference in response to childhood illness or disability.

The concept of chronic sorrow is reflected in the voices of two parents from the study by Marsh (1992):

> It is constant grieving throughout our lives. Feelings of frustration because [of] fighting the system and seeing very little progress. (p. 123)

> The pain's there, it never leaves. I am to the point now where I'm kind of over the self-blame part of it. Every once in a while it will crop up. I tried hard to give her the best that I had at the time. I tried to make the best decisions I could for her. Given what I had, what I knew then, I think I've done a good job. But I always think maybe I could have done a little better. So it's painful. I hope the day comes that I can close my eyes and get a little bit of peace. (p. 123)

PSYCHOSOCIAL STRESSES ASSOCIATED WITH CHILDHOOD ILLNESS OR DISABILITY

The previous section addressed parental response to the period of time subsequent to diagnosis. Some family members may take longer to reach acceptance, and as noted earlier, others may experience a mild yet chronic sadness. We now explore five stresses commonly experienced by families as a consequence of chronic illness or disability. These stresses are intellectual, instrumental, emotional, interpersonal, and existential (Brinthaupt, 1991; Chesler & Barbarin, 1987).

INTELLECTUAL STRESS

Intellectual stress is mainly associated with the process of first information when determining an accurate diagnosis occupies the parents' attention. It is not uncommon for parents of children with certain disorders (e.g., cystic fibrosis, rare and multiple disabilities) to engage in the frustrating process of visiting a number of medical specialists. With some disorders, there can be several misdiagnoses before a correct one is given. Once the diagnosis is made, however, parents usually experience a compelling need for information (Hobbs, Perrin, & Ireys, 1985).

The parents' quest for information regarding etiology, prognosis, and treatment options helps to enhance their sense of control in a very anxiety-provoking situation. Parents may engage in "doctor shopping," which may make them susceptible to "quack" treatments, although some shopping may be necessary to reach a professional who can make a definitive diagnosis.

According to Brinthaupt (1991), various intellectual stresses are imposed as parents attempt to comprehend their child's disorder. Parents may be required to integrate vast amounts of information about disease physiology, timing and type of treatments and the rationale for them, symptoms of decline or improvement, complications, and side effects of treatment. In writing about childhood cancer, Chesler and Barbarin (1987) observed, "The stress of wondering if they are handling treatments and side effects properly is escalated by the stakes involved—the child's comfort and even life may hang in the balance" (p. 42). Brinthaupt (1991) added, "The overriding task of learning the skills necessary to effectively operate within a medical subculture is an intellectual stress not to be underestimated for its difficulty as well as importance" (p. 301).

INSTRUMENTAL STRESS

Instrumental stress involves tasks that are necessary to incorporate the child's medical care and treatment into the lifestyle of the family. The goal is to achieve as much equilibrium as possible in the family system. Parents become frontline caregivers of their child and, as a result, become proficient in providing management of the child. While simultaneously attending to their child's needs and their own needs, they must also be vigilant of the needs of other family members, such as other children or their spouses. Brinthaupt (1991) listed the following instrumental challenges:

1. Managing finances
2. Determining the division of labor in the family so that adequate care is provided for the child with a disability
3. Accomplishing necessary household chores in addition to caretaking
4. Becoming aware of signs that indicate a negative impact of the illness on family members
5. Knowing when and how to seek assistance
6. Fostering a sense of normalcy despite the demands of the illness or disability

The financial demands on a family are instrumental stresses that are often given short shrift in the professional literature. Both direct medical care and in-home and self-care expenses as well as expenses for special diets, special schools, time lost from work, home modifications, and the like constitute significant sources of stress. Also, one parent, usually the mother, often relinquishes a career to remain at home to care for the child. A decision to stay at home necessitates a sacrifice and negates a second income that could help to meet uninsured expenses. It may also mean that a parent must forego pursuing more challenging, fulfilling, or lucrative career opportunities if such a choice would remove the family from a treatment facility. These financial demands can interfere with potentially restorative and interpersonally rewarding family activities, such as vacations (Brinthaupt, 1991).

EMOTIONAL STRESS

Emotional stress encompasses both psychogenic factors and reactive responses to the demands of caregiving. Responses might include lack of sleep, loss of energy, and excessive worry and anxiety (Chesler & Barbarin, 1987). A key factor contributing to the emotional response to illness or disability is uncertainty regarding disease prognosis and responses to periodic exacerbations (Jessop & Stein, 1985; Perrin & MacLean, 1988). Furthermore, the uncertainty and ambiguity that can accompany illness or disability can compromise one's sense of perceived control (Pollin, 1995; Wright, 1983).

Parents of children with rare disorders can feel isolated, which increases emotional stress, because it is unlikely that they will encounter another family with a child who has the same condition. A useful resource for parents of infants who have rare disorders is the "Readers Forum" in the magazine *Ex-*

ceptional Parent. Letter writers often offer to correspond with other parents who have an infant or child with the same uncommon disorder as their child. Another contributor to emotional stress is the heart-wrenching experience of watching a child suffer and not being able to relieve that suffering. Also, heightened vigilance for signs of relapse or disease exacerbation can add to stress and anxiety.

INTERPERSONAL STRESS

Interpersonal stress can follow on the heels of pediatric disability or illness. Interpersonal stress can involve family members, friends, and medical or educational personnel. Although divorce rates among these families are virtually equivalent to those of families in which there is no illness or disability (Brinthaupt, 1991; Kalins, 1983; Sabbeth & Leventhal, 1984), there does appear to be evidence of marital distress. More research is needed to clarify the role of marital distress in these families in comparison to families with nondisabled children. Brinthaupt (1991) speculated that marital distress may not necessarily be maladaptive and that, at times, it may serve an adaptive function, in that problems that had not been broached before can be addressed. There is some suggestion, however, that high–recurrence risk diseases serve as a threat to marital stability (Begleiter, Burry, & Harris, 1976).

It was observed that the incidence of divorce in families in which a child has a nonhereditary disorder (e.g., leukemia) or a low–recurrence risk disability (e.g., spina bifida) is lower than the national average whereas the divorce rate in families with a high–recurrence risk illness (e.g., cystic fibrosis) is comparable to the national average (Brinthaupt, 1991). It is important to acknowledge once again that marital distress in some families may be related more to problems the marital partners have with each other than to problems with the child who has the disability.

I believe that one needs to be careful about attributing marital conflict or divorce to the presence of a child with special needs. The decision to dissolve a marriage is a complex one, made up of personal styles and values, family of origin issues, external factors, and the like. My suspicion is that the general public believes that a child with a disability creates enormous tensions within the family, eventually culminating in divorce. On the other hand, parents who speak and write about their experiences with their child project the notion that a child with a disability marshalls constructive forces within the family system and eventually brings family members together. My guess is that the truth probably falls somewhere between what the general public seems to believe and what some parents have projected in their public utterances and in their writings. We need to openly address this issue so that the public is better informed and that parents who have experienced divorce are not filled with guilt and shame due to the perception that most other families are actually brought closer. (Seligman, 1995, pp. 178–179)

Interpersonal distress can appear in other family members as well because nondisabled children and extended family members are also affected by childhood disability, a topic that will be explored more fully later in this chapter. Finally, interpersonal stress can emerge from potentially stressful encounters with the public (Siegal, 1996; Wikler, 1981). Depending on the extent to which parents "go public" with their child's disability, they must negotiate the sometimes stressful and awkward transactions with strangers.

EXISTENTIAL STRESS

Existential stress refers to the family's ability to construct an explanatory meaning framework for its experience. Childhood disability is an affront to an assumed developmental order of the family life cycle. "Childhood is supposed to be a time of well-being, or, at worst, a period of self-limited, transitory illness, and not a time of threats to viability or function" (Stein & Jessop, 1984, p. 194). Parents grapple with such existential issues as "Why me?" or "Why my family?" (Kushner, 1981). Cherished notions about God, fate, and a just world are challenged (Chesler & Barbarin, 1987).

> If the child is seen as a divine gift, the unexpressed question, "why did this happen to me"? has the corollary "why did He do this to me?" and raises the age-old philosophical question, "If God is good He would not have done this. (Ross, 1964, p. 62)

An infant or a child with a disability may be perceived as a reflection of the mother's adequacy. In situations where a child is viewed as salvaging an unstable marriage, the birth of a child with a disability may be another indication that the marriage is doomed to failure. On the other hand, the infant may be seen as a divine gift, a sign of grace (Ross, 1975). Such a child may be viewed as a sign of special grace because only the most worthy would be entrusted with his or her care. One study showed that an ability to endow the child's illness with meaning and a sense of optimism seemed to characterize highly functioning families (Venter, 1981).

Some parents appear to be able to explain their child's disorder within the framework of a particular life philosophy whereas others alter or abandon their prior religious or spiritual commitments. It is apparent that existential stresses are a formidable challenge for parents of children with chronic illnesses or disabilities (Brinthaupt, 1991).

THE MEANING OF CHILDHOOD DISABILITY: A MULTICULTURAL PERSPECTIVE

Using an open-ended questionnaire design, researchers interviewed 63 families that have children with disabilities to discover how they explained their child's disability to themselves (Garwick et al., 1997). The study group consisted of 21 African American, 20 Hispanic American, and 22 European American families. Although these families offered disparate explanations, all three groups found an explanation that made sense to them in a way that fit their belief system.

Forty-five percent provided biomedical explanations for their child's condition, mostly associated with pregnancy or birth factors. Some families reported that the environment caused the disability, which included exposure to secondhand smoke, cold, air dust, and pollutants. Other families relied on folk explanations. The authors noted that two Hispanic American families believed that strong emotions such as fear and anger caused the disability. Families whose definitions took on positive attributions were better able to cope than those that gave negative reasons for their child's disability or experienced considerable family disagreement. A negative attribution could be something like the father blaming his wife for the disability because she started a fight during the period of conception.

Some families gave spiritual or religious explanations such as, "God had a purpose or reason for the child's condition." These parents felt that religion helped them cope. Others enlisted more fatalistic explanations of their child's disability. "That's just the way it is" or "Disability is just a part of life"—such explanations helped families to closure about why the condition happened.

The researchers felt that these observations require professionals to listen for negative attributions that family members give to a child's disability, especially when they blame themselves or other family members. Clinicians can help foster the development of positive attributions by focusing on the child's strengths and abilities, and for families that are coping poorly, to suggest a referral to a mental health professional.

MARITAL ADJUSTMENT, DIVORCE, AND SINGLE PARENTHOOD

There is a growing population of single parents in society in general, and single parents of infants and young children with disabilities would appear to experience greater stresses than parents in two-parent families (Simpson, 1996; Vadasy, 1986). In regard to parents of children with autism, Siegal (1996) was unequivocal in her position that single parenthood presents enormous challenges. A particular danger is the possibility that healthy children may become parentified siblings.

> In the absence of an adult helpmate, mothers, often without realizing it, depend a great deal on help from the autistic child's brothers and sisters. Seeing a three-year-old take her autistic five-year-old brother firmly by the hand as they are about to cross a busy street gives a picture of how much the life of the three-year-old can be affected by having an autistic sibling. (Siegal, 1996, pp. 139–140)

Yet, as noted earlier, most of the assumptions about single parenthood and childhood disability are intuitive; empirical data are scarce. Also, when considering divorce and single parenthood, one needs to bear in mind that divorce does not have the same impact on all family members and that the effects of divorce may depend on when in the family life cycle it occurs; the degree of dysfunction in the family before marital breakup may also be a factor (Schulz, 1987; Simpson, 1996). Furthermore, one cannot necessarily assume that the parents are not involved with their child after a divorce. It is possible that divorced parents can devote more time to their child once the issues that led to the dissolution of their marriage are resolved.

One outcome of divorce exists in families in which one or both parents in the original family remarry (Visher & Visher, 1988). New rules and roles need to be adopted, issues of loyalty to the biological and nonbiological parents need to be negotiated, new lines of authority need to be established, financial responsibilities may need to be reconsidered, and the like. When a child with a disability resides in a blended family, issues such as caretaking and primary responsibility for the child need to be negotiated, among other issues.

As suggested earlier, information regarding marital problems and divorce in families of children with disabilities is sparse and contradictory (Crnic et al. 1983; Patterson, 1991a). Gabel, McDowell, and Cerreto (1983) reported that the onset of marital difficulties is one of the more frequently reported adjustment problems. Their research review showed that marital problems included more frequent conflict, feelings of marital dissatisfaction, sexual difficulties, temporary separations, and divorce. Siegal (1996) estimated that for families of infants and children with disabilities the divorce rate is about 20% higher than in families of nondisabled children. In his landmark study, conducted a number of years ago, Farber (1959) found marital conflict to be common, especially in families containing a boy aged 9 or above who has retardation. Conversely, some families of children with disabilities report no more frequent problems than comparison families (Bernard, 1974; Dorner, 1975; Martin, 1975; Patterson, 1991b; Weisbren, 1980) and some marriages have been reported to improve after the diagnosis of an infant's disability (Schwab, 1989). Conclusions about divorce rates among parents with or without an infant or young child with disabilities are affected by the presumptions researchers make about divorce rates. Some report that one-half of marriages end in divorce, whereas others cite figures closer to one-third.

Although the data regarding marital satisfaction and divorce in families of children with disabilities are contradictory, we do know that some marriages are under stress but remain intact, others simply fail, and still others survive and thrive. The task of researchers should be to understand why some families do well whereas others do poorly. Some believe that future investigations should seek to differentiate the child and family characteristics and other ecological factors that distinguish families that cope well from those that do not (Crnic et al., 1983).

As noted earlier, a family's focus on the infant or child with a disability as a source of family problems may in fact be a "red herring" that leads the parents away from more fundamental issues about their relationship (Harris, 1983). It is important for professionals to discriminate between family problems related to the stress of coping with childhood disability and those that would have arisen under any circumstances. Problematic marital relationships can be made considerably worse, however, by the birth of a child with a disability. It is a myth that such a child, or any child for that matter, can bring a troubled marriage together (Lederer & Jackson, 1968).

Siegal (1996) noted that parental adjustment to childhood disability may be related to whether a child was planned for or desired. She also observed that parents who have planned their children very carefully often experience a greater sense of "unfairness" at having a child with a disability when they compare themselves to others who live their lives in a less planful way. Furthermore, she observed that younger couples appear to be able to cope somewhat better than older couples because their lifestyle preferences are not as fixed, because they can decide to have more children, and because of the greater physical energy available to them.

After a thorough review of the literature on families of children with severe disabilities, Lyon and Lyon (1991) concluded that these families must contend with a number of stressors, but in general the research revealed mixed conclusions regarding the impact an infant or child with severe disabilities has on the family. Like other contributors to the literature, these authors made note of the major methodological problems inherent in much of the existing research and concluded that in the absence of clear evidence that these families are coping badly, professionals should focus on such practical matters as concrete information, respite services, financial help, and other supportive services to help with practical and logistical problems. Others have made a case for providing psychotherapeutic services for some families (Elman, 1991; Laborde & Seligman, 1991; Marsh, 1993; Siegal, 1996).

From this overview, what can we conclude about marital harmony and dysfunction among families of children with disabilities? One conclusion may be that marital dysfunction can occur even without the presence of disability. Still another is that in some families an infant or young child with disabilities may aggravate latent problems. Perhaps an acceptable conclusion is that many families can cope successfully with the help of family and community supports.

FAMILIES OF A CHILD WITH DIFFERENT DISABILITIES

Although research on and observations and personal accounts of families of children with different disabling conditions is increasing, the available research is, again, too contradictory to draw any definitive conclusions. Nevertheless, there are some reports of infants or children with dissimilar disabilities that provide a glimpse of the concerns their families face. For example, the unpredictability of the behavior of some autistic children and the social-interpersonal ramifications experienced by families can cause considerable stress (Bristol, 1984; Harris, 1994; Schopler & Mesibov, 1984; Siegal, 1996). Even as we learn more about the biological bases of certain conditions, parents of children with autism and childhood schizophrenia (albeit very different conditions) are still often enough considered responsible for their child's illness and thereby suffer the social stigma that accompanies this disorder. Schizophrenia was initially explained by a theory of family interaction that was flawed because it was not based on scientific evidence (Dawes, 1994). For families with autistic children, the following constitute high-risk factors: ambiguity of diagnosis, severity and duration of the illness, and lack of congruity with community norms (Bristol, 1984). Cantwell and Baker (1984) cited research that indicates that families are impacted by the most severely disabled child, that spousal affectional bonds tend to be weakened, that siblings are affected, and that family difficulties do not diminish as the child grows older.

The unpredictability of seizures in children with epilepsy may result in family members' constant vigilance for seizure activity (Lechtenberg, 1984). Public attitudes toward persons with epilepsy resemble those toward persons with mental illness, thereby creating a major stressor for the family. Families with a hemophilic child need to be constantly vigilant of their child's bleeding episodes and families with children with heart disease need to be cautious about bringing home infections (Travis, 1976). All of these characteristics of the child's disability may cause stress in the family and precipitate a major family crisis when there are other existing family problems. As Tartar (1987) pointed out, the contribution of the parents' characteristics together with the demand characteristics of the child's disability, "underscores again the complex dynamic and reciprocal relationship between parent and offspring with the characteristics of one affecting the reactions of the other" (p. 83).

As with most disabling conditions, the effects on the family of a child who is deaf or significantly hearing impaired are mixed (Luterman, 1984). Hearing-impaired children are often also impaired in their communication, however, which can be a source of considerable frustration for family members (Sloman, Springer, & Vachon, 1993). Fewell (1991) reported that the degree of visual loss in blind children has important implications for the child and the family's reaction to the child. Just as children with low vision try to pass as normally sighted, parents, too, are caught in the dilemma of not wanting to identify their children's differences. Although children who are blind may struggle with their mobility, and there is some evidence of delayed and immature social behavior, the fact that a child with blindness can think, communicate, and carry on with the chores of daily living may make blindness less stressful to the blind child and the family than other disabilities (Fewell, 1991).

For children with physical disabilities, it is their mobility that is most affected, which, in turn, depending on the severity of the disability, may affect their ability to perform self-care functions. As with most conditions, however, there can be psychological and social factors that are directly tied to the disability. For example, some children with physical disabilities may shrink from interactions with nondisabled peers, fearing their negative response. By isolating themselves from others, they may become despondent. Physical impairments can take a variety of forms, such as a loss of limbs or a paralysis due to accident or disease. The nature, characteristics, and severity of the physical impairment may determine the type of adjustment the child and the family must make (Marshak & Seligman, 1993). For example, quadriplegia holds numerous implications for how family members contribute to frequent caretaking duties, such as lifting, feeding, and transporting. Muscular dystrophy, a degenerative disease, means that the child and family need to adjust to an increasing level of dependency as the disease progresses. Numerous other physical disorders, many that are rare and leave the family with few others to identify with, may cause problems for the family.

Mullins (1979) reported that the physical needs of children with cancer affect the entire family: "The medications, hospitalizations, repeated transportation for treatment, and extended care at home will be a drain on family finances and physical resources" (p. 266). If the cancer is terminal, the family needs to prepare for the child's imminent death (Sourkes, 1982). This can be a crisis of major proportions and requires considerable family adjustment before and after the child's death occurs.

Cystic fibrosis, one of the most common chronic diseases of childhood, requires the family to comply with a prescribed home regimen. This disease results in pulmonary dysfunction and also involves the pancreatic and gastrointestinal systems and presents serious challenges for the coping skills and adjustment of the family (Brinthaupt, 1991). The home care of the child is difficult and chronic; failure to carry out treatment can contribute to the progression of the disease and eventual death (Dushenko, 1981). Communication in these families may decline in a situation that is difficult and requires the continued expression of hope and mutual support (Patterson, 1985). McCracken (1984) reported that families of children with cystic fibrosis have multiple problems; Offer, Ostrov, and Howard (1984) argued that adolescents' problems are exacerbated by short stature and the appearance of lower maturational level. Social stigma, as noted earlier, adds to the disability.

It is impossible to conclude with any certainty how the type of an infant or child's disability will affect the family. Factors other than type may play an important role in determining family adaptation (Crnic et al., 1983). We know from Rolland (1994) that onset, course, and prognosis, as well as other illness- or disability-related variables, may influence family response. Researchers report that the quantity and quality of community resources and family support have an impact on the family's ability to cope with childhood disability (Darling, 1991; Korn, Chess, & Fernandez, 1978; Wortis & Margolies, 1955). More recently, researchers have sought to determine how and which aspects of social support are most helpful to families (Kazak & Marvin, 1984; Kazak & Wilcox, 1984; Krahn, 1993).

According to one study, mothers of children with disabilities experienced significantly more stress if their offspring had a greater number of or unusual caregiving demands, were less socially responsive, had more difficult temperaments, and displayed more repetitive behavioral patterns (Beckman, 1983). Beckman's research is important in that it represents a departure from other studies by examining specific child characteristics rather than medical labels. Beckman's results support those of Tartar (1987) and of Siegal and Silverstein (1994), who reported that it is the behavioral aspects of a condition that can be the most distressing to the family.

In a study of 111 parents of children who have hemophilia, researchers found that the burden caused by their child's illness was small (Verekamp et al., 1990). In fact, 45% of the parents reported that their marriage had improved, in contrast with 4% who felt that the marriage had gotten worse. With hemophilia, bleedings are mostly unexpected and require immediate attention. The risk of bleeding, which places the parents in an internal struggle between wanting to protect the child and also wanting to avoid limiting the child's bleeds, seems to be less problematic to parents than dealing with children who isolate themselves, do not communicate, have outbursts, and experience behavior problems (Harris, 1994).

In the face of inconclusive research data, it is important to educate service providers regarding the numerous variables that affect family adjustment and to persuade them to keep these variables in mind when evaluating a family's level of functioning.

SIBLINGS, FATHERS, AND THE EXTENDED FAMILY

Much of what we know about childhood disability and the family comes from research on mothers. More recently, however, there have been studies that include fathers. There is also a growing number of studies on siblings and a modest literature on grandparents. The following section will briefly review these family roles.

FATHERS

With the historical emphasis on mothers and attachment, the role of fathers in child development and family functioning has been undervalued. Although there have been marked changes in gender roles, men and women were historically cast into instrumental and expressive roles. The relaxation of sex roles in society has enabled some family members to respond more flexibly to changing family needs. As a result of role flexibility, fathers are more willing to adopt nurturing roles and they are also now considered capable alternative caregivers for children. Furthermore, they have more time to spend with their children due to the shortening of the work week and flextime schedules (Pruett, 1987). Although there are differences in the way fathers and mothers interact with their children, both parents are now accepted as competent nurturers and caretakers (Lamb & Meyer, 1991).

There is only a modest research base on fathers of children with disabilities and some of the studies that exist have been compromised in a number of ways (Hornby, 1995; Lamb & Meyer, 1991; Marsh, 1993). Some of the research shortcomings include the absence of control groups, the use of retrospective information, and reports about father functioning from mothers. From the research and from personal accounts of fathers' experiences, some information about fathers is available, however.

It seems that fathers and mothers initially respond differently to the news that they are parents of a child with a disability. Fathers tend to respond less emotionally at the time of diagnosis and to focus on long-term concerns, whereas mothers respond more emotionally and are concerned about their ability to cope with the burdens of child care. Generally speaking, fathers seem more concerned than mothers about the adoption of socially accept- able behavior by their children—especially their sons—and they are more anxious about the social status and occupational success of their offspring (Lamb & Meyer, 1991).

Because of the high expectations fathers have of their sons, they may be particularly disappointed when they have a boy with a disability (Farber, 1959; Grossman, 1972). As a result, some fathers manifest extremes of in- tense involvement and total withdrawal with their sons; they seem to have limited, routine involvement with their daughters who have disabilities (Chigier, 1972; Grossman, 1972; Tallman, 1965). A more recent study does not support this conclusion, suggesting that more research is needed in this area (Houser & Seligman, 1991).

Fathers' reactions to their children with disabilities may have implications for other family members. One older study found a high relationship be- tween the degree of paternal acceptance of the child and the amount of ac- ceptance and rejection generally observed in the home (Peck & Stephens, 1960). Not only is the development of the child with a disability likely to be affected when fathers choose to withdraw, but the entire family suffers. As the father withdraws, the burden of care generally falls to other family members, particularly the mother.

A problem for some fathers is their discomfort with strong emotions. Men are supposed to "fix" things, be stoic, and be in charge (Smith, 1981). Hav- ing a child with a disability is a profound challenge for some fathers who adhere to traditional male values and as a result may suffer more than their spouse from having a child with a disability (Seligman & Darling, 1997).

In spite of these negative indicators of fathers' ability to adapt to child- hood disability, there are fathers who cope well and, in fact, become in- volved in helping other fathers come to grips with their special circumstances (Meyer, 1995). One example of this is the fathers program that began in 1978 at the University of Washington (Meyer, Vadasy, Fewell, & Schell, 1985). This program has become national in scope as fathers and pro- fessional facilitators are being trained to provide workshops for fathers of children with disabilities. The workshops integrate discussions with infor- mation and opportunities for fathers to learn how to socialize and play with their sons and daughters who have disabilities.

The research from these workshops is encouraging. One study reported that fathers who completed the workshops experienced lower stress and depression and higher satisfaction levels than parents newly entering the program (Vadasy, Fewell, Greenberg, Desmond, & Meyer, 1986). Another evaluation, of 45 sets of parents, found that both mothers and fathers reported significantly decreased depression and fathers had a decrease in stress and grief (Vadasy et al., 1986).

Fathers have a need for information about their children's disability and about programs, services, and treatment options that is equal to that of mothers (Darling & Baxter, 1996; Seligman, 1995). It is important that organizations serving children with disabilities encourage the involvement of fathers in the family and include them in programs developed by the organization.

In his book *Uncommon Fathers: Reflections on Raising a Child With a Disability*, Meyer (1995) collected a series of poignant essays by fathers on their experiences of parenting a child, adolescent, or young adult with a disability. The contributing fathers reflect considerable diversity in background: a rabbi, a retired police officer, attorneys, a Christian missionary, a parole officer, authors, and college professors. In the preface Meyer wrote,

> The opinions and experiences of fathers of children with special needs are anything but monolithic. As might be expected from such a diverse group of men, the authors hold differing religious and philosophical interpretations of their children's disabilities. They possess a wide range of coping strategies. Some are up beat and optimistic; others are still struggling; most are somewhere in-between. (p. vii)

Although research is essential to the understanding of fathers' reaction to their child's disability, there is a richness and a depth of understanding that appears in personal essays that simply cannot be replicated by research data and tests of statistical significance.

SIBLINGS

Until recently, siblings constituted forgotten family members (Siegal & Silverstein, 1994). In the late 1960s and the 1970s, however, there was a trickle of research devoted to sibling adjustment to having a brother or sister who was disabled or ill. The 1980s and 1990s witnessed a surge of interest in sibling adjustment, as evidenced by the spate of books devoted to the subject (Harris, 1994; Meyer & Vadasy, 1994; Moorman, 1992; Powell & Gallagher, 1993; Siegal & Silverstein, 1994; Stoneman & Berman, 1993). Sibling relationships are often the longest and most enduring of family relationships. As Powell and Gallagher (1993) noted, "Siblings provide a continuing relationship from which there is no annulment" (p. 14).

Being the brother or sister of an infant or child with a chronic illness or disability constitutes a risk factor for some nondisabled siblings. Siblings who are expected to provide care for a brother or sister with a disability may show signs of resentment, anger, and rebelliousness, as well as guilt at having such feelings. One sometimes finds an ambivalent relationship between disabled and nondisabled children due to powerful and conflicted feelings of love, obligation, anger, and resentment. Some siblings feel that their lives are "on hold" while they and their family pool their resources to take care of the ill or disabled family member.

It seems that a key variable in how troubled the nondisabled sibling is depends on how the parents handle the situation. A particularly toxic situation is where parents expect their children to continuously care for a son or daughter with a disability while neglecting their needs. Modest and appropriate caretaking accompanied by parental attention (love, concern, support, and guidance) provides a sound foundation for the nondisabled children. In the absence of good parenting, Siegal (1996) estimated that about 50% of siblings view their childhood as compromised in some substantial way by the stresses associated with the presence of their disabled sibling. The remaining 50% feel more neutral about the experience or believe that it has actually helped them.

Age-appropriate information for young children helps them understand their brother or sister's condition (Powell & Gallagher, 1993; Seligman & Darling, 1997). Ambiguity about a child's disability creates fear and anxiety about the transmissibility of a condition, how long it will last, whether it is a taboo topic within the confines of the family, and whether the well sibling may have actually caused the disability.

Some believe that excessive caretaking, parental inattention, and lack of open communication in the family provide the foundation for psychological problems in adult life (Siegal & Silverstein, 1994). And since sibling relationships are lifelong, involvement with a brother or sister may actually become intensified during adulthood (Moorman, 1992). Adult siblings worry about caretaking duties as they and their siblings with disabilities enter middle and old age. Some single siblings wonder if a prospective spouse will be accepting of a brother or sister with a disability. Nondisabled siblings may worry about the social stigma that their parents may have shielded from them. Recent years have witnessed an increased interest in adult siblings. As a result, we will elaborate on this topic in subsequent chapters.

Siegal (1996) believed that some siblings exhibit discernible patterns of coping that are reflected in certain roles that these children adopt. As an illustration, the *parentified child* is a fairly common role that siblings assume as caretaking issues inevitably emerge in the family. These children act more like parents than brothers or sisters to their siblings with a disability. These children may become the "keepers" instead of the "kept." Some parentified children may accept this role with little adverse effect, whereas others may be resentful and feel guilty about their resentfulness. Parents and professionals working with families should be aware that parentification can deprive a child of his or her own childhood. It is important that siblings have opportunities to be children.

Some siblings do not try to earn parental attention by helping. Instead they may become *withdrawn children*. They may be overwhelmed by parental demands for help or they may be driven away by their brother or sister's behavior. Siegal (1996) noted that often withdrawn children are younger siblings who never had much attention from their parents. These children are slow to warm up to new situations and usually are not very gregarious. "With the added stress of minimally available parenting, they psychologically give up" (Siegal, 1996, p. 152). Withdrawn children can benefit from individual counseling and from more empathic attention from their parents.

The *superachiever* or *family mascot* compensates for the loss that family members experience. When one child has a disability, parents may feel better about their circumstances if another child is developing normally or, even better, is an exceptional achiever. Sometimes too much is expected of the other child when the parents' goals for that child exceeds his or her abilities. Just like parentified children, superachieving children realize that by succeeding in activities that their parents value, they can garner parental attention. Siegal (1996) noted that many parentified children are also high achievers. The "mascot," who may not be academically or otherwise talented, tries hard to establish an identity that parents pay attention to, for example, by using humor or being a show-off. In capturing the four coping styles, Siegal (1996) wrote,

> Parentified children can be worrisome—because they subjugate their own needs so easily. Their behavior is similar to the pattern sometimes described as "co-dependency" in the literature on adult children of alcoholics. Co-dependents don't feel like worthwhile human beings unless they are helping someone who is helpless or out of control. On the positive side, parentified children grow up to be special education teachers, pediatricians, and social workers in disproportionate numbers. On the less positive side, they get into relationships with spouses who abuse drugs or alcohol, or who are chronically unemployed—in this way they continue to have someone dysfunctional to take care of. The super-achieving and mascot children probably have the healthiest adaptations because they operate with an intact sense of self that derives either from achievements outside the home or from a certain ability to view family dysfunction at a distance as reflected by their ability to use humor to describe their own difficult situations. (pp. 153–157)

The conclusions that can be drawn from the research on siblings are mixed (Seligman & Darling, 1997; Stoneman & Berman, 1993). Generally speaking, the impact may be for better or for worse depending on numerous mediating variables. We concur with Lobato's (1990) observation after an extensive literature review:

> To many parents of young children, it may seem as though the child's illness or disability will do nothing but harm to the other children. However, this is actually quite far from the truth. As young siblings mature, evidence is clear that they usually do not have more problems than other children. In fact, many siblings show areas of great social and psychological strength. Their relationships with and behavior toward one another also tend to be more nurturing and positive than between many other sibling pairs. (p. 60)

In terms of helping siblings cope, there has been a major push across the United States to invite siblings to attend workshops and support groups (Meyer & Vadasy, 1994). These workshops help siblings express repressed or suppressed emotions, contribute to their knowledge about disability, and provide a social context where they can experience the company of others struggling with similar issues. Siblings of infants and children with disabilities are sometimes referred to as "forgotten children" (Seligman, 1996), but more will be said about these children in subsequent chapters as siblings enter adolescence and adulthood.

GRANDPARENTS AND OTHER EXTENDED FAMILY MEMBERS

Much of the literature on families has focused on the nuclear family, with little mention of grandparents. To think of the family apart from its ancestral past is to ignore an integral aspect of the family's present life. Generally speaking, grandparents are a source of much pleasure, support, and guidance to the nuclear family. There are exceptions, however, when grandparents are experienced as meddlesome; providing little support; and, in some cases, contributing to disruption and conflict in the family. An issue that may be especially frustrating for the family is the grandparents' difficulty in grasping the seriousness of the impact of a child's disability on the family (Harris, 1994).

A concern of parents of infants with disabilities is whether their parents will be accepting of the baby. On the other hand, a source of consternation for grandparents who are accepting of their grandchild is how to help and be supportive of their children. They may be in a position of wanting to support the nuclear family while grieving over their own loss of a healthy grandchild. Unless there are preexisting unresolved issues between the grandparents and the parents, the grandparents can be the source of considerable emotional and instrumental support for the rest of the family. In fact, grandparents can at times be more accepting of a grandchild with a disability because they are one step removed. One must not minimize the potential devastating impact a grandchild with a disability can have on the expectations of grandparents, however.

Some grandparents have difficulty accepting their grandchild, which may be expressed by neglecting the parents, trivializing the disability, or denying it (Meyer & Vadasy, 1986). Strong negative reactions from extended family members can lead to triangulation and cutoff between and within generations (Walsh, 1989). Grandparents siding with one or the other parent can lead to triangles that harm family functioning (Farber & Ryckman, 1965; Kahana & Kahana, 1970; Pieper, 1976).

In general, grandparents are often in a position to provide both instrumental and emotional support. In working with families, providers should consider grandparents as major sources of guidance and support while being aware that extended family members who are conflicted about the child can disrupt family functioning (Hornby, 1995; Seligman, 1991).

Like grandparents, aunts and uncles can provide emotional support and concrete help. Siegal (1996) observed that sisters of mothers who have autistic children tend to provide helpful social support if the relationship between the sisters is a good one. An older sister with experience raising children can be particularly helpful to the parents. Although brothers or sisters can be supportive, sincere attempts to be helpful can be seen as criticism, especially if the siblings are competitive with one another. Generally speaking, when siblings have reasonably good relationships with each other, they can be of considerable support to the nuclear family.

CONCLUSION

In this chapter we have elaborated on the family's response to a disability in an infant or young child. From this discussion one can see how disability in the family touches both nuclear and extended family members. It appears that most families cope well under these circumstances, yet a minority of families, due to the lack of familial support and community resources or because they are not particularly resilient, experience difficulties coping. Subsequent chapters will explore the family response to disability as the child grows and negotiates the later stages of childhood, then moves on to adolescence and adulthood.

CHAPTER 3

School-Age Years

D uring infancy and toddlerhood, the focus of the child's life is within the family constellation as the child interacts primarily with parents and immediate family members. In this situation, the child is usually the object of specific attention by caregivers within the family unit as parents and other family members bear primary responsibility for nurturing the child's cognitive, emotional, and social needs. Entrance into preschool and formal schooling, however, includes increased exposure to peers, teachers, and other adults outside of the family boundaries. One of the major developmental tasks in childhood is learning to interact in social and academic situations with increased independence and to separate from parents. Although parents want their children to have increased opportunities, this time period may impose anxieties on children with disabilities and their parents.

Academic or social behaviors that set the child apart from peers are easily identified by other children and may result in early exclusion from opportunities to socialize. Behavioral delays or irregularities in terms of immaturity or atypical behavior can become a major source of concern. Parents who recognize subtle differences in behavior and learning ability may try to mask them from view while still providing social opportunities for their children and maintaining a life for themselves. Parents who have children with invisible disabilities need to decide if and when to "go public" about special needs. They may experience an ongoing need to protect their child and feel ambivalent about turning the child over to a teacher who may have 25 other children in the classroom and no sense of their child's history. At this point, parents of all children with disabilities must learn to be informed advocates, to interact with educators, and to locate sources of support while facilitating positive outcomes for their children.

During this time period, sending the child beyond the protection and security of home and family simultaneously creates new opportunities and
presents risks over which parents have decreasing control. In this chapter,
we discuss the ongoing process of adjustment and readjustment for families
and their school-aged children with disabilities.

Stress, chronic sorrow, and some other issues introduced earlier reappear in
this chapter. Rather than being redundant, this continuous coverage documents the dynamic process of growth and development of individuals and
families over the life span. Needs identified in early years may continue to exist, although changed in form and intensity, while new issues emerge during
each developmental period. The critical nature of family and social supports
as coping resources during school-age years will be explored, as well as
changes in philosophy reflecting the current search for family strengths, capacity, and resources. Experiences with socialization and exclusion for both
children and their parents will be described through parents' anecdotes. Ongoing concerns about support, advocacy, stigma, education, and interactions
with professionals will be reviewed in the context of the child and the family.

GOING PUBLIC

"Going public" is an issue faced by parents as soon as their child is old
enough to separate and engage in informal or formal settings away from the
family's watchful eye. Early decisions "to tell" or "not to tell" may be based
on parental acceptance, comprehension of the disability, societal acceptance,
and visibility. Play groups, swimming lessons, day camps, and preschools
are examples of typical settings in which children are involved prior to the
initiation of formal schooling.

If the disability is apparent because of its visibility (e.g., Down syndrome,
cerebral palsy, or limb deformities), then the child is "exposed" whether or
not the parents wish it. Parents must be prepared to anticipate such questions as "What's wrong with him?"; reactions of pity or fear; or blanket assumptions that because the child may have a disability he or she must also
not be able to hear, see, speak, think, or feel.

Parents who have children with invisible disabilities such as mild developmental delays, language-processing disorders, attentional deficits, seizure
disorders, and mental illnesses may face a different situation in the decision
to go public. The child's "normal" appearance provides camouflage in many
situations, which may delay disclosure. Parents frequently struggle with
when and who to tell and what the implications will be. One mother re-
members her daughter's first-grade experience:

She was a bright child, but had processing difficulties we saw at home. All the teachers in the preschool, however, described her as a "free spirit" rather than as a child with significant problems. Only one student teacher even mentioned that we might anticipate difficulty in first grade because of processing and attention difficulties. Rather than plant negative expectations from the outset, we decided that maybe we should take a wait and see approach. After all, only one teacher out of many even noticed any difficulties at all. Maybe she would blend in, maybe the summer was a time of maturation, maybe the teacher individualized so much that it wouldn't matter. But it did. Within the first three months of first grade, our daughter was behind in everything, couldn't attend to a task, and came home with a daily note in red across the top of her reading worksheets which said "Will not listen!" When we agreed that she definitely needed school-based assistance, the school evaluators said she scored too high on some tests to have a justifiable problem. We had to threaten to take it to the state level in order to obtain an independent evaluation and when we finally received services they were a waste. Although the wait and see approach may not have been successful, I firmly believe that going public at that time in that setting would have resulted in lowered expectations before my child ever reached the classroom. (Anonymous, personal communication, 1994)

A parent of a 12-year-old son with attention deficit hyperactivity disorder (ADHD) said,

His intelligence and our intervention masked his problem to a degree. I worked on social skills with him from a very young age and basically programmed him on a daily basis with "What do we do if" scenarios. I worked so hard with him that when he entered school as the model, respectful child, it came back to haunt me. I almost regretted what I had done because people didn't believe there was really a problem and I was exhausted from dealing with it. I sometimes thought I should've given them the raw material to work with and then they'd see. (Anonymous, interview, January 1996)

It has been documented that teachers' expectations of children are reduced if the child has a label (Richey & Ysseldyke, 1983). Parents who are aware of this may have mixed feelings about whether their child would be better off without formal identification. A school board member in a rural area recently saying at a televised board meeting that children in special education are the "dregs of society" documents the perpetuation of damaging attitudes and beliefs and one of the negative consequences of labeling. Comments such as these from educators or community members inhibit parents from either "telling" or "asking" if they suspect a problem. Professionals should be aware that there is no set protocol or solution for this problem, as each situation varies not only with the child and family but with the school. Professionals can assist parents by ensuring that they have current information on disabilities and educational rights. Assertiveness training and role-playing interactions with professionals can be helpful. Involvement of an advocate as an outside party is often supportive for parents and facilitates information sharing.

Parent concerns about going public relate not only to school settings. Parents are very concerned about whether or not their children will be rejected socially by peers. Again, in the case of invisible disabilities, sharing information is not a onetime decision but an ongoing one. The parent of a son with ADHD said,

> My decision to tell or not was determined by each situation. It depended on the particular setting, who was in charge, and what difficulties I could anticipate if I did share that he had a disability as opposed to the possible problems that could arise if I said nothing. (Anonymous, parent interview, January 1996)

A parent of a child with well-controlled seizures shared the following:

> Almost up through adolescence, I was still deciding how public to be on a case-by-case basis. My daughter's seizures were under good control and she only experienced a problem once every few years. We knew that sudden equilibrium shifts, strobe lights, and oxygen–carbon dioxide changes that accompanied sudden and dramatic exercise could be triggers when her resistance was low or when a fever was present. We knew that the sight of a seizure could be frightening to people who had never witnessed one and we knew that many people still had misinformation about what to do, like giving someone a drink of water or sticking a pencil in their mouth so they wouldn't swallow their tongue. Every time she went on a sleep-over at a new place or an overnight excursion with an organized group, I had to make the conscious decision about whether or not to tell. It disturbed me to tell because I knew that telling would expose her and the chances were remote that a problem would occur, but on the other hand it was important to be sure that a responsible adult would be prepared if something did happen. It was also important to know that someone would check to be sure she took her medication. Each time I told, I wondered if I had just restricted future social opportunities because of stereotypic reactions others might have. (Anonymous, personal communication, 1994)

Professionals need to recognize the issues faced by parents and children in their efforts to disclose needed information. Parents' fears are understandable and in many instances justified. They may rightfully be concerned about the stigma of labels and the effect on the attitudes and resulting actions of peers, other parents, and teachers. Some parents also resist disclosure because of their own embarrassment or lack of acceptance of their child. The implications of telling range from being helpful to being negatively stigmatizing and depend on what needs to be told and to whom, current level of knowledge, attitudes, and so on. Empathetic professionals can help parents determine what information should be shared and how to effectively accomplish that while still optimizing rather than restricting opportunities for the child.

EFFECTS OF CHILDHOOD DISABILITY IN SCHOOL-AGE YEARS

CYCLIC OR RECURRENT GRIEF DURING SCHOOL-AGE YEARS

As discussed in Chapter 2, the concept of chronic sorrow was a major contribution to the disability-related literature because it increased awareness about normal parental reactions to offspring with disabilities, in contradiction to prevailing professional beliefs. Prior to Olshansky's (1962) use of this term, the professional misconception was that grief was time limited and would resolve with final parental acceptance of the disability. Olshansky demonstrated progressive insight, which over the past three decades has impacted professional views and assisted parents in recognizing that acceptance does not finalize grief and that recurring grief is normal and does not indicate parental dysfunction. Interestingly, Olshansky's work also reflects negative attitudes associated with the societal norms of the time period in which he wrote. Discussion of the "tragedic" component of the disability and the goal of counseling to increase the comfort level of parents in managing their "defective" children reflected the view that children with disabilities were burdensome, limited, and totally dependent on parents and had bleak outlooks for the future. Legislation guaranteeing educational rights was not even in place at the time.

Olshansky's (1962) castigation of professionals for urging parents to take prompt interventional action when they faced an entire lifetime to deal with this child might be inappropriate today given our knowledge of the benefits of early intervention. Similarly, the term chronic sorrow, though it was coined to effectively describe normal parental feelings, today seems to imply a state of ongoing sadness. Perhaps terms like cyclic, periodic, or recurrent grief more adequately illustrate the roller-coaster pattern of positive and negative emotions experienced by parents over time (Wikler et al., 1981). As parental anecdotes reveal, children with disabilities frequently bring joy, satisfaction, and rewards to families as well as frustration, anger, and grief. Professionals should recognize that educational, medical, and social advances have enhanced the lives of children with disabilities and their image and acceptance in society. Their lives do not represent ongoing doom and gloom for themselves or their families.

The issue of recurrent grief does continue to be relevant for parents today and Olshansky's (1962) recommendations for repetitive contact to address reemerging issues continues to be timely advice that professionals should heed. In the progression from infancy through school-age years, children pass through numerous social, cognitive, motor, and educational developmental milestones that are triggers for periods of recurrent feelings of grief or frustration. These milestones can be identified and anticipated by professionals, who should be able to provide information and support for families experiencing these normal reactions (Wikler et al., 1981). As one parent said,

> You spend years teaching your child how to throw and catch a ball. She finally gets it right and you are ecstatic. It is one of those moments of joy and satisfaction and confirmation that your child can learn and progress with attention and practice. Suddenly your joy is tempered by the realization that while you have spent years mastering the simple task of throwing and catching, your child's peers have worked on batting, basketball, soccer and are now playing football. That very accomplishment which was for an instant a supreme high is now yet another cause to grieve. I realize that this will recur throughout my child's life and makes me realize how emotionally strong parents of children with disabilities have to be. (Anonymous, personal communication, 1993)

Professionals working with families of school-aged children must recognize that parents are not constantly sad, that they do experience happiness, satisfying relationships and accomplishments, yet also are subject to understandable periods of emotional upheaval. These episodic periods of grieving are not indicative of a lack of parental acceptance but of parental awareness of normal developmental advances in comparison to their own child's development. Parents' needs for support will depend on their own internal and external resources, which will be addressed later in this chapter.

STRESS ON THE FAMILY UNIT

> His disability has affected every aspect of our lives. I had to watch everything he did. I was so tense all the time and we couldn't go anywhere where there wasn't a problem. I oversaw everything. There was nothing I would've rather

done then turn my head away for even a minute but if I did it turned out to be a horrible situation. I feel like I live under constant pressure. Everything is a pressure and that's terrible. We got to the point that we isolated ourselves because it was easier than explaining his behaviors and being embarrassed and going home feeling awful. There has been a negative cumulative effect on the family which has affected the way the kids look at everything. It has put a strain on our marital situation. If we had a less stable relationship we never would've made it. (Anonymous, parent interview, January 1996)

As discussed in Chapter 1, it has been well documented that families who have children with disabilities experience significant stress (Boyce, Behl, Mortensen, & Akers, 1991; Farran, Metzger, & Sparling, 1986; Frey, Greenberg, & Fewell, 1989). One only needs to talk to a few families like the previous one to confirm this. It is not difficult to see how a family in this situation might be at risk. It is a jump, however, to assume dysfunctionality based on increased stress alone. The preceding quote does testify to the increased pressure, social isolation, and negative effect resulting from the child's disability, but on the other hand the family is still intact, fights for the child, and remains strong because of a stable relationship.

In the previous chapter on infancy, five types of stressors were described. Stress continues to affect families and is cumulative during this developmental period. When children enter school and social settings, new challenges specific to school issues emerge and may exacerbate existing problems. The way in which stress has been treated in professional literature and practice is important because of the ramifications for research and treatment.

Historically, a stress reaction model approach postulated a direct relationship between stress related to parenting a child with a disability and family dysfunctionality (Erickson, 1969). Later research suggested, however, that clinicians might actually be observing typical parental reactions and misinterpreting them because of a trained predisposition to look for pathology in families where there is a child with a disability (Antonovsky, 1993; Freidrich & Freidrich, 1981). Practitioners and researchers have expected dysfunctionality and designed both research studies and family intervention within limited and biased parameters. Innocenti, Huh, and Boyce (1992) cited this explanation for the paucity of studies that examine family dynamics through a normality approach.

Examining the lives of individuals without disabilities shows that stress is also present but is not always dysfunctional. At a basic biological level, a degree of stress may serve as a protective feature. For some, a degree of stress increases alertness or helps to focus thoughts or actions. Higher levels of stress may at times motivate individuals to take risks that they would not ordinarily take, which in some instances may be productive. Although families of children with disabilities face increased stress related to the extra demands regarding evaluations, caregiving, education, and social development, it does not necessarily follow that all reactions to stress are dysfunctional. As one mother of a child with a disability reasoned,

> I do feel stressed, which may not always be particularly healthy for me, but helps my family in numerous ways. It seems to me that the stress associated with constant dealing and concerns forced me to prioritize and focus on things important in the larger scheme of things. "Take time to yourself" is a handy credo, but when there isn't enough time in the day to do everything, something's gotta give. So my house isn't particularly neat, my bills are usually paid late, and I forget little things like putting enough money in the parking meter, but I am well informed, I'm a good advocate for my child, and I work to sensitize others while trying to maintain all that is necessary for a perhaps hectic, but supportive family life. Stress has demonstrated how much endurance we have as a family. I feel fortunate that we are all together and committed to each other while families who don't have concerns about disability issues are falling apart around us. (Anonymous, personal communication, March 1997)

Based on stress research, efforts to compare families with and without children with disabilities in terms of dysfunctionality have not demonstrated significant differences on measures of depression, marital dissatisfaction, or family dysfunction; significant differences may exist, however, when both maternal stress and maternal marital satisfaction are taken into consideration (Kazak, 1987). These findings suggest the need for professionals to identify sources of familial and maternal stress.

Time demands related to caregiving and worry about the future are major sources of stress identified by parents (Harris & McHale, 1989). Another major source of stress frequently revealed by parent anecdotes is parents' frustration or feelings of helplessness that stem from observing their child fail at social attempts or academic undertakings:

> There's a helpless feeling that you get when you pick up your child at 3:00 in the school parking lot and watch her going from child to child inviting each one over only to be refused. If you only had the power to create a friend, you would do it. How many times can you tell her that they must have other things to do today and maybe they'll be free another day before she catches on they just don't want to play with her? And then what do you do? (Anonymous, personal communication, September 1997)

Dyson (1991) found that families that have school-aged children with disabilities share many positive interactions and that these shared relationships may be among the most critical factors in strengthening the ability of the child and family to withstand any negative effects related to disability. Historically, insufficient attention has been given to these family strengths, attitudes, or functional adaptations. Researchers failed to recognize that individual reactions to stress vary depending on personal resources, personality characteristics, mental health, and outlook, as well as cumulative effects of stress from other life challenges. Ferguson (1997) revealed that his perspective as a parent increased his awareness of limitations in research studies used to describe families and document needs.

STRESS ON THE CHILD

Stress, like grief, should be viewed as cyclic and longitudinal rather than as static, due to the changing nature of the family constellation as it moves through different developmental periods. In addition to stress on the family unit, the school-aged child with a disability may experience ongoing stress that varies depending on the time, setting, and situational demands. Stress may be more pronounced if cognitive skills are less affected, because the children are aware enough to recognize discrepancies between their educational performance and that of their peers. They may also be more attuned to their failure to fit socially with peers. Children feel frustrated and angry, with their self-esteem deflated. Constant failure may perpetuate learned helplessness rather than self-efficacy (Seligman, 1975). Some of the manifestations of these emotions are withdrawal, aggression, displaced responsibility or blame, passive-aggressive behaviors, overdependency, clowning, or depression (Silver, 1984; Smith 1991).

Frequently, educators and other professionals fail to realize the effect of situational and time demands as significant stressors on the child. According to one parent,

> In order to keep up with the mainstream classes, the child's homework workload sometimes exceeded 5 hours a day. Five hours of sheer torture. This was after spending a full day in school and coming home feeling frustrated, defeated, and exhausted. Other kids played outside, did things with friends, joined clubs, or relaxed while our child worked from the time she came home until we made her go to bed. The only break was for dinner. We felt justified in requesting homework modifications, but the need for that accommodation really didn't strike the teacher or principal until we were asked at an IEP [individual education program] meeting, "When does she play?" My husband and

I looked at each other, at the teacher, at the principal and said, "That's what we've been trying to tell you. She doesn't play. There's no time." They were amazed that she never plays but that's exactly what we had been complaining about for quite some time. We came as close as possible to having them follow her around to realize this. It was like talking to egocentric children who couldn't see beyond their own space. Their recognition of the fact that her social life had been severely limited because of school expectations was like an epiphany for this group of supposed experts who had been giving us advice. (Anonymous, personal communication, December 1995)

In this situation, the parents had requested modifications to the child's program and tried to justify them by explaining the significant stress experienced by the child on a daily basis and its threat to her overall status. It was not until the family actually kept a written log tracking the number of hours engaged in homework and the limitations that put on other aspects of the child's life that the school agreed. Although this child needed both social opportunities and academic remediation, she maintained herself academically only at the cost of social opportunities.

Robert Brooks (1994b), a clinical psychologist who uses client anecdotes in his presentations and publications on self-esteem and resilience, recalled that many of his clients explain their dislike for school as "school is the place where their deficits rather than their strengths are highlighted" (p. 335). His remark pinpoints the stress that school-aged children with disabilities must experience on a daily basis.

During this developmental period, school and homework are often a source of frustration for children with disabilities. In addition to the stress placed on the family unit as a result of meetings, educational plans, excessive homework, test preparation, and so forth, the child experiences personal stress sometimes to a degree unimagined by others. Parents and professionals must realize that although the family stress load is significant, at least one or two independent adults are usually members of most families. In most families, parents have the ability to discuss their feelings and concerns with other adults. Children may feel more isolated in their stress, and their limited worldview may cause them to think they might be the only one with such problems. The pressure of understanding academic work, meeting teachers' criteria for classroom behaviors, isolation by peers, and completing homework on time may consume a large portion of a child's waking thoughts. Under those circumstances, withdrawal, avoidance, depression, or other debilitating side effects may appear to be reasonable emotional reactions.

One parent recalls her daughter's first exposure to an elementary school class in which several children had hearing losses:

She came home in amazement and told me about all the other kids in the class who had hearing aids too. She said "They were just like me." It was like she never believed that she was not alone and there were actually other children with hearing loss. (Anonymous, parent interview, 1995)

OTHER EFFECTS ON FAMILY INTERACTIONS DURING ELEMENTARY SCHOOL YEARS

Despite increased parental stress, changes in family routines, and effects on interfamilial relationships, Dyson (1996) found positive self-esteem in siblings of children with disabilities. Siblings have been shown to exhibit mixed responses to their brothers and sisters with disabilities, which may be indicative of sibling adjustment in the population at large. Dyson's research with families yields some interesting findings regarding siblings. Although almost half of the parents reported siblings as being sensitive to their brother or sister's special needs, the parents expressed feelings of guilt about the excessive time spent on the child with the disability and were concerned about possible sibling resentment. Parents also indicated concerns about the ramifications of younger nondisabled siblings academically surpassing the older school-aged child with a disability. Informal anecdotal reports voicing these concerns are heard frequently, as in the following examples.

A college student known to one of us (F. P.) described the impact that a course on exceptionalities had on her view of her family during her school-age years. She admitted that her younger brother's learning disability had always been a source of frustration to her. When she brought home A's on her tests or report cards, they would be acknowledged with a "Good job," but when her brother came home with barely passing grades, her parents would jump for joy and tell him how proud they were. After looking more closely at the obstacles faced by children with learning disabilities in regular schools, she finally understood how much he had to struggle to get those passing grades and how much harder he really did work. At the time, though, it just seemed unfair.

The parent of a child with a learning disability and a younger child labeled mentally gifted reported,

Sometimes it upsets me that my child with the learning disability was the firstborn. If she were the younger of the two, I would've benefited more from observing normal developmental and academic milestones before she arrived on the scene. An older brother without disabilities could've been a role model for her. The worst thing is that I have a difficult time enjoying the opportunities and accomplishments of my younger child because his successes always make me think of her struggles and the inequity of it all. Then I feel guilty because my thoughts seem unfair to him. At a recent parent meeting at the middle school, I heard about a great course offering in career options that would be available to gifted students. I thought that was a great idea but immediately became angered that such a program had not been available to my daughter, who needed it more. (Anonymous, personal communication, 1997)

Professionals are advised to maintain an awareness of the entire family and to pay attention to sibling issues and parental worries about sibling relationships and resentment during the elementary school years. Finding ways to plan special times with the nondisabled sibling may be helpful even if they do not balance out in actual time allotment. Helping parents to appreciate the merits of each child without feeling guilty and exploring methods of assigning family responsibility to each child to ensure a sense of competence and reduction in the feelings of being burdened or ignored may alleviate some common problems.

It is important for professionals and parents to be alert to the learning potential of younger siblings and attuned to teacher expectations based on potential rather than association with the learning difficulties of an older brother or sister. Of interest is an infrequently reported research finding regarding an educational side effect for younger siblings of children with disabilities. In two investigations, Richey and Ysseldyke (1983) found that educator expectations for younger siblings of children with learning disabilities were lower than anticipated performance estimates for younger siblings of students without disabilities. This intriguing finding may or may not be related to teachers' understanding of characteristics and causation of learning disabilities.

SOCIALIZATION AND EXCLUSION

Peer Interactions

Increased exposure to other children usually provides numerous and varied opportunities to practice peer interaction. Learning to initiate contact with peers, to enter ongoing social situations, and to maintain positive interactions and conversations are developmental skills characteristic of this period and are usually acquired incidentally through increased exposure rather than formal instruction. For young children with disabilities, the reactions of others to overt characteristics that signify "difference" or behaviors that are immature may actually result in a reduction of opportunities to practice socialization at a time that is critical for the development of such skills. Children are usually quick to identify group members who stand out. One only needs to observe a class at recess or lunch to identify the outcasts. One parent said,

> There was nothing more upsetting to me than to observe my daughter's class at recess from a distance and see that she was the only one off by herself. Any overtures she made were quickly rebuffed. To add insult to injury, she was taunted and teased. Why didn't any of the teachers notice or do something? Was I just sensitive to it because I felt helpless? Can you imagine going to a party by yourself and everyone else is in couples or groups? People are laughing at your clothes or the way you look and no one will talk to you? You really want to leave and can, but that kid at recess must stay out there until the bell rings. (Anonymous, personal communication, 1995)

Parents may try to mask social problems while still providing social opportunities, structured activities, or engaging social outings to facilitate interaction for the child (Dane, 1990), as this mother described:

> Any play dates with one other child ended up with the children playing separately and not interacting at all, or when more than one child was around, mine would end up being left out. I began to plan trips to McDonald's or the park as a way of enticing children to join our little group. I began structuring and monitoring activities to assure turn taking. This of course meant that I was always part of the group, which in retrospect doesn't seem very normal. (Anonymous, personal communication, 1994)

Behaviors like poor turn taking, misunderstanding of game rules, inability to wait or follow directions, and difficulty with conversation are among those that exacerbate interactional difficulties with childhood peers. It may become difficult to determine whether the child's behaviors trigger negative reactions from other children or whether ongoing negative reactions trigger the behaviors, but they feed on each other in a vicious cycle. Motor delays or physical limitations may further limit opportunities and increase the risk of exclusion since childhood is a time period that is typically movement and play oriented. Cognitive delays or developmental delays in communication skills may present other risks in situations in which children cannot be understood or when their comprehension of childhood verbal exchanges is limited.

Children with disabilities become aware of their social status at early ages. Frequently, the children who have difficulty establishing friendships are the same children who are isolated in school. Loosely structured group activities or those in which children select partners or times when participation is neither defined nor monitored tend to typify the situations in which children with disabilities are most excluded. These periods may be the most desirable times of the day for children who are socially accepted, but are often the most painful times for those who are always rejected and left to stand alone and stand out. Many parents and children could identify gym class, recess, and lunch as examples of those times. The following comments were reported by parents of two girls who were always left out in gym class:

"I hate gym because I'm always the last one picked to be a partner." (Anonymous, personal communication, 1996)

and

"The gym teacher was my partner today because there were none left for me." (Anonymous, personal communication, 1995)

Another parent reported what her daughter had to say about school assemblies:

At assemblies, all the girls say to each other, "So-and-so, come sit by me," but no one ever invites me except for this one girl who doesn't walk well. Last time, I had to sit near two boys who did everything they could not to get too close to me. (Anonymous, personal communication, 1996)

Lunchtime is another difficult period:

There was an empty seat at this table and when I asked if I could sit there, the kids said no, that the seat was reserved. One of the kids spit on me and pushed me and told me they didn't want me at the table. (Anonymous, personal communication, 1993)

After repeated such incidents, the child finally sought help from the guidance counselor, who told her to toughen up because all kids act like that (Anonymous, personal communication, 1994). Responses like this tend to reinforce the exclusion of children and, in addition, imply that children who cannot stand up to physical or social rejection are weak and helpless.

Related to the exclusion and peer rejection of children with disabilities, researchers have examined the experience of loneliness (Margalit, 1997; Parker & Asher, 1993; Vaughn, Elbaum, & Schumm, 1996). Loneliness has been described as the perceived discrepancy between desired and actual social involvement (Peplau & Perlman, 1982) and as a result of unmet needs for intimacy and belonging to a social group (Margalit, 1997). Loneliness may occur as the result of poor peer acceptance in social groups, lack of friendship relationships, or both. In her studies of children with learning difficulties in Israel, Margalit (1996) found that they experienced more loneliness than their peers without disabilities.

Low peer acceptance and low social functioning have been noted as problematic for children with varying types and degrees of disabilities (Salisbury, Gallucci, Palumbaro, & Peck, 1995; Vaughn et al., 1996). This is significant to note since acceptance is a critical factor in influencing adaptation to peers (Parker & Asher, 1993), self-esteem, and a sense of belonging to a peer community. Since children with disabilities already constitute an at-risk population, it is important to foster self-esteem, acceptance, and belonging to increase the likelihood of positive outcomes and to facilitate personal interaction skills and satisfying relationships. Development of positive social relationships in childhood may contribute to development in communication skills, cognition, and emotions as the child develops (Hartup, 1996; Parker & Asher, 1993).

Although peer acceptance and friendship seem intimately related to one another, current work reveals that peer group acceptance and friendship may be separate phenomena in childhood. Although better accepted children were more likely to be involved in friendship dyads, this finding did not necessarily indicate that children with low acceptance rates had no friends (Parker & Asher, 1993). It was found that children with low levels of acceptance were involved in friendships, although they identified a very best friend with lower frequency. Friendships fulfill human needs for intimacy, companionship, and social contact, which can buffer the effects of stress in at-risk children (Hartup, 1996; Ladd, Kochenderfer, & Coleman, 1996). Contrary to what some may believe, children with disabilities do not select friends based on labels but on common interests and experiences (Mest, 1988; Schnorr, 1993). Strully and Strully (1992) stressed the need for professionals to address friendship development as a primary goal. They noted a tendency in educational systems to focus on skills at the expense of socialization due to the belief that skill development will lead to positive outcomes.

Development of friendships is an important goal for children with disabilities as a mediating factor against stress and to improve their quality of life and sense of belonging. Professional efforts that focus on social inclusion and acceptance in integrated settings are important, but attention should also be directed to developing friendships as a related but distinctly different developmental task. Implications for professionals are critical in terms of time. To wait until a child has already been isolated and rejected is almost too late. It is imperative to take preventive and proactive measures. Using peer matching, cooperative learning, or "Circles of Friends" (Pearpoint, Forest, & Snow, 1992) is helpful in facilitating individual friendships. Circles of

Friends refers to a proactive structuring of friendship based on the idea that the people in our lives surround us in an arrangement of circles. The innermost circles contain the people most important in our lives, such as family and close friends. The outermost circles are more distant and may include paid professionals. Pearpoint et al. (1992) discuss the absence of people from the inner circle in the lives of people who have labels. Developing circles requires volunteers to participate in becoming part of the child's inner circle.

The child with the disability often becomes a magnet or target for peers whose behaviors are less than desirable. While talking the talk about collaboration, compassion, and brotherhood, as a society we more frequently model behaviors that represent ultimate competitiveness, one-upmanship, and social hypocrisy. School professionals should engage more actively in social skills development, with the recognition that acceptance, concern for others, and teamwork among children can and should be encouraged as important developmental building blocks. Schools should adopt a zero tolerance policy for bullying and exclusionary behaviors that demean any child. Strategies to facilitate social inclusion in elementary settings described by Salisbury et al. (1995) include active facilitation, building community in the classroom, and modeling acceptance.

Modeling acceptance may be an important way to set a tone in a classroom community that welcomes all children. Prezant and Filitske (1993) conducted a project in 70 rural schools based on parent concerns about children's attitudes and lack of exposure to positive role models with disabilities. It was observed that school libraries had few literary selections that portrayed children with disabilities and even fewer that portrayed them well. Stereotyped images were perpetuated, particularly in less progressive schools where inclusive practices were not integral to school functioning. The project involved identifying children's books that highlighted differences or portrayed children with disabilities as positive role models. The books were then donated to school libraries in the context of hands-on workshops that combined discussions about differences, disability simulations, and reading from some of the selections. Children were asked to identify physical attributes, hobbies, interests, and cultural traditions that made them different, and those differences were highlighted in a positive manner. Simulations were interactive experiences to demonstrate different learning styles and book discussion activities focused on identifying positive and negative feelings that result from differences. Participating teachers and librarians were surprised at how insightful the children's comments were, which tied into the secondary objective of sensitizing faculty.

Professionals should explore with parents opportunities for capacity building in the community and for identifying children's strengths at young ages and capitalizing on those. Additionally, professional efforts to sensitize parents, teachers, and community groups to the value of friendship and belonging is important.

Teachers

School-aged children with disabilities are often excluded not just by their peer group but by teachers as well. Although their behavior is usually unintentional, educators are frequently unaware of the impact of their comments. The following teacher comments have been reported by parents: One math teacher said, "This is so easy you don't even need a brain to do it" (Anonymous, student communication, 1997). He may have intended to demonstrate that the problem was easy, but for the child with the math disability, such a comment reinforces to the child and others that he or she does not fit in or is too stupid to figure the problem out. One elementary teacher made the following comments on a regular basis: "Will all the normal kids please raise their hands?" and "How many times do I have to tell you? If you were listening in the first place you would understand," and "Are you always the last one to finish?" (Anonymous, student communication, 1995). These comments were demeaning children on a daily basis and effectively excluding them from their own peers while demonstrating that it is tolerable to treat others with disrespect. Finally, the parent of a third grader said,

> His teacher would only let the kids out for kickball if they scored 100% on the spelling tests, which my son couldn't do. I used to hear him praying at night saying "Please let me get 100% tomorrow." His self-esteem was tied into his school experiences and the teacher's reaction to him. (Anonymous, parent interview, January 1997)

Teachers should be aware of the power of suggestion and the negative or positive impacts resulting from their statements. Preprofessional training of teachers should include this information in university training programs.

Neglect and Abuse by Caregivers and Others

Rejection, isolation, and exclusion increase when child abuse occurs. History has demonstrated that a disability is a characteristic that puts children at risk. It follows that people with disabilities may have increased susceptibility to becoming victims of abuse and violence (Tharinger, Horton, & Millea, 1993). Dependence on others, lack of power, and emotional and social insecurity are some of the reasons for increased vulnerability to sexual abuse in children with mental retardation (Tharinger et al., 1993). Children with other disabilities may become targets for abuse as well. Children with severe physical disabilities who require excessive amounts of time in caregiving may provoke frustration and abuse. Abnormal crying or whining in children with disabilities has been associated with negative reactions by caregivers (Frodi, 1981). Behaviors demonstrated by children with emotional disturbance may prove challenging to caregivers (Herrenkohl, Herrenkohl, & Egolf, 1983). An inability to recognize what is happening or to tell others because of severe cognitive, motor, or communication disorders may be an attraction for a potential abuser.

Although the personalities of abusers may be characterized by inability to deal with stress, lack of control, or past personal history of victimization (Morgan, 1987), some forms of abuse occur at the hands of respected authority figures and are perpetrated upon children in ways that may not result in bruises or sexual violence. In some situations, they may not even be considered to be abuse. School is one of those settings. Corporal punishment, now banned in many schools, is an example and does continue to occur. Children with disabilities who may not understand the rules, may have challenging behaviors, or may deviate from school expectations may be punished for their behaviors in ways that are abusive. Pouring hot pepper juice on a child's tongue for speaking out of turn, throwing a child off the school bus and making him walk 3 miles because he dropped his books on the floor, or locking a child with disabilities in a closet-sized, unventilated space for not completing his assignment appropriately are real occurrences that were reported to parent advocacy groups and legal advocates (Anonymous, personal communications, 1997).

Exclusion and Isolation of Parents

Exclusion and social isolation affect not only children with disabilities but their parents as well. Sometimes this may be the result of perceived insensitivity or intentional avoidance by other adults who may be uncomfortable or uninformed. Exclusion of parents may also be self-imposed and related to excessive time demands in families with a child with a disability, inability to locate child care, fatigue, embarrassment, or the overwhelming needs of the child. In some families, respite care is in the form of separate vacations for the parents. Conscious or unconscious withdrawal by parents may also be a factor.

A parent of an elementary school–aged boy discussed her own withdrawal from social groups:

> I noticed a change in our friends, or maybe I just started noticing the kinds of things they were saying about kids with problems and didn't like what I was hearing. I just stopped seeing them. When it became apparent that people didn't understand our son's behaviors, it just became easier to stay at home. (Anonymous, parent interview, March 1997)

Another parent commented,

> My main discouragement was in my own friends. I wanted them to understand and I spent so much time and energy, which was wasted. At this point I have a few close friends I can call but I'm much more careful now before I expound or unload. (Anonymous, parent interview, January 1997)

The following parent reported teacher reactions that resulted in anger and feelings of exclusion:

> At the time, I had returned to college to get a degree in Education of the Hearing Impaired. I also had a daughter with a severe hearing loss. As part of my degree requirements, I had to observe in numerous regular classroom situations. I happened to be assigned to observe a teacher who I already knew my daughter would have during the following year. The teacher did not know me or my child ... yet. After observing her class, I met with her about what I saw. After she answered my questions, the topic moved to special education. I will never forget what she said. Her words were, "The parents of special needs students will suck the lifeblood out of you and then come back for more!". At that point, I informed her that I was the parent of such a child and that she was going to be her teacher the next year! (Anonymous, personal communication, 1994)

As in this example, stigma, labels, and negative attitudes sometimes used to exclude children with disabilities are extended to the parents as well. Feldman, Gerstein, and Feldman (1989) reported that teachers viewed parents of children with disabilities more negatively than their peers who did not have children with special needs. Findings suggest a teacher belief system that attributes the child's deficits to problems and characteristics of the parents.

Not only do the labels of children seem to be revisited on their parents, but the same deficit model appears to guide professional interpretation of parent reactions to their school-aged children (Lipsky, 1989). Parent behaviors may be viewed as a maladaptive response to the disability rather than as normal reactions.

The exclusion and social withdrawal of parents may serve as an additional stress factor for professionals to be alert to since it essentially removes potential sources of support from families. Professionals should address the issue of exclusion of both children and their parents in working with families. Heightened awareness may pave the way for strategies and actions that enhance inclusion rather than exclusion. It should be noted, however, that targeting strategies for family action alone are insufficient and may prove fruitless. Teaching a child to smile, say hello, or enter a social situation may be giving them useful and important skills to have in childhood but will have little real effect in an environment that views the child as the source of the problem. Progress must involve individual change as well as system change. Suggested strategies that ignore stereotypes, demeaning behaviors, bullying, and rejection at the hands of others are incomplete.

MANAGING DURING THE SCHOOL YEARS

RESILIENCE

For some time, researchers have noted that some children bear up well under adverse or traumatic circumstances whereas others do not (Brooks, 1994a). As discussed in Chapter 1, resilience is a term that has been used to describe the characteristic that allows children to buffer themselves against the effect of adverse events and stressful situations and to thrive in spite of them. The incidence of negative events in one's life does not seem to predict resilience, although such events may increase risk of failure. Since disability is a characteristic that puts school-aged children at risk, it is important to examine sources of resiliency during this developmental period and foster those to enhance children's achievement of potential.

Self-esteem, a child-centered resource, is identified as critical in the development of resilience. Brooks (1994a) defined this construct as "feelings and thoughts that individuals have about their competence and worth, about their abilities to make a difference, to confront rather than retreat from challenges, to learn from both success and failure, and to treat themselves and others with respect" (p. 547). According to Brooks (1994b), whereas children with high self-esteem view positive occurrences as a result of their actions or efforts, children with low self-esteem feel powerless and inept and may attribute even the most positive occurrences to random chance rather than to any efforts or actions of their own. This is significant during the elementary school years, when students become motivated by success in school. Children with disabilities, who so often fail both academically and socially, may not give themselves credit when they do experience success. They may continue to feel impotent while other children are encouraged by their own gains.

Implications for parents and professionals involved in child counseling, family casework, or therapeutic or educational intervention are clear. Efforts should be made prior to school entrance to facilitate positive self-esteem and a sense of self-worth in children. This can be done best in conjunction with joint efforts with parents to identify strengths and accomplishments.

If children with disabilities learn that positive occurrences may directly result from their own efforts, they may be in a better position to learn from both school successes and failures without damaging their self-esteem. Based on Weiss and Hechtman's (1993) determination that it was a significant adult who was most helpful in developing resilience in children, Brooks suggested consideration of adult attitudes conveyed to children regarding what we think about their attempts, efforts, and abilities to cope. He stressed locating "islands of competence" in each child and the responsibility of significant adults to foster these as sources of strength and resilience. Practitioners may benefit from his suggestions for strategies, including encouraging contributions, providing opportunities for problem solving and decision making, providing positive feedback, and helping children learn that mistakes are part of the learning process.

COPING

More important than assessing the degree of stress associated with having a child with a disability during the school years is examining the way in which the family copes with that stress. Each of us handles stress in a different way and the same situation may evoke differing levels of perceived stress depending on the individual. The family's perception of stress, cognitive appraisal of the situation, ability to manage it, and resources that assist the family in coping successfully are factors to be considered by professionals.

The mother of an elementary school child responded to the question, "How do I cope?"

> I used to be in a crafts group but I couldn't take the conversations I was hearing. I was tired of hearing about the dumb kids and the demanding parents, and whether it had anything to do with me or not, I was fighting for my kid against that same mentality. I got to the point where the group was no longer an outlet. I came home more frustrated than when I left so I quit. I lied about why I quit but I have no desire to go back. My outlet is now getting information, reading, talking to people. Talking to new parents makes me realize we've come a distance. (Anonymous, parent interview, March 1997)

Although it might seem to some that this parent has no social outlets, her coping strategies served her well. Once her initial outlet became counterproductive, she left it and went on to something else that promoted self-perceived competence and control. Her coping strategy became helping others and in the process she reinforced her own ability to handle stress in a functional way.

Another parent said,

> I get mad sometimes because I feel like I'm the cement that holds everything together and I'm not allowed to have a bad day. When I do, everybody crumbles.

I've had to be strong. I have no life except this. (Anonymous, parent interview, November 1996)

This parent seems to be under a great deal of stress, but perhaps the role of protector she plays is her coping strategy and provides a sense of power despite her complaints about it.

DELAYS IN IDENTIFYING DISABILITY

As addressed in the previous chapter, finding out that a child has a disability can be difficult news to accept, and parents go through a variety of stages and reactions in the process of developing coping strategies. Much of the literature focuses on the parents of children identified at birth or shortly thereafter. When there is a delay in the identification until well after infancy and into the childhood years, the coping process may be more problematic for parents. Delays may occur for various reasons. Parents may be suspicious but unable to have a problem confirmed by experts, invisible disabilities may be present but not obvious until formal schooling begins, or children who appear to be normal acquire disabilities.

The mother of an elementary school–aged daughter with Down's syndrome said,

I thought as soon as I saw her that she had Down's syndrome but the physician wouldn't say anything. When I asked, he said, "Let's wait awhile to see what happens." When I came in for her 9-month checkup and asked the nurse if the doctor would be doing some testing at this visit, the doctor overheard me and ran away. I didn't even get to see him. When she was about a year old we finally forced the issue and insisted on testing, which confirmed the diagnosis I had suspected all along. It was almost a relief to know for sure and that I wasn't imagining something. (Anonymous, parent interview, January, 1993)

Parents like this one may go through the anomie-related stress mentioned earlier, when they think a problem exists but no one else sees it or can identify it. Parents describe this as a time when they question their own observations or intuition, rationalizing that if there were a real problem, surely someone else would see it too. Lack of an early diagnosis when the methods are available to make such a diagnosis results in missed intervention time and may result in increased anger on the part of a parent. Experiences like the one just described, however, may be instrumental in developing confidence in intuition as an effective coping strategy.

Invisible disabilities such as learning disabilities, hearing loss, attentional deficits, or mental illness pose special problems because they are not evident at birth, and unless the disability is severe or the parent a keen observer, the child is assumed to be normal until found otherwise. In the process of learning to cope with unexpected information, many parents are plagued by guilt after they find out that they may have punished their children for behaviors related to their undiagnosed disability.

> I had no idea that she couldn't hear me. I thought she wasn't listening. I used to get angry when she grabbed my face as I was reading to her. It was later that I realized she was trying to read my lips. (Anonymous, personal communication, 1995)

Diagnosis in these situations occurs when (a) it dawns on the parent that certain behaviors may actually signify disorders, (b) a specialist or even a friend notes significant milestone discrepancies that are increasing, or (c) entrance into formal schooling puts the child in structured situations with increased task demands that exacerbate the symptoms of a disorder and make it more obvious given the changed context.

In the case of later diagnosis because the disability is acquired, the parent has no reason to consider disability. The parent whose son had a surgical procedure and encountered complications due to the anesthesia that resulted in severe perceptual difficulties did not anticipate a problem. This parent discovered a whole new world, changed expectations, and needs for information that were not present only a few hours earlier. The parent whose child gets hit by a car or flips head first off a bike has not had any reason to deal with childhood disability in the past and has a set of expectations based on previous ability and performance. The need for coping in these situations is not gradual but sudden and unexpected.

INTERNAL AND EXTERNAL SUPPORTS

Internal and external supports are those resources that families mobilize to help refine their perspectives, analyze the challenges they face, strategize their action plans, request help, receive camaraderie and alliances, and obtain feedback and validation. Most of us rely on both internal and external resources on a daily basis through personal reflection, religious participation, talking with friends, reading, and a variety of other activities. For parents of children with disabilities and for the children themselves, these sources of support may be significant determinants of successful outcomes. Personal beliefs and cognitive appraisal, family integrity, problem-solving ability, and financial security are examples of internal resources that serve as the basis for successful coping and adaptation (Alper et al., 1994; Lian &

Aloia, 1994; Turnbull & Turnbull, 1990). Friends, support groups, and professional and organizational assistance constitute formal and informal external supports.

Parental appraisal of challenging situations and the perceived ability to exert some control are critical in determining responses to disability and subsequent successful outcomes (Frey et al., 1989). The severity of the disability is not necessarily a factor in negative or positive appraisal, but the family's estimation of its ability to address the child's needs, as well as its interpretation of the meaning of the disability, may be very significant. This explains why some families in which a child has a severe disability have more positive outlooks than families with children who have mild disabilities. The family's definition of the negative or positive nature of the disability may be predictive of family crisis (Bristol, 1987) or successful adaptation.

Cox (1981) described demand, capability, and coping significance as determinants of an individual's cognitive appraisal of stressful situations that are changeable rather than fixed. This is consistent with the notion that adaptation is a balance between the demands posed by the disability and the support provided by the combined internal and external resources (Frey et al., 1989). Because demands posed by the disability, as well as internal and external resources, change over time, coping ability varies as well.

Family structure and relationships serve as another internal source of support. Numerous studies have documented the importance of maternal perceptions and attributions in maintaining family stability and marital satisfaction (Bristol, 1987; Freidrich & Freidrich, 1981; Frey et al., 1989). Maternal self-blame is associated with higher distress in families (Frey et al., 1989), whereas the ability to externalize blame (Hill, 1958) is associated with a more satisfactory marital relationship and reduced maternal depression (Bristol, 1987). Excessive caregiving demands in terms of time and restricted freedom, identified by parents as significant stresses, usually apply to mothers rather than fathers (Harris & McHale, 1989). In addition, Harris and McHale found that even activities typically considered recreational in nature were time intensive for mothers.

The ability of parents to actively participate in decision making with regard to their school-aged child varies greatly and depends on the problem-solving abilities of the parents. Proactive engagement in evaluations, educational meetings, and consultations with physicians or helping professionals requires assertiveness, information, and excellent communication skills. The type of problem-solving skills required in parenting a child with a disability is highly specialized and may require formal coaching and role playing to develop. Turnbull and Turnbull (1990) described four tasks inherent in good problem solving. First, the parents must be able to define the problem and recognize factors that are changeable and factors that are fixed. Next parents must be able to generate, or brainstorm, a menu of possible options. The family must then agree on options by evaluating alternatives and finally must be able to select options for further action.

External supports may be formal or informal but originate outside of the family unit. Support may be planned and organized or serendipitous, as one of us (F. P.) described:

> I was in the bookstore searching for a gift and overheard a woman ask the clerk for anything by Dr. Larry Silver, who is a nationally known expert in learning disabilities and ADHD. She didn't even have a title, but I observed that she already had an armload of books on disability-related issues. I tapped her on the shoulder, introduced myself as an advocate for this population, and informed her that our office housed a lending library as well as providing advocacy services. She opened up to me immediately, giving me details about her child's difficulty with school and about her own difficulty in accessing services. We talked for about 15 minutes as if we were old friends and exchanged names and phone numbers. This is a frequent occurrence for me. I have just as many "professional" conversations with parents in parking lots, grocery stores, and malls as I do in formal meetings. What I find so interesting is that in this day and age when people are so careful about interacting with or giving out information to strangers, two strangers who find that they have disability in common often strike up an immediate relationship that benefits one if not both.

Informal support networks (addressed later in this chapter) may be loosely bound and organized based on need and desire and utilize natural supports in the community. The informality of the network is in its flexible yet supportive nature and the minimization or absence of paid services by professionals doing their job. Friends, extended family members, and community members who also have children with disabilities are woven into informal support networks. They are nonexclusive. In addition, informal support groups provide a context and framework for shared concerns, training, information seeking, and collective advocacy efforts.

State developmental disabilities councils, which are independent state agencies funded through federal monies, understand the value and strength of informal supports so well that they fund numerous grassroots groups each year that advocate for people with disabilities by finding creative ways to establish and nurture informal relationships and connections between families that have common needs. The number of these groups has increased with national parent-to-parent efforts. Many groups have been founded on the premise that there is information available to parents that is not necessarily accessible unless one can connect with the appropriate resources. It is not uncommon to find that these groups have been formed by parents who have worked in the helping professions and are now using their dual experiences as professionals and parents to assist other families.

More formalized external supports include structured organizations that provide assistance to families. Disability-specific organizations provide printed information and referrals; social service agencies may provide clinic-based intervention or home-based programs for preschoolers; public or private professionals such as counselors, therapists, and public health nurses provide services; government offices may provide financial subsidies; and the educational system should provide an appropriate education that has been developed in conjunction with the parent as a team member. Although external supports are valuable to parents, it is not uncommon to find families receiving numerous supports from several agencies, yet due to lack of communication between agencies, there are either gaps or duplication in services.

Given the value of internal and external supports, professionals, rather than focusing on dysfunction or change in child behaviors, should target proactive adaptation through the use of effective formal and informal networks to support parents and children (Bristol, 1987).

Based on reports indicating increased stress but fewer helpful social supports in families of children with disabilities, practitioners should focus on increasing opportunities for social interactions for parents (Freidrich & Freidrich, 1981).

FINDING SERVICES

How to locate appropriate services or even know which service is needed may vary greatly depending on types of internal and external supports as discussed previously. This is particularly true for children who have educational needs, medical needs, counseling needs, public assistance needs, and the like. The parent attempting to meet these different but related needs may have to negotiate various service systems with distinct and separate eligibility criteria, jargon, and procedures. Some families with good support systems, coordinated services, and the assistance of advocates are more informed about types of service and access to them. Other families, however, are lost in this maze of systems and services. For instance, the family with a preschooler who has a severe communication disorder looks for speech and language therapy and uses its limited private insurance to pay for services. Because the family has no contact with other agencies, educational systems, or advocates, the family is unaware that the child may be entitled to these services through free, school district programs rather than depleting the family's insurance policy.

Families frequently report that they are referred from one professional to another but never make headway (Covert, 1992) while each professional passes the buck. This may explain the frustration of parents who have attempted for weeks to get a single answer to a question and instead have communicated with countless message machines or voice mail recordings. Intrasystem differences in structure, function, physical location, and process may present obstacles to parents and to professional collaboration. In addition, in rural or economically disadvantaged areas, transportation and finances may be barriers.

Effective management during school-age years requires good coordination among providers and families to ensure access to needed services. All service providers for school-aged children, as well as advocates, should consider this involvement integral to their roles.

MULTICULTURAL ISSUES IN THE EDUCATIONAL SETTING

Several landmark lawsuits in the 1970s called attention to the interface between disability issues and multicultural concerns (e.g., *Diana v. State Board of Education*, 1973; *Larry P. v. Riles*, 1974; *Mattie T. v. Holladay*, 1977). Cultural bias in assessments resulted in higher numbers of minority children on the special education rolls in the nation's public schools. To more accurately identify children with disabilities, subsequent legislation mandated revised testing procedures, assessments in the child's native language, and culturally nonbiased testing. These issues focused attention on existing racial and cultural stereotypes in the disability arena. Professional assumptions that the prevailing Anglo culture dictated the norm may have contributed to these stereotypes.

Over the past three decades, multicultural influences and public awareness have increased significantly. It has been estimated that within the next few years, the non-Anglo population in the United States will constitute one-third of overall population figures. Despite the growing diversity, however, a high percentage of special educators, other professionals, and agency administrators continue to represent Anglo culture and develop policies accordingly (Lynch & Stein, 1987; Turnbull & Turnbull, 1990). Middle- to upper-class Anglo values also continue to be represented as the standard in many curricula and text materials (Mehan, 1991).

Bias was present not only in assessing children but in professional approaches to families due to lack of awareness about sociocultural differences that impact relationships between families and the professional community. This is particularly significant because children who have disabilities and are members of nondominant cultures may be in double jeopardy. The therapist, educator, or other professional assisting the child and the family requires additional insight into the most effective ways of collaborating given specific cultural beliefs, values, practices, and communication styles. Teachers and other professionals may assume that a child is noninteractive or, conversely, aggressive, when cultural variation dictates behaviors that differ from traditional Anglo expectations.

Tharp (1989) cited social structure, sociolinguistic differences, cognition, and motivation as four major culturally based variables that may directly impact a child's ability to function adequately given traditional expectations in school settings. For example, whereas Native Hawaiian children may learn best by engaging in small group discussions during instruction, in Navajo culture children may be taught to wait until other speakers are finished before responding (Bos & Fletcher, 1997; White & Tharp, 1988). Hispanic American culture may encourage close physical contact and proximity in situations that demand distance and lack of touching in other cultures. Similarly, although eye contact is demanded or expected in many professional interactions with children and their parents, in some Asian cultures direct eye contact, particularly with elders or those in authority, might be considered disrespectful.

There is documentation that parent involvement in school decision making by culturally diverse parents is restricted (Misra, 1994). Barriers to proactive engagement and ongoing collaboration are in part due to professional insensitivity and lack of information regarding culturally different verbal and nonverbal communication styles. Misra provided examples of culturally based behaviors that may be misinterpreted by professionals, thereby presenting obstacles to open communication. Parents who do not respond with verbal or nonverbal acknowledgment during communication with school-based professionals may be perceived as lacking interest when in fact responding unless requested may not be part of the parents' cultural communication norms. Discomfort when greeted or when attention is called to oneself, though common to some other cultures, may be perceived negatively by professionals. A lack of questions posed by parents may be perceived as passivity instead of respect for authority. Whereas one- or two-parent families dominate Anglo culture, Native American families may include numerous extended family members who may act as caretakers (Turnbull & Turnbull, 1990). American middle-class families may be achievement oriented and focus on competition and control and prize verbal interaction whereas Native American culture values cooperation and nonverbal expression (Seligman & Darling, 1989).

Turnbull and Turnbull (1990) listed numerous cultural considerations for professionals working with families of school-aged children. Among those are two that pertain to cultural views on disability and on attitudes toward professionals. The way in which particular cultures view disability may determine its "acceptability" and subsequent overt family reactions to professional efforts because disability may be viewed as a disgrace in some groups. Disgrace, shame, or embarrassment may inhibit parents from acknowledging the need for help, seeking help, or accepting help from outsiders. Similarly, the way in which a culture views human service professionals with expertise in disability issues is important for professionals to understand how to find the best ways to get the family needed information. In some cultures, because professionals are seen as authority figures, families may be reluctant about questioning, asking for help, or disagreeing.

Although recent surveys reflect the views of average Americans regarding minority group members to be somewhat derogatory, with terms *ignorant, unintelligent, uneducated, unmotivated,* and *apathetic* used, the reality may be that these views are representative of some helping professionals and therefore color the way professionals approach families (Foster, 1997). Foster advocated that professionals, in this case, teachers, need to change their behaviors because schools have failed to educate minority students in an adequate manner.

Professionals are advised to learn about different cultural beliefs and enlist community support groups to provide necessary information and training to parents in ways that help them to advocate for their children. Professional recognition of personal biases is a necessary step in leveling the playing field. Sharing information about different cultural systems as part of school and community programs might facilitate the involvement of families from nondominant cultures. Honest discussion with families, inquiring about family practices and values in efforts to advocate, may be helpful. Locating other families who share the same cultural values and linking them as mentors may also facilitate trust, respect, and willingness to engage in proactive action planning.

Also related to cultural diversity are the significant issues of poverty, single-parent families, and families in which there is abuse. A child who is in fear for his or her safety or a parent who is concerned about how to feed the children, pay the rent, or provide child care while he or she works may accurately conclude that professionals do not really understand the obstacles he or she faces.

THE EDUCATIONAL SYSTEM
AND HELPING PROFESSIONALS

INCLUSIVE VERSUS SEGREGATED SETTINGS

Upon school entrance, parents may have concerns about whether their child will be in integrated or segregated programs. Informed parents may be very vocal about this issue whereas other parents may abdicate their rights and leave the decisions to school officials or feel grateful that their child is receiving any assistance at all.

The term *inclusion* is never actually mentioned in the special education legislation but it is based on the "least restrictive" clause of the Education for All Handicapped Children Act of 1975 (P.L. 94–142), later renamed the Individuals With Disabilities Education Act of 1990 (IDEA; P.L. 101–476; see discussion later in this chapter). This clause guarantees a free, appropriate education without undue restrictions of opportunities and with integration into regular classroom programs to the maximum extent possible. Inclusive philosophies are based on the premise that individuals with disabilities are people first, who can learn, become self-sufficient, secure a job, and contribute to society. They have the same desires for friendships, needs for belonging, and right to be treated with respect and dignity that other people experience throughout their lives. Over the past two decades, proponents of inclusion (integration of children with and without disabilities) have identified the pitfalls of segregated education and as a result most children with disabilities are in regular classrooms for part, if not all, of their school day.

Even after the passage of P.L. 94–142, children with disabilities were educated primarily in segregated settings. These included residential programs, center-based separate schools, and self-contained classes in regular public schools. The children who attended public schools may have been forced to attend a school in another community to access the special class. This meant the child did not attend school with the children who lived in the neighborhood, join after-school clubs, or play ball down the street. Classrooms for children with disabilities in public schools were isolated in the basement or in a trailer behind the building. The children had separate teachers and separate programs and had lunch, gym, and recess at different times. School did not prepare these children for the real world, only for a segregated one. These practices perpetuated stereotypes and negative attitudes on the part of students and teachers.

Through the efforts of parents, advocates, legislation, and the public visibility of people with disabilities, it became evident that these individuals could learn, earn a living, become self-sufficient, and be equal partners in society if given the opportunities. Parents began to push for more inclusive settings and wanted their children in regular classrooms, recognizing that exposure to peers without disabilities was more natural and provided opportunities for children both with and without disabilities. As will be discussed further in Chapter 5, information on school outcomes revealed that segregated programs were not always preparing students with disabilities for the world of work or independent living. Schools began moving toward more inclusive practices, and according to a recent survey (Department of Education, 1996), 72.9% of identified children are indeed educated in the regular classroom for part, if not all, of their school day.

Inclusion remains a controversial issue for many reasons. Inclusion necessitates restructuring school policy and practice. This includes coteaching, service delivery in the classroom (e.g., therapies, resource assistance), and shifting roles for regular and special educators. This requires change and established institutions are notoriously resistant to change.

Having children with disabilities in regular classrooms poses new challenges to regular educators who have no background at a preprofessional level regarding adapting curriculum, teaching practices, or including students with diverse needs. And instituting inclusive programs confronts societal attitudes and stereotypes about disabilities. Teachers, administrators, parents, and students without disabilities are part of that society.

Professionals may have different operational definitions for inclusion that result in conflict. Programs that boast inclusive practices may not be inclusive. Below are a few examples in schools known to one of us (F. P.):

- A child with spina bifida is allowed to attend regular classes if her mother attends school with her.
- All of the students with learning disabilities in a local school are placed in the same science class, instructed by a regular classroom teacher with no background in special needs. They are taught primarily through worksheets, and test scores of 65%, which would earn failing grades for other students, receive A grades in this class. It is called a mainstream class.
- A student with a severe hearing loss is placed in a regular "inclusive" classroom and is graded on an assignment that involved taking notes from a filmstrip that does not show the narrator's face. An interpreter, though specified in the child's educational plan, is not provided.
- A child is left at school during a class field trip because his behaviors would require additional attention.
- A school administrator tells parents that special education evaluations are no longer being done because the school is adopting inclusive practices and all children will be in the regular classroom. (The use of inclusive practices does not negate the need for evaluations or specialized services.)
- A high school yearbook places the photos of all identified exceptional students on the last page although all of the other students are pictured in alphabetical order.

Other school programs that may appear to be segregated provide inclusive and appropriate opportunities. A local school has a class for students with severe hearing loss and deafness. Although this would seem to be a segregated program, the children receive instruction in regular classrooms and support from a specialized educator, and the children assist in teaching a sign language class that is available as an elective for all students. These children have the opportunity to not only receive an appropriate education with needed supports but also experience social opportunities with children who do not have disabilities in a setting that capitalizes on their strengths rather than deficits.

Inclusive programs are those that include a child educationally, socially, and physically in the context of the school community while also providing an appropriate education that leads to meaningful progress and real learning. A child with a physical disability in a wheelchair may participate in a regular program given physical accommodations, the use of an elevator, and adapted physical education. It is not necessary to label, categorize, and separate children who have disabilities solely on the basis of their identification.

The placement of a child in the regular classroom without needed supports does not constitute inclusion. Nor does provision of special services define segregated programs. Parents and professionals must explore options and needs to determine the appropriate program for each child. Whereas some parents feel strongly about their child's participation in regular programs, other parents may feel that the level of need requires intensive services available in more segregated programs. Still other parents may not have the information they need to make these important decisions and will need the assistance of informed professionals.

THE SIGNIFICANCE OF EDUCATORS AND OTHER PROFESSIONALS

Gary Vermeij, an internationally recognized paleontologist and evolutionary biologist, is known for his extensive research on mollusks and their shells. He is also blind. The fact that he is successful in his career is not remarkable. Many individuals with disabilities are successful. But his chosen career has been considered challenging even for sighted individuals because the identification and description of mollusks requires very fine discriminations usually considered to require vision as well as superior intellect, drive, and determination. In addition, academic preparation for this field is extensive, with much time spent in laboratory work, field experiences, reading, and written work. Vermeij has exceeded the boundaries of what many would consider possible by achieving expertise without the use of vision—and in the process demonstrating the value of tactile senses in this type of scientific work. Many professionals, scientists and helping professionals alike, considering his blindness and his interest in shells and mollusks, would surely have attempted to dissuade him or steer his interests in different directions due to his lack of sight, an assumed prerequisite. (Vermeij successfully completed his academic preparation through his doctorate with scholarships and degrees from Princeton and Yale Universities.)

In his book *Privileged Hands* (1997), Vermeij discussed his childhood, the advocacy efforts of his parents, his education, and the significant impact of educators on his life. As a child, he emigrated from the Netherlands to the United States, so in addition to being a child with a disability in the 1950s (before special education legislation) he faced language and cultural adjustments as well. Some of his comments about elementary school teachers bear repeating. Of his third-grade teacher he said,

> Whatever the shortcomings of third grade in America might have been, Mrs. Saplow saw to it that I became a fully responsible member of her class. Her sunny extroverted personality created a forgiving atmosphere in which integration was natural, even inescapable. My classmates never uttered rude remarks about blindness, and the enterprising Mrs. Saplow never met a project or an activity in which I could take no part. When the time came for the class play to be performed in front of the whole school, including my mother, I spoke my lines along with the other would be actors and actresses, and I played the recorder I had brought from Bussum. *Full inclusion* to Mrs. Saplow was not merely an empty phrase or distant bureaucratic mandate; it was the state of mind, the manifestation of a deep conviction that the blind should be treated with equality and dignity along with everyone else. (p. 42)

These comments are a testimony to dedicated, caring, and accomplished teachers who did not need special education legislation to tell them all children needed to be included and taught. Unfortunately, many children, even in this era of legislation and due process rights, are excluded or relegated to menial tasks indicative of low expectations for success. Vermeij went on to describe the ways in which another teacher inspired and motivated him to have a dream and pursue it:

> Mrs. Colberg told of the beaches on which one could casually gather these works of art. I daydreamed of such places. They would bear exotic names and gentle waves of warm water would reach up from below, depositing shells in which corrosion never compromised textural complexity. . . . My fourth grade teacher had not only given my hands an unforgettable esthetic treat, but she aroused in me a lasting curiosity about things unknown. None of it was in the

books; there was no expensive conspiracy to teach science, no contrived lesson plan painstakingly conceived by distant experts. Instead, Mrs. Colberg captured the essence of her task. She created an opportunity, a freedom for someone to observe, an encouragement to wonder, and in the end a permissive environment in which to ask a genuine scientific question. (p. 5)

If Mrs. Colberg harbored doubts about my ambitions, she kept them to herself. My obsession must have looked like any boy's fanciful dream of becoming a fireman, baseball player or spaceman. Sooner or later, this blind boy would settle on a career, to put it discreetly, more consistent with his limitations. Yet none of this was said. Instead, there was unanimous and unreserved encouragement. If that autumn day in 1956 passed unnoticed for Mrs. Colberg and the rest of her class, for me it was like no other. On that day, a wonderful teacher set the course for one man's life. (p 7)

Future planning does not begin with high school or postsecondary training. It begins with the seeds planted, nurtured, or quashed by significant adults in children's lives. In addition to parents, educators and other professionals must realize their unspoken power and their responsibility to use it well. When a family has a child with a disability, professionals may play a pivotal role in shaping expectations and facilitating or obstructing the attainment of future goals. Prezant, Marshak, Cerrone, and Seligman (1997) discussed parental perceptions regarding helpful or obstructive professional actions based on responses from 120 parents of children with disabilities. Using a critical incident technique, the respondents were asked to identify and provide examples of times when professionals helped children toward their potential or were obstructive. They were asked to identify categories of professionals engaging in such actions and to describe desired professional actions that would be helpful in the future. By asking parents to elaborate on a specific event and to describe specific actions, meaningful situations served as the basis for parental comments rather than forced choices. Interestingly, of 12 professional categories derived from the responses, teachers were the professionals designated most frequently as instrumental in either helping or obstructing children's ability to reach their potential. Thirty-seven percent cited a teacher action as helpful whereas 40% cited nonhelpful actions by this group. Of note is that principals were cited over three times more often in performance of nonhelpful rather than helpful actions and that physicians were more than twice as likely to be identified as performing nonhelpful rather than helpful actions.

It is striking that when parents were asked to identify specific helpful actions, the most commonly cited (approximately 40%) simply fell within basic job requirements. Professional actions that reflect exceeding job requirements (i.e., going the extra mile) were identified by only 10% of the sample. Approximately 9% indicated that a professional had never engaged in any helpful actions on their behalf. In addition to a basic job well done, parents identified the following actions as helpful (in descending order of frequency cited): supporting child and parent, encouraging inclusion, enhancing self-esteem, having high expectations for the child, exceeding one's job, teaching parents, making accommodations, advocating for the child, and learning from the parents.

Of the nine categories of nonhelpful actions, poor performance of basic job requirements was cited most frequently and was closely followed by holding low expectations for youth with disabilities. Other nonhelpful actions identified were not complying with recommendations and accommodations; discouraging inclusion; demeaning the child, the parents, or both; abusing power; ignoring parental input; recommending institutionalization; and physically abusing the child.

An important implication of this study is that within this sample of parents, teachers were perceived as having the most significant role (of all professionals) in whether children reach their potential. Some of the most valuable findings with implications for all professionals are in the suggestions parents provided regarding what they would most like to have a professional do:

I would like professionals to be aware that their contact with a child is usually temporary. If the child's case becomes too difficult, they can refer the child to another agency. A parent's role is a lifetime role. We will never stop being parents.

Listen to me. I've been a parent for over 23 years. I'm not stupid, overprotective or extreme. I don't lack parenting skills, I just have a son with problems and he is hard to deal with on some issues. I can tell you what I've tried and what worked or didn't—Don't make me do it all over again!

Focus on my child's abilities not disabilities. Listen respectfully and consider the information I give is based on my knowledge about her. Be a part of the team which includes me, to help my child learn, grow, and have success.

Respect my opinions—my vision for my son's future. Stay up to date on best practices that are enabling children with disabilities to work, live, and recreate in the community. Learn how to work with families. Learn how to listen with empathy and communicate effectively. Treat parents as valued partners with important information and skills to share. Focus on my child's strength and potential. Work hard to keep ongoing home/school communication going. (Anonymous, parent survey responses, 1996)

PARENT-PROFESSIONAL RELATIONSHIPS—
BUILDING BLOCKS OR STUMBLING BLOCKS?

I wish professionals had trusted my instincts as a parent. I knew something was not right. Something was too hard. I didn't know where to go. Nobody said anything encouraging. I wish they would've told me about the help that was available. I did it on my own. I called people who I had inklings that their children also had problems. Nobody pointed me in any directions. I saw support group ads in the paper and called them in desperation. More information was needed. (Anonymous, parent interview, 1996)

When I went to the IEP meeting at school,* they made me feel stupid and treated me as if I was wasting their precious time. They told me that my requests would do more harm than good and that I was babying my son and they couldn't just grant favors to all parents who asked for special treatment. They told me I was fighting for things that shouldn't be fought for. But I was upset that his teachers had not read his previous IEPs on file. I was told that they weren't allowed to see them due to confidentiality. And when I went to the guidance counselor for assistance, she told me I'd have to see someone else because she really didn't know anything about my son's disability. (Anonymous, personal communication, June 1997)

Literature reviews, parent interviews, and the rising number of support and advocacy groups evidence the ambivalent and sometimes adversarial relationship between parents and professionals. Good parent-professional relationships, however, are integral in planning for children with disabilities during the elementary school years. What is it that makes this relationship so difficult for some? Although family-professional relationships are covered in Chapter 8, the following discussion will focus on such relationships during school-age years. Families may work with many professionals over the course of their child's life, but during this specific period there are increased interactions with professionals that relate to educational and school issues.

As a prerequisite to further discussion about this issue, it is important for professionals to understand three givens about basic differences between parents of children with disabilities and professionals:

1. *Parents have no choice—professionals do.* Professionals in education and other human service professions have consciously selected their profession based on professional interests, training, and job availability. Professionals may switch jobs, change professions, or retire. Parents of children with disabilities in most instances have not selected this role by choice. Most in fact have no prior training, have not been asked, and are frequently surprised and shocked to find they will be intricately involved with a child who has a disability in a unique way.

---

* See descriptions of the individual education program (IEP), later in this chapter.

2. *Parents are permanent; professionals are transient.* No matter how well trained or dedicated a professional is, he or she is a transient in the life of a child with a disability. Particularly in a school setting (but also in mental health, medical, social work, and other settings), a professional's direct involvement with a child and his or her family may be for as little as one year. Consequently, the goals set by professionals may be time limited and short-sighted. The child continues to move through a series of professional educators and paid service providers, each with different perspectives, attitudes, and approaches to both the child and the family. Parents on the other hand are permanent fixtures, continually observing and readjusting to changing needs over time. The parent moves with the child through life transitions, through different systems, and through different professionals. In most families, the parent is the holder of the history and the key to effective future planning.

3. *Parents and professionals are concerned in different ways.* Although ideally parents and professionals both focus on the child's needs, their concerns may vary by nature of their differing roles. Educators may be concerned about the child from an academic perspective, whereas counselors may be concerned about mental health issues. Some families may see six, seven, or more providers who all have different concerns relating to the child. Each professional is assumed to have the child's best interest at heart, but additional concerns may relate to professional obligations, doing the job well, self-validation, and so on.

Parents need to look at the whole child and frequently act as a case manager of sorts in integrating objectives, information, and suggestions from each provider. Parent concerns are tied to plans for the future; implications for the family; and validation as an effective advocate, protector, supporter, and emotional provider. In addition to these concerns, parents frequently must deal with housing, employment responsibilities, time management issues, and other daily concerns.

Additional factors that impact parent-professional relationships are the nature of professional training and myths or assumptions about both parents and professionals.

Professional Training

Professional training is designed for a specific purpose. In the education and helping professions, professional preparation imparts information, specific skill training, and experience in practical application. Certificates and degrees imply a certain level of expertise in a specific field. What sometimes happens when professionals and parents interact is that the relationship, rather than being a partnership, is viewed by one or the other member as a two-tiered system that consists of opposite poles of the spectrum, one positive and one negative: superior-inferior, helpful-helpless, knowledgeable-ignorant. Such a relationship is nonproductive.

Families like those quoted earlier may have negative experiences with professionals that serve to confirm and reconfirm their notions that professionals may not care, do not respect them, are uninformed, and will not be helpful. These parents may not seek assistance or become involved unless necessary and may develop a mind-set about the value of professional involvement that restricts or limits progress.

Professionals may have been cautioned about the dangers of becoming too involved with their clients (see discussion in Chapter 8) and, lest they risk sacrificing objectivity, are warned to maintain professional distance (Sonnenschein, 1981). Yet it is their very involvement that makes parents feel that professionals are concerned and interested. When one considers the reasons or attributes that lead a person into the helping professions, care, concern, interest in individuals' welfare, and skill in working with people are traits that would rise to the top of the list, yet we attempt to squash those very instincts in the name of professionalism. There certainly are good reasons to avoid becoming overly involved with client needs but being devoid of emotion does not serve any purpose. In fact, professional distance is viewed by many parents as an obstacle to parent-professional relationships because it denigrates empathy, which parents may feel the need for above all else in such relationships (Sonnenschein, 1981).

A newly trained mental health professional who felt that too much professional distance had its drawbacks had this to say about being reprimanded for overinvolvement:

> I was told that I was feeling too much compassion for the child I was working with because I wanted to wait until his situation was resolved before taking on a new client. My supervisor said that she was afraid for my well-being. I tried to tell her that it wasn't about me but it was about the child, my client, the person we were supposed to be helping. I was castigated for crossing the boundaries and being too involved in order to meet my own needs. (Anonymous, personal communication, June 1997)

Myths and Assumptions About Parents and Educators and Other Professionals

Preconceived notions held by parents or professionals about each other may have a deleterious effect on interactions regarding the child. A group of parents participating in a workshop was asked to characterize professionals both positively and negatively by ascribing attributes to them. A group of professionals was asked to do the same for parents (Prezant, 1996). Among the positive traits listed for parents were caring, concerned, and knows child well. Positive characteristics of professionals included intelligent and competent. Negative traits listed for professionals were unprepared, arrogant, unreceptive, ignores needs, inconsistent, and negative. Negative traits used to describe parents included unrealistic, lacking in expertise, poorly educated, uninformed, pushy, demanding, and frustrated.

Assumptions about professionals and parents develop because of experiences, information level, and word of mouth anecdotes. The importance of perspectives and experience became apparent during this workshop when a school administrator indicated that he was present at a meeting to which a parent brought an advocate and he felt this was an adversarial and challenging move. Unbeknownst to him, the parent was present at the workshop. She responded by telling the group that she brought an advocate because she knew that she was not well informed about her rights and wanted somebody with her who would know what to ask and say. She thought doing so was not challenging or adversarial but rather a sign of a concerned parent who wanted what was best for her son. In this scenario, the same action was viewed differently because of perspectives, experiences, and assumptions.

Numerous myths and assumptions regarding parent participation are prevalent among professionals and should be recognized as sources of bias and negative mind-sets. Some of these commonly held myths and assumptions include parents do not know what their child needs, parents are uninformed, parents are too emotionally involved to be objective or realistic, and parents are troublemakers.

Despite the fact that parents may not use professional jargon or know what the latest curriculum is, they usually know their child's likes, dislikes, strengths, and needs better than anyone else. They may not know the child's math level or at what grade level the child reads, but they can tell that the child is a great reader or has no mind for numbers. They have observed over time the way their child follows directions, participates in conversations, makes friends, and accepts responsibility. The parent is a storehouse of information for professionals who know how to access it in a meaningful, proactive manner.

Some parents may not have the information they need, either because their prior experiences have reinforced passive behaviors or a sense of inferiority or because they have not been linked to appropriate informational sources. Once they understand how to get information, however, many parents become more informed than helping professionals and are in a position to provide information to them (Dane, 1990).

Emotional involvement with the child has been used as an excuse to demean parents and omit them from educational decision making. Emotional involvement is precisely why parents should be active participants in parent-professional partnerships. They care enough about their child to make decisions, take risks, and invest time and effort in the child's learning.

Some parents feel that they should have had more confidence in their own instincts. This may occur when parents follow up on professional sugges- tions but feel that no one is listening to them. In situations when profes- sional recommendations do not yield desired results, parents may become more assertive and may be labeled as troublemakers.

Parent-professional relationships are complex in nature and based on as- sumptions, training, and experiences. As such, they are partially defined even before the parent and professional ever meet. Once the relationship is initiated, three aspects of the relationship that are either obstructive or facil- itative are information level, communication skills, and administrative is- sues (see Table 3.1).

Information Level

Lack of information about the disability, about educational rights, or about appropriate strategies and inclusive practices may propel a relationship into a tailspin from the outset. If parents and professionals begin the process with different information, defensiveness and conflict may result. Parents who lack needed information may feel intimidated or ignorant. If parents have more information than the professional, the result may be defensive posturing or the perception of threats to the skill and expertise of the teacher or helping professional.

In initiating relationships, a good jumping-off point would be to determine what information is available about the child, about characteristics of the dis- ability that pose obstacles, and about what can be done to facilitate progress. Parents at times do not have sufficient information. It may also be the case that classroom teachers have little understanding of either the disability or laws protecting the child. Mental health professionals may hold an equally dismal track record when it comes to their knowledge of how to use educational rights to access services, programs, and accommodations that a child may need. Such misinformation may affect a teacher's estimation of children's abil- ities or mean that children will not receive services to which they are entitled.

Parental resistance to follow-up on well-intended but time-consuming suggestions may be indicative not of lack of interest but of overwhelming demands in the face of limited resources (MacMillan & Turnbull, 1983). It is imperative that professionals be knowledgeable about family dynamics. It is of equal importance that parents have information regarding daily demands on a teacher, including the strong possibility that the teacher has had no for- mal training in disabilities, educational law, or how to make modifications for children with disabilities in regular classrooms.

TABLE 3.1   Parent-Professional Relationships: Stumbling Blocks or Building Blocks?

Obstacles to Positive Relationships

Informational	Lack of knowledge re disability, laws, services
	Lack of understanding of family dynamics
	Differing goals for child
	Jargon
	Stereotypes
Communication Skills	Lack of respect, acceptance, empathy
	Poor listening skills
	Emotionality, defensiveness
	Inflexibility
	Confrontation, blame
	Minimization of concerns
	Lack of encouragement
Administrative Issues	Poor provision of rights and procedural information
	Bureaucratic delay
	Time issues
	Turf issues
	Insufficient teacher in-service
	Negative attitudes

Proactive Steps to Foster Positive Relationships

Informational	Be informed
	Level the playing field: share information
	Recognize biases
	Recognize parents as source of information
	Understand family dynamics
Communication Skills	Convey respect and empathy
	Listen, explain, clarify, question
	Request feedback
	Be flexible and creative
	Engage in shared problem solving
	Focus on child
	Facilitate transition as a resource, liason, advocate
Administrative Issues	Be sure parents understand rights and process
	Provide time
	Minimize delays
	Collaborate and coordinate
	Be sensitive to disability training

The excessive use of professional jargon is a sure way to obstruct rather than facilitate a healthy relationship. Parents frequently report discomfort participating in meetings at which they are the sole "nonprofessional" and everyone appears to be speaking a foreign language with no interpreters. Parents in this situation feel left out, disregarded, and either ignorant or angry. If specialized or shorthand terms are used, everyone should have a clear understanding of what the terms mean.

Communication Skills

Good communication skills are critical to any relationship, and professionals should be able to identify the communication styles of parents. Lack of respect, empathy, or acceptance are frequent concerns of parents who participate in meetings during their child's elementary school years. Parents perceive that professionals, through their communication style, minimize their concerns, are not active listeners, and become defensive when questioned. Professionals may feel that parental communication is confrontational, challenging, and affected by high emotions. Meetings that are characterized by poor use of communication skills may result in beliefs that nothing has been accomplished.

Basic rules of good communication should be observed by all parties to the relationship. Conveying respect and empathy are primary. Listening is an aspect of communication that is frequently violated yet integral to the communication process and tied in to information sharing. Listening paves the way for questioning, clarifying, and explaining. Requesting and providing feedback gives each person an opportunity to contribute and assists in the process of shared problem solving.

Administrative Issues

Administrative regulations and guidelines may pose barriers. Comments like "We can't do that because it's never been done before" or "It wouldn't be fair to the other children" or "We can't provide that because that service isn't available in this building" are statements that reflect a larger administrative framework guiding what children should receive rather than their own individual needs. Some major administrative issues that negatively impact parent-professional relationships, particularly in school settings, include bureaucratic delays, time issues, turf issues, and confusion about how procedural information is imparted to parents.

Despite the fact that school-based evaluations should be completed in a very specific time period under the law, it is a frequent finding that children have waited a year or more to be tested and placed due to bureaucratic delays, paperwork, and staff shortages. Scheduling parent-teacher or IEP meetings is often problematic due to individual scheduling issues. Parents are understandably upset when they prepare for what they consider to be an important meeting about their child to find that half the people asked to be present are not and the rest come and go during the meeting. One parent described her feelings and actions about these problems:

> Having teachers walk in and out as they pleased was very disruptive. Here you had spent so much time preparing what you wanted to say to the teachers and someone would stroll in during the middle or, worse yet, would get up and leave. You felt like you needed to begin again each time and the continuity was destroyed. It gives you the feeling that nobody really cares about your child or values what you have to say. After a few years of that, I began requesting that the meeting be scheduled at a time when all teachers could come and if I was told we only had 20 minutes for the meeting, I made it clear that I would be happy to schedule another session to complete the meeting. (Anonymous, personal communication, May 1995)

Turf issues surface when a specific need is addressed but assigning accountability is debated either because of overlapping areas of expertise or lack of collaboration. Procedural safeguards, a legal right of which parents should be informed, are more often than not provided in jargon through a written document with no follow-up to check parent comprehension.

To minimize obstacles due to administrative regulations, professionals should be sure that parents understand their child's rights by discussing them. Scheduling meetings that include needed personnel at times when they can fully participate in the meetings and provide needed information as well as receive useful information is critical. Minimizing delays will reduce parent anxieties about lost time. Collaboration and coordination, though easier said than done, will help avoid duplication of services or areas that have been overlooked.

BUILDING BRIDGES BETWEEN PARENTS AND PROFESSIONALS

In her lectures for preprofessionals, a parent of a child with a disability who advocates for others based on her own learning experiences explains just what it is that parents expect from relationships with educators—for themselves and their children—by using the acronyms "share" and "learn."

S = Share information by communicating and listening
H = (helper)—Let me help you to help my child
A = Assess and adjust so my child will learn

R = Respect confidentiality and be courteous

E = Educate yourself so you can help my child experience growth and success

and

L = Listen to my child, nurture interests, use strengths to improve weaknesses

E = (exciting and innovative)—Make learning fun, provide options

A = Accept each child as a whole person, not a label

R = (role model)—Show respect for everyone by your actions, set guidelines, do not tolerate exclusion or abuse

N = Nourish the desire to learn so my child becomes a lifelong learner

Several other strategies to improve parent-educator relationships are initiating contact, making periodic reports, and recognizing educator efforts.

Initiating Contact

Either the parent or the educator initiating contact by phone or note makes the other party aware of an interest in collaborating. It is frequently recommended that parents request initial meetings with teachers early in the school year. Similarly, teachers who call or write parents to introduce themselves convey a sense of caring concern to families. Although counselors, therapists, and mental health professionals maintain ongoing contact with families, their suggestions can facilitate improved relationships with school-based professionals.

Periodic Reports

Schools are in contact with parents through report cards several times a year. For children with disabilities, whether in inclusive or noninclusive settings, more frequent contact is desirable. Academic or social problems cannot wait until the end of the quarter. Periodic reporting, sometimes as often as every two weeks, will keep parents abreast of school progress.

On the flip side, a helpful strategy has been a parent report card or parent feedback note. When parents provide regular feedback to the teacher about satisfaction with the educational program, increased collaboration is reinforced. If parents are not satisfied, teachers will also know and teamwork will facilitate readjustments in curriculum, service, or scheduling. One member of a parent network reported that each year she sends a letter to each of her child's teachers in appreciation of their efforts. She also sends the principal a letter outlining positive and negative feedback for each teacher each year. In this way, regular feedback is provided and the parent is perceived as a team player rather than someone who only complains when things go wrong.

Recognizing Educators

Like the rest of us, educators are not often acknowledged when a job is well done, but always hear about mistakes or missed opportunities. Maybe this is human nature, but it is also human nature to enjoy knowing when someone has been helped through our efforts or that something we have done has made a difference. Horror stories about professional treatment of children with disabilities abound but they do not represent the experience of the majority of families.

The Parent Information Project, a parent network and advocacy group for families of children with disabilities at Indiana University of Pennsylvania, challenges parents to think about the positive events, practices, or changes occurring for their children to increase the frequency with which they occur. Parents in the area network have been asked to identify educators who have had a significant positive impact on the life of their child and nominate them for recognition by describing exactly what it is that they have done. The teachers, counselors, therapists, principals, psychologists, custodians, and classroom aides are then recognized at a formal reception, along with the parents who submitted their names. In addition to public recognition and receipt of a certificate of appreciation, their supervisors are notified by mail and regional media cover the event.

This type of recognition has several purposes. First, it commends the nominee, reinforces previous efforts, and creates an awareness that someone is taking notice. Second, it gives the parent the opportunity to locate sources of support in teachers, increase collaboration, and recognize that there are dedicated professionals facilitating optimal progress. Most important, it presents a teacher as a role model for peer educators.

The following is one nomination letter:

There was one such teacher in our child's life. Our son was diagnosed with ADD [attention deficit disorder] when he was in the third grade. He is now a seventh grade student. Through the years we have found that each teacher handles our son in much the same way. Their attitude usually makes it clear to my husband and myself that our son merely has a behavior problem. Once they have a chance to take control of him, everything will be better.

However, the year that our son was diagnosed, he had a wonderful teacher . . . one who took an active interest in our son. It was he who helped us to realize just how bright our son really is and how to best help him. He discovered that our son does his best work when given a challenge and lots of encouragement. He not only talked to our son, he listened—really listened to our son. In those nine months with this teacher, our son discovered that his thoughts, feelings and abilities really are important! The encouragement and self worth that his father and I just couldn't seem to convey to him at home, came from his teacher. Sadly, since that time, the few teachers who have shown interest in our son have lost that interest when they realized what a challenge he would be to them. I know it's just too much to hope for, but what a wonderful learning experience all our children would have if they could have at least one teacher like this man in their lives! (Anonymous, parent nomination letter, 1995)

ADVOCACY FOR FAMILIES OF SCHOOL-AGE CHILDREN

Many parents of children with disabilities do not realize the power they possess to effect change because they are overwhelmed by their child's needs, intimidated by the educational process, uninformed, or feel that they have no control. The advocacy movement, however, has been responsible for many advances in rights for individuals with disabilities. The Individuals With Disabilities Education Act of 1990 (IDEA) and the Americans With Disabilities Act of 1990 (ADA) are prime examples of major pieces of legislation enacted through the efforts of ordinary people.

Among the most well known landmark advocacy efforts that paved the way for dramatic changes mandated by these two laws was *Pennsylvania Association for Retarded Children v. Commonwealth of Pennsylvania* (1972), a case in which parents of children with mental retardation in Pennsylvania banded together to protest a denial of access to public educational programs. It has only been through such efforts that systems change has occurred over time.

Advocacy means to take up another's cause. The definition for an advocate does not specify necessary degrees, titles, or job descriptions as prerequisites. Most advocates have no preprofessional training in advocacy and may not even be trained professionals at all. Numerous individuals serve as advocates, including parents, teachers, therapists, mental health professionals, friends, and so on.

Parents of children with disabilities need advocacy efforts for various reasons, all centering on meeting the needs of the child with disabilities. Advocacy provides information, training in assertiveness and communication strategies, linkages, lobbying opportunities, and parent networking, among other supports. Effective advocacy, although it may be a lifelong need, demonstrates to individuals how to advocate for themselves and others. It is a process that provides individuals with tools and skills to improve conditions, in this case, the quality of life.

In their description of advocacy types, Alper, Schloss, and Schloss (1995) noted that the most formal types of advocacy may not be as effective as informal approaches due to the confrontational nature of legal proceedings. The four types of advocacy they describe are *self-advocacy*, which is the use of self-assertiveness to meet needs; *social support*, or citizen, advocacy, which involves efforts to improve conditions for a group; *interpersonal advocacy*, which entails direct involvement on behalf of specific individuals; and *legal advocacy*, which uses the legislative and judicial systems to ensure preservation of individual rights.

For parents of children with disabilities, interpersonal advocacy may be the key to all forms of advocacy. The parent who asks for a teacher meeting because appropriate things are not happening for a child, the friends who inform a parent about what worked for them, the counselor who helps a parent practice a strategy to use, or a parent support group that provides assertiveness training all meet the definition of interpersonal advocacy. Interpersonal advocacy can help parents and children to become more effective self-advocates, create an awareness for a community need, and inform parents about legal options they may wish to pursue.

Parent support and advocacy groups are increasing in number due to the gaps in our system that leave parents out of the process. The discrepancy between ideal and actual services provided to school-aged children is a factor that stimulates parents to seek support outside schools or agencies (Hamre-Nietupski et al., 1988). These groups may range from small, informal groups that meet monthly at someone's home, to grassroots organizations backed by funding and a physical facility, to branches of national disability-specific advocacy organizations with high public visibility and financial campaigns. Examples of such associations are the Association for Retarded Citizens, Learning Disability Association, Down's Syndrome Society, Epilepsy Foundation of America, and Children and Adults With Attention Deficit Disorder. The groups may differ in size and formality but overlap on type of advocacy support provided. A family's decision about what type of help to enlist may depend on whether it lives in an urban or rural community.

Assuming that parent advocacy groups originate from an observed need, there are variations of basic steps that guide advocacy efforts. The first step is identifying the problem. Are all the children with disabilities made to sit at one table in the cafeteria? Are there several parents in the group assigned to a school guidance counselor who has no information on disabilities? Is there a parent whose child's rights have been violated because of an inappropriate education? Do parents need to know more about the laws so they know what to say at a school meeting? Has a child been denied services based on lack of staff or a "This is the way we've done it here" attitude? These are some examples of problems to identify.

The next step is to think about goals and objectives to improve the situation. Does the school need information on inclusion? Do the guidance counselors need additional training? Does the family understand how to discuss inappropriate versus appropriate education according to the law? Do the parents know what educational rights their child is entitled to? Does everyone know that it is illegal to deny needed services because they do not appear to be available at present?

Strategies to use in meeting the objectives might include asking the school to sponsor a workshop or meeting for parents and teachers, bringing a legal expert to a parent support meeting who can explain the laws, or teaching parents how to be assertive when they feel their child's needs are being glossed over.

Finally, taking action is the implementation of the first three steps.

Every advocacy group is slightly different from the next, but all are dynamic because to be effective they must respond to the needs of the members over time. If the group becomes a fairly stable force in a community, it has recognition value—parents access it based on word of mouth; schools, practitioners, and agencies may use it as a resource; awareness is increased; and change will occur.

In addition to tools like information, assertiveness training, and communication training, advocacy groups may share specific helpful strategies that parents can practice with each other and implement in their meetings with school professionals. Most of these are simple, easy to learn, and inexpensive. Basic information on how to dress, what to bring, where to sit, and who to take with you may seem simplistic but these things do make a difference. Suggesting that parents take their child's photograph to a meeting helps to personalize the situation and reinforces that the child is the common focus of all. A parent known to one of us (F. P.) always brings her daughter's photo as well as a picture of the entire family. As the meeting begins, she places them on the table in a way that introduces the child as an integral part of a real family. Discussing a child in terms of strengths exhibited and areas of interest and life outside of school tends to remind participants that the meeting is about a whole child and not just the child's math or speech problems.

Despite the fact that professionals frequently complain about inordinate amounts of paperwork, it is surprising how many parents do not keep records. The simple act of demonstrating why records are important and how to keep a chronological record of evaluations, progress reports, medical notes, notes about meetings, and copies of correspondence may be helpful for numerous parents who discard important information or throw it in a pile never to be found.

Some parents are not aware that they should go to school meetings prepared, rather than as passive observers. They may need to be prompted to think about what their child's needs are; what objective they would like to see addressed; or what accommodations the child may need, such as homework modifications or an extra set of textbooks at home. They should have questions ready about what the school staff will do to meet the child's needs or how the child is doing in the present program. They should come with notes in case they forget, lose their train of thought, or become emotional during the meeting. They should also take notes that can be reviewed after the meeting or if possible have a spouse, friend, mentor parent, or advocate attend with them.

Parent advocacy groups always remind parents to write letters that document phone conversations or requests for evaluations. Sending such letters by certified mail with a return receipt provides documentation that the message has arrived and helps to avoid responses like, "I never got that letter." Parents should be reminded to date the letters, keep a copy, and file the copy in a safe place.

EVOLUTION AND IMPACT OF
ONE PARENT ADVOCACY ORGANIZATION

Parent information and advocacy groups have impacts on communities that cannot be measured in number of direct contacts tracked. The Parent Information Project at Indiana University of Pennsylvania has received funding since 1990 to provide information, support, training, and peer advocacy for parents of school-aged children with disabilities in a rural area. The group began with 10 families attending the University Speech and Hearing Clinic, where it was recognized that the parents lacked information that would help them to advocate for their own children. Word of mouth and minimal publicity has increased the size of this group from 10 parents to over 750 families and 400 agencies. Provision of printed information, telephone support, the availability of a mentor parent who attends IEP meetings, and trainings have indirectly impacted thousands of families. In addition, the focus has increased based on needs expressed by parents. For example, concerns about ADHD led to grant funding that supported the project's in-servicing of over 500 teachers on this topic. Concerns about children's attitudes resulted in funding that supported the donation of "sensitization" materials and workshops to more than 70 rural schools. Faculty and preprofessional students at the college level became frequent users of a lending library and requested lectures for their education classes. Recognition that education majors had insufficient information and training to teach children with diverse needs paved the way for the Teacher Preparation Program funded by the Developmental Disabilities Council. The purpose of this program is to collaboratively enhance the type of information that college education majors receive about students with disabilities. Parents in the project are directly involved as frequent guest lecturers who bring an experiential perspective to theoretical course content. Students interviewed as part of this project have indicated significant needs for more fieldwork and coursework related to disabilities.

Numerous other unanticipated activities, such as national presentations, representation on organizational boards, Internet connections, and requests for information from other state agencies and countries, have developed and continue to grow exponentially, resulting in systems change. All of this stemmed from a small band of parents in a rural community, committed to improving the lives of their children and looking for appropriate resources to help in that process.

IDEA, THE SPECIAL EDUCATION LAW: FOR SPECIAL EDUCATORS ONLY?

It is critical that every professional working with children who have disabilities understands special education laws. Counselors, therapists, physicians, social workers, classroom teachers, guidance counselors, and numerous other human service professionals may all be involved in the process of evaluating or providing service to children with special needs. This puts them in a position to make recommendations that may be school based. Far too many children are falling through cracks because private and public service providers do not understand the child's legal rights to the educational process and how they can impact programs.

Mental health professionals may recommend modifications to the school day, suggest homebound instruction, or request regular contact with a school professional; physicians may recommend occupational or physical therapy; and developmental specialists may determine a need for a classroom aide, assistive technology, or sign language instruction. Any one of these professionals, among others, could impact the educational evaluation or program. Knowing that all these resources can be integrated should not be the sole responsibility of the parents. They are the ones seeking assistance.

Below are some examples of basic information related to special education legislation that professionals working with children should know:

- A parent must give permission before a school can evaluate, place, or change the placement or program of a child.
- If transportation is necessary for a child's program, it is the school's responsibility to provide it.
- Parents have a right to disagree with a school evaluation and under certain circumstances may request an independent evaluation at public expense.

- If a child attends a private school and is in need of specialized instruction, the home school district is required to provide it.
- Waiting lists for evaluations are illegal and the law specifies timelines for evaluations, educational plans, program implementation, and annual reviews.
- Requesting preferential seating, teacher in-servicing, an extra set of books at home, homework modifications, extended time on tests, or alternate methods of taking tests can all be justified if the child needs them.
- A school may be obligated to provide assistive technology or interpreters for children who are visually or hearing impaired. Large print or braille books, specially designed computers, FM units, and oral and sign interpreters are examples.
- Suspending or expelling a child for behaviors that are due to his or her disability may be illegal.
- Not permitting a child to take a class that meets on the second floor because the child is in a wheelchair is a violation of the child's rights, as is making the child eat lunch in the classroom because there is no ramp that allows access to the cafeteria.
- The wording used in professional recommendations may make the difference in whether or not the child receives a needed service.
- Classroom teachers who ignore the contents of an IEP have been fined with monetary damages.
- A school administration who informs teachers that they may not see their student's IEP because of confidentiality may actually be violating the child's right to an education.

WHY IS SPECIAL EDUCATION LAW NOT COMMON KNOWLEDGE FOR ALL PROFESSIONALS?

Prior to passage of the Education for All Handicapped Children Act of 1975 (P.L. 94–142), children with disabilities had no entitlements to education and were frequently excluded. Services provided were through private practitioners, public agencies other than schools, or costly private schools that were limited to those who could afford it. After P.L. 94–142 was passed, children were entitled to an education, but it was typically a segregated one in which children with disabilities were relegated to special self-contained classes. Special educators and associated therapists were the only professionals who taught children with disabilities in schools. Preprofessional training in special education and regular elementary education took the form of two distinct strands of preparation that did not overlap (see discussion in Chapter 5). Differences in training and turf issues gave rise to the idea that elementary educators taught typical children and special educators taught the others. Each professional group became territorial; special educators were seen as the experts and noninvolvement of regular educators reinforced stereotypes and the need for separate systems. Simultaneously, there was little interaction between school-based and private practitioners or human service agencies.

Although passage of P.L. 94–142 paved the way for changes in the education of children with disabilities, teacher preparation programs did not change quickly enough. There still exist university programs that do not require even a single course on disabilities or related legal issues for elementary teacher candidates, guidance counselors, school psychologists, or other mental health and family service professionals. Currently, classroom teachers usually have children with disabilities in their classes but may not understand the children's needs, the methods by which to teach the children, or the laws that pertain to the process. Situations like this promote fear, resentment, and poor relationships among such professionals and with parents. Relevant information from outside agencies and practitioners should also be part of the record, creating the need for an increased knowledge base on the part of the professionals working with families outside the school setting.

What Is IDEA and What Does It Say?

Given the constraints of time and space, it is impossible to fully cover IDEA here, but all professionals should know that a copy of each state's standards and regulations (all of which must comply with the federal mandate) may be obtained from their state's Department of Education, Office of Special Education. All practitioners should have a copy available as a resource. In addition, every state has a Federal Parent Training and Information Center that can provide the same information, as well as other resources and printed information.

The original act passed in 1975, the Education for All Handicapped Children Act (P.L. 94–142), called for a free, appropriate public education designed to meet the unique needs of the child in the least restrictive environment for children with disabilities ages 6 to 18. Amendments and reauthorizations resulted in the Individuals With Disabilities Education Act of 1990 (IDEA; P.L. 101–476), which guarantees needed services and education to children from birth through age 21. From birth to age 3, services are provided under Part H of this law and are family-focused services that revolve around the infant or toddler as part of the family unit. Many of the services provided to the under-3 population are home based. Part B refers to school-aged children (3–21); in addition to ensuring an appropriate education that includes special education and related services, it guarantees the involvement of parents as partners in the process and ensures their due process rights.

It is important to understand how children with disabilities are defined and what terms like *free, appropriate, unique needs, special education, related services,* and *least restrictive* mean. According to the law, the following categories are used to define exceptionalities: mental retardation, hearing impairments and deafness, speech or language impairments, visual impairments and blindness, serious emotional disturbance, orthopedic impairments, autism, traumatic brain injury, other health impairments, specific learning disabilities, deaf blindness, or multiple disabilities.

It is important that practitioners recognize that these labels may not be exclusive. For example, many families of children with attention deficit (hyperactivity) disorder have been denied services on the premise that ADHD is not one of the previously mentioned categories. It is true that there was an effort to create another category. The information that frequently is not passed on is that there was no need for an additional label because ADHD fits in existing categories (other health impairments or, sometimes, learning disabilities and emotional disturbance). In addition, some children who are intellectually gifted may also have disabilities. The gifted status does not exclude a child from services.

IDEA guarantees that appropriate programs will be designed for children with disabilities to meet their unique needs. This means that children should not be placed in programs or assigned services based on availability but based on needs determined by a multidisciplinary evaluation team. This may include the need for special education and related services. Special education is specially designed instruction that can be in the classroom, at home, in hospitals, in community-based settings, and so forth. Related services are transportation and other services necessary for the child to benefit from specialized instruction and may include transportation to and from school; physical, occupational, or speech or language therapy; counseling services; social work; parent counseling; and others. Free means that the parent does not bear the cost of the services and that if a district cannot provide what the child needs it must fund the services by either creating an appropriate program or sending the child to a private one.

The "least restrictive" concept is based on the idea that government intrusion on individual rights should be minimized. For example, to place a child who is blind in a life skills class with children who have severe mental retardation because the blind child cannot read the classroom textbooks would constitute a needless restriction of opportunities. (The rights of the other children may be jeopardized as well in a segregated program.) Informing a parent of a child who needs toileting assistance that the child may only come to school if the parent accompanies the child would also be an unreasonable restriction. Placing a child with a severe hearing loss in a classroom with no interpreter, trained teacher, or any other supports instead of meeting the child's needs in a nearby program that has the necessary supports is too restrictive. Providing detention rather than counseling for a child with known emotional problems who is receiving outside professional assistance could be viewed as overly restrictive.

The unique needs of children with disabilities are defined through a very specific process outlined in federal standards and regulations. An evaluation, which may be requested by the parent or a school-based professional, is completed by a multidisciplinary team (MDT). This team includes a teacher, specialized personnel such as a school psychologist or a speech and language pathologist, resource personnel, and the parent. Assessments that may include formal tests, observations, and family history are used to evaluate sensory and motor functioning, intellectual ability, academic achievement, communication skills, and social and emotional status. Reports of assessments from outside professionals also may be included in the evaluation.

The evaluation results are then shared by the team (and should be provided to the parent in written form) and an evaluation report recommends that the child is or is not eligible for special education based on whether the child meets eligibility criteria for a specific category and whether the difficulty demonstrates a need for specialized instruction.

If special education is warranted and the team is in agreement, an individualized education program (IEP) is written by the IEP team, which includes the parents, classroom teacher, a representative of the district, and specialists. This process facilitates communication, problem solving, and planning to meet the child's needs. The IEP itself is written documentation of the process and must include the following information:

- A description of the child's present levels of performance
- Annual goals and short-term objectives for the child to target during the coming year
- A description of the services and specialized instruction to be provided
- The amount of time the child is in the regular program
- Information on who will provide the services and how they will be provided, criteria and methods for evaluating progress, and dates of initiation and review

Every IEP must be reviewed at least yearly and each child must be reevaluated at least every 3 years. This process occurs more frequently for preschoolers.

EVALUATION AND PLANNING FOR A CHILD WITH DISABILITIES

The child's needs are what should drive the IEP and program, not administrative convenience, availability of service, or the way things have been done before. Decisions about placement of the child can only be made after needs and services are determined. The parent has a right to disagree at any stage in the process and the law specifically delineates parent rights to notification, permission, and options if there is a disagreement during the process. Mediation and due process hearings are part of the continuum of options.

The following is a hypothetical scenario to exemplify how this process works:

A child with learning disabilities, attentional deficits, and a bipolar disorder is doing poorly in school. An evaluation is requested and assessment results indicate the child is functioning at low levels academically. The team fails to request parent input even though the parent has demonstrated interest. The parent has no knowledge of due process rights to be involved. Limited testing is conducted in the area of achievement, with no assessments of the child's intellectual potential. Observations reveal a child who does not follow classroom directions, does not pay attention, and is frequently reprimanded by the teacher and excluded by classmates. The team decides that the child has some disciplinary problems due to lack of parental interest and that the child does not meet eligibility requirements for any specific category, but could use more discipline and attention at home.

A meeting is scheduled and for the first time the parents are invited to participate in the process. At the meeting, they are astonished to hear the findings and finally share information regarding outside help the child has been receiving. The team sticks by its decision. The parents consult with their mental health professionals and someone puts them in touch with a local parent advocacy group. When they find out about their rights, they ask for an independent evaluation, which the school denies. A prehearing conference ensues and then a hearing. It is then up to the school district to prove that its evaluation was appropriate. Upon finding that the parents rights were violated, that they were not part of the process, and that the evaluation was incomplete, the hearing officer agrees that an independent evaluation is needed and the school district must pay the cost. The family has the child thoroughly evaluated by a neuropsychologist, incorporating reports from the psychiatric and other mental health professionals who have been serving the child. This comprehensive evaluation demonstrates that the child may meet the criteria for three categories (other health impairments, learning disability, and serious emotional disturbance) and that there is a indisputable need for specialized instruction. The fact that these professionals write that the child *needs* these services to make meaningful progress rather than saying only that the child *might benefit* from them is significant.

An IEP is written with input from the outside professionals whom the parents invite to the meeting. The IEP is implemented and the child receives language therapy, school-based counseling in conjunction with outside consultation, resource room assistance for two periods a day, and regular classroom placement for the rest of the day. It is decided that periodic reports will be forwarded to the outside professionals and to the parents to coordinate efforts.

Clearly, not all IEPs are developed under such adversarial conditions. Most run smoothly and schools in general do a good job of evaluating children and involving parents in the process. To ensure that everyone understands his or her role and impact, it is critical that all parties comprehend the rights, the rules, the process, and the purpose of the IEP.

IDEA's rules also apply to preschoolers, although timelines differ, the focus is family based, and agencies other than schools may be providing services for infants and toddler. IDEA also applies to teenagers and young adults (through age 21) going through transition by directly involving them in their own planning. This will be addressed further in Chapter 5.

CONCLUSION

The elementary school years are a period of growth; exploration; and exposure to peers, other adults, school settings, and the community outside the home. As the child is exposed to more opportunities and takes more risks, the family continues to be watchful as it readjusts to ongoing and changing needs. The combined and collaborative support of school professionals, physicians, mental health professionals, friends, advocates, and family members is critical as the child approaches adolescence.

CHAPTER 4

Adolescence

*Individuation and Separation
in the Context of Disability*

A dolescence has been described as "a time of seeking: a seeking inward to find who one is; a searching outward to locate one's place in life; a longing for another with whom to satisfy cravings for intimacy and fulfillment" (Lidz, 1983, p. 306). The entwined processes of *individuation* and *separation* are at the heart of adolescent development. The adolescent is faced with shedding the primary role of being someone's son or daughter and becoming a person in his or her own right (Lidz, 1983). The struggle to define oneself as an individual is generally bound up with attempts to loosen familial ties in terms of both emotional attachments and parental authority. During this time, there are often strongly conflicted feelings about freedom from and dependency on one's family. As a result, attempts to separate are often clumsy and involve varying types of rejection of one's parents.

Peer groups are often instrumental in helping adolescents cope with individuation and separation. Adolescents often informally band together to provide mutual support, security, and emotional nourishment as they try to become less emotionally dependent on their parents. Peer groups may provide relatively safe arenas for testing out new behaviors as part of social and sexual exploration. Relatively small separations pave the way for eventual larger separations (Turnbull & Turnbull, 1985). For the majority of adolescents, driving plays an important role in these small separations and provides opportunities for exploration of all types. Physical separation is a common means of establishing independence, through "hanging out" with peers in the community and spending large amounts of time at the homes of others.

As illustrated in the following comments of an adolescent boy, the processes of individuation and separation are generally considerably more complicated for adolescents with disabilities:

> For me, one of the hardest things during my teenage years was that I wanted to challenge and defy my parents, as many teenagers do. However, because I was physically dependent on them for personal care, my desire for independence seemed thwarted. I couldn't run away from home or even stay in my room alone all day; it was obvious that my parents had considerable control over me because I needed so much of their help. This added extra pain for my parents and me during my teenage years. I couldn't simply break away from them, and they couldn't simply allow me to be alone. (PACER Center, 1993a., p. 20)

Adolescence is a time that challenges the psychological resources of most youth and their parents because of the breadth of issues being examined and the depth of emotions involved. The reader is undoubtedly aware of the standard changes that introduce upheaval during this developmental period, such as pubertal changes, increased peer pressures, heightened sexual impulses, and a questioning of basic values and assumptions. A host of additional factors converge in families that have a son or daughter with a disability.

For families with a child with a disability, the period of adolescent development has been described as a "threat to normalization" (Seligman & Darling, 1997). The family and adolescent, through denial, may have been able to maintain somewhat of a fiction that the child with the disability is essentially the same as others. Families that have minimized the impact of the disability in infancy and childhood find this increasingly difficult to do because problems of dependence are much more striking in adolescence when active caretaking is no longer the norm as it is in childhood. In addition, it is typical for parents to become more anxious about their children's future during this developmental stage because their experience of middle age generally includes an increased awareness of their own mortality (Colwell, 1984). As the child matures physically, an awareness of an adolescent's differentness from more typical age mates becomes more apparent. In addition, the parents may once again confront some of the strong emotions experienced during the phase of initial identification of the disability. Families that have adopted a "one day at a time" approach to cope during childhood often find themselves fearfully facing the vast expanse of the future. For some, this may include the recognition that major caretaking responsibilities will not end.

Adolescents may also have a "dawning" of the impact of their disability even if they had previously been largely at ease with it. Intensified negative feelings about one's disability may surface with force at this time. Although the capacity for abstract thinking varies, it is not unusual for adolescents to experience far-reaching changes in their intellectual abilities as they gain the ability to think conceptually and hypothetically.

Lidz (1983) described the newfound ability to hypothesize as follows: "The adolescent can reason 'If x is true, then y must follow,' and also "Had x been true, y would have been a possibility"(p. 324). This newly found cognitive ability often leads to hypothesizing about what life would have been like if one was born without a disability or did not develop a disability (Wright, 1983). What had been accepted simply as fact now is examined from different angles. This newly acquired ability for abstract thinking often leads to other types of comparisons—particularly comparisons with age mates. The adolescent with a disability consequently may feel the impact of his or her disability in new ways and may feel devalued or mournful as a result of these comparisons. Adolescents with congenital physical disabilities that were not previously experienced as devaluing may now find their bodies intolerable. Furthermore, Zetlin and Turner (1985) wrote that adolescents with developmental disabilities may now become aware of and troubled by their intellectual limitations.

As will be discussed more fully later, wrestling with what it means to be different (yet not devalued) is an important part of adjustment to disability and one that typically is successfully resolved over a period of time. The impact of disability is often acutely felt during adolescence, however, and may be accompanied by dysphoric feelings.

When one considers the interface between issues of separation and individuation and a heightened emotionality about the impact of disability, it is apparent that this period of development is of critical importance. It is unusual for the developmental processes of individuation and separation to be completed by the time adolescence chronologically draws to a close. Many issues are carried into adulthood for the individual with a disability. Strax (1991) noted that adolescents with disabilities almost always experience a "prolonged adolescence." Adolescents with disabilities and their families are often faced with the need to address these developmental tasks under conditions that differ from the norm. This gives rise to many questions. How does an adolescent establish a positive identity in a society that generally views people with disabilities in distorted ways? How are the processes of individuation and separation mastered if the adolescent does not have the same access as others to peers and mobility? What meaning does separation have if an adolescent appears unable to negotiate this physically or mentally? This chapter will focus on these questions and a discussion of other developmental tasks and realistic problems faced by adolescents with disabilities and their families.

IDENTITY FORMATION

Answering the question, "Who am I?" preoccupies adolescence and is wrestled with on both a conscious and an unconscious level. As expressed by Lidz (1983), "Young people are in the process of finding themselves even when they give it little thought" (pp. 354–355).

Distorted Perceptions

The process of identity formation is particularly complicated for adolescents with disabilities, partly because so many distorted identities are projected onto them. Much has been written about the manner in which people's own fear of disability results in strong, irrational reactions to people with disabilities. Perceptions of them are often distorted and they are made "heroes or tragic victims, larger or smaller than life" (Brightman, 1984, p. 45).

Distorted perceptions of persons with disabilities and their potential are present in childhood; we have chosen to address them in this point of the life cycle, however, because the damage of such stereotypes snowballs during adolescence and can have a destructive impact on socialization, intimacy, and vocation. Within the confines of this chapter, it is not possible to comprehensively cover the full range of ways in which persons without disabilities have misconceptions about people with disabilities. We briefly discuss some of the most pronounced ones.

Spread is a powerful perceptual phenomenon that underlies most of the other distortions. It is defined by Wright (1983) as "the power of single characteristics to evoke inferences about a person" (p. 32). Disability is such a powerful characteristic that (through spread) persons both with and without disabilities generally make numerous, subconscious inferences about people with disabilities. Through spread, the perception of one impairment leads to the inference that other impairments invariably exist. For example, this gives rise to the common phenomenon of talking loudly to people who are blind, as if they must also have hearing problems. A college student described this common manifestation of spread:

> When I tell a professor that I have a visual impairment (excluding the rehabilitation field), they always start talking louder, and this is true for other blind individuals I have asked. I wonder if the hearing impaired are thought to have blindness? (Anonymous, personal communication, 1996)

Similarly, spread leads people to infer impaired intelligence when there is impaired physical functioning. This pattern is all-too-evident in the stories of families with youth with physical disabilities who have been inappropriately placed in classrooms for students with mental retardation, despite average or above average intelligence.

In addition to inferences of additional impairments, spread often results in distortions about personality; professionals and the general public hold stereotyped views regarding the effects of disability on personality. The adolescent or adult with a disability may be regarded as extremely virtuous (or saintlike) for coping so well. Although the general public may regard this perspective as positive, it is still a distortion that sets the individual apart from others in detrimental ways. For example, adolescents with disabilities who are experiencing an emerging sexuality clearly will not benefit from being regarded as saintlike by their peers when their adolescent desire, by nature, is to have their sexuality recognized by others.

More often, however, personality inferences by the public and professionals are ones of maladjustment (Siller, 1976). The tendency to infer negative personality characteristics as a result of disability is embodied in the old saying, "Twisted body, twisted mind." Because (as outsiders to a situation) those of us who do not have disabilities cannot imagine how we could cope with a severe disability, we project our feelings onto others and tend to assume that they also would feel inferior, bitter, perpetually frustrated, and the like. This assumption is pervasive despite evidence to the contrary. Research studies largely conclude that these inferences are inaccurate. For example, Wright's (1983) meta-analysis of studies on adjustment to disability concluded, "On balance, research shows that people with a disability fare as well (or as poorly) on general measures of personality adjustment as do their able-bodied counterparts, provided that socioeconomic status and other confounding factors are eliminated" (p. 151). Shontz (1977) came to a similar conclusion after a systematic review of numerous studies:

> Though many efforts have been made to correlate disability with overall personality maladjustment, no systematic evidence has yet been published to show that reactions involving psychiatric disturbance occur any more frequently within a truly representative sample of people with disabilities than within the general population. (p. 208)

In addition to assumptions of additional impairments and personality maladjustment, life is often assumed to be invariably tragic for persons with a severe disability. Once again, this automatic inference is inaccurate. Studies on life satisfaction generally conclude that although life is more difficult, disability per se does not have a major negative impact on life satisfaction; in fact, other factors such as socioeconomic status have a greater impact on quality of life ratings (Cameron, Titus, Kostin, & Kostin,1973; Stensman, 1985). The interested reader is referred to Marshak and Seligman (1993) for a more extensive discussion of these findings.

The pervasive assumption that persons with disabilities have tragic lives leads to passivity on the part of some professionals and families with regard to preparing adolescents for a satisfying life outside of the family. The mother of a daughter with a spinal cord injury talked about the pervasiveness of this view among other parents she had contact with in the rehabilitation hospital:

> They have a different perspective on things. Sometimes they can depress you. Some would say their kids' lives were over and that they were stuck with the kids forever. I thought that was terrible. First of all, your kid's life is not over and you are not stuck with them. When the kids hear the parents say that, the kids believe it. (Anonymous, interview, 1995; quoted in Lasher & Marshak, 1995)

The view of life with a disability as invariably tragic can be attributed to the differences between the perception of insiders versus outsiders. In this context, insiders are persons with disabilities and outsiders are observers. Family members are classified as quasi-insiders. Those of us who are outsiders tend to overlook the forces that enable people to adjust to severe disabilities and the solutions that are more apparent to insiders. Consequently, we tend to see problems as insurmountable and situations as hopeless that from an insider's perspective are not. For example, an outsider might easily look at an adolescent's particular vocational goal as fraught with insurmountable problems, whereas the insider might realize that numerous problems exist but are individually manageable.

SELF-ESTEEM AND BEING "DIFFERENT"

Research on adults with disabilities indicates that they do not necessarily internalize distorted images others often hold of them (Fichten, Robillard, Judd, & Ansel, 1989; Kriegsman & Hershenson, 1987). Distorted projections are more powerful for the adolescent because the sense of self is not cohesive. Furthermore, many adolescents lack viable role models—an important factor in identity formation. Although the body of research literature on adults with disabilities is sufficient to clearly conclude that their problems with self-esteem are no more widespread than in the general population, the research on adolescents is far from conclusive. Some investigators report that these adolescents' levels of self-esteem are on a par with adolescents in general, but these studies were generally done with chronically ill adolescents (McAnarney, 1985). The dynamics of illness (including life-threatening illness) are different from those related to a disability that may barely impact health but may render one "different." Leslie Milk, a woman with a paralyzed arm, described part of the crux of the matter when it comes to adolescence and disability: "To be different when every adolescent instinct begs for sameness, is to be denied the protective coloration that helps other kids endure the teen years, the mean years" (quoted in Kriegsman, Zaslow, & D'Zmura-Rechsteiner, 1992, foreword).

During adolescence, identity formation and one's physical self are closely linked and one's own physique is often scrutinized (McAnarney, 1985). Reflecting back on her own adolescence, Milk added,

> Adolescence is the ultimate disability. All teenagers hate their hands or their hair, feel stupid or awkward, and are certain that their tiny flaws and foibles are the only things that others see about them. So to be a teenager coping with adolescence and a disability is to be doubly disabled. (quoted in Kriegsman et al., 1992, p. v)

The general population (and many professionals) assumes that self-esteem is inversely correlated with severity of disability, but this contradicts the findings of research studies (Shontz, 1977). Actually, it appears that persons with a milder disability may often have a harder time with adjustment due to their ability to avoid ("hide") the disclosure of their disability and therefore avoid "wrestling" with what it means to be different (Macgregor, 1951; Seligman & Darling, 1977). In addition, the ability to hide a disability leads others to expectations that they might not be able to achieve with regard to behavior, cognition, or socialization.

With regard to positive self-esteem, the adolescent with a physical disability is faced with a psychological task that has been termed *subordinating physique relative to other factors* (Wright, 1983). This requires the individual to accept that nonphysical attributes are genuinely more important than physical ones (Wright, 1983). This psychological task is germane to the eventual psychological adjustment of all of us, but if we do not have disabilities, we often do not feel a need to develop this attitude until much later in life when we age and our physical appearance begins to deviate more from cultural definitions of attractiveness (as portrayed in advertising and other media). Some adolescents with disabilities are able to successfully engage in this psychological task essentially 20 years before most are faced with it in middle age. This is well illustrated in the comments of one adolescent with quadriplegia: "God let me live. Just in *a different form*"(Anonymous, interview, 1995). Others cannot attain (or maintain) this attitude toward themselves.

Many of the difficult aspects of adjustment are due to differing from the social norm during a time in which there is a great desire for conformity. The matter of how families deal with "differentness" is a difficult one to address because the general public has consistently exaggerated the differences of people with disabilities. As discussed earlier, even in situations where impairment is relatively limited, people infer many differences in wide-ranging characteristics such as personality, mental abilities, and desires. This exaggerated sense of differentness (combined with stigmatization) has been a source of segregation and second-class treatment of persons with disabilities. On the other hand, to ignore all differences is not useful. Sometimes families communicate a viewpoint that there is nothing different about their child, a perspective that sometimes stems from denial and sometimes from an awareness that disability is often largely a social rather than a physical phenomenon. Nevertheless, it is the social phenomena that are often the greatest obstacle. As Olkin (1995) wrote, "There is no diagnosis that says, 'I'm counter to societal expectations and having a hard time of it'"(p. 40).

One female adolescent with a disability discussed the usefulness of acknowledging differences:

> I didn't get sheltered, at least not like a lot of other people with disabilities who have able-bodied parents. I find they often don't learn about themselves, or the disability, until they're 20 or beyond because they are taught to ignore it. No one ever talks about it because they think if you ignore it, it will go away. You are kind of brainwashed that you aren't different. Well, yes, you are different, and it's OK to be different. (PACER Center,1993a, p. 21)

If the differences are not acknowledged, families lose the opportunity to help adolescents place these differences into perspective and contain them. The position of "no difference" generally contrasts with adolescents' actual experiences. They are often treated differently and may feel different from others. Adolescents may feel that parental avoidance of the disability indicates that it is so awful to them that it cannot even be talked about. Furthermore, most problems loom larger when they are hidden.

To summarize our position on this topic, the danger is not in acknowledging differences, it is in inferring additional differences that do not exist. Wright's (1983) writings on adjustment to disability present a useful way to address differences. She referred to the importance of "containing disability effects." This psychological task concerns the ability to differentiate for oneself between those abilities that are and are not affected by one's disability. Adolescents and their families both need to learn to make these differentiations.

One mother's comments about her daughter who has quadriplegia reflected mastery of this task:

> I think we are fortunate that we have something to relate this to. My daughter [name deleted] has a cousin who has a brain stem injury. She has only a shell of a body with a full working mind. She cannot move any part of her body. She can blink her eyes and move them up and down. . . . So here she is trapped inside herself. So her life is TV and books. My daughter has 100, no, 1000 times more than that. Yes, it is too bad. But she can still talk, have friends. She can have a car. She can move. She can do a lot of things a normal kid can do. (Anonymous, interview, 1995, in Lasher & Marshak, 1995)

Acceptance of a disability, an important aspect of adjustment, hinges on integrating the disability as a single nondevaluating aspect of one's personal identity. The family is faced with the equivalent task. Acceptance is a process that takes place over a period of time and often involves grief and mourning. The parent just quoted also reflected an acceptance of disability when she said (in reference to her daughter's quadriplegia), "It is tragic but it is not a tragedy" (Anonymous, interview, 1995). This differentiation is critical. It preserves the understanding that *all* of life is not affected by disability without pretending that the disability is not also grievous.

GRIEF AND MOURNING

As noted previously, adolescence may precipitate a sense of loss and mourning in adolescents and families even when the disability has been long-standing or congenital. Coping honestly with feelings of loss and mourning may facilitate acceptance of a disability. When mourning occurs for youth and families, it involves grieving for the loss of "What might have been." But it is important to understand that mourning is *not* a precondition for adjustment.

Because the experience of loss and mourning is so common (and because we often assume life with a disability is tragic), many practitioners make the serious mistake of assuming that the individual or family must go through a state of mourning to accept the disability. There is no research to support this assertion. There appears to be great diversity in how persons cope. It is our experience that this may be particularly true with adolescents. Many adolescents with suddenly acquired disabilities, such as spinal cord injury, may need to cope as they did previously, though high levels of activity. Another comment from the mother quoted previously provides an illustration of the disregard of diversity in mourning by a professional. She described how the psychiatrist involved in her daughter's care did not seem to understand that overt expression of mourning is not a prerequisite for adjustment:

> I think she would come in and not understand that my daughter [name deleted] had the state of mind that she did have. So she would continually try to break her down and say that she was in denial and all of this stuff. And [name deleted] was trying to tell her, "I'm not in denial and I know what reality is. I could lay here and get depressed but that doesn't get me anywhere." And that was just her attitude. And that has always been her attitude. If she wanted something, she worked at it until she did it. And the lady [psychiatrist] would just come in and continuously say how "tragic" everything was and used all these negative terms. That really bothered my daughter. (Anonymous, interview, in Lasher & Marshak, 1995)

The daughter's comments about the handling of grief were similar. She began with a reference to the psychiatrist in the rehabilitation hospital:

> And she would be telling me, "You should be depressed. You should be taking this real badly." And I go, "I am not going to be depressed! And if you don't like it, get out of my room! I don't like you and I'm not going to talk to you." She felt I had to be depressed. I said, "Yes," granted I had my nights where I kicked and screamed, "This is not fair!" and "Why did this happen to me?—I don't deserve this!" Yes, I had my moments and had to get this out of my system to keep going. If you dwell on it you will be miserable. You will never want to get out of your room, out of your home. You'll do nothing with your life. So, I got over it! (Anonymous, interview, 1995)

She added (in reference to the psychiatrist):

> I think she forgot that people do not deal with things the same way. I choose not to deal with depression. She may meet someone who is depressed. Okay, she is depressed, so you try to help her through it. Maybe you can show her people who are coping. But I was one of those that kept thinking, "I got to get out of here." So I did. (Anonymous, interview, 1995)

The comments of this mother and daughter illustrate the importance of respecting the ways people choose to cope with their situations and feelings without imposing rigid beliefs about the adjustment process and the role of mourning. Although these quotations pertain to traumatic injury, these points are equally applicable to disorders acquired at birth or during childhood.

REVEALING ONESELF

Healthy identity formation requires honest expression of one's feelings and opinions, but adolescents with disabilities often experience a greater number and variety of constraints regarding emotional expression than do other adolescents. Olkin (1995) described strong societal controls regarding how persons with disabilities are to regulate affect, including a "prescription for pluckiness and courage and a prohibition against anger" (p. 41). The adolescent with a disability may end up essentially donning a mask in the belief that parts of their emotional selves are not acceptable to others. There may be a hiding of grief, anger, a sense of differentness, or adolescent sexuality. The mask, first embraced in adolescence, may continue into adulthood. Donovan (1995) wrote,

> Many people with a disability whom I have seen in therapy have expressed feelings of having to wear a mask to the world. The mask reflects what the world wants to see, not the true self. The true or real self, never having been reflected or mirrored back, is lost. Recovering these missing pieces of ourselves can sometimes be arduous and time consuming. (p. 184)

It is our experience that it is not just the individual with the disability that often wears a mask; families conceal too. Although others tend to understand parental grief around the time of diagnosis, sustained sadness or chronic sorrow is less tolerable to others.

Sometimes adolescents hide their feelings in an attempt to protect their parents. In addition, parents may discourage the expression of emotions because it is so painful for them. In essence, there is collusion not to talk about sadness or grief. One of us (L. M.) encountered this situation quite often working with adolescents with spinal cord injuries and their parents; the parents often appeared to be more depressed than the children. If a parent is rigid and absolute about inhibiting grief, the adolescent will also be inhibited in progressing with aspects of mourning that may need to be resolved.

The therapeutic benefits of revealing rather than concealing aspects of oneself related to disability often extend to physical characteristics. Part of what may have been helpful to the adolescent quoted previously about her refusal to be depressed was her willingness and ability to reveal rather than hide parts of her physique that were disturbing to her. For example, she "made" herself wear shorts despite the apparent scars from multiple skin grafts.

IDENTITY FORECLOSURE

Adolescence serves the critical function of keeping future options open while the youth gains enough experience to better decide what to do with his or her life (Lidz, 1983). Failure to keep options open results in what has been termed *identity foreclosure*. This is a particular risk for adolescents with disabilities if they have internalized societal injunctions about their place in society. They lose the freedom to explore personal desires. They may fail to dream about their future or may be too quick to compromise their dreams away rather than work toward them. So that adolescents do not foreclose their future, it is empowering to have role models with disabilities who are coping well and involved in personally meaningful activities. As one adolescent commented in an interview, "seeing is believing" (Anonymous, interview, 1995). Several parents also cited role models as the most instrumental factor in their own ability to set challenging goals for themselves.

PARENTAL PROTECTION

Adolescent identity formation and the family's ability to facilitate separation are interwoven developmental tasks. Parents are often described as overprotective and unable to master this developmental task, but this situation needs to be understood in social and historical context.

The emphasis placed on youth with disabilities making a transition to adulthood is "historically new" to this generation of parents. This is particularly true for parents of youth with severe disabilities (Ferguson, Ferguson, & Jones, 1988). In individual families, child-rearing practices are often transmitted from one generation to another. For the preceding generations, disability and independence were still largely viewed as antonyms. Child-rearing concerns often focused on resolving questions of who takes care of the child with a disability. Central concerns focused on whether the child could be cared for at home or needed to be placed in an institution. If the child had a mild disability, a common practice in many families was to assume this child would never establish his or her own family. Such children were often socialized into the role of looking after the parents as they aged and required help themselves. Families that helped children with disabilities achieve independent adult status were the exception rather than the rule.

Rolland (1989) wrote of the importance of understanding an individual family's history with disability or illness as a way of shedding light on family members' responses. The value of this perspective was apparent to one of us (L. M.) when working with a woman who was struggling with issues of adolescence although she was well into her 30s. The central conflict with her family was her desire to live independently despite frequent grand mal seizures. She had a measured IQ in the range of mental retardation due to the effects of intractable seizures. In a joint session with her mother she stated, "I'm not my Uncle Louis!" and expressed her anger and fear that her mother was going to shape her life to conform to how her maternal grandmother raised her uncle

Louis, a man described by the family as "slow." Louis was expected to not marry and to stay at home and be a comfort to his mother in her old age. Exploration of the family's history with disability was a major factor in lessening the tenacity of the conflict about the daughter's independence.

Zetlin and Turner (1985) described the negative effects for this generation of parents of youth with mental retardation of a lack of role models:

> Because parents are uncertain or in conflict as to what retarded adolescents' adult roles will be, they are unsure how to prepare their teenagers for the transition to adulthood. They are more likely to encourage dependency, obedience, and child-like behavior rather than independence, self-direction, assumption of responsibility, and sexual awareness. (p. 571)

Uncertainty regarding what to expect from their children in adulthood is not restricted to parents of youth with mental retardation. For example, parents of sons and daughters with spina bifida have virtually no role models because so few children in preceding generations survived into adulthood. Similarly, with advances in health care, the future for youth with spinal cord injuries holds radically different opportunities than as recently as a decade ago. In the absence of easily visible contemporary models, we tend to look at outmoded ones. Historically, people with disabilities have been largely socialized into a social role that is asexual and passive and where they are expected to be "grateful" for what they receive. Although professionals are quick to judge parents of adolescents with disabilities as overprotective, it is important to bear in mind that our society has also largely cast adults with disabilities in a childlike role. With regard to the portrayal of persons with disabilities in the media, Peters (1985) referred to the childlike image depicted in fundraising telethons: "Telethons are society's largest purveyor of what disabled people are like. The picture isn't very dignified. It is difficult to view oneself with dignity when you are being patted on the head by a movie star several years your junior" (p. 16).

Many parents long to be able to become less involved but do not dare stop struggling to obtain needed services and places in society for their sons and daughters. Families face a period of time in which education will no longer be an entitlement and they will face a terribly inadequate system for adult services. Blotzer (1995) summarized her perspective on this matter, gained from years of working with families of young adults with developmental disabilities: "The collision between developmental imperatives and inadequate social supports could not be more striking. Just when young adults are seeking greater independence from their families, they are forced into a position of greater dependency" (p. 155). Blotzer (1995) described the impact of the transition from an entitlement to an eligibility system:

Once their educational entitlement ends in their 21st year, these young adults have no guarantee that they will have a place to go during the day, work that gives them a sense of accomplishment and identity. . . . To both them and their parents, the future looms as a black hole that threatens to swallow their hopes and dreams, and even their sense of self. (p. 20)

It is not merely a matter of "falling between the cracks" as a transition is made from educational entitlement and adult services. In some states, the crack could more appropriately be described as an abyss. Blotzer (1995) described the situation in her state as follows:

Faced with limited funds, Maryland's policy has been to prioritize funding for adults with developmental disabilities—first priority going to those who are homeless or about to become homeless due to the death of their parents. Practically, this means that parents in their 50s, 60s, 70s and even 80s are still caring for their now-adult children. (pp. 20–21)

The demands facing these parents are paradoxical. Just as there is a developmental need to let go, external reality demands that parents become very involved to help their child obtain appropriate services and carve a good-sized niche in society for himself or herself.

It is not unusual for a professional to indicate to a family that it is overly involved and too protective of an adolescent or young adult. This message may stem from several sources—some more legitimate than others. Interviews with parents of youth with disabilities conducted by Ferguson et al. (1988) bring into focus a very important viewpoint on the issue of professional requests to relinquish behaviors that appear to encourage dependency:

For most of the parents we interviewed, the issue of adult status was really an issue of control, not independence. That is, as parents interpreted the process, the status transitions of their sons and daughters often became translated from a "child—or adult" question to a "parent control—or professional control" question. (p. 185)

One parent wrote,

I don't think any of us want to totally control our children's lives as far as what they do by the day. But for the future, we do. . . . Ultimately the family has to be involved. This total schism between family and the retarded person is unnatural, it doesn't happen in any other part of your family. (Ferguson et al., 1988, p. 185)

PROCESSES OF SEPARATION

The process of separation for most adolescents is set in motion in a variety of ways and is most typically initiated by physical changes in the son or daughter, such as the development of secondary sex characteristics. In most families, this process is propelled by the allurement of hanging out with peers, having a car, and expressing one's sexual desire; parents often follow the adolescent's lead to separate. Unless there are undue complications (such as disability), the family generally goes through a role reorganization during this time and the adolescent assumes greater responsibility within the family and increased control over meeting personal needs. Discord with parents is often inherent in this aspect of development as parents and youth struggle to find appropriate levels of freedom and responsibilities. There are important rites of passage, most notably high school graduation, that often communicate to parents (and others) the beginning of adult life; this results in "legitimizing" adult activities and freedoms. For those who do not remain in high school for graduation, official status as an adult may be established through joining the military or moving into one's own apartment.

Families with an adolescent who has a disability face increased difficulty with matters regarding achieving adult status because the rites of passage are not nearly so clear. Referring to Neugarten (1976), Turnbull and Turnbull (1985) wrote, "Many adolescents and their families dealing with dissonant development do not have the same 'punctuation marks along the life cycle' to cue them to the need for developmental reorganization" (p. 112). The tensions of separation are generally felt by adolescents and their families despite the existence of very different disabilities. For example, Zetlin and Turner (1985) found more than half of adolescents with mental retardation experienced conflicts with their parents over independence. Zetlin and Turner (1985) noted that these individuals faced the same conflicting role demands that distress many adolescents, but they face them with relatively more cognitive difficulties.

The term *separation* implies a parental letting go as the youth develops into adult status. For families with adolescents with severe disabilities, the concepts of changing roles and facilitating *interdependence* are more realistic. Regardless of the type of disability and whether or not the youth will likely leave home someday, there are general principles that are useful for facilitating this aspect of development. These cut across type and severity of disability and (as will be discussed in the following section) include (a) redefining separation and independence, (b) reconsidering decisions on the risk versus protection continuum, (c) modifying the organization of family roles, (d) encouraging adolescent self-expression, (e) facilitating peer relationships, (f) addressing sexuality, and (g) future planning.

REDEFINING "INDEPENDENCE"

In American culture, independence tends to be thought of in simplistic terms and associated with self-sufficiency in physical functioning and finances. When parents and professionals use this framework, the prospects for a child's independence may become a moot point because self-sufficiency is often not realistic. Turnbull and Turnbull's (1985) definition of independence is more useful; they defined independence as

> choosing how to live one's life within one's inherent capacities and means and consistent with one's personal values and preferences. Independence, thus, is synonymous with freedom of choice, self-determination, and autonomy from outside interference. . . . Independence is the converse of being obliged to live one's life as others want that life to be lived. (p. 108)

In this framework, facilitating independence becomes a relatively more workable concept. It is important to also recognize that independence is rarely an all-or-nothing state. The concept of interdependence more accurately describes the state most people in the general population achieve. Consequently, the parents' task is not so much to let go as to redefine the appropriate way to be involved.

Modifying the Risk Versus Protection Equation

Blatt (1987) is one of many who have argued for the rights of persons with disabilities to include choice and risk. Blatt stated that freedom to make choices, even choices that may result in harm, is a freedom that most people cherish. Freedom of choice is one of the highest American ideals. Why then, asked Blatt, should we hold a different set of ideals and values for people with disabilities? (quoted in Schloss, Alper, & Jayne, 1993, p. 216).

In theory, few would argue with this view of independence. In practice, many parents and their sons and daughters are conflicted about self-determination because of the close relationship between independence and risk taking. Vash (1992) noted that freedom and protection are both essential for survival and happiness but represent two polar ends of a continuum; she added, "To get one you usually have to give up some of the other" (p. 59). The necessity of accepting a trade-off that requires a lessening of protection to enhance personal freedom may be very difficult for parents of youth with disabilities.

Out of necessity, parents may have become used to assuming the role of protector. The mother of one adolescent provides a compelling description of the roots of her protectiveness:

> After five hours of repeated attempts to get my daughter a sedative for a CAT scan procedure, I saw a fear in her that I'd never seen before. Even though they had given her enough medication to sedate a 200-pound man, her anxiousness

prevented the medicine from having an effect. I worried that if I allowed her anxiety to continue, I would destroy part of her spirit that was so important to her whole-health person. I refused to give permission for the treatment.

With 60 limp pounds in my arms, we checked out AMA (against medical advice). My daughter's pediatric neurologist approached us at the exit. He agreed that the CAT scan could wait for a less anxious moment. It was the first time I had defied a medical order. On the drive home that night, I said to myself, "no one will ever put her through that terror again. I will protect her." *That became a major part of my identity. I was her protector* (italics added). (PACER Center, 1993b, p. 5)

A useful intervention is to help parents consciously examine the relative benefits of protection versus risk and reevaluate decisions that may have grown out of natural instincts to protect a child as well as responses to acts of medical mistreatment such as the one just cited.

It is sometimes helpful to graphically depict a risk-versus-protection continuum in the form of a line drawing for parents to think more concretely about types of trade-offs between risk and freedom in several domains of their adolescent's life.

Often, protection has little to do with bodily risks. Adolescents may be protected from " making mistakes" although mistakes are an inherent part of adolescent development. Some parents fear that their adolescent with a disability "can't afford" them. For example, one adolescent with a quite visible disability wanted to dress in a casual, eccentric manner typical of adolescents. Whereas the family went to great lengths to buy carefully coordinated clothes, the son's understanding of his parents' admonitions was that he needed to be "more careful" than others. This attempt to protect him socially may actually have led to additional self-consciousness over his differentness of appearance.

We have seen many parents be overly vigilant about protecting their child or adolescent from social rejection and loneliness. Sometimes efforts to protect the child from the risks of rejection involve attempting to fill the child's social needs through the family. The end result is a social isolation that is often more damaging than occasional rejection. Our clinical experiences with parents underscore the extent to which parents fear the loneliness of even their grown children with disabilities and the manner in which the desire to protect them against loneliness becomes an issue when young adults want to move into their own residence.

One parent stated,

I worry about her being alone but she wants to be alone. I am afraid that she is lonely but she never is. I think that is the only conflict we have. She is content to sit and play with the computer. How many kids her age sit down and watch TV? I think that is normal. . . . But there is this concept in your head that there is something wrong with your kid so she must be lonely. You need to constantly make sure that it is not true. I know it isn't true but I have to make sure. I don't know where it comes from. (Anonymous, interview, 1995, in Lasher and Marshak, 1995)

Sometimes the parents' reluctance to progress with increased separation masks the adolescent's own fearfulness. It is one thing to rail against parents who want to keep you at home—it is another to face moving out on your own. When this occurs, it is useful to help the youth articulate their fears in a more conscious manner so that they can be addressed more productively.

REORGANIZATION OF FAMILY ROLES

The family system naturally becomes transformed to some extent when children reach adolescence. Parental relationships change to lessen parents' control and exercise of authority and this permits adolescents to develop more autonomous functioning and an increased capacity for decision making. Ideally, adolescents gradually assume increased responsibility for decisions while parents provide the security of supportive guidance (Carter & McGoldrick, 1989). Heightened disorganization, discord, and strain are often felt in the family system as the adolescent's development stimulates the family to meet new demands.

During this time, parents are often coping with stressors that are common in middle age. Marriages may undergo scrutiny and this developmental phase is often a time of relatively lower marital satisfaction (Summers, 1986). It is not unusual for middle-aged parents to feel a sense of urgency to make changes in their personal and work lives. In addition, middle-aged parents often experience changes in their relationships with their own parents. Roles may be reversed, as parents are often required to become the caretakers of their own parents. The demands of taking care of aging parents may introduce additional stressors into the marital relationship as conflicting demands tax individuals' resources. It is often in this context that the adolescent and family members face the challenging tasks of adolescent separation.

When families are faced with the increased conflict that is often generated during this period, they tend to return to solutions that worked in earlier stages of development (Carter & McGoldrick, 1989). They do more of the same (i.e., more control, more use of parental authority, etc.) although the demands of the situation actually require new solutions.

Families with children who have disabilities often struggle to find solutions to problems—and it is natural to want to return to strategies that worked before. Patterns of interaction in families that have a child with a disability may develop as a coping mechanism and become relatively entrenched even if they are no longer adaptive due to developmental changes. Ritchie's (1980) study of families of children with epilepsy illustrates this point. Ritchie found that families of children with a seizure disorder formed more efficient problem-solving units in contrast to other families, partly by suppressing disagreements between family members to quickly achieve a group consensus. In addition, these families tended to have a more rigid hierarchy of authority, with the mother being prominent and the child being somewhat withdrawn from family interaction. Ritchie noted that although this pattern of interaction may develop as an important means to initially cope with disruptions in family life, it may cease to be adaptive and begin to be maladaptive when continued for long periods of time. A similar pattern was found by O'Connor (1967) in a much earlier study. Both studies are consistent with crisis theory regarding family behavior, which states that families change their behavior to meet threats to the group's integrity (Ritchie, 1980). This is not meant to imply that *most* families with a child with a disability necessarily respond in this manner; rather, some will. For these families, it is useful to help them examine whether their habitual means of coping with problems have outlived their usefulness.

For example, a mother one of us (L. M.) worked with did a wonderful job of advocating for her son. Unless she had assumed this role, it is unlikely he would ever would have become so well adjusted vocationally. But her active involvement, which had once been critical, became a source of antagonism to her son. She still wanted to monitor his job because she was aware of his propensity for interpersonal problems with coworkers and supervisors. She was able to successfully resolve the situation by accepting that more would be lost than gained if the old pattern persisted.

Adolescents are sensitive about monitoring messages that reflect on self-worth and adequacy and families may be unaware of the type of messages they are transmitting in this regard. For example, families with adolescents who have disabilities need to be alert to the need for the adolescent to have a functional role in the family. All parents know that it is often easier to perform a task rather than watch a child struggle to do the task—consequently, it is all too easy to take over. The need for each member to have a contributing role in family life is described by Turnbull and Turnbull (1985) as "one of the most important quality of life determinants for persons with mental disabilities" (p. 112).

EXPRESSION OF ANGER

Expression of anger toward family members is often a part of adolescence because it serves as a vehicle for the processes of both individuation and separation. Challenging parents is one way to define oneself. It is easier to separate emotionally from someone with whom you are angry. Adolescents are pulled in two directions, wanting to remain childlike and dependent on parents and wanting to be free of them; attempts to separate include searching out flaws in parents. Lidz (1983) wrote of the propensity of adolescents to separate through conflict: "Arguments can become wildly irrational in order to help overcome the contradictions and the longing to remain attached. The inability of parents to understand are magnified and grudges are reinstated" (p. 338). Similarly, it is common for parents also to respond with anger and hurt and perceive the child as an "ingrate upstart" (Lidz, 1983, p. 338).

The expression of anger is especially complicated for adolescents with disabilities. The adolescent is often aware of many of the additional strains and demands experienced by the parents by virtue of his or her disability and sometimes also aware of major sacrifices on the part of parents and family members. This raises difficult developmental quandaries. How does one rebel without being ungrateful? How does one separate emotionally under these conditions? Does the instinct for adolescent rebellion disappear with disability? It is doubtful. Similarly, how does a parent express anger at a child who may be viewed as vulnerable? Under less complicated circumstances, anger also helps parents with separation. Professionals may be helpful in supporting families who may need help to accept anger and rebellion as a normal part of the developmental process.

SOCIALIZING

Peers

Peers play a critical role in the processes of separation, individuation, and sexuality. The social experiences of adolescents with disabilities generally differ greatly from those of age mates who do not have disabilities. For students with physical disabilities that interfere with mobility, there are fewer opportunities to participate in after-school socialization. In addition, social attitudes present formidable barriers to socialization.

Adolescents are often rejecting of those who are different. Friendships formed and maintained during preadolescent years often do not survive adolescent years. A study of adolescents with spina bifida reported this phenomenon and found that by adolescence half of these youth were severely socially isolated (Dorner, 1973). Social rejection may be overt or subtle. It often takes the form of social distance being maintained, especially in activities that are relatively intimate. Although adolescents with disabilities may be superficially well accepted as classmates, they are not well accepted as romantic partners or best friends.

This pattern was evident in interviews conducted by one of us (L. M.) and L. Lasher with adolescents returning to school following spinal cord injuries. They often found themselves initially surrounded by many peers but had more difficulty identifying more intimate relationships. In addition, a relatively increased social rejection experienced during adolescence may not only be from other students. Stephens and Brown (1980) found teachers in seventh and eighth grades were more rejecting of students with disabilities than were teachers of lower grades.

The social problems of adolescents with severe disabilities are often intensely painful for adolescents and their parents. One young man with cerebral palsy recalled his adolescence as follows: "Everyone was playing football; I was on the porch with my Lincoln logs and my Legos. I felt terrible peer isolation. I cried a lot, and I didn't know it then, but I made my mother cry a lot too" (Kriegsman et al., 1992, p. 43). Problems with social rejection and social isolation do not necessarily primarily affect persons with severe disabilities, however. Many youth with invisible or marginal disabilities experience significant problems in this regard (McAnarney, 1985). Colwell (1984) noted that it may be relatively harder for peers to understand and empathize with the problems of adolescents whose disabilities are largely invisible, such as those with mild mental retardation.

We have found that adolescents sometimes hide the extent of their social problems, partly to protect their parents from pain. This leaves them without important resources to address these problems, however. Parents may be helpful in finding alternate sources of socialization outside of school, including volunteer positions, scouts, or membership in organizations.

Limited opportunities for socialization may result in social skills deficits. As further discussed in the following chapter, addressing these is an essential aspect of making the transition from high school to the world of work. In addition to systematic instruction when needed, parents and professionals need to be careful to provide the type of corrective feedback that will build social skills. Strax (1991) identified a vicious cycle that may develop for adolescents with disabilities, triggered by the combination of increased dependence on parents and social isolation. He noted that this may result in immature social interactions, which lead to a cycle of even more social isolation:

> In an attempt to find friends and attract attention, teens with disabilities are prone to turn toward inappropriate behavior such as loud talking and foolish behavior. The individual who is able-bodied and turns to these types of behaviors usually gets instant feedback from family, teachers and peer-group members. This is not the case with the physically disabled, for whom the social response tends to be to ignore inappropriate behavior. (p. 508)

This reluctance to provide corrective social feedback stems, in part, from a phenomenon that Wright (1983) described as the "norm to be kind." The norm to be kind is based on the assumption (described earlier) that suffering is so great (because life is assumed to be tragic) for the individual with a disability that it is better to withhold anything that would make the person feel worse about his or her life. This attempt to spare a person any more pain actually results in withholding the type of information the person often needs to function better socially. The withholding of corrective social feedback may also be motivated by low expectations that a youth will ever be accepted socially—a sense of futility when it comes to genuine social integration.

NEGOTIATING SOCIAL SITUATIONS

In addition to correcting social skills deficits, it is often advantageous to help adolescents develop additional specialized social skills, because they are faced with a far greater number of situations that are inherently difficult to handle. Adolescents with disabilities need well-developed skills in assertiveness in particular because they encounter so many situations in which others overlook, disregard, or misconstrue their needs, opinions, and feelings. In addition, they can benefit from the rehearsal of solutions to anticipated problem situations. Other adolescents with disabilities are a rich source of specialized (informal) social skills training. Kriegsman et al. (1992) provided a resource of advice from adolescents with disabilities about handling difficult situations. For example, in regard to the problem of friends being overprotective, these adolescents wrote:

> Most likely your friends treat you this way because they care about you and don't want you to get hurt. They may think they are saving you the embarrassment of admitting you can't do something. But in reality they may have jumped to the wrong conclusion. You can easily clear up these misunderstandings by communicating your abilities. Tell your friends what you can or can't do. Be specific. For example, tell them: "I can dress myself," "I do my own hair and nails," "I am able to push myself in my chair," "I know what to say to jerks who stare," and "I'm a very strong swimmer." Stating your abilities up front will help your friends understand that in most cases you are not fragile. If you have osteogenesis imperfecta and your bones *are* fragile, it is even more important to let people know your physical limitations. . . . Perhaps you might want to have one simple rule with your friends to put everyone at ease: if you need help, you will ask for it. They don't have to try to read your mind. (pp. 66–67)

The adolescents in Kriegsman et al. (1992) also suggested strategies to help with problems such as handling pity from peers and dealing with people who focus excessively on one's disability and overlook all other aspects of oneself. Our experience has been that adolescents who anticipate and discuss problem situations are less likely to become socially avoidant, because preparation militates against feeling overwhelmed by social difficulties.

The impact of a role model with a disability who is coping well can accomplish more in terms of instilling hope than most other experiences. But adolescents with disabilities are often reluctant to associate much with other adolescents with disabilities. Partly, this is a phenomenon of internalizing the societal devaluation of persons who differ from the norm. In addition, avoidance of other adolescents with disabilities may be motivated by denial. Strax (1991) wrote, "It is difficult to deny one's physical disability when one walks toward a reflecting image or enters a crowd of people with similar disabilities. Many people with severe gait and mobility problems see themselves in their dreams as walking normally" (p. 509). This can be a classic double bind since peers with disabilities may be their only "accepting" peer group.

At a time in life when identity formation is so critical, it is important that adolescents not be pressured to attend groups with others with disabilities, but if initial barriers to contact with others with disabilities can be surmounted, the gains are often most valuable. Affiliation with other adolescents with disabilities has the potential to alleviate feelings of being the only one in the world with a particular condition or problem. The Internet may be a useful vehicle for contact with other adolescents while maintaining the distance a particular adolescent may desire.

Although the problems of social isolation are complex, sometimes very simple solutions have a great impact. When asked for a recommendation for personnel in rehabilitation and educational settings, one adolescent responded, "It sounds so simple, but just have a place for them in the class. It makes it easier to just have a place to go and sit like a normal person, and even aisles, where you can go up and bring your paper to the desk. It sounds little, but it's not" (Mulcahey, 1992, p. 331).

Some of the social problems of adolescents with disabilities have roots in the lack of community resources and adaptability. For example, the lack of accessible transportation has a more devastating effect on adolescent social involvement than many other factors. It precludes involvement in after-school activities, the ability to "hang out" with peers, and the acquisition of part-time jobs. Transportation problems are most pronounced in rural communities.

SIBLINGS

Relationships with siblings may also undergo changes during this period of development as siblings also respond to the strong pressures of conformity that are often the hallmark of adolescence. As a result, there may be a new-found self-consciousness over having a brother or a sister with a disability (Siegel & Silverstein, 1994). In addition, adolescent siblings are likely to experience an increase in anger at parents as part of the separation process; sibling rivalry may increase and include criticisms that parents focus too much on the adolescent with the disability.

SEXUALITY

We tend to compartmentalize sexuality as if it were a separate aspect of identity formation, yet it is interwoven with and facilitates the completion of other developmental tasks. The self-identity of adolescents is "greatly connected to their feelings about being male or female" (Carter & McGoldrick, 1989, p. 261). This is important to bear in mind because parents and professionals tend to avoid the sexual development of youth with disabilities.

Chilman's (1990) definition of healthy adolescent sexuality will be used as a framework for our discussion of this aspect of adolescent development:

> Adolescent sexuality is based on esteem and respect for the self and other people of both sexes. . . . Sexually healthy adolescents take pleasure and pride in their own developing bodies. As they mature, they have an increasing ability to communicate honestly and openly with persons of both sexes with whom they have a close relationship. They accept their own sexual desires as natural but to be acted upon with limited freedom within the constraints of reality considerations, including their own values and goals and those of "significant others." (p. 124)

Adolescents with disabilities experience more limited opportunities for exploring their sexuality than do peers without disabilities. This stems from a variety of sources, including the view of persons with disabilities as asexual. Furthermore, adolescents with disabilities find they experience more rejection in terms of physical intimacy with peers with disabilities than in regard to more casual interaction. Geri Jewell, a well-known comedienne with cerebral palsy commented on her adolescence:

> When you watch telethons, you probably hear handicapped people say that their handicaps don't get in the way of their sex lives. Whenever I hear that I start to laugh. The truth is, one of the reasons that . . . regular class kids were so afraid to get close to me was that they were afraid that things might get sexual eventually . . . [and] nobody was identifying me with the idea of sex at all. (Baroff, 1991, p. 181)

Additional social barriers include problems "circulating" and more limited opportunities for privacy.

Despite these social barriers, problems with psychosexual development are not an inevitable consequence of disability; parental expectations are an important factor in this regard. Nearly all relationships and activities in families transmit messages (overtly or covertly) to children about aspects of their sexuality, such as sex role, sexual feelings, values, and interpersonal relationships (Chilman, 1990). In this manner, a shaping of attitudes and feelings toward one's sexuality occurs in an ongoing manner often long before adolescence.

In families in which an adolescent has a disability, parents may be even more reluctant than in other families to help their children view as themselves as sexual. Sexuality may be viewed as a Pandora's box and avoidance is sometimes felt as one way to keep it unopened. Many fear that discussion of sexuality will only open up a longing that can rarely be fulfilled because they underestimate the frequency with which love relationships and marriages actually do occur in adulthood. Parents also fear exploitation and abuse. This fear is based in reality, but it is a serious error to believe that avoidance of children's sexuality will protect them from exploitation.

Adolescents with disabilities are naturally alert for messages about their sexuality and often interpret avoidance as parental pessimism about this area of their life's development. One adolescent, commenting on avoidance of his sexuality wrote, "Even parents often neglect discussing sexual relationships with their children. This could be because of society's general embarrassment about sex, but many of us feel it also has to do with our disabilities or chronic illness" (PACER Center, 1993a, p. 40). Another wrote:

> We have to remember that our parents have grown up in a society where the word "sexy" means a healthy, strong, able-bodied man or woman. This could be why our parents might think it's impossible for us to ever have a sexual relationship, since we have a disability or chronic illness. Likewise, if our chronic illness or disability makes us physically vulnerable, our parents might fear that we could be taken advantage of and hurt more easily than a person who is able bodied. It could be these and other fears combined that cause parents to simply choose to avoid the topic of sexuality with us. It's very sad, because although I do not think this is a good decision on a parent's part, it is nevertheless unmistakable that they are acting out of their pain and sorrow for us. They want us to be happy, but they're afraid we may never have a love relationship. (PACER Center,1993a, p. 41)

It is unfortunately paradoxical that adolescents with disabilities often get less parental and professional attention paid to their sexuality because they actually need more than their peers. They are faced with much more to sort out regarding their sexual feelings, desires, and capabilities than peers without disabilities. For example, many adolescents with disabilities generalize the impact of their disability and are fearful that their sexual organs are impaired as well. McAnarney (1985) noted that this attitude often leads these adolescents to early sexual experimentation in attempts to prove they are "normal."

Rousso (1988) wrote that parents are generally far less concerned with the sexual development of adolescent daughters with disabilities in contrast to their achievement in educational and career domains. She wrote that the daughters' limited heterosexual involvement may be experienced by parents as a "relief" and as "the best form of contraception" (p. 140).

One woman with spina bifida said in an interview, "My parents made it clear that I was destined to become a career woman" (Anonymous, personal communication, November 1994). It is important that by encouraging this option, parents do not send the message that other options are excluded. Rousso (1988) emphasized that despite changing roles and goals of women, adolescent girls continue to see social success as relatively more important than academic achievement. Consequently, their perceived failures in this area carry a great personal meaning. The resultant damage is a further weakened ability to appreciate one's body.

An appreciation of one's body is hindered for adolescents whose disabilities may cause their pubertal development to differ from their peers (Blum, 1984). Early maturing females, in general, have been found to have more problems in adjustment than their peers. Chilman (1990) described early maturing females as experiencing associated problems, including feelings of inferiority and social and sometimes academic problems. This is pertinent to adolescents with spina bifida because this disorder often results in a precocious onset of puberty. Boys, on the other hand, have been found to be proud of early sexual development and associate feelings of inferiority to delays in this aspect of physical development (McCandless, 1970). Males with some disorders, such as cystic fibrosis, often experience delays in this regard.

Preoccupation with one's body peaks in adolescence. Efforts to mitigate this preoccupation are important, however. Adolescents with disabilities offered this advice: "Most likely you already realize that, as you get older, looks are not going to be as important to you or others as they seem now" (Kriegsman et al., p. 41). As noted earlier, this requires a subordination of the importance of physique relative to other attributes (Wright, 1983). It is clearly not easy, as illustrated by Jewell's reflections: "Others had fully formed figures. . . . I was a stick. I couldn't stand to take my clothes off and take showers with these girls. I felt so inadequate, so ugly, so handicapped" (Baroff, 1991, p. 181).

An important aspect of adolescent sexuality for females is the self-image formed regarding the ability to parent children in the future. In interviews with adolescents with physical disabilities, one often-repeated concern is the prospect of having children who are embarrassed or teased because of them (Kriegsman et al., 1992). A representative comment reflects this point of view:

> I'm not sure I'd like to have children. My kids would probably ask me, "What's wrong? What happened?" and it would be hard for them. If I picked them up at school, their friends would ask and it would be hard for them to explain. (Kriegsman et al., p. 27)

SEXUAL ABUSE

Adolescents with disabilities clearly have the same sexual desires as other youth but differ by virtue of often having less sexual education at the same time that they are often at far greater than average risk of sexual abuse. In the general population, it is estimated that 20% of all male and female children and adolescents are sexually abused. It is generally agreed that rates of sexual abuse of those with disabilities is much higher than the general population (Cole, 1991; Gardner, 1986; Marshak & Seligman, 1993). One study reported by Moglia (1993) indicated that by age 18, more than half of women with congenital blindness report at least one forced sexual experience. A Canadian study reported similar findings with a 50% rate of sexual abuse among children and adolescents with a wide range of disabilities (Niagra Regional Police Services, 1996).

Many variables converge to result in these grim statistics. They include the fact that the disability itself tends to make people "easy prey." Lack of education is a contributing factor, as is the fact that these youth often are exposed to so much touching (in the context of caretaking) that it is even more difficult for them to differentiate between appropriate and inappropriate touch (Cole, 1991). In addition, people with disabilities are often taught to be more passive and accepting than others and may lack the assertiveness needed to set limits or refuse inappropriate requests (Rosen, 1984). It has been established that more than 99% of the perpetrators of sexual abuse of persons with developmental disabilities were known to them (Cole, 1991). This of course includes family members, teachers, caretakers, and so forth. Rosen (1984) noted that it is most often the primary caretaker who is the perpetrator. Regarding persons with physical disabilities, Cole (1991) described the dynamics that increase risk as well as decrease the ability to notify others of the abuse:

> The mere fact that they are in many ways more dependent on the care-providers to assist them in activities of daily living creates multiple opportunities for them

to be vulnerable in ways that the able-bodied are not. Not only do they lack privacy, but they also lack the ability to be spontaneous in protecting themselves. Many individuals are without speech or language abilities and limited in or without mobility. Some may be so totally dependent on others for health care needs for daily survival that to consider resisting anything from a care-provider or family member may seem too frightening for their own existence. They may also not know in whom to confide for assistance were they to try to identify abusive behavior. They may also have already experienced a disenfranchisement from society and might not be willing to risk a further separation. It is understandable that handicappers may predict that their stories might not be believed because their credibility will be pitted against that of an able-bodied person. (p. 231)

Cole (1991) pointed out that the self-containment or isolation of many families that have a child with a disability poses an additional significant barrier in obtaining help—particularly in cases of incest.

The pervasiveness of sexual abuse is one more reason why sexuality is so critical to carefully and comprehensively address in childhood and adolescent development. Gardner (1986) wrote that it is

ideal for parents to offer sexual information to their children with developmental disabilities very early in childhood and to continue so throughout their adolescence into adulthood. A home where parents can talk openly and confidently about sex with their children, whether disabled or not, is the best possible protection against unnecessary risks and dangers. (p. 55)

Gardner (1986) provided the following guidelines for professionals to work most effectively with parents:

1. Involved parents probably know more about their son or daughter than anyone else. Respect their expertise.
2. Encourage parents to think about the sexual needs of their sons and daughters as they plan for the future.
3. Include parents in planning sex education programs.
4. Help parents get more training in sexuality and disabilities by providing materials workshops, parent discussion and support groups, films and so forth.
5. The goal of all training is the empowerment of the consumer. For many adults, self-advocacy will include making their own choices about sexuality. Help consumers feel safe and confident enough to discuss their choices with their parents. (p. 55)

EMOTIONAL ASPECTS OF FUTURE PLANNING

For adolescents with disabilities, in many ways the future represents both a potential enemy and a potential savior. A belief in a better future can help adolescents cope with some of the very painful aspects of adolescence. Adolescents with disabilities may also recognize that the future brings about a lessening of the cruelty of some peers and relief from social pressures. But fear of the future is also at the heart of some of the darkest adolescent despair—despair that a husband or wife will never be found, despair that one's body will never "measure up," despair over the prospects of supporting oneself in a world where disability is not well accepted.

Families, in general, may fear the changes that are required in response to the developmental tasks of adolescence; some have been described as attempting to "stop time" when these developmental tasks seem overwhelming (Preto, 1989). The prospect of increasingly letting go of adolescent sons and daughters as they make some type of transition from the family home is threatening because they see the world as an "unsuitable" place for their children (Tingey, 1988).

Emotional confrontation with a child's deficits may be unavoidable when plans for future residential, educational, or vocational options are formulated and initially implemented. A parent of a 7-year-old with attention deficit disorder commented, "I try to think the worse for the future so I don't have a big let down if things don't get as good as I feel they should" (Anonymous, quoted in Prezant, Marshak, Cerrone, & Seligman, 1997).

As a result, some families only superficially engage in these planning activities and skim over deficits, focusing almost exclusively on the youth's attributes. As a result, plans may be vague, unrealistic, or delayed. For example, some parents have kept their adolescent children out of situations where any deficits would be apparent. Although this behavior could be seen as supportive, it also masks the problems that need to be addressed for a healthy transition to adulthood to occur. Avoidance of future planning may occur in some families due to parental hopelessness (i.e., "If your chronic illness or disability is severe, you or your parents may think it futile to plan for the future" [PACER Center, 1993a, p. 20]). Parents whose children have life-threatening disorders such as cystic fibrosis may face a particularly difficult emotional struggle as they engage in future planning. Orenstein (1989) is one resource that is useful this regard.

For some parents, grief is pivotal in their ability to plan for their child's future and to begin to take steps toward this transition. The parents of a young woman with a developmental disability wrote,

We firmly believe that what is often referred to as the grief process is a critical component of transition planning for parents, even for the entire family, including the individual with a disability. Because we and others think, "We have already been through the grief process," or "They should have been done with that a long time ago." We don't understand our own reactions, nor are we understood by professionals in the field. Thus we can seem uninterested, uncaring and unwilling to be involved in our child's transition process. (Pettitt & Pettitt, 1993, p. 48)

Addressing parental denial is also conducive to successful future planning. Failure to do so can result in significant vocational problems, as illustrated by this woman with a severe progressive visual disability who described the results of attempting to pass as not having a disability—a practice she believes prolonged her denial that she will eventually lose all functional vision:

I could talk about many times in my life that I have tried to pass as nondisabled. The one thought that enters my mind was when I attended beauty school. I looked like I knew what I was doing, but the results never came out quite how the clients wanted. I tried to pass off too much as a person with perfect vision. When I had to mix the colors ingredients for a tint, it was the wrong color and the outcome was green hair. Another bad experience occurred while I was giving a perm. I left the perm solution on too long. When I was rinsing the solution into the sink, the curls came out along with the lady's hair. Needless to say, the woman never returned and I was told that this was a bad occupation for me. . . . In the thirteen years that I have known about my condition, I have been in denial as well as my family. I only deal with my disability when I have to. (Anonymous, personal communication, 1995)

CONCLUSION

The experiences of the woman just quoted underscore the necessity of vocational planning and a transition process during adolescence that takes into account desires, attributes, interests, and functional limitations. At this point in her life (mid-20s), this woman has completed undergraduate college education in a field that is gratifying and does not require vision. The following chapter will be devoted to a discussion of this transition from adolescence to adulthood, the time during which such planning should take place.

CHAPTER 5

The Bridge Between Adolescence and Adulthood

Changes in societal attitudes about individuals with disabilities, increased visibility in the workplace and community, and the first generations of children with disabilities having completed high school have focused public attention on the transition of youth with disabilities to adulthood. Self-determination, choice making, employment, and future planning are concepts that were ignored several generations ago because young people with disabilities were not educated, were dependent, and were mostly unemployed. Social activism, advocacy, and legislation have resulted in altered views of people with disabilities and a recognition that each individual has a contribution to make, a desire to belong, and a need to exert control over his or her own life.

Transition refers to a change process that affects individuals throughout the life span. In this chapter we address the transition from school to postschool outcomes for youth with disabilities. This discussion is framed in the context of the historical and legal foundations for transition, the changing needs of the family, and the challenges and opportunities faced by youth with disabilities in their approach to adulthood.

TRANSITION TO ADULTHOOD: A CONCEPT

Transition from high school to life beyond constitutes a major life change for most young people. Completion of high school signifies the end of formal required schooling; the onset of careers, employment, or further education; adult relationships, including marriage and parenthood; responsibility; and general admittance to the world of adulthood. This is a time when many youth leave their parents' home permanently in search of their own independence. The physical and emotional nurturing, as well as the financial support of the past, usually change with this bridging into adulthood.

Levinson (1978) viewed early adult transition as the metamorphosis from the preadult self to the beginning of numerous adult stages of life. This period has been identified as a stressful life stage in adulthood for families with children who do not have disabilities (Olson et al., 1984). Since most families plan for their child's eventual social, emotional, and financial independence, one of the most significant threats to families is the failure of a child to achieve independence and self-sufficiency with the peer group and in the adult world.

Completion of high school signifies a transition. For youth with disabilities the type and success of transition varies with the severity of the disability; preparation for life after school; level of independence; self-advocacy skills; family supports; and community opportunities for friendship, employment, and residence.

Although research and programmatic implementation in the area of transition from school to adult life is relatively recent in the history of individuals with disabilities, it signifies an increased awareness of the obstacles to adult independence faced both by young people with disabilities and by their families, who have supported them emotionally and financially. The current "transition" movement has been driven by parent outcry and by legislation. Positive results have been realized, but the longitudinal, developmental basis of transition and the implications for individuals, families, and professionals are frequently ignored in the bureaucratic hodgepodge of guidelines and mandates that currently exist.

Through high school graduation or the age of 21, education law mandates the delivery of appropriate school- and community-based services to youth with disabilities. At the completion of formal schooling, these youth are no longer protected by a comprehensive entitlement system of educational services but are thrust into an adult service system governed by different guidelines and funding streams. They are no longer entitled to services and supports based on their disability label but must meet eligibility and severity guidelines. Numerous youth with disabilities become lost in this system and opportunities for training and employment, community participation, and independent living are also lost.

Until recently, educational entities and adult service systems (vocational rehabilitation, mental health agencies, etc.) operated in isolation despite the fact that many youth with disabilities move directly from one system to the other. Children with disabilities are the responsibility of the schools, mandated to provide appropriate programming in the least restrictive environment (see discussion in Chapter 3). Upon entrance into the adult world, youth with disabilities who were able to successfully navigate the resources available to them were able to connect with the Office of Vocational Rehabilitation (OVR) to obtain assistance, training, and employment if they were eligible for services. Numerous young people with disabilities, however, fall into a gray zone in which their special needs pose significant obstacles to their future employment, education, and independent life but are not obvious or visible enough to qualify for adult services. Moderate learning disabilities, mental illness, epilepsy, or other "hidden" disabilities are excellent examples of this.

Although these two systems seemed to represent a natural progression, there was no thread connecting educational life and vocational endeavors; there was no one individual to shepherd families into a new system unless they had prior knowledge. The following situation exemplifies the impact of such gaps in our services:

A local group known to one of us (F. P.) that specializes in advocating for families of children with disabilities received a call from the parent of a 25-year-old young man looking for help. When told that the agency served families with school-aged children only, the mother responded that her son, who had cognitive limitations, had completed high school in accordance with all the recommendations the specialists and educators had made. The family did everything it thought it was supposed to do, everything it was told it needed to do. High school graduation came and went, and here he sat, years later, still without a job, without friends, without a place in the community outside of his parent's home, and without anything to do. The parent, at a loss to help her son and clearly unknown to any educational, social service, or vocational rehabilitation agency, feared a dead end and began calling phone numbers in the Yellow Pages that listed "parents" in the organizational name.

If transition is defined as the passage from one life cycle stage to another, then it is an evolution of sorts characterized by numerous changes, with each one serving as the foundation for the next and in effect shaping future possibilities and outcomes. Super's (1953; quoted in Blalock, 1988) model of career development proposed that developing self-concepts are molded throughout childhood stages, which in turn shape decisions about future occupations. The process of transition is initiated in infancy and affects the individual and the family in roles that vary throughout the life span with critical groundwork initiated in preschool and elementary school years (Szymanski, Turner, & Hershenson, 1992). Szymanski (1994) supported this concept by refuting the notion that a single point in time or even a limited period in time could be called a "transition" but that there exist "critical antecedents" to transitions that occur long before concrete career or vocational transition planning. These appear in the facilitation or discouragement of skills, interests, and opportunities for young children with disabilities.

For instance, restricted opportunities in peer interactions for young children with disabilities may delay the development of, or hinder, appropriate social skills, whereas positive opportunities for interaction may foster those skills that will be necessary in the future. In using this developmental perspective of transition, it is reasonable to think that extreme overprotectiveness because of a disability-related concern might result in limited opportunities that could impact the individual's future. Negative views of the future held by either parents or professionals might result in lowered expectations, again limiting the child's choices, anticipation, and outlook for the future. Repetto and Correa (1996) recommended teaching academics that have functional applications in the real world so that children at young ages have the opportunity to begin to see connections between employment, community, social skills, and school-related learning.

Current transition guidelines ensure that a school-based team (which includes representatives from adult service agencies and parents as well) help to outline a positive road map to adult life by assessing and addressing current skills, needs, and interests prior to high school graduation and by providing navigational skills (training, opportunities, and connections to adult agencies) for life beyond school. Practitioners involved with young adults with disabilities and their families should have a good understanding of this process to elevate transition planning above the realm of a "paper process" and to retain a sense of purposeful participation.

TRANSITION: THE LEGAL MANDATE

RECENT HISTORICAL FOUNDATIONS

> Mental defectives with little sense of decency, with no control of their passions, with no appreciation of the sacredness of the person and the higher reference of life, become a center of evil in the community, and inevitably lower the moral tone. . . . Modern methods of preventing unemployment and poverty, such as vocational and industrial education, labor bureaus and industrial insurance have little or no application to the feeble minded. Their vocation is in institutional life where they alone can be employed and happy. (MacMurchy, 1916, p. 59)

Negative attitudes like MacMurchy's followed the "handicapped" as they approached adulthood. In 1916, the "feeble minded" were blamed for the deterioration of the home, unemployment, and poverty and were depicted as a source of health problems and alcoholism. Such individuals were characterized as having a lack of self-control and contributing to the moral decay in society (MacMurchy, 1916). It was noted that they should not be employed in the outside world or be allowed to raise offspring, but instead institutional life would be most appropriate for feebleminded adults.

Prior to 1975, children with disabilities were routinely denied entrance into public school programs or placed on waiting lists on the premise that either they could not benefit from learning or there was no available staff or facility to deal with them. Many of the decisions to exclude children from schools were arbitrary. Children were kept home or institutionalized with little chance of future opportunities for positive outcome and increased probability of long-term dependency on parents for both financial and emotional support. Children with disabilities—and adults for that matter—had limited visibility in public places and employment opportunities were bleak at best. The vocational rehabilitation system was inaccessible to those with severe disabilities.

The passage of the Education for All Handicapped Children Act (P.L. 94–142; see Chapter 3) in 1975 gave rise to the most dramatic and controversial yet productive changes in the history of the treatment of youth with disabilities in the United States. Under this landmark federal mandate, brought about largely through the efforts of parent advocacy groups, children with disabilities were suddenly entitled to a free, appropriate public education in the least restrictive environment that was designed to meet their unique learning needs. Children with disabilities were guaranteed, or "entitled," to an education with needed supports and services until the age of 21. The families who were trailblazers during this time period were the first such group to wage and win such dramatic entitlements for their children with disabilities.

Perhaps the families and professionals were too absorbed with the changes to consider the implications for the future, but by the mid-1980s the first round of children entitled to school services under P.L. 94–142 were completing high school. Parents began to recognize that although their children had finally gained the rights to a free, appropriate public education, they were not necessarily getting what they needed to become independent, contributing members of society who were respected, valued, and included.

INFORMATION FROM EMPLOYMENT DATA

Employment figures emerging in the decade after passage of the 1975 special education legislation led us to look more closely at the programs we had created and their outcomes. For instance, in 1983, the U.S. Commission on Civil Rights reported that 50% to 80% of people with disabilities were not employed. The President's Committee on Employment in 1985 estimated that only 21% of students with disabilities leaving school would be fully employed, and a significant number of those would be in poverty (Blalock, 1988). In the state of Vermont, a study of students with mental retardation completing formal schooling in the early 1980s found that the employment rate was 46% (for women it was only 23%) and the majority of them continued to live with parents (Hasazi, Gordon, Roe, Hull, et al., 1985). It became increasingly clear that special education programs were not successfully preparing youth with special needs for competitive employment or independent living (Everson & Moon, 1987).

Okolo and Sitlington (1988) reported that youth with learning disabilities were employed at the same rate as peers without disabilities, but their employment was usually in entry-level positions that were not full-time and salaries were often at minimum wage. The 1994 Harris Survey reported that two-thirds of all adults with disabilities aged 16 to 64 were not working and 60% lived in households with incomes of less than $25,000.

In a sample of 900 young adults with learning disabilities, Sitlington and Frank (1990) confirmed previous findings regarding low-status positions, differences in employment between men and women, and continuing residence with family. Only 6% of the sample indicated that their school was a source of assistance in securing a postschool job. Judging "successful adjustment" by criteria that included (a) employment, homemaker, or student status; (b) living independently, with family or friends, or buying a home; (c) paying a portion of living expenses; and (d) involvement in at least one leisure activity, 50% of the sample were successfully adjusted. This study raised several important concerns. If these criteria truly measure successful adjustment, is a 50% rate for a group of high-functioning individuals with "invisible" disabilities a good success rate or a positive comment on years of special education and labeling? Does living with parents; holding a low-paying, unskilled job; and participating in one leisure activity constitute success in terms of fulfillment and satisfaction with one's life?

Professionals and parents should note that research suggests that particular attention should be paid to the needs of women with disabilities. The employment data (Haring & Lovett, 1990; Harris, 1994) revealed higher unemployment rates for women with disabilities and significant discrepancies between the employment rate for nondisabled women versus women with disabilities. We might ask why there is such a discrepancy between rates of employment for men and women with disabilities and what are we doing during the critical learning years to prepare these youth for the future? Efforts to "shelter" women from the real world for fear of victimization, although understandable, may not be particularly helpful. Families and professionals must address needs for recreation, residence, and employment regardless of gender. Employment rates and salaries are higher for men with disabilities than women, but in addition it appears that more men receive vocational services (Fulton & Sabournie, 1994; Wagner, 1992). Wagner (1992) also found that men with disabilities held more part-time jobs prior to school completion.

Benz, Yovanoff, and Doren (1997) discussed four variables predictive of successful employment for youth with disabilities. They included two or more work experiences in the last 2 years before graduation, exit from high school with high-level social skills, exit with good job-search skills, and no vocational instructional needs after 1 year postschool. Lack of vocational training, lack of opportunities to gain employment experience, and a preponderance of low-paying part-time jobs, when viewed in terms of statistics on early marriage and parenting in women with disabilities (Wagner, 1992), highlight needed areas of focus for practitioners working with young women with disabilities. Societal stereotypes about disabilities and also about the role of women may compound these problems and further restrict opportunities unless specific attention is targeted by parents, advocates, educators, and other professionals. Young women with disabilities must have increased opportunities for job training and employment experience prior to high school completion.

There are several reasons why adequate employment remains low for all youth with disabilities transitioning to adulthood. Perhaps the two most important are perpetuation of negative stereotypes and inadequate preparation for the world of work. Recent educational and civil rights legislation for persons with disabilities has increased opportunities and awareness, but it takes more than legislation to change attitudes. And although students with disabilities are graduating from high school in numbers greater than ever before, we need to question whether they are graduating with usable skills. Okolo and Sitlington (1988) cited poor interpersonal skills and lack of both vocational skills and job-related academic skills as reasons for unemployment. They identified school-based educational practices as lacking in skill development for employment and recommended more direct strategies that focus on employment-related social skills, job-related reading, and increased vocational preparation. This emphasizes the needed involvement of parents, educators, and well-trained rehabilitation professionals. In addition, it highlights the needed deviation from traditional academics, as well as the additions to vocational tracks, that will incorporate skill training, applied reading, math skills, and social skills.

SHAPING OF TRANSITION LAW

In the early 1980s, attention to transition services was discussed by the Office of Special Education and Rehabilitative Services (OSERS) as a necessary bridge between secondary school programs and adult life (Will, 1984). Madeline Will, then the deputy director of OSERS, felt that transition was a process that would result in employment for youth with disabilities. Although the initial focus of early transition work was on employment, Halpern (1985) suggested broadening the primary target of transition to include community adjustment, quality of residential environment, and adequacy of social and interpersonal networks.

In 1990 when the Education for All Handicapped Children Act (P.L. 94–142) was reauthorized, its name was changed to the Individuals With Disabilities Education Act (IDEA; P.L. 101–476) to reflect more current and acceptable terminology. Several changes were instituted with the reauthorization. Among them was a requirement stipulating the introduction of transition planning for identified youth by the maximum age of 16, but earlier if necessary. What this meant in practice was that for every child who had been receiving special education services of any type (whether in a special class with a severe disability or only consultative services with a mild disability), a new type of formalized planning would occur. The intention was not only to consider immediate academic needs and goals but to begin to address postschool outcomes related to employment or education, independent living, preparation and support needs, anticipated involvement with community agencies, and participation in the community at large. The most significant change with the introduction of the transition plan process was the direct, mandated involvement of the youngster. Formerly, annual education plan meetings included a teacher, principal, and parent who spoke on behalf of the child. This new concept of transition planning recognized the need for the children to express their own opinions about current interests, future aspirations, and perceived needs to attain their goals. (Transition law will be discussed in further detail later in this chapter.)

Other transition legislation that supports the concept of transition services includes the Carl Perkins Vocational and Applied Technology Act (P.L. 101–392) and the Americans With Disabilities Act of 1990 (ADA; P.L. 101–336).

The Perkins Act provides for the assessment and assistance of students in special populations to complete vocational education programs, including modifications of curriculum, equipment, and classrooms; the provision of instructional aids and supports; and counseling and career development activities by specialized personnel.

The Americans With Disabilities Act is landmark federal legislation that ensures equal access to individuals with disabilities in employment, public accommodations, transportation, telecommunications, and government services. This law has far-reaching effects since it not only refers to schools and government agencies but spans social, community, and medical services and opportunities afforded to all individuals.

IMPLICATIONS OF TRANSITION REGARDING
LONGITUDINAL PERSPECTIVE AND FAMILIAL ADJUSTMENT

For transitions to be successful, professionals and parents must consider early exposure, attitudes, choice making, interest development, and future options earlier in an adolescent's life than the close of formal schooling. Just as the effects of early experiences and societal attitudes have been documented in the literature as having an impact on personality development in children, these same factors should be viewed as impacting personal skills, expectations, interactions, and future outcomes for youth with disabilities.

As the parent of two teenagers, one in college without a disability and one in high school with an invisible disability, revealed in retrospect:

> When my older daughter engaged in behaviors which I felt were annoying, aggressive, or bothersome as a teen, I attributed them to maturation and age-appropriate struggles to be treated as an individual. When my son with ADD exhibited the same behaviors, I related them all to his disability and perceived them in a more negative way as if they were aberrant behaviors. This perspective made it difficult at times to separate normal maturation from abnormal behaviors. I wonder if my negative reactions to his possibly "normal" behaviors affected his own view of himself. (Anonymous, personal communication, fall, 1996)

Comments like these represent the feelings of many parents who raise a child with a disability to adulthood, particularly when nondisabled siblings are present.

The importance of the family in future planning cannot be overestimated. In addition to engaging the family in the process, however, professionals must be cautious and consider the implications of their own professional perceptions, attitudes, and predictions regarding social, educational, or vocational potential. It is essential that professionals attempt to be proactive in providing pragmatic suggestions without unnecessarily limiting outcomes and expectations, as in the following example:

A parent of a teenager with a severe hearing loss had been proactively advocating for her child for all of her school years. A professional with expertise in assessment judged the girl to have mental retardation because of a numerical score received on a test that did not account for her hearing/language problem. Even though it was determined later that the child had average intelligence, the specialist told the mother of the child (then 9 years old), "Do you think you're being realistic about your daughter's future? I think that if your daughter can go to the store, buy bread, and make change, then you should be satisfied." He went on to inform the parents that higher expectations would be unreasonable and irresponsible for them as parents to have. His professional recommendations included "preparation for menial work." Fortunately, due to the assertive efforts of the family and their involvement in obtaining accurate information from reliable sources, this young woman, now 18 years old, is receiving appropriate educational services in the classroom and is planning to receive postsecondary training (Anonymous, personal communication, September 1993).

To some families, this misguided professional assessment would have resulted in reduced expectations and parental guilt for appearing "irresponsible and unreasonable." It is important for helping professionals to provide accurate assessments, appropriate counseling, and realistic options for the future, although it may be difficult at times to find the balance between limited outlooks and false hope without a crystal ball. A combination of professional assessment, past experience, knowledge of the individual, and understanding of the family dynamics should be used as a guide and not a ruler in attempts to assist parents with future planning.

Had this family accepted the advice and accompanying limitations of the specialist from the outset, their daughter's preparation for the future over the subsequent decade would have been quite different. Fortunately, the combination of the parents' assertive stance and their ability to connect with appropriate parent support and informational resources resulted in a better outcome than the professional predicted.*

It is also important to consider the great number of families who have no community or family supports, no sources of information, and insufficient assertiveness to disagree with "expert" opinions. For this reason, the impact of proactive involvement, accurate assessment, and intervention on behalf of youth with disabilities becomes highly significant when viewed as a contributing factor in their long-term adjustment.

Even for those who consider transition as a single discrete time period surrounding the completion of formal schooling, it should be recognized that this major change signifying entrance to adult life does not occur at the same time for all youth with disabilities. Some students complete high school and nothing changes for them except an absence of schooling. Does this constitute healthy adjustment to adult life? Others' lives may change drastically upon school completion via entrance into training programs, higher education, or job placements.

A 23-year-old man with significant mental and physical involvement known to one of the authors (F. P.) entered a therapeutic activity center upon

---

* It is interesting to note that the recommendations were based on invalid test results since no testing accommodations were made for this young woman's severe hearing loss.

school completion but continued to live at home under the care of his mother and other caregivers. Although some aspects of his life had changed, he really had not progressed in social or community adjustment. It was not until a local group home had an opening several years later that his true transitions were actualized. He was able not only to work but to leave his childhood home and caretakers to live with peers and at a higher level of independence, despite the ongoing need for support and assistance.

It is interesting to note that as a result of the son's transition, the mother's life was also affected. As a divorced parent and sole caretaker for over a decade, this mother had scheduled her every activity in accordance with the needs and schedule of her son. This included employment, higher education, social relationships, and activities. Even the purchase of family vehicles was influenced by his presence. Despite her happiness and excitement at the prospect of her son's new opportunities, she responded to his transition by saying, "They should design transition plans not just for the kids but for parents like me" (Anonymous, personal communication, December 1996). The realization that she no longer had to plan life around her son was overwhelming. Hobbies, free time, socialization with peers, and vacations had never been an option for her as they are for other families. It was clear to those who knew her that this adjustment was a difficult one to make, for in the shadow of a vast array of new opportunities was the reminder that the entire role and function that had defined her as a person and mother for most of her adult life would never be the same again.

Variations in expected life changes pose additional challenges in the transition to adulthood for parents and youth. Spekman, Goldberg, and Herman (1993) addressed the critical nature of "off task early or late events" as factors that increase susceptibility to further failure. They cited early school failure, prolonged schooling for individuals approaching adulthood, and overdependence on families as examples of such events. The following two situations also reflect the impact of skewed milestones for both youth with disabilities and their parents:

> A mid-fortyish father of a young woman with significant academic delays returned to school with the goal of obtaining a college degree. He enjoyed the learning experience and found the competitive atmosphere stimulating. One day, several months into the semester, a classmate arrived in class in a jovial mood and indicated that she had been celebrating. When asked what the occasion was, she responded that it was her 18th birthday. It was at that point that the father suddenly became painfully aware that many of his collegiate peers were approximately the same age as his daughter who academically and socially was in a different world. (Anonymous, personal communication, spring 1997)

The mother of the same young woman frequently shares the following story when speaking to future rehabilitation professionals: In many rural towns, the approach of the school prom signifies a traditional milestone and is a celebrated and publicized social event synonymous with bridging the gap between childhood and adulthood. Everyone who is anyone goes. Like the other young women in town, her daughter planned on participating in this ritual passage. Many young women, in fact, attended several proms before their own senior one if they were asked by older males to attend. Each year her daughter removed a fancy prom dress from the closet and dreamed aloud about the year's upcoming prom, what she would wear, and the imaginary escort who would be on her arm. And each year, the prom dress was put back in the closet unworn, a distinct reminder of missed chances. There are now few opportunities remaining for the prom dress to be worn and then this will be yet another milestone not just delayed, but denied. This annual, unfulfilled dream marks the passage of time for both the young woman and perhaps more insightfully for her mother (Anonymous, personal communication, spring 1997).

Delays like the one just mentioned further isolate, exclude, and restrict youth from common opportunities that stimulate growth and expanded experiences. For these reasons, professionals must consider the whole individual in treatment and not just the psychological problem, the medical concern, or the educational approach, for all are intertwined with the life outside the therapy room, examination room, or classroom.

Other transitional rites of passage expected for the typical young adult, such as dating, driving, voting, or part-time employment, are also frequently skewed temporally and occur later or not at all for youth with disabilities. The younger teenage sister of the individual discussed above remarked to her mother that she was concerned that "F. isn't doing the things that most young women did. She should be dating, going to dances and proms, driving and hanging out. I'll probably have my first date before she does" (Anonymous, personal communication, fall 1996).

This sibling realized that her older sister, who ideally should be her role model within the dynamics of the family structure, was missing out on normal social activities and in fact was more like a younger sister because of this. In previous years, she had been intolerant of her sister's idiosyncrasies and resentful of the attention she received. Her own maturation increased her ability to look beyond her sister's impact on her personally and sensitized her to her sister's plight and its resulting effect.

Siblings and the Transition Process

Although it is addressed in previous chapters, the issue of siblings deserves mention at this point. The topic of siblings in families that have a child with a disability is frequently covered in terms of resentment, embarrassment, and negativity on the part of the nondisabled brother or sister. Interviews with families and the current literature (Turnbull & Turnbull, 1990) also note positive outcomes for siblings. The following family interview touched on negative aspects related to siblings but it also discussed the positive change in family relationships over time. The mother of 18-year-old twins, one with a disability and one without, shared this insight:

> Bea, as a child, was often embarrassed by her sister's difficulties. The fact that they were identical twins exacerbated the problems and Bea was particularly upset when she wasn't invited to social happenings because other kids were afraid they'd have to invite Jay also. Bea was resentful of this and of the fact that everyone seemed to depend on her to take her sister somewhere or that they expected her to help Jay with something. But eventually Bea began getting angry at the other kids who teased and taunted her sister and she spoke up for her. She became more aware of what the difficulties meant in Jay's life and became stronger, more accepting, and definitely more sensitive. They both still live at home and share a room. Bea has become more supportive of Jay and they have talks in which Jay shares problems with Bea that she never tells me about, which I think is good. Bea is concerned about what Jay will be doing next year but at the same time is excited about her own future plans. (Anonymous, personal communication, May 1997)

Many reports of sibling problems focus on negatives as they occur at one point in time without consideration of a longitudinal perspective. Young siblings may not be cognitively or socially mature enough to understand why a sibling might seem to get more attention, accommodations, and so on, but nevertheless recognize that it happens and respond on a very personal level. It would be difficult to find any family in which sibling problems do not occasionally occur. Such problems are a normal aspect of maturation. It is important to follow these relationships over an extended period to discover ways in which they evolve and change as siblings approach adulthood. Families like those described earlier discuss positive results and close-knit siblings who support each other. Some siblings of persons with disabilities, in fact, may select career options that are related to their experience and sensitivity with their own siblings.

Transition Planning

Transition planning suggests that professionals and families should actively focus on a set of coordinated activities that will assist in the adjustment to adult life. Professionals must engage the family in true consideration of future planning since it has been well documented that the family poses a more significant influence on the outcome than does educational success (Dowdy, Carter, & Smith, 1990; Morningstar, Turnbull, & Turnbull, 1995). Too often, though, transition planning becomes yet an additional paperwork task with little real meaning and little real parental input.

Szymanski (1994) noted that common transition practice contradicts what is known about career development for all individuals, specifically that youth without disabilities usually are not ready to make career or occupation choices in high school. Why then should we expect students with disabilities to be able to, unless we provide more supports that allow them to think about their own strengths, interests, and future possibilities. Transition counselors at the high school level indicate that many students with special needs have no idea what they want to do in life (Anonymous, personal communication to F. P., 1995), but some counselors only inform the parents and child several days prior to the scheduling of a transition meeting that they should begin thinking about their future and that the child will be asked questions at the meeting pertaining to interests and strengths. It is unrealistic and unfathomable that a directive from a counselor to "think" about the future for the next few days would suddenly clarify in a student's mind whether he or she wants to go to college, look for supported employment, and the like. This seems akin to heading toward the runway in an aircraft without ever having looked at the flight manual. The purpose of a transition meeting is to discuss and project interests, activities, and services to prepare for a long-term future rather than just the next academic year. Szymanski stated that we should be using the transition period to plan long-term career development rather than to find a job. Professionals and families must focus on a set of coordinated activities that will assist the person in adjusting to adult life in the community rather than targeting one specific job.

Professionals and parents should pay attention to social rites of passage and make efforts to enhance participation to foster expanded opportunities. The daily bus ride to school, as described by this parent, can be such an activity:

> The simple everyday act of riding the school bus was problematic for my daughter. Because of her difficulty with timed tasks and basic disorganization, she was fearful of missing the bus. So I drove her, rationalizing that it was easier, allayed real fears, and that I had to travel in that direction anyway. We did notice though that this approach did not expand her limited social circle. Towards the end of high school we arranged her schedule to alleviate some of the timing problems and insisted she try the bus. Who would've thought that riding the bus made such a difference, but that act was associated with more adult status like traveling without parents and using your key to let yourself in at the

end of the day, unattended. This simple change, which added a degree of adult-like responsibility to her life, also added flexibility to my work schedule, thereby decreasing some of the frantic rushing around I did in the afternoons. (Anonymous, personal communication, September 1994)

OBSTACLES TO SUCCESSFUL TRANSITION

INADEQUATE SOCIAL SKILLS AND SOCIAL NETWORKS

Although many parents of children with disabilities focus on obtaining academic remediation and training in preparation for adulthood, the development of adequate social interpersonal skills is critical to positive self-concept and successful interaction with others in social and employment settings. Successful socialization at a young age provides children with opportunities to learn experientially about social relationships and promotes further development using an interactive approach. In contrast, poor early socialization skills without remediation or opportunities to practice interacting with others contribute to developmental gaps between children with disabilities and their peer group. As a child's social differences become more apparent to peers and as peers become old enough to select their own social partners, chances to socialize tend to decrease and limit opportunities to acquire acceptable and rewarding interactional behaviors.

Although employment, residence, and social integration are three targets of any transition planning, Halpern (1990) indicated that social interactions are examined in less than half of current studies on transition outcomes. Chadsey-Rusch and Heal (1995) identified three critical reasons to measure social aspects of transition for youth with disabilities: Socialization is related to quality of life, positive interactions may be associated with other aspects of life, and specific social behaviors are required in specific employment settings. For most adults, life devoid of social relationships is unsatisfying. Having a job or career and earning an income contribute significantly to one's ability to be self-sufficient, but life entails more than working and paying bills. Many transition efforts have focused on job preparation, but how many have examined the quality or even existence of someone's interpersonal relationships? This is an extremely difficult variable to quantify and measure but it is clearly intertwined with a person's self-assessment of life.

Most personal relationships for youth with disabilities are limited to other youth with special needs or paid professionals (Nisbet, Covert, & Schuh, 1992), further restricting opportunities to make choices about social partners or to be valued and respected by peers without disabilities. The child with a disability who is excluded or regarded as a social outcast by peers may continue to have similar difficulties during later developmental periods. A prior history of limited or inadequate social relationships does not vanish as a young person exits school and begins to embrace the future.

Unfortunately, for various reasons, socialization is an area that has not been addressed adequately throughout the school years for youth with disabilities. Despite the fact that most youth with disabilities are in the regular classroom for a part or all of their day, most regular classroom teachers have little information on teaching students with disabilities. Therefore the critical need for positive social interaction and development of self-esteem may not seem as pressing to them as it should.

School-Based Socialization

In addition to attending to academic matters, programs in school settings need to directly address the issue of social skills as part of the educational process to ensure positive social and employment outcomes. Social skills of youth with disabilities should be assessed to determine needed areas of attention that will facilitate the development of social relationships and employment relationships. As the parent of a young woman commented in retrospect,

> When it was clear that she would need academic remediation, we focused on her studies, therapy, school modifications; all of the things that seemed important to her academic success. Although we attempted to provide opportunities that would address social skills, the school never included this in their planning or even recognized a need for it or for their involvement in this aspect of life. Looking back, I wish we spent less time on the academics and more on the social end of the spectrum. Being a teenager without a social life appears to be more devastating than receiving poor grades in subject matter which fulfills some arbitrary academic requirements but may not even be preparatory in nature. More attention to physical presence, eye contact, initiating conversations, and interacting with others or developing friendships in my mind would have resulted in a far happier, more well adjusted young woman. (Anonymous, personal communication, September 1994)

Social skills are not a focus of formal academic preparation because most children acquire functional social skills through incidental exposure and experience. Gaps in social development for youth with special needs usually do not close on their own. It is damaging enough that children with special needs are made to feel excluded and demeaned by their peer group, but by transition age resulting socialization skills may not serve to assist in the successful transition to postschool outcomes.

One parent said,

> My daughter won't try new activities like clubs or dances that involve talking
> to people because of years of negative school experiences related to peer vic-
> timization or unintentional teacher victimization. When my daughter was a
> young teenager, children with special needs were assigned to sit at the same
> lunch table in the cafeteria and other children who were punished were ban-
> ished to that table. Teachers and students alike would walk away while my
> daughter was speaking because they couldn't understand her. (Anonymous,
> parent interview, fall 1996)

Another parent reflected that with her daughter almost 18,

> All my daughter's friends have major home problems and are not good role
> models. This was not by choice but the result of years of being treated as an out-
> cast from the mainstream by kids and teachers. You can attempt to optimize op-
> portunities for friendship, but can't guarantee friends who are a positive
> influence. (Anonymous, personal communication, fall 1996)

Parents like the one just described wish that one of the numerous professionals providing service to their children would look at their child as a
whole and see the need for opportunities to socialize with others rather than
be the recipient of isolated, individual therapy. There are limitations to the
extent that parents can be social organizers for their offspring (particularly
older ones approaching adulthood) without being intrusive.

As well, parents' efforts to engage their children in social activities sometimes backfire. In attempts to be sure their youngsters have "someone" in
the absence of many friends, parents frequently assume the role of "friend"
or "peer playmate," attempting to fill a void for the child and increase feelings of inclusion. Although some benefits do result, the youngster becomes
dependent on adult companionship, which may further restrict peer social
opportunities and social maturation and may extend into the transition period and adult life. What may have been acceptable for children is no longer
acceptable for budding adults, nor is it appropriate for their parents, who
also have lives to lead. On this note, although some parents manage to maintain their own lives, friends, and jobs, others may feel overwhelmed by the
time and emotional demands of their children. This may occur to the degree
that social relationships, family relationships, and employment are affected.
As the parent of a teenager said,

My daughter's social isolation is even more pronounced in comparison to her younger sibling's social life. He is always making friends, organizing groups and could be out all day from dawn to dusk with friends. She has few friends and little motivation to initiate solo activities even though she has the ability. In my efforts to combat her loneliness, I have spun a web in which I am the worker, parent, tutor, friend, and social organizer. The benefits to her are questionable, in the process she has become more reliant on me, and I feel like my life is not my own. If she only had a small group of friends, I feel that her outlook would be much more positive. While many parents who have children completing high school years are concerned about their kids going out to parties, or dating or socializing too much, I would be thrilled to have some of those concerns. My hope is that once she graduates, she no longer has to be faced with a school cafeteria filled with people sitting together, school dances or sporting events that she doesn't attend, or peers who look down on her because she missed the question in class. My hope is that she won't find solace in the television like she does now. I desperately want to see her satisfied with some personal relationships so I don't worry about what will become of her when I'm not around. (Anonymous, personal communication, fall 1996)

Employment-Related Socialization

Employment-related social skills are another area of social interaction that must be addressed in transition-aged youth. For most young adults, social behaviors do not pose obstacles in finding or maintaining paid employment. They have acquired appropriate social skills through experiences with peer relationships and other normalized social activities. By the time they are young adults, most individuals can distinguish inappropriate from appropriate behaviors and also recognize that peer relationships, familial relationships, and work-related relationships may call for different sets of behaviors and what works in one may fail in another. It might be acceptable for a young man to roughhouse with his friends but not with his mother, a delivery person, or his employer. Although you would be expected to give your grandmother a hug, you would not think of demonstrating the same behavior with the cashier in the grocery store after he or she gives you your change. It might under some circumstances be understandable to haul off and punch someone who physically attacks you or your family on a dark, deserted street, but it would be inappropriate to react in the same way to someone saying your tie was ugly.

Young adults with disabilities may have poor or unevenly developed social skills, not as a direct result of the disability itself, but for the many reasons mentioned in this section: isolation; exclusion; lack of friendship opportunities; and misconceptions on the part of peers, teachers, and parents. Unfortunately, this issue is frequently omitted from school-based intervention and bounced back into the parent's court because it is not a traditional academic area. Practitioners should remember that although parents must be involved advocates, some issues left for the parents alone to deal with result in children's overdependence on their parents. For this reason, direct instruction and practice in social skills should always be considered for youth with disabilities.

Appropriate work-related social skills rely not only on well-developed interaction skills but on cognizance of the level of formality or informality and unwritten rules regarding various workplace behaviors. The appearance of neatness and good personal hygiene skills, physical presence, posture, and facial and body expressions that convey friendliness are factors that figure into initial impressions and may be determining factors in competitive job interviews. The ability to get to work on time; follow directions; complete tasks; ask for clarification; work unassisted; accept criticism; be productive, considerate, and cooperative; and interact with coworkers appropriately are important skills in most job situations. The absence of social behaviors that are perceived as negative, such as fighting, cursing, and being uncooperative, is also important. The employee who comes to work unkempt and in need of a shower, who belches loudly, swears when given a job task to complete, and keeps to himself or herself rather than interacting with peer colleagues will probably not be welcomed in the workplace. Hanley-Maxwell, Rusch, Chadsey-Rusch, and Renzaglia (1986) reported that in a sample of individuals they studied, most job terminations were the result of social difficulties. In summarizing several studies related to employment for individuals with disabilities, Chadsey-Rusch, Rusch, and O'Reilly (1991) cited good social skills, absence of asocial behaviors, and presence of positive attitude as attributes associated with successful employment.

Self-Determination, Control, Choice Making, and Self-Advocacy

According to Szymanski(1994), transition is really about empowering society. Instead of viewing employment, place of residence, or recreation as end results of transition for youth with disabilities, we should be viewing these transition components as vehicles for promoting interdependence, self-worth, and respect in a world where all individuals are viewed as members of the group capable of making contributions. Consistent with this view, Ozer and Bandura (1990) stated, "Personal and social change rely extensively on methods of empowerment" (p. 472). People must be given knowledge, skills, and self-beliefs of efficacy to assert control over portions of their lives. Bandura (1977) discussed the perception of self-efficacy as a factor in initiating and maintaining motivation, cognitive resources, and follow-through to alter circumstances. In interviews with individuals regarding what it might be like to have a disability, responses were characterized by concerns about helplessness, loss of independence, and lack of self-determination skills (Van der Klift & Kunc, 1994).

Autonomous adults in our culture have to function within some societal constraints to be considered successful and well adjusted. Throughout one's life, it is not unusual to feel limited by one's family situation, education, job, or place of residence, but it is assumed that autonomous individuals have the ability to make certain socially acceptable choices that will improve their quality of life. Self-determination is one of the characteristics associated with adult status and refers to the ability to plan, modify, and pursue goals determined by individuals regarding their own life choices. Self-determination implies self-knowledge and an ability to exert some control over planning future goals and acting on them based on personal needs, interests, and desires. A self-determined individual defines and takes initiative to pursue goals through assertiveness, self-evaluation of progress, performance adjustment, and problem solving (Martin, Marshall, & Maxson, 1993).

Prior to legislation asserting the rights of individuals with disabilities, self-determination was not a priority issue in determining how to best serve, care for, or meet the needs of people with exceptionalities. Perhaps this is due to the historical medical model approach to persons with disabilities, which categorized and depersonalized such persons and focused on deficits (Groce, 1985) and treatments to maintain, fix, or care for them. This model is also associated with the idea that people with disabilities cannot make decisions for themselves (Lipsky & Gartner, 1989). As society has moved away from this model over the past several decades, we have recognized that people with disabilities need to be viewed in the same context in which the rest of us view our own lives and rights to live them. Advocates should be facilitating a sense of efficacy, control, and choice making rather than removing it.

Although young adults without disabilities use self-determination to advance themselves through further education or employment, this is often not the case for those with disabilities. Youth who have been involved in special education programs and services for their entire school career (and sometimes longer) have had others, usually paid professionals and parents, determining their needs and at times their interests. Special education programs, although designed to improve outcomes for students with special needs, may actually pose obstacles to preparation for adulthood and result in limited choices and perpetuation of dependence rather than independence (Wehmeyer, 1992). Numerous researchers in the past decade have concluded that children with disabilities are offered limited choices even as they approach the end of formal schooling and that motivation is decreased in educational situations characterized by control rather than autonomy, but that self-efficacy can be enhanced when students are able to assist in goal setting (Bandura & Schunk, 1981; Deci, Nezlek, & Sheinman, 1981; Schunk, 1985).

A college student with a learning disability who was majoring in education told of her high school guidance counselor who insisted she would not be able to complete the appropriate college prerequisites because she of course would not be able to register for biology. The reason he used to discourage her from signing up for this course was that she had a learning disability and therefore could not possibly succeed. With the support and assistance of her mother, who recognized her capability and determination, she not only registered, but aced the class. Success motivated her to proceed and she later successfully completed college-level preparation to become a teacher (Anonymous, personal communication, fall 1993).

This story could easily have gone the other way if an advocate, whether parent or professional, had not seen and objected to externally imposed limitations in choices that were arbitrary and based on one person's misconceptions. To develop effective self-advocacy and self-determination skills, individuals must perceive that their choices mean something or make a difference. According to Seligman (1975), it is critical that children have some sense of control at an early age. The lack of opportunities to choose or initiate, the sense of loss of control, a sense of incompetence, and the need to undertake actions because of external locus of control rather than an internal locus are detrimental to the development of self-determination skills.

Despite the fact that, by law, each child's special program is reviewed annually through the IEP process, many youngsters have never participated in these meetings, which are intended to target their needs, strengths, and interests. Based on interviews with students who had disabilities, Morningstar et al. (1995) found that students were not actively involved in transition planning. Reasons cited were irrelevance to future planning, negative experiences with past meetings, or student perceptions that the meetings held no real meaning. Students also revealed a lack of any unified parent-child planning prior to IEP meetings.

Entitlement to special services and programs can be a mixed blessing. Some might consider themselves fortunate that mandated planning to accommodate special needs and improve educational access is an option, but the process at times inadvertently minimizes the individuals while maximizing services, placements, expenditures, and bureaucratic paperwork.

The process, designed to foster growth and independence, may in fact perpetuate an unnecessary dependency on services and people and discourage the development of personal interests or desires to determine one's future. Mandated transition planning that includes the youngster may be the beginning of major changes related to the development of self-determination as a critical aspect of preparation for future life for youth with disabilities.

Although self-determination skills should be considered in all formal transition planning for youth with disabilities, it is important to note that these skills do not develop overnight, only in school, or only at home. Effective enhancement of self-determination skills must be a concerted, collaborative, intentional effort implemented through thoughtful and proactive planning. This is much easier said than done. Many parents only begin to realize when their children are nearing the age of peer departure for independent lives that their offspring with disabilities may be passive noninitiators who are ineffective at asserting choices or desires. A history of parents doing what may have seemed expedient or protective may in fact have eliminated the choice making, risk taking, or self-initiated planning critical to the development of self-determination skills.

Providing unnecessary help is a major impediment to effective self-determination skills. Although it may have been necessary to offer physical assistance, to help interpret homework assignments, or to intervene in a child's social life to optimize opportunities, it is sometimes difficult for a parent to objectively observe a cycle of dependency that may inadvertently develop over time. A parent of a teenager with a learning disability commented on self-determination and independence:

> It occurred to me when the other neighborhood kids began to drive that at seventeen, my daughter is still asking me if she can make a phone call or get a snack. When she tries to arrange a social outing with a friend and I am in the room while she's on the phone, she independently plans about 50% of the time and asks me what to say the other half of the time. She has the ability, but I find myself frequently concerned about whether she will meet her potential in asserting or even recognizing what she wants in social situations, in job interviews, in life at large. Her own self-determination skills would be stronger if she had been forced to do more independently or make her own choices, but I feel that if I didn't assist her in the ways I had, she would have experienced more academic and social failures at a younger age, which would've been devastating to self-esteem. (Anonymous, personal communication, fall 1995)

Another parent, currently an advocate for families with children who have disabilities, discussed her 20-year-old daughter. She reflected on transition problems occurring after years of assisting her daughter with monitoring and time management, which at the time was both necessary and helpful. The daughter was accepted at a local university but dropped out shortly thereafter:

> Through all of our efforts she was accepted in college but staying there was another story. The class content wasn't as problematic as the newfound independent living demands associated with college and dorm life. Meeting deadlines and monitoring her own time when she was used to me checking in on her was a major change. Most young people would welcome that change but for her it was detrimental. Having to share a room with a roommate, studying with other people, or trying to work in a noisy dorm environment was more than she could handle. She since has returned home, is receiving technical training in a vo-tech program and has a part-time job. She seems happy. (Anonymous, personal communication, January 1997)

Residential Planning

The examples in the previous section raise the issue of residence in association with self-determination and self-advocacy skills. Hanley-Maxwell, Whitney-Thomas, and Pogoloff (1995) found that residential issues are a major concern for parents of youth with disabilities and that needs for independence on the part of both youth and their parents are often in conflict with inadequate residential options outside of the family home. The parents surveyed viewed a safe, independent residence as critical in further development of independent functioning, but for youth who needed supervised or group home settings, limited options and availability created a prolonged dependence on families.

Residential plans are usually made in terms of considering independent, semi-independent, or group home situations. In group homes, nonparental supervision and structure are built into the program. In independent living, it is assumed that the person needs no or relatively few informal supports. But what about the person in the gray zone who probably has the potential to live independently but who has relied on supports over the years that have become a part of daily living? The function of job coaches in supported employment programs is to teach job-related tasks until a person can handle those tasks independently. It appears that for many young people with disabilities, "living coaches" may be even more basic. Such a person could act as a liaison between intense family supports and independence, with a gradual fading of supports.

Barriers and Windows to Developing Self-Determination

Parental reflections like those quoted earlier document the ongoing need for professionals working with families to see the bigger picture of the individual as part of a dynamic family system and to facilitate the ability of parents to see it as well. Parents may easily become entrenched in their child's immediate needs, which subjectifies the situation. It is the responsibility of the "helping" professional to use objectivity to help the parent step back and problem-solve in ways that will be productive not just at the moment but over the long haul. Because parents may feel overwhelmed in dealing with the present, the professional's responsibility is to demonstrate to the parents how present actions influence long-term futures and to help them develop strategies that serve present needs but do not diminish independent planning, choice making, or self-assertion skills.

On the other hand, self-determination sometimes is unintentionally enhanced when a parent feels unable to continue to be ultimately responsible for all planning, caretaking, and day-to-day tasks involved in the delayed nurturing of an almost adult and in response takes action that inadvertently results in increased efficacy, self-determination, and self-advocacy: The mother of a transition-aged teen with a significant disability described her son as extremely independent and willing to self-advocate, despite the fact that his behaviors were not always appropriate and his disability posed many obstacles to relationships with others. He had stayed at home alone since the age of 9 and had fixed meals, done laundry, and independently accessed urban transportation since that time as well, despite the fact that the mother continued to receive notification from the school because of behaviors exhibited by this young man. His independence, she said, came from the fact that she just could not handle all the overwhelming details any more and felt forced to relinquish not just control but the constant provision of help and assistance. He was forced to deal with many issues for himself, not predicated on long-term future planning for self-determination, but instead based on parental need to cope (Anonymous, personal communication, 1996).

Other parents who may be more passive, tolerant, or unable to refuse requests from their child without feeling guilty may in fact perpetuate overdependence and lack of control by giving second chances, doing for, playing offense and defense in all situations, and denying ownership of any problems to the youngster. In other words, such parents overfunction, which leads to the underfunctioning of their child.

In addition to unnecessary help, unnecessary control at home or in the educational setting has devastating effects on a person's ability or willingness to take risks involved with making personal choices. Teachers conducting controlling classrooms with externally dictated goals may never even be aware that a young person's ability to self-determine his or her future may have been influenced negatively. The focus may be on completing educational curriculum requirements to the exclusion of recognizing the critical need for youth with disabilities to exercise self-determination skills.

Lack of self-determination skills poses difficulties with reference to choice making, goal pursuit, or envisioning a future in which one sees oneself as successful. But when an individual with a disability has limited self-determination skills, the results are also reflected in the ways others view and subsequently interact with the person based on their perceptions:

> My daughter's lack of self-determination and self-advocacy skills is readily evident to others despite the fact that her disability is an "invisible" one. It struck me again this week when an acquaintance walked up to my family. He addressed my 11-year-old son, engaged him in conversation and instead of talking to my older daughter, he asked me, "How old is she now? How is she doing?" as if she were not there at all. Although my immediate reaction was discomfort and disturbance at the friend, I recognized that she might as well be wearing a placard that said, "Don't talk to me. I don't assert myself, communicate, or make active choices." It was easy to see that her perceptions about herself could be "read" by others and, in turn, their lack of direct engagement with her and vice versa contributed to a vicious circle. (Anonymous, personal communication, March 1997)

SELF-DETERMINATION AND SEXUALITY

Sexuality is another area related to self-determination and control over one's life, one that is frequently ignored. Needs for intimate relationships, expression of emotion, and recognition as a sexual being are basic to human nature, although it is common to assume that individuals with physical or cognitive limitations cannot be sexual or have needs for sexual intimacy. According to Marfisi (1996), society's understanding of sexuality as a quality associated with "normalcy," has contributed to misconceptions about sexuality in individuals with disabilities. The treatment of members of this group as "asexual" by omission sends yet another message about the nonperson status of individuals with disabilities and serves to further limit their control over choice and self-determination. As discussed in the preceding chapter, sometimes good intentions based on desires to shield from physical abuse or emotional harm result in denial of sexuality through limited information offered as well as limited opportunities to explore sexuality. Studies indicating that sexual development and interest in youth with mild and moderate mental retardation parallels such development in young people without disabilities substantiates the need for accurate and responsible provision of information regarding normal sexual development and relationships in young adults with disabilities (Haavik & Menninger, 1981; Szymanski & Jansen, 1980, quoted in Nagler, 1993).

Spruill (1996) described the insensitivity of professionals and family who ignore normal needs for privacy on the part of individuals with disabilities or who joke about their physical characteristics in their presence as if they were not there or did not care. She also pointed out that failing to provide information on sexual matters increases susceptibility to sexual abuse, which is based on abuses of power and control. As discussed in the previous chapter on adolescence, this issue can continue to be problematic through the transition years and into adulthood. Practitioners should recognize the need for transition-aged youth to receive information on sexual behavior and sexual abuse.

Morningstar et al. (1995) advocated emphasis on developing autonomy and self-determination skills at much earlier levels through the use of school-parent partnership models and further conceptualization of family roles to ensure more active collaboration in decision making.

INADEQUATE PARENT INVOLVEMENT IN THE TRANSITION YEARS

There is extensive documentation in the current literature regarding the importance of parent involvement and input in the transition process as well as the preceding time periods (Hasazi, Collins, & Cobb, 1988; Morningstar et al., 1995), but lack of parent involvement is frequently cited as an obstacle to effective planning for, implementation of, and follow-through to targeted goals. Studies indicate that parents are relatively uninvolved (MacMillan & Turnbull, 1983) and frequently the implication is that parents are uninterested, irresponsible, or unintelligent. There are numerous plausible explanations, however, for parental uninvolvement that should be considered but often are not. It seems easier to label the parents as "unconcerned" and then use this factor as a reason for unmet goals or failure of a program.

Lack of Information

As mentioned in Chapter 3, for parents to be effective advocates for their own children they must have necessary information regarding their child's disability. In a 1992 survey of 440 parents of children through the age of 21 with disabilities, 38% indicated that they did not have enough information to effectively engage in meetings about their child with special needs and that professionals appeared defensive when parents asked questions (Prezant, Borman, & Walker, 1991).

Parents' calls to networking and advocacy groups in search of advocates are commonplace because they recognize the need for support and information. Parent involvement during the transition period is critical, but many parents have no information regarding mandated transition plans and multiagency responsibility to assist in planning for postschool outcomes. Upon whom is it incumbent to ensure that appropriate information is provided to the parents, particularly at this stage of the game? Or are parents assumed to somehow access the information alone? It is possible that some parents choose not to be involved, but based on information from parent networks across the country, it is likely that many parents have never been informed of their right to be part of the process. The implication for practitioners is that rather than assume a parent is unconcerned or oblivious, efforts should be made to ensure that parents have information necessary to make effective, proactive decisions about their child's future.

Frustration with System

Another possible explanation for insufficient parent involvement with bureaucratic systems (e.g., schools, agencies, human service organizations) is the increasing frustration that parents have experienced by the time their child with special needs transitions to adulthood. In a parent survey of 120 families in Pennsylvania (Marshak, Prezant, Cerrone, & Seligman, 1997), parents of older youth appeared more dissatisfied in interactions with professionals than parents of younger children. Is it because programs have improved so much since transition-aged students entered school? Is it because parents of younger students are just beginning their journey through a system that they believe will hold all the answers and cures? Or have the parents of older students come face to face with many questions about the impending future of their offspring entering adulthood?

Parents of young children with disabilities may welcome any information relating to the disability or available services, but by the time youth reach adulthood, many of the same parents have been frustrated by perceived roadblocks in obtaining accurate information, education services for their child, or relevant preparation for life. The recognition of fleeting time and impending entrance into adulthood adds to this frustration with the system. In addition, over time, parents who by need become very well informed about their child's disability may be struck by the frequency with which professionals lack information. It is both frightening and frustrating for parents to become aware that they may have more information than paid professionals they consult. The following parent statement about several such revelations is illustrative:

Our child's neurologist enjoys talking with us because we are well informed and ask stimulating and challenging questions but there are never answers to our questions.

A consult to a private psychiatrist regarding the possibility of depression included a 15-minute interview with our teenager, a 5-minute interview with us, and conclusions that not only didn't address our questions adequately but were clearly based on scanty and inadequate information.

Our daughter's transition plan was a test case because the school-based professionals who organized the team didn't really know how to write such a plan. We ended up with some appropriate objectives and activities but it was because we developed them and brought a consultant with us.

Repeated experiences like these have taught us to be wary of professional consultation and that seeking additional professional opinions may in fact be harmful rather than helpful if all they do is emphasize to our daughter that she is different without providing any concrete information that could help. (Anonymous, personal communication, September 1993)

Insufficient Efforts to Engage Parents in the Process

Parents often complain that their involvement in the transition process appears meaningless and that at times the extent of their involvement is a requested signature on paperwork. Parents feel insignificant and unheeded in such situations. Planning for entrance into adulthood, a process that requires a great deal of thought and collaboration, is reduced to a brief meeting. Parents are not always informed of the nature of the meeting, which does not foster advance planning; students are not always involved; and the timing is not always conducive to parents' work schedules.

The preponderance of the disability-related literature that focuses on dysfunctionality in such families may contribute to the idea that parents may not have important contributions to make. Turnbull and Turnbull (1993) observed that only rarely does the literature address successful coping strategies used by families. If more studies investigated the strength, resilience, and capability of families, professional efforts to engage families might be more persistent.

Poor Relationships with Professionals

Much of past research and documentation regarding families of youth with disabilities has been negative (see earlier chapters) and tends to focus on dysfunctionality, problems, and deficits. This approach is inconsistent with treating the person as a whole and contributes to fragmented fixes. This approach also parallels the way in which individuals with disabilities have been viewed by society in general and may help to explain many family comments about professional incompetence and insensitivity, such as the following comment from an advocate who is the parent of a young adult:

It's up to the parent and kids to forge their way through this. Our transition plan was a farce. The formalized plan was a checklist to nowhere. The school professionals focused on problems and worked in a box with graduation as the foreseeable boundary. They hoped that things would go okay after that, but if not, their professional responsibilities were over. Transition to a parent and child has a different meaning and focus in terms of time span. I wish I knew then what I know now. When I meet parents of younger children today, I am always surprised that they think everything will be taken care of. Sometimes I want to shake them into action. It makes me wish that someone had provided for me the information and support I provide for other parents. (Anonymous, personal communication, January 1997)

Another parent expressed her dissatisfaction with professional attitudes:

Throughout my daughter's education, the school psychologist has been a negative influence. He questioned my ability to know and understand my child's disability. He has always downplayed my importance in her education. "Leave it to the experts" is his motto. (Anonymous, personal communication, October 1995)

It is imperative that professionals working with transition-aged youth understand their strengths or "islands of competence" and needs for targeted training in career orientation (Brooks, 1994a). The father of a young man with a learning disability who was expected to graduate from high school but was held back because of an administrative technicality stated the following in a press release:

There are but a handful of irreplaceable moments in a person's life. A high school graduation is one such moment that, if missed, can never be replaced or repeated. In perspective, it commonly ranks among the most significant events in a person's life. B. will hopefully go on in life to do other important things. With enough dedication, his family may even see him graduate from college some day. But the unique moment of high school graduation is lost forever to all. A time that should have been filled with pride and joy—a day that B. would have learned an important life lesson; that hard work really does have its eventual rewards. Instead, graduation day for B. and his family, was a day of overwhelming dismay and disappointment, and one filled with a sense of hopelessness. It was also a day that a very discouraging message was sent to a young man whose achievement is always hard won. Who knows the ultimate effect that such unconscionable rejection will have on a person whose confidence is, understandably, as fragile as B's? (Anonymous, personal communication, spring 1996)

If objectivity has any place in our professional behaviors, it should be used first and foremost to monitor our own beliefs, judgments, and practices in terms of how they are used either proactively or destructively in dealing with those we purport to be helping.

Other Family Issues

Raising youth with disabilities to adulthood in an atmosphere that fosters optimal outcomes can be a challenging and overwhelming task in time, effort, and personal stamina. Other family issues may also need attention. In two-parent, nuclear families, which occur with less frequency, parents must also resolve employment issues of their own, possible relocation, and sibling issues and frequently at this point in time they must negotiate the increasing demands of their own aging parents. Travel time frequently becomes an issue if families and youth are receiving multiple services from providers in different locations. Providing academic or self-help assistance at home is often not considered by those outside the family but adds to stress levels when time is a limited commodity. In the case of severe physical, mental, or behavioral disabilities, parents must be concerned about constant supervision and may require respite care for some relief. For single parents, poor parents, and culturally different or socially isolated parents, these problems and others become magnified.

The approach of adulthood is usually accompanied by growing independence of youth and parents from each other and similar increases in control and self-determination by both parties. The situation for families who have children with disabilities facing adulthood frequently follows a reverse pattern in view of the lack of adult services (Nisbet, Covert, & Schuh, 1992), termination of mandated educational services, and departure of peers and siblings. One could wonder about Seligman's (1975) concept of learned helplessness in relation to the parent role when a disability in the family has resulted in a sense of loss of control over life by the parent. By the time the child approaches the threshold of adulthood, the parents may be faced not only with unfulfilled dreams regarding the child's future but with a reckoning of the impact on their own lives as adults. This may be emphasized by the observation that other parents at similar stages in life are gaining freedom and independence to once again pursue their own interests. Hanley-Maxwell et al.

(1995) described the internal conflicts experienced by parents who recognize their offspring's ongoing dependence despite parental desires to see them as more independent adults. Frustration and fatigue may be factors that cause parents to give up at a time when their persistence may be most critical.

Lack of Teacher Preparation

As mentioned in Chapter 3, regular and special education have grown as separate strands at all levels. The preparation of teachers in each field has followed different paths. This has contributed to fragmentation, defensiveness, and turf problems.

Regular education teachers still receive little or no information regarding disabilities, particularly at the secondary level. At the critical juncture during the transition from school to work, when students need opportunities and increased self-esteem to succeed, many are relegated to low-level tracks. The reason is frequently that high school teachers do not have sufficient information on how to make accommodations or vary learning strategies and as a result feel unprepared for or threatened or angered by placement of students with disabilities in their classes. It is assumed that because youth with disabilities may deviate from the norm in learning style, they might not be capable of learning and subsequently are not challenged or included.

On the flip side, special educators and related professionals in rehabilitative fields have received training to deal with disability-specific issues but are often seen as providing fringe services or transient. School-based specialists, particularly at secondary levels, are frequently viewed as tangential to the real work of the program. For example, speech and language pathologists or counselors who work with students on a pullout basis in several schools might be providing valuable services that allow the student to make academic and social progress. Because that specialist may not have a regular class or a full-time presence in that school, he or she may not be considered an integral member of the faculty. It is also common that secondary-level special educators have little training in secondary issues, which would include socialization, sexual relationships, vocational issues, and the like. Paralleling the need for regular educators to receive more applicable and relevant information, secondary special educators as well must receive preservice instruction in issues specific to teens and young adults to help with postschool adjustment.

Visibility Versus Invisibility

It is commonly assumed that the more visible the disability, the more disadvantages will be present in terms of the child's attitudes and integration in the mainstream (see Chapter 1 discussion of stigma), but some parent reports are mixed.

The mother of a teenager with cerebral palsy, unintelligible speech, and cognitive impairments known to one of us (F. P.) reported in retrospect that her daughter's disability posed definite disadvantages but was also advantageous in some respects. When she needed to speak or engage in other motor movements, her disability was apparent and contributed to exclusion, low expectations, and discrimination based on appearance. On the other hand, the visibility of her disability resulted in school recognition that she had some needs. Evaluations were completed expeditiously and services (although not always the appropriate ones) were provided in a timely manner.

> No one ever argued that a problem existed, because it was apparent. This was helpful in our quest for services. However, whenever H. experienced any new problem, it was always blamed on her existing disability as if that was a catchall reason for anything that occurred. This was not helpful as it precluded the ability to obtain good diagnostic information, gain new perspectives, or alter services. (Anonymous, personal communication, spring 1997)

Youth with "invisible" but real disabilities are often unidentified or mislabeled because of the invisibility of their disorder to the untrained professional. Youth with these disorders who remain unidentified by transition age are probably achieving far below potential or out of frustration with repeated failure have allowed their behaviors to meet the preconceived notions of their "judges," who may be teachers, parents, or peers.

Need for Employment or Community-Based Experience Prior to School Completion

Although legislation has brought about changes in secondary education for youth with disabilities, many are still completing high school without paid or unpaid job experience. Lack of such experience increases the likelihood of difficulty in acquiring or maintaining employment because now these individuals not only have to face obstacles posed by the disability but must do so in a competitive job market where many nondisabled job seekers have previous experience in part-time or summer employment. Studies over the past decade indicate that paid work experience prior to high school graduation is a positive indicator of future employment success (Hasazi, Gordon, & Row, 1985; Kohler, 1993).

This reality should again reemphasize the need for students with disabilities to receive direct skill training and work experiences in real settings through the mechanism of transition planning. Implementation of such experiences requires collaboration between schools, families, and agency providers as part of the transition team for each individual. Transition teams may recommend community-based learning, which provides learning outside of traditional classroom settings in actual job sites. An extension of this exists in transitional and supported employment programs that help locate positions for adults with disabilities, provide on-the-job training with a job coach, and gradually remove the job coach when the job tasks and job-related social skills are mastered.

Gerber et al. (1990) obtained self-reports from 133 adults with disabilities and concluded that the difficulties experienced in the school years related to their learning disabilities persisted into adulthood. These persistent difficulties may affect job acquisition and maintenance and therefore further substantiate the need for specific preventative and interventive approaches prior to school completion.

INADEQUATE COLLABORATION BETWEEN PRACTITIONERS, AGENCIES, AND EDUCATIONAL ENTITIES IN CAREER OR VOCATIONAL PLANNING

The aforementioned obstacles of inadequate teacher preparation and lack of employment experience are related to poor multiagency collaboration in the development of effective transition plans. Individual transition plans (ITPs) should specify anticipated outcomes and should identify community and other resources that can be accessed to address those outcomes. This might include vocational assessments and education, work-based learning, or vocational or rehabilitation counseling. Planning such as this requires the educational system charged with monitoring the ITP to have a good working knowledge of which agencies, family supports, and community resources should be accessed and to have the ability to actively engage them in transition planning. Although this is beginning to happen with more frequency and efficiency, several problems arise from the mandate that one entity monitor what it cannot necessarily control. The educational entity can invite other parties to the ITP but cannot enforce their presence. Many state vocational rehabilitation offices will not serve youth until they are 18 years old and may not actually attend an ITP meeting until the youth is almost finished with school. Parents may be receiving assistance from various private practitioners, but if the parents are unaware that those practitioners have valuable input, or if the practitioner is not knowledgeable about transition law, then critical information may be omitted from the planning process.

Such gaps in collaboration further evidence the need for changes in pre-professional training to include information that may cut across service roles. Everyone must be on the same page.

NEED FOR EFFECTIVE FUTURE PLANNING BY PARENTS

Families with children with disabilities approaching adulthood may be unsure as to how to prepare for the future and uncertain as to what the possibilities are for their children's self-sufficiency. Halpern (1985), in his examination of the foundations of transition, identified needs to improve effective transition planning. He pointed out that one of the most negative results of inadequate connections to the future for youth with disabilities lies in the low or nonexistent expectations parents have for their children's futures: "Their knowledge of both their children's capabilities and the services that would be available left them unable to predict either success or failure" (p. 571). Zetlin and Turner (1985) stated that parents may be unprepared to face transition issues. This should not mean that parents do not think about the future for their children with disabilities, but future planning may depend on a variety of factors, which may include type and severity of disability, prior experiences with professional systems, educational programs, and family support. In addition, for many parents, future planning may be anxiety provoking.

Asked when a parent of a child with disabilities begins to plan for the future, the mother of a 16-year-old with multiple disabilities responded,

> I know that at some point I seriously began to think about the future but it was a gradual process. When H. was born, we knew there were serious problems. For the first few months, we were so concerned with whether or not she would even live that we really were unable to consider even short-term future plans or to anticipate what types of difficulties she might encounter in school let alone any long-term plans for the future. (Anonymous, parent interview, November 1997)

Another parent of a child with a severe disability explained,

> Our present concerns are so important to us at this time that we are not able to dwell on what the future may bring! We are doing the best to see that she has an opportunity to develop to her fullest potential and staying healthy and remaining in our home and community that we cannot even fathom thinking about romantic relationships or career goals! If she can just become more independent than she is today, we will be thrilled. (Anonymous, interview, April 1997)

Brotherson et al. (1988) found that families do plan for the future and are most concerned about residence, vocation, and opportunities to socialize. Turnbull and Turnbull (1988) considered "low parental expectations" as more a result of years of societal shaping rather than as isolated opinions about their children's limitations. They perceived parental expectations as being affected by the expectations and actions of educational programs, the community, professional opinions, and recommendations that accumulated over time.

INDIVIDUAL TRANSITION PLANS

The advent of mandatory transition plans in special education legislation appears to have facilitated future planning for several reasons. Mandated transitional planning for students identified as having special educational needs has by necessity increased awareness on the part of both educational professionals and families who must be involved in the process. Bridges between school and vocational or employment settings have been strengthened, including a move away from automatic segregated settings as desired outcomes and further explorations of all options instead. Increased representation of individuals with disabilities in community activities, higher education, and employment settings has resulted in gradual changes in societal expectations.

Despite advances over the past decade in the area of transition planning, it remains an overwhelming task to attempt to sort through the policies, laws, and regulations as well as the maze of adult social service and vocational rehabilitation organizations unassisted. If parents are to help their children make decisions about the future and assist in facilitating opportunities that will increase the likelihood of adjustment, they need access to available information on options early and often at various developmental phases.

Embedded in transition legislation is not just the involvement of the parents but the recognition that the child's desires for the future are of critical importance in the planning process and need to be included and addressed. Therefore transition plans invite and demand the participation of the student as well as the parents. It is of utmost importance that parents and professionals invite youth with special needs to consider their likes and dislikes and their visions of their own future. Dowdy et al. (1990) investigated self-perceptions of students with learning disabilities regarding future goals. The results showed that parents provided the most assistance in decision making regarding vocational career choices for the future. Friends were listed as next most helpful, with special educators and vocational rehabilitation counselors listed as the least helpful. When asked about desires for additional assistance regarding vocational educational options, learning-disabled students did want further assistance in career exploration, job seeking, and independent living skills. The study results imply that despite higher numbers of students with learning disabilities entering postsecondary programs or jobs, more relevant assistance is needed by professionals to optimize choices regarding the future.

In discussing future planning, families identify residence, socialization, and employment as the areas of their greatest concern (Brotherson et al., 1988). Morningstar et al. (1995) found that students identified their families as most influential in career plans, but through "informal role models" rather than through any formalized planning process. It is noteworthy that extended, as well as immediate, family members seemed to influence future planning. In the same group of students, few identified school vocational experience as having a major effect regarding decisions about the future. Students in the sample envisioned living and working near family or extended family in the future and considered this factor in decisions about where to attend postsecondary training programs. Few identified adult service systems as a planned source of support for independent living skills.

Families, whether they are cognizant of it or not, may be the most important support and advocacy system for future planning. Parents, however, indicated needs for more formalized assistance in providing work experiences, educational support, and location of future residence for their children (Hanley-Maxwell et al., 1995).

At times, future planning may be facilitated by exposure to past experiences of others and reflections on the all-too-quick passage of time. When asked about regrets, the parent of a teenager said,

It was apparent fairly early that support services would be needed to ensure an appropriate education. Our family moved to another state to ensure this. Despite years of self-advocacy, involvement of professionals, and assistance to our child, my regret is that we accepted too many compromises in light of fleeting time. Perhaps we felt that being proactive, nonadversarial, and giving the system new chances each year would eventually pay off. Perhaps we felt that moving to another state and starting over was the compromise that would ensure appropriate services. It wasn't. We had searched for a place where we could engage in our chosen professions and where good educational programs existed. In retrospect I would have to say that we should've investigated the best private program and gone wherever that was even if it meant renegotiating our own positions and careers. It is difficult to reconcile that faced with a teenager soon to be making her own way, years of inadequate programs despite glorious written documentation, have resulted in untapped potential, decreased self-esteem, and social isolation. The sum total of the person she ends up being is in part a result of the opportunities or lack thereof that we did or didn't provide. The enormity of this realization is overwhelming and makes other aspects of life pale by comparison. I would love to have the opportunity to turn the clock back. (Anonymous, personal communication, October 1995)

The pervasive effects of special needs are cumulative and cut across all areas of functioning. Although this may be evident to those family members who have witnessed the results, others may assume that the youngster's behaviors are the cause of the problem rather than the result.

STRATEGIES FOR PROACTIVE ENGAGEMENT IN THE TRANSITION PROCESS

Since the great majority of practitioners are transients in the lives of individuals with disabilities, it is reasonable to assume that contact with the student-client has been initiated at some point along the life span continuum of the individual and is limited in duration. Therefore, to make the most expeditious use of time, it is imperative that professionals working with transition-aged youth not only understand the specific obstacles faced in the past but employ proactive strategies from the outset that are likely to result in positive outcomes.

TREAT THE CLIENT AS AN INDIVIDUAL

When we lost the concept of the family doctor to specialization, we also lost a great deal of knowledge and personalization. The family "doc" who made house visits and treated sisters, brothers, and parents knew a great deal about the nuclear family, intergenerational dynamics, environment, habits, and interests that is missed in today's highly specialized society. Although in many other ways we have seen great technological advances, we have become less personal and more fragmented in the process. This situation parallels changes in human service professions over time. Our increased specialization has promoted the idea that we should identify the disorder and see if it can be fixed. Although this may be the method of choice for diagnosing an automotive problem, this approach has not proved as successful in working with individuals with disabilities.

One of the greatest obstacles faced by those with disabilities is that the disability is seen first rather than the person. This approach sets the stage for the subsequent analysis of limitations or dysfunctional behaviors and tends to preclude seeing "the person" as a whole. Many parents who have endured intimidating IEP meetings (see Chapter 3) may liken the experience to that of a lab dissection in which their child is analyzed part by part. Since transition law is based on improving outcomes for individuals with disabilities in employment, independent living, and community participation, practitioners must understand the "whole person" first in terms of personality, strengths, and interests. In this way, characteristics related to the disability become an integral part of the person rather than a sole identifying factor.

INVOLVE THE FAMILY

As noted in Chapter 1, the individual with a disability has not developed in a vacuum but in a family system that is unique. Attitudes and involvement of the parents, the presence of siblings or other family members, opportunities provided, exposure afforded, dependency issues, work demands of family members, and living environment are just a few of the factors that must be considered in actualizing potential. The critical nature of family involvement has been well documented as a source of support, advocacy, and information integral to potential success, yet families routinely report that their input has been minimized or ignored or that professionals are condescending to them (Marshak, Prezant, Cerrone, & Seligman, 1997).

In addition to using parents as a good informational source, practitioners need to help parents understand how to access and effectively use information (see Laborde and Seligman, 1991, model in Chapter 8). Parental knowledge of rights is a good place to begin. Parents are frequently amazed on being informed of the numerous rights they have. One of those rights, of course, is to act as part of their child's transition team, provide and solicit feedback, and assist in developing objectives. Practitioners should encourage families to attend these meetings; ask questions; take notes; bring someone with them to support or advocate; and obtain copies of all evaluations, transition plans, and other documents that may be part of the child's school records. Parents should also be informed that they have the right to have test results explained, to agree or disagree with professional opinions, and to request independent evaluations (see Chapter 3). Although most parents welcome such information, there are parents who do not have the time, inclination, or personal resources to deal with these issues. To assist their children, it may be necessary for professionals to address these underlying issues. Sometimes connecting parents to other parents with similar concerns is helpful.

INCREASE LEVELS OF AWARENESS AND INFORMATION ABOUT TRANSITION LEGISLATION AND COMPONENTS OF TRANSITION PLANNING

To effectively involve the family in transition planning, the practitioner must understand the multiple systems with which the family typically interacts.

Developing a good working knowledge of transition law under both the Individuals With Disabilities Education Act of 1990 (IDEA; P.L. 101–476) and the Rehabilitation Act of 1973 (P.L. 99–506) is extremely important. The interaction of private practitioners with transition planning can be a critical factor in developing effective plans. The need to understand adult service system eligibility and operations is critical and enhances envisioning the bigger picture regarding postschool outcomes.

In 1990, IDEA provided a federal definition of transition services as

> a coordinated set of activities for a student, designed within an outcome oriented process, which promotes movement from school to post-school activities, including post-secondary education, vocational training, integrated employment (including supported employment), continuing and adult education, adult services, independent living, and/or community participation. (Section 602[30], 20 U.S.C. 1401)

This definition put teeth into recommendations that had been made by practitioners, researchers, and families for years. The inclusion of outcomes beyond high school completion made it possible to explore modifications to programs and community-based experiences beyond the walls and requirements of traditional high school settings. IDEA went on to describe transition services, activities, and regulations regarding monitoring focused on the needs and interests of the student rather than on graduation requirements of a particular program.

The written documentation of transition services is accomplished through the already-existing individualized education plan (IEP), which needs to include

> A statement of the needed transition services for students beginning no later than 16 and annually thereafter (and when determined appropriate for the individual, beginning at age 14 or younger), including when appropriate, a statement of the interagency responsibilities or linkages (or both) before the student leaves the school setting. (Section 602A, 20 U.S.C. 1401 A)

In other words, a formal transition plan must be developed for students whose IEPs in the past have documented needed educational services.

Employment

The transition team must consider the interests and skills of the student and examine the likelihood of competitive versus supported employment. If the student has specific career interests, it is important to assess his or her present skills related to success in that field. Determination must be made of the preparation the student will need and any accommodations that are required. Some students may be able to anticipate competitive employment whereas others will require supported employment programs involving job coaches. In some instances, preparation may not be for a specific job but for general employment-related skills.

Postsecondary Activities

The team must consider possible training options beyond high school, whether they be college, vocational programs, or other skill training, and identify needed skills and accommodations in anticipation of these outcomes (i.e., assistance in identifying possible programs, extended time on college placement tests, vocational assessments, postsecondary training programs, shadowing experiences, etc.).

Independent Living

Some students with disabilities continue to live with their families after formal schooling ceases and this must be considered in transition planning. Personal preferences of the individual and family are of the utmost importance here. Although some individuals may be able to live independently without supports, others may need group homes or skilled care facilities. The transition team needs to consider the level of daily living skills and needs for further assistance in school, home, or community settings.

Adult Service Systems

The transition team must identify possible adult service organizations that the student might anticipate receiving services from and involve representatives of those agencies in efforts to achieve a smooth transition from entitlement programs to eligibility programs. Examples of such agencies are vocational rehabilitation, mental health/mental retardation (MH/MR), Social Security, supported employment programs, and adult advocacy groups.

Community Participation

To enhance full inclusion in the community, consideration must also be given to recreation and leisure activities, opportunities for social interactions, and development of personal and social skills.

Implications of Transition Legislation

A good working knowledge of IDEA's coverage of transition is of the utmost importance when practitioners are working with families who have children approaching adulthood. Agency evaluations that document needs but recommend only "whatever the school has available" or that totally omit recommended services that the youngster needs but the evaluator does not believe are available in typical schools do a great disservice to the individuals with disabilities who rely on such agencies as specialists and to the parents who may or may not have the necessary information.

Two points should be noted here for practitioners and families. The first is that according to IDEA it is the student's individual needs that drive the transition plan rather than some other convenient method of determining services. This does not necessarily mean the child must be provided with the best program, but the plan must meet the child's needs so that he or she can make reasonable progress. It does mean that a high school senior with a severe hearing loss who uses sign language may need that service to make progress and so it must be provided at public expense. Many youngsters in need of specific services (not all educational) have had to forgo them because professionals may have told the parents that the child needs a service, but when it comes to documenting this in writing, the resulting evaluation phrases like "may benefit from" rather than "needs" fail to ensure delivery of services. Despite the fact that many people would "benefit from" a vacation abroad, not many actually "need" one to progress with life in a successful manner, but it is an everyday occurrence for real needs of youth with disabilities to be described only as services they "could benefit from." It is imperative that practitioners, whether they are counselors, psychiatrists, physical therapists, vocational educators, classroom teachers, or others, understand the implications of the specific wording they use in their recommendations and evaluation reports. Terms like "may benefit from" or "could be beneficial" frequently are ignored because of the understatement or lack of emphasis and result in no service being provided, which may negatively impact the long-range outlook for an individual. It is a professional's obligation to firmly state needed services rather than to project what might be reasonable or expected from an agency, provider, or educational entity.

The second point relates to the fact that transition law is relevant not only for educators in the school setting but for all practitioners working with families. Practitioners reading this text whose expertise may be outside the direct educational setting may assume that this information is not applicable to them because of the school-based terminology. This is a frequent misconception, which occurs because transition law is framed in special education legislation. It is just as important, however, that the rehabilitation counselor, psychologist, state vocational rehabilitation specialist, and representatives of other related disciplines understand the components of transition law, for they are integral to its success. The education agency is charged with monitoring development and implementation in collaboration with other agencies.

The intent of transition legislation is that of a vision beyond traditional educational programs and therefore must involve individuals outside of traditional educational settings. This requires modifications not only in school instruction but in a host of other areas as well. For instance, if a high school senior with disabilities had an interest in becoming a store clerk, he or she needs more than an academic knowledge of rudimentary reading and writing skills and may need to sharpen social skills and time management skills. The student might need on-site experience with a job coach to learn the specific job tasks or counseling related to self-esteem. Furthermore, the student may need information and experience with the public transportation system. Consideration would need to be given to whether the student will live with parents or in a group home or what skills might assist him or her with independent living. There is a need to be concerned with the student's social life and place in the community. In other words, the goal is to access needed supports and services that are necessary to facilitate the student's integration into the community.

Transition plans allow students to design such programs to meet their needs while they are still in school. Job shadowing, auditing programs, work-study, vocational assessment and training, learning interview strategies, and community-based instruction are just a few of the items on a menu limited only by imagination. In fact, it may even be easier to accomplish the plan when a student has a more rather than less significant disability. Students with mild disabilities may be more able to pursue higher education, but to do so must meet certain criteria in academic coursework. Because of this, they may have less flexibility in deviating from traditional academic curriculum.

Numerous family and professional supports (many outside of direct educational instruction) may be required to ensure a smooth transition, and no one person can be responsible for implementing all required transition activities in isolation.

FACILITATE UTILIZATION OF VOCATIONAL ASSESSMENT, SPECIAL EDUCATION, AND COUNSELING AS OUTCOME-RELATED TOOLS

In addition to written guidelines pertaining to planning and writing transition plans, IDEA also increased the need for collaboration between three related fields, vocational assessment, special education, and counseling, that have served individuals with disabilities, but often in a fragmented way.

If vocational assessment is a process that helps delineate vocational interest and capability, this is a tool that should be used in planning for all transition-aged youth. Informal and formal vocational assessments and inventories used prior to high school completion can be invaluable in targeting vocational future planning for training, technical education, or further academic preparation. Because this type of assessment can occur across professional roles, it is imperative that someone on the transition team addresses this issue. Parents should be encouraged to ask about present vocational assessment options in the school and initiate such assessment through the transition plan process; explore careers with their youth; encourage prevocational electives in high school; and request the inclusion of career preparation and exploration activities like shadowing and internships (National Information Center for Children and Youth With Disabilities [NICHCY], 1990). As discussed in the next chapter, vocational assessment outcomes are greatly affected by the perspective of the practitioner. A practitioner who is not creative and used to solving disability-related problems often discourages viable options.

FOCUS ON DEVELOPING SELF-DETERMINATION, SOCIAL NETWORKS, AND EMPLOYMENT EXPERIENCE

Because lack of self-determination, poor socialization skills, and lack of work experience are three factors that have been repeatedly identified as major obstacles to transition, these are areas that practitioners, educators, and families must specifically and intentionally address. These are the gaps that exist, in part, because of fragmented methods of service delivery, and addressing these issues requires the concerted effort of families and providers working in tandem. We should be assessing present levels of self-advocacy, choice making, and sense of self-esteem or control. What can we do to assist this person become more independent? What types of informal, social opportunities are available to enhance community participation? What types of employment experience can be designed? The transition plan team is the perfect vehicle for this cross-analysis and discussion. Becoming a counselor in training for the local YMCA, doing volunteer work in a nursing home, or joining a local youth group are community-based experiences that could address needs in this area.

ACT AS A LIAISON OR NETWORK ORGANIZER

Families of youth with disabilities may be involved with numerous service providers in various systems and settings (see Laborde and Seligman, 1991, model in Chapter 8). This can be confusing, particularly when providers do not communicate with each other and the information they provide to the family and individual might either reinforce or conflict with previous recommendations made by other professionals. In some states, additional professional roles have been created to ensure that families and individuals do not fall through the cracks. Unfortunately, this becomes another bureaucracy with yet another set of user-unfriendly rules and regulations introducing more professionals and agencies into the mix. Professionals must reevaluate the boundaries of their "jobs," and when they are working with youth with disabilities, those boundaries must extend beyond four walls of an office. Professionals must be able to link families to needed services or individuals and to other families that can provide support. It is also critical that all professionals working with a family during this period should be actively involved in the transition planning team. If the youth has not yet graduated from high school, professionals should ask about the transition plan and indicate a willingness to be involved regardless of status as a teacher, therapist, psychologist, and so on.

Assist the Family in Formulating Future Visions

Because youth with disabilities tend to rely on informal family networks in planning their future, decisions about residence, schooling, and employment may be influenced more by this person-centered network than by an array of formalized educational systems or service agency bureaucracies. For this reason, conveying accurate information and initiating long-term planning with parents is essential. Professionals can assist families in defining future visions by helping to identify current beliefs or practices in the family dynamics that may either facilitate or obstruct future progress. If parents believe that the educational system or service agency system is ultimately responsible for their child's success or failure, they may not be as actively engaged. Regardless of our professional efforts or the parents' knowledge level, they, at times unknowingly, appear to be the conduit to the future. Professionals should be utilizing this information and viewing parents as a type of "middlemen" who require an array of formal and informal supports to act as informed but informal role models for their children.

Ensure That Parents Have Information on Adult Service Systems

Because procedures and implementation of transition plans vary from school to school, professionals must be sure that families will be able to assist their youth in accessing adult services if they have not already been ruled eligible. The two major systems to know about are vocational rehabilitation, which provides job training and placement, and the Social Security Administration, which helps with medical coverage and monetary assistance for individuals with disabilities (NICHCY, 1993). Vocational rehabilitation offices in each state were empowered to assist people with disabilities prepare for and enter the workforce in gainful employment. Eligibility for services is based on the existence of a disability that presents substantial barriers to employment despite a desire and capability to work. Available services may include diagnosis and evaluation, rehabilitation counseling, restoration services (e.g., physical therapy, technology services), job training, and placement. In addition, in some areas, local MH/MR agencies provide significant support through counseling, social opportunities, and linkage with supported employment programs.

SYSTEMS CHANGE STRATEGIES

IMPROVING MULTIAGENCY COLLABORATION

Despite the vision and intent for interagency collaboration to pave the way for successful transition to adulthood, restructuring to effectively accomplish this continues to need refinement. Among the more obvious obstacles to interagency collaboration are differing preprofessional preparation, agency structure and regulations that may conflict, movement from entitlement to eligibility systems, and gaps in some services and duplication in others in the face of limited funds and increased demands.

Currently, schools are charged with monitoring and facilitating the multiagency collaboration integral to the transition planning process, but other than identifying and inviting appropriate professionals to transition meetings, they have no power to mandate involvement. According to Gloekler (1993), transition has presupposed that schools could access agency resources and systems that were already inadequate, resulting in fragmentation and gaps in services. Patton and Browder (1988) suggested a series of preliminary stages necessary to facilitate interagency collaboration. They sequentially include a commitment to collaborate through interagency agreements; increased organizational and procedural flexibility; mutual agreement across agencies regarding roles, responsibilities, and funding; and, last, an agreed-upon implementation strategy. They also proposed a "transition specialist" or liaison to support the youth and family in connections with school personnel, adult service systems, and long-term outcomes planning. The increasing frequency of interagency agreements and the use of transition specialists evidence attempts to improve on past practice, but further changes are required.

The introduction of transition specialists provides an anchor person with good working knowledge of transition philosophy, transition law, special education practice, and available resources and services in the community. The concept is a proactive step, but in some states, intermediate units tie geographical areas together with shared resources. Intermediate units in large, rural areas may encompass 10 to 15 separate school districts. Because one transition specialist would be a woefully inadequate resource when shared among 10 to 15 districts, transition coordinators have been appointed to cover local secondary programs. Variations emerge depending on who the transition coordinator is. This may be a person with no training, experience, or comprehension of transition beyond the surface level. This person may be an attendance officer, coach, or other staff member who can take on a few hours more per week. Although the intent is to provide increased coverage, the results may be very inconsistent. Efforts must be made to ensure that individuals responsible for development and orchestration of transition planning in each school have an in-depth understanding of underlying principles, transition needs, effective strategies, and adult systems.

The interagency agreements implying commitment must have teeth in the form of mandates or incentives to guarantee active, consistent engagement of the agencies while youth are still in high school. It is certain that the need to address transition issues will not decrease. Given improved awareness regarding factors critical to positive outcomes, increased family and professional advocacy, and successful efforts to integrate individuals with disabilities into society, current practices and programs will undergo reshaping and refinement. Systems change will result from further definition of needs, yet at the same time will function as a powerful trigger for additional changes in implementing transition.

MODEL PROGRAMS

Due to current legislation and disability advocacy, transition programs that include community-based opportunities, shadowing experiences, vocational and social skills training, modification of traditional curriculum, and assistance with linkage to postsecondary training should be standard operating procedure in high school programs. Legislation has provided the framework and flexibility, which has given rise to variations on a theme and a multiplicity of innovative programs at various levels to facilitate successful transition.

Students with disabilities may be eligible for educational services until the age of 21 or high school completion, and although at one point this option was reserved for students with severe disabilities, it has recently been used in providing transition activities for students with milder disabilities.

Thirteenth year, or transition year, programs for students with learning disabilities run by private educational facilities have increased in popularity. These programs are frequently residential and provide a one-year program beyond high school completion to increase functional academic and vocational skills; improve social skills and self-help skills; and assist in preparation for adult living, working, and possible entrance into postsecondary educational programs.

Disability-specific post–high school programs also provide short-term residential situations focusing on rehabilitation and independence training that address obstacles common to that disability (e.g., spina bifida, deafness). These programs (usually 6 months to 2 years in duration) focus on assessing present skills, examining options, choice making about the future, and developing necessary skills. These programs are funded by a variety of sources, including grants, OVR, MH/MR, private donations, and fees for service.

Colleges across the country have begun to address the issue of students with disabilities who have the potential to complete degree programs and have responded in several ways. In addition to providing services for students with mobility or sensory deficits, many colleges are providing an increasing array of opportunities for young adults with learning disabilities. Precollege summer programs are being offered so that students with disabilities who have plans to enter college can become acquainted with college life prior to actual entrance. Study skills, independent living, and other skills are addressed during such programs. Most colleges, in compliance with the Americans With Disabilities Act of 1990 (ADA), have offices for students with disabilities and provide supports ranging from note taking, tutoring, and test accommodations to comprehensive programs. Commercially available guides (Mangrum & Strichart, 1994) provide detailed descriptions of hundreds of programs and services countrywide.

In many communities, supported/supportive employment programs have evolved from the sheltered workshop concept. These programs, funded by a variety of sources including grants, OVR, MH/MR, and other community resources, function to enhance the employability of adults with disabilities through assessment, training, and placement with the support of job coaches. Individuals who desire and are capable of maintaining paid employment are matched with participating employers and placed either in transitional short-term job experiences or in long-term employment with a job coach who teaches the job task and supports the individuals until they can function independently in the job setting. Several noteworthy model programs have been highlighted in current transition literature.

LIFELINK: A TRANSITION LAB

Lifelink, a program for high school students with mild disabilities, is based on the premise that transition-aged students need opportunities to practice decision making, problem solving, and independence in a controlled but realistic setting while supports are still available to them. In this program students apply transition skills by taking turns living in an apartment for brief periods of time (3–5 days) with a transition coach who assists in teaching on-site living skills and monitors the experience. The apartment is viewed as an education lab experience similar to a cooking or science lab in which learned theory is applied to real situations. Through this innovative strategy, common problems for youth leaving home have been identified as fear of functioning without familiar supports, loneliness, making new friends, coping with problems, dealing with parental concerns, and being expected to have learned independent living skills when in reality school had not prepared them. Competencies addressed through this program are practical living skills, money skills, social skills, organizational skills, medical and personal safety, and community living (Penn State University, 1995; Sparrow, 1996).

PUTTING YOUTH WITH DISABILITIES TO WORK

Putting Youth with Disabilities to Work, a 3-year demonstration project funded by OSERS (Balser, Harvey, & Hornby, 1993), created a business-education partnership administered by a hospital that bridged the gap between the employment community and participating public schools. The project goal was to increase the number of youth with severe disabilities who acquire and maintain paid employment by graduation. Targeted activities to accomplish this included evaluating students' work competencies, assisting with career exploration, providing work experiences, identifying specific supports required, and developing a work history through paid employment. Curriculum development, the business-education partnership, and community integration were the three major program strands. The curriculum development strand incorporated a career development sequence and a social skills program into the high school curriculum. These programs focused on skills necessary for the workplace. The business-education partnership used a combination of job shadowing, community-based assessments, employers in classroom settings, and paid job experience through summer employment. The community was involved through the formation of a business advisory committee, parent forums, and agency agreements. Data collected from this demonstration project identified paid employment as the single project intervention significantly related to postgraduation employment.

PROJECT WORK

Project Work, a comprehensive high school transition program piloted in Southern California, included four components: employability skills training, family involvement, adult agency referral, and on-the-job support. In implementing an "employability skills curriculum" in the classroom, instruction targeted self-advocacy, family involvement in employment plans, and methods for job search and retention (Patton, de la Garza, & Harmon, 1997). Some specific employability skills addressed were identifying jobs of interest, job interview strategies, qualities of good employees, and job-related social skills. These skills were taught in the context of a 15-week class, during which students were placed in community-based jobs to apply classroom-based instruction with the support of a job specialist. The job specialist involved families through home visitations and provision of information regarding adult agency referrals. Educational activities and support for families encouraged continuity. A vocational rehabilitation counselor worked with the students to begin referrals for services that might provide supports while the students were still in school.

Analysis of the pilot program revealed that 80% of the students were placed in paid job sites and 88% became clients of the vocational rehabilitation system prior to graduation. This program has been replicated in numerous locations in California and Florida.

DISABILITIES, OPPORTUNITIES, INTERNETWORKING, AND TECHNOLOGY (DO IT)

To address the underrepresentation of individuals with disabilities in science, math, and technological fields, the University of Washington, with primary funding from the National Science Foundation, developed DO It, which uses the Internet to link high school students with disabilities to mentors, faculty, scientists, college students, and mathematicians (many of whom have disabilities). These role models support and encourage students to pursue interests in science, math, and technology. DO IT participants are loaned computers and other hardware to enable electronic communication. Through this process, students not only link up with mentors but learn to use Internet resources to explore career options, develop friendships, and do research for school or community projects. Students may then participate in a 2-week precollege summer program at the university that provides opportunities to participate in adapted labs, live on a college campus, and practice social skills (University of Washington, 1996).

COMMUNITY LIFE OPTIONS

A field-initiated research grant from the National Institute on Disability and Rehabilitation Research, Community Life Options developed a supported recreation program for individuals with developmental disabilities. Based on lack of evidence to indicate that integrated employment ensures social opportunities in personal life (Gliner & Sample, 1993), this model focuses on increasing awareness of community social activities, encouraging and supporting participation, facilitating relationship building, and developing long-term support networks. A recreation specialist acts as a liaison between the individual, the Life Options team, and the community by assessing needs, designing interventions, and assisting the client in developing social skills.

CONCLUSION

Proactive strategies on the part of professionals, systems changes, family support, and multiagency collaboration are prerequisites to successful transition to adulthood for youth with disabilities. Regardless of how sophisticated or tolerant our society becomes, people with disabilities will continue to need to be viewed as people first. As long as society's sole focus is on "fixing deficits" or "normalizing," we will fail to truly integrate youth with disabilities into the adult world on an equal level. Respect, value, dignity, and high expectations must be part of the message that youth with special needs receive. As one parent said:

> The greatest challenges my child faces are not in the limitations posed by his disability but those posed by the restricted and narrow views of others who see him as less worthy or able, who see him through his disability first rather than the person he is. Society preaches tolerance, acceptance, and goodness but is hypocritical in practice. (Anonymous, personal communication, November 1995)

To ensure effective transition for all youth with disabilities, we must not wait until they are 16 or even 14 years of age to think about future plans or determination of interests. We must begin with young children, capitalizing on their strengths, providing opportunities, and encouraging positive visions of the future in their minds' eyes. We must encourage the collaboration of related disciplines in understanding each other's roles and the ways in which we should mesh to complement rather than contradict each other. We must attend not only to employment outcomes or skills but to socialization, lifestyles, and that which determines a sense of belonging for each individual. We must make efforts to ensure a sense of self-direction, determination, and efficacy for young adults with disabilities. We must constantly reinforce the notion that each person is unique and has untapped potential. If there is a shred of truth to the concept of self-fulfilling prophecy, then it is critical that we offer a positive prophecy as a starting point for youth entering the world of adulthood.

CHAPTER 6

Adult Children
with Disabilities

As discussed in preceding chapters, the developmental needs of individual family members naturally differ, sometimes conflict, but are always interwoven. The divergence of developmental needs of individual family members is striking by the time a son or daughter with a disability reaches adulthood. Typically, adulthood is characterized by immersion in vocational life, making marital choices, and establishing one's own family. This pattern holds true for some adults with disabilities. Others engage in these activities but find the timelines for establishing family and vocation to be delayed in comparison to the norm. Still other adults with disabilities have lives that differ significantly because of lack of access to the same life opportunities or lack of capacities for certain activities. In adulthood there is a need for productivity and generativity. Erikson (1982) used the term *generativity* to describe the need to feel that when one's life is eventually finished, one has left behind a meaningful accomplishment—that is, one feels one's life has made a difference.

The awareness of one's mortality that often accompanies middle age frequently results in increased parental desire (and sometimes urgency) to "get things settled" with adult sons and daughters who have disabilities. Circumstances related to disability often conflict with the desire for settled matters, however. First, feelings of mastery regarding parenting often decrease as the child matures and are at a relatively low point when the offspring reach adulthood (Heller, 1993). This lack of mastery is evident in the following observations of one father, who described how he changed as his son with disabilities physically matured:

> I feel more frustration in that I can't relieve his frustration, so my feelings about Robin and my attitudes towards him are certainly much different than they were when he was young. Simply, as he has changed, I have changed; not in a way that makes me less accepting. As I just mentioned, I feel more frustrated about Robin now than I ever did before. . . . I just wish I could help him recapture the kind of attitudes he displayed as a youngster. I wish I could relieve his frustration. I wish I could make him a happier person. But I don't know how to do this and I don't know whether anyone can do it. It just bugs me; it is a constant thing. (quoted in Helsel & Helsel, 1978, pp. 105–106)

In addition to diminished feelings of mastery, many parents (particularly fathers) feel an increased sense of stigma about their grown child (Gumz & Gubrium, 1972). Brotherson, Backus, Summers, and Turnbull (1986) wrote, "Pushing a 4-year-old child with a severe disability through a shopping mall is far less stigmatizing than pushing a 34-year-old man or woman with a severe disability" (p. 29).

Furthermore, some families experience burnout by the time their children reach adulthood. Mallory (1986) described the skewed nature of timing in the family life cycle:

> For most families, the peak of involvement with formal organizations occurs at the middle of the family life cycle when children draw their parents into school-related or recreation-related associations or networks. Families with handicapped children may experience an acceleration of this pattern by being compelled to interact with formal organizations much earlier in their life cycles. This, in turn, may lead to a desire on the part of families to decrease their involvement as their children approach school age. (p. 323)

Given that families often feel depleted by childhood challenges, one can imagine how this is compounded by the time the offspring reaches adulthood. For some, financial drain contributes to this sense of depletion. The average family of an adult with developmental disabilities was found to spend 20% of its pretax income on related expenses that could not be reimbursed (Fujiura & Braddock, 1992).

Because individual developmental timelines are often skewed when disability is present, some adults with disabilities who live with their parents settle in and adapt to the lifestyle of their parents, who are 20 to 40 years older and may be weary from struggles to obtain appropriate services and dealing with a cadre of professionals on behalf of their child. As a result, adults with a disability may be living a lifestyle more suitable for someone a generation older.

Referring to families with a son or daughter with a developmental disability, Fewell (1986) noted,

> When a handicapped child becomes an adult, decisions must be made as to where the person will live, and the level of care he or she will need. These decisions will often determine how the child will spend his or her adult life, and the changes will be relatively few during the ensuing years. (p. 18)

The lifestyle of persons with physical disabilities may similarly be at odds with their developmental needs. For example, it is not unusual for adults with disabilities that impair mobility who require adaptive housing to find accessible residences only in buildings that are primarily established for persons who are elderly. A terrible lack of synchronicity between developmental needs and unnatural lifestyle restrictions is evident in the lives of relatively young persons who live in nursing homes due to the lack of more age-appropriate alternatives.

QUALITY OF LIFE

The propensity toward premature "settling in" contributes to a tedium that characterizes the lives of all too many adults with disabilities. In midlife, less attention is directed to the quality of life, developmental growth, and social roles of persons with developmental disabilities (Seltzer, 1993). Seltzer (1993) noted that this pattern fosters the perception that little can be done to help adults with developmental disabilities reach their potential after they have reached age 30 or 35. As the individual ages further the tediousness of activities often mounts.

> Advancing age is an experience where close relationships are few, and growing fewer, where daily activities, whether in the residential or vocational setting, are characterized by the sameness day by day and where leisure-time activities are limited to watching television, going on occasional shopping trips, or attending day programs in agencies. . . . The looking forward to which most of us have been acculturated seems to reveal nothing but a blank page for retarded persons entering middle age. (Koch, 1986, pp. 1–2)

Persons with developmental disabilities have long been characterized as having less desire and relatively fewer needs for meaningful activity. This is all too well illustrated by the comments of the Attorney General in Saskatchewan in 1944 as he campaigned to temporarily house persons with developmental disabilities in airport buildings: "Nothing could be better for the mentally defectives than having the monotony of life broken by the taking off and landing of aircraft" (quoted in Schwier, 1994, p. 35). Although this comment is dated, the basic premise unfortunately carries on relatively unchanged. Currently, many professionals feel that persons with developmental disabilities can hold jobs that are too boring for others. Although there are always some individuals (with or without disabilities) who acclimate to tedious work, the association between developmental disabilities and tolerance for boredom is a myth. Graffam and Turner's (1984) study of social interactions at a sheltered workshop suggested that some seemingly inappropriate behaviors are actually resourceful attempts to escape boredom:

> The restricted mobility and heightened dependency that characterize the lives of workshop clients precludes, to a large extent, the possibility of increased social activity. Given the limitation of social resources, it does not seem surprising that workshop clients might attempt to construct an event-filled life from the resources that are available by maximizing the eventfulness potential of seemingly commonplace occurrences or other events of apparently little significance. (p. 127)

Graffam and Turner (1984) described an informal social system governed by social norms that reciprocally accept and encourage attempts to raise the level of "eventfulness" in the workshop setting (which serves as the hub of many people's social lives):

> By elevating mundane events to a more profound level of experience and by generating or exaggerating personal problems from events in the daily routine, individuals may gain immediate attention and support from peers, as well as gaining a sense of having an event-filled existence. One then appears loved or successful, as well as "busy," all of which are considered characteristics of the ideal normal adult. (p. 129)

It is important to point out that not all persons with developmental disabilities experience unusual levels of tedium. Edgerton (1988) found persons with mild mental retardation who were deinstitutionalized and living in the community (without services from the mental retardation service system) had levels of adjustment that paralleled those of persons in the general population with similar socioeconomic status and education.

The problem is not simply ensuring "eventfulness" and preventing tedium; it is recognizing that the need for meaning in one's life is not diminished due to disability. The comments of Michael Dalziel, who was interviewed (at age 32) regarding his life at Orillia, a state institution where he was placed due to mental retardation, reflect this drive for meaning in life:

> I'm gettin' old you know. I try to be nice all the time, but I run outta patience. I want the world to listen to me. I want the world to understand I'm here for a reason. What did God put me here for? Cause I'm a teacher. I'm a student and a teacher and I teach people things. I know a lot about history and stuff, and I can teach them about what Orillia is like and it isn't all that great. (quoted in Schwier, 1994, p. 43)

Adults with mental retardation, who are not likely to have a spouse or children, may be in particular need of a sense of generativity (Seltzer, 1993). Referring to the developmental stages described by Erikson (1982), Seltzer (1993) pointed out that we rarely provide them with the opportunity to assume civic and social responsibility, thereby hindering their abilities to progress with the developmental need of generativity versus stagnation.

PREDICTIONS

Tedium and the failure to encourage options in life is, in part, due to predictions of what will be feasible and what will result in failure. These predictions often take the form of assumptions that have a great bearing on whether adult children are prepared for and encouraged to pursue major life activities. Under the most ordinary of circumstances, humans are poor at predicting outcomes, however, and when the element of disability is added, predictions tend to be even less accurate. As discussed in Chapter 4, the phenomenon of *spread* greatly affects the accuracy of our perceptions of people with disabilities. The reaction of most persons (who do not have disabilities) to disability is so strong that it serves as a catalyst for automatic inferences about a person's abilities and character. These inferences often involve the assumption of additional impairments and emotional problems. For example, impaired speech often leads to automatic inferences of impaired intelligence and personality disturbance.

PROFESSIONAL BIAS

Professionals have been found to be no different from the general population with regard to the extent to which they exhibit biased perceptions (Meehl, 1960). The extent to which a disability causes a person's appearance to deviate from the norm becomes the basis of judgments regarding "attractiveness." Through spread, these judgments become the basis for far-reaching judgments and predictions. Research has extensively documented how attractiveness evokes positive inferences and a relative lack of attractiveness evokes negative inferences about unrelated characteristics. Professionals in the fields of health, education, and social service all are vulnerable to the "beautiful is good" stereotype (Dion, Berscheid, & Walster, 1972). For example, attractiveness has been found to bias psychologists' appraisals of intelligence (Sandler, 1976) although there is no correlation between these two characteristics (Feingold, 1982). Decisions made by school psychologists regarding inclusion of students with disabilities in regular classes have also been found to be influenced by an attractiveness bias (Elovitz & Salvia, 1982). Persons who are judged as less attractive (by cultural standards) are often seen as having greater degrees of emotional disturbance despite a lack of correlation between these characteristics (Jones, Hansson, & Phillips, 1978). Even prognosis for recovery from traumatic physical disablement has been found to be affected by the extent to which a person fits cultural norms of attractiveness (Bodieri, Sotolongo, & Wilson, 1983).

Parents need to recognize the extent to which professionals' judgments are often subjective and inaccurate. This is especially true in consultations where families may tend to defer to professionals in making some important decisions. In fact, the impact of bias in perceptions of persons with disabilities is strongest in initial encounters, when assessments of potential are often conducted (Felson, 1981).

These biased judgments have a significant impact on planning in adult life. Although the transition process discussed in the preceding chapter emphasizes future planning and making a transition from school to work, these developmental tasks often actually extend far into adulthood. This is due partly to delays stemming from the number of problems that need to be resolved to launch a vocation and partly to the fact that plans created in adolescence often have fallen apart by adulthood. Consequently, plans for the future often have to be reconsidered (or sometimes considered anew) in adulthood.

PSYCHOMETRIC TESTING

Particularly if the individual has a physical disability, family members and professionals need to be wary of professional predictions based on psychometric testing. It is easy to give too much credence to test results. For example, it is well known that performance on intelligence tests has little ability to predict success in a wide range of domains of life, including vocation (McClelland, 1973; Power, 1991). Most of these tests, including those of personality and intelligence, are based on comparisons to norm groups that do not include people with disabilities. Skewed outcomes are often quite striking with tests that attempt to assess psychological variables such as emotional health. For example, questions on instruments such as the Minnesota Multiphasic Personality Inventory (MMPI) that focus on preoccupation with bodily functions may indicate hypochondriacal characteristics in the general population but may reflect realistic concerns for persons with health-related disabilities. Responses of persons with disabilities to many standardized instruments that do not include persons with disabilities in their norm groups often result in overly negative judgments (Allen & Sligar, 1994). In addition, psychometric testing is often conducted without regard for the manner in which a disability affects the reliability and validity of test results. A student of one of us (L. M.), a woman with a severe visual impairment, wrote about her experience with psychometric testing in the course of the Bureau of Visual Services (BVS) deciding whether it was appropriate to encourage and fund her college education:

> I had to go through a series of psychological testing that would determine if I could attend college. I was twenty-three years of age at the time and the psychologist persisted in talking to me as if I were an adolescent. . . . My IQ score was significantly low but the section I scored highest in was grammar. They could not understand how I scored so well in grammar when my reading skills were so low. . . . Because my BVS counselor believed in me, I was given the opportunity to attend college. The psychologist's diagnosis would not have even given me a job at McDonald's. My self esteem concerning my intelligence looked grim until I attended my rehabilitation classes. I was so elated to find out that IQ testing was inaccurate and uneasy to determine for persons with visual impairments, hearing impairments, etc. *Another significant factor to my low IQ score was the fact that the psychologist offered me no accommodations during the testing* [italics added]. (Personal communication, 1996)

The performance of this woman on a test she could barely read because she is legally blind was compared to that of persons who could read the test print and see the test material without difficulty. Furthermore, no attempt was made to understand that low scores were a result of physical disabilities rather than intellectual limitations.

ENVIRONMENTAL FACTORS

A third factor that hinders the accuracy of predictions about the capabilities of persons with disabilities is related to a tendency to overlook the impact of environmental factors. Lewin (1935) described behavior as a function of the person and his or her environment as summarized in the equation $B = P + E$. This basic equation is a useful reminder that we cannot simply look at behavior that is considered inadequate without considering whether modifying the environment will alter the behavior in ways that may open up possibilities for meaningful opportunities. The term environment needs to be used broadly to subsume factors including whether the environment provides high-quality skill training that could remediate behavior or skill deficits. Research on impression formation (Wright, 1983) indicates that when someone deviates from the norm, we are unlikely to consider the impact of the environment in drawing conclusions about his or her behavior. In essence, we overlook the E and believe $B = P$ in a shortsighted manner. The practical implications of this are manifold. For example, we have known adults with developmental disabilities who have difficulty maintaining concentration on sheltered workshop piecework and consequently are told they cannot concentrate long enough on a task to be considered for other kinds of jobs or work in the community. In this manner, the short attention span is considered an intrinsic part of the person, not a possible reaction to a task (or environment) that has grown boring over the years or a meaningless wage.

The term *retarding environment* is pertinent to this discussion. The retarding environment was described by a member of a self-advocacy group for persons with developmental disabilities as follows (as rephrased by Rosenberg, 1994):

> The Retarding Environment means having only other disabled people who have learned how to act retarded as your role models. It means having keepers rather than real teachers. It means that professionals who ought to be helping us to grow and develop and learn how to solve our own problems are trying to manage us as if we are the problem. It means people having low expectations and training us to live *down* to these low expectations. . . . When I graduated from high school, they put me in a sheltered workshop, and promised me they would teach me to be a carpenter. But then I spent the next four and a half years sitting next to the Coke machine sanding blocks of wood, and learning to rock back and forth, and how generally to act retarded like the others. Finally I started *liking* the rocking and the humming of the Coke machine. (p. 177)

The concept of retarding environment is useful also when we think about the life experiences of some people with physical disabilities and the interwoven effects these have on their abilities and the consequent judgments others make of them. Edgerton (1994), who has spent much of his career studying the lives of persons with mental retardation, described the gross inaccuracy of most predictions:

Before I made the first restudy of the 48 individuals released from Pacific State Hospital to live independently, I carefully made predictions about the ways their lives would prove to have changed over the period of a decade. I was right only about half the time and then usually for the wrong reasons. (p. 55)

He also noted that sometimes a spouse who appeared relatively less capable actually did surprisingly well when the more intellectually dominating spouse died.

When predictions are made, families and professionals tend to err on the side of constraints rather than risking failure. The net result was well described by Edgerton (1994):

It is quite clear that the lives of mentally retarded people who live with their parents or residential care providers are overdetermined, one might say, because not only is their present day organized, arranged and regimented by other people, so is their tomorrow and future. What is more, there is very little that mentally retarded people can do in most of these living arrangements that can make a significant difference in their lives. As our years of research in community residential facilities have made only too clear, the lives of people like these are *depressingly predictable* [italics added]. (p. 57)

Personal Impact

A final comment from an adult with a developmental disability (rephrased by Rosenberg, 1994) underscores the personal impact of predictions:

I have learned that being retarded just means being slow, but nobody really knows how far you can keep going, even if you go slow. The other kids learned to read when they were six. I didn't. But if my parents and teachers had decided that because I didn't learn to read when I was six I'd never learn, I never would have learned. . . . I learned to read when I was twelve. (p. 179)

Families and professionals fail to prepare children for activities they assume or predict the children will never be able to handle. The lack of preparation often becomes a self-fulfilling prophecy—that is, if we fail to prepare someone to handle a major life activity, it is quite likely he or she will not be able to manage it. But we are often unaware that the performance deficit may be a consequence of lack of preparation; rather, the failure is attributed to the disability itself. This is one way that negative stereotypes are further solidified.

These observations of factors that undermine the accuracy of predictions regarding the capabilities of persons with disabilities have important practical implications. They pertain to issues of independent living, instrumental roles such as parenting, and vocational choices.

IMPACT ON VOCATIONAL LIFE

Despite the passage of the Americans With Disabilities Act (ADA) in 1990, the rate of unemployment for adults with disabilities remains far higher than that of the general population. According to the U.S. Census Bureau, as of 1994, 52% of adults with disabilities were employed in contrast to about 82% of persons without a disability. The employment rate for women with disabilities was even lower. Only 26% of persons with severe disabilities were employed. In addition to very low rates of employment, those persons with disabilities who are working, are often underemployed. Frank, Karst, and Boles (1989) found that although a college degree certainly helped employment prospects, after graduation only 65% of college graduates with disabilities were employed, in contrast to 89% of college graduates without disabilities. For those employed college graduates with disabilities, a far greater proportion were employed in positions outside of their chosen field of study.

Several factors contribute to this pervasive problem. As stated earlier in the chapter, it is important to understand that behavior is a function of the person and his or her environment ($B = P + E$). Vocational behavior (i.e., performance) of persons with disabilities is impacted by the environment, which includes barriers, attitudes, services, training, and available accommodations. One of the implications for families, professionals, and persons with disabilities is that it is often difficult to predict what will be feasible until one thoroughly examines the numerous resources found in the environment.

Gold's (1978) work with persons with severe and profound levels of retardation illustrates the power of systematic training to make apparently impossible situations possible. Through the use of task-analytic training, he was able to train persons with severe or profound retardation to perform complex assembly tasks so accurately that their error rate was lower than industrial standards. It is important to note that this training was not contingent on the use of highly trained professionals. Gold (1978) found that he could easily train persons with mental retardation to serve as trainers themselves. Although his focus has been on training, his work also pertains to the topic of predicting capabilities.

An important resource, described in Chapter 5, is the vocational rehabilitation system, which provides mandated services in each state. One study of college graduates with disabilities found that those who received services through the vocational rehabilitation system had a 21% rate of unemployment, compared to 67% for those who did not receive services (Frank et al.,

1989). Other valuable resources include the Job Accommodation Network (JAN), an international toll-free consulting service established to provide information so that functional limitations from disability can be circumvented in a way that does not obstruct job performance. The service can be accessed through the Internet at http://www.asel.udel.edu/at-online/. Similar sources of help include Assistive Technology On-Line, which is partially funded by the National Institute on Disability and Rehabilitation Research through the U.S. Department of Education and the National Science Foundation. Resources are also available through the ADA Information Line: 1–800–514–0301(voice); 1–800–514–0383(TDD).

PLANNING FOR THE FUTURE

Making adequate plans for one's offspring generally enables aging parents to face the prospect of their death with greater equanimity (Smith & Tobin, 1989). Some parents do not believe this is possible. One father wrote,

> I suppose that the biggest worry that a parent of a severely handicapped child has is—what happens when I die? And there is no answer to that. As far as I know, there is no way to provide properly for him in the eventuality—at least I don't know of any. . . . You can't amass enough capital to set up a private home for such a person. There just isn't an answer or a way to provide properly for such a child after your death. (quoted in Meyer, 1986, p. 59)

Such concerns over the future of their offspring were echoed by several parents in response to our survey question asking what services parents felt most in need of from professionals. One wrote, "Assure me of good care for him when I die. I have turned down CLAs [community living arrangements] and TLAs [transitional living arrangements]." Another wrote, "Help him be independent enough to work or have further education and learn to be responsible to a job coach or a significant other—so that we can die in peace without worrying about his care as he gets older" (Marshak et al., 1997).

The pain of recognizing that after their death no one may care for their child as well as they do contributes to the fact that a significant proportion of elderly caregivers have not engaged in active planning for their child's residential, financial, and legal security in the future (Smith & Tobin, 1989). An additional factor is that the most common coping strategy of families of persons with disabilities has been found to be consciously maintaining a strong present orientation and choosing to take one day at a time (Turnbull et al., 1986). This pattern coexists alongside a pervasive worry about the future (Heller & Factor, 1994).

Because planning often involves placement outside of the family home, reverberations are often felt throughout the family system. Some elderly parents may not feel they have the strength to face one more loss, such as the loss of their child's companionship. Smith and Tobin (1989) wrote,

> One of the many examples of this phenomenon from our own interviews was an 86-year-old widow who absolutely refused to discuss placement options for her only child, a moderately retarded 60-year-old daughter who helped her mother with housework, prepared snacks for her, and was her sole source of companionship. Only after encouragement from a psychiatrist could this mother bear the pain of being separated from the daughter just long enough for her to attend day programs during the week. For this elderly woman permanent separation from her daughter was unthinkable! (p. 50)

It is not unusual for elderly parents to become dependent on the help with daily tasks and chores that an adult child with a disability can provide (Smith & Tobin, 1989). These parents face the painful dilemma that their ability to retain their own independence in the community may be jeopardized if their child leaves the home (Smith & Tobin, 1989). Other barriers to future planning include guilt, overprotectiveness, a loss of one's primary role as caregiver, loss in supplementary income from disability, and concern over offspring's reaction to environmental changes (Smith & Tobin, 1989).

Without advance planning for care after the death or deterioration of a caretaking parent, the adult with a disability and surviving family members are at risk for devastating disruption. A lifetime of caring can fall apart, as illustrated by a former neighbor of one of us (L. M.), a man in his 50s with Down syndrome. He lived with his parents until their death and then lived in the home of his elderly married brother and his wife. It was clear that they expended a great deal of effort to provide him home-based care even though he was progressively becoming more difficult to manage. When the elderly brother fell and broke his hip, the brother with Down syndrome very quickly was placed in a state institution. Not only was he not prepared to move swiftly from the family home to a large institution but the choice of facilities was made in haste. The facility was too far from the home to monitor the quality of his care or facilitate his adjustment. He died within 6 months from pneumonia following injuries, including broken ribs, from altercations in the state-run facility.

Placement in an appropriate group facility, when precipitated suddenly by parental loss, is also hindered by the fact that this is a particularly bad time during which to assess self-care and social skills. Because of the emotional trauma of loss, the son or daughter may appear to intake workers quite different from the way he or she would under better circumstances (Hollins, 1995).

For these reasons, there is a great need to engage families in the planning process. One project reported significant success in attracting elderly parents of children with developmental disabilities to workshops focused on permanency planning. Because many of these families were apprehensive about using services associated with traditional mental retardation services, these planning workshops were offered through other, more generic social service agencies. For this reason, they were perceived as both useful and nonthreatening (Smith et al., 1994).

Future planning must incorporate the needs and perspectives of the adult child with a disability, the parents, and adult siblings. This often does not occur, however. There appears to be a widespread inattention to the preferences of dependent adults with disabilities. Gold, Dobrof, and Torian (1987) found that many parents of grown children with mild or moderate mental retardation never broached the topic even though some of these adult children had raised it indirectly by discussing the experiences of their peers following parental illness or death. Adult children with disabilities may be anxious while discussing their future, yet it must be recognized that many have thought about the future and have definite preferences. In this regard, Smith and Tobin (1989) found that even when parents understood the preferences of adult children with developmental disabilities, these preferences were often disregarded if they were incompatible with the parents' preferences. For example, parents often place priority on the continuity of a "loving home environment" over other factors, including opportunities for peer interaction (Smith & Tobin,1989).

Plans that are made are often vaguely formulated. Aging parents, particularly those who have remained outside of the formal delivery system, most often hope or assume that a sibling will assume the caretaking role upon their own deterioration or death. Typically this sibling is the oldest female child in the family (Smith & Tobin, 1989). Seltzer and Seltzer (1985) pointed out, however, that there is little research regarding the ability or willingness of siblings and other relatives to accept caretaking responsibilities. Although parents often regard siblings as the best future caretaking option, they often do not engage them directly in the planning process (Heller & Factor, 1993). Reasonable sibling involvement may ease the stress of eventual separation from parents (Seltzer et al., 1991).

Financial planning for the future needs of a grown child with a disability is complex and needs substantial consideration. Professional expertise is often invaluable for a family because of many complications that families may overlook. For example, consideration needs to be paid to the impact of trust funds and alternatives on eligibility for sources of assistance such as SSI and Medicaid. Interested readers can find more comprehensive discussions of this important topic in Turnbull, Turnbull, Bronicki, Summers, and Roeder-Gordon (1989).

CORESIDENCE OF PARENT AND ADULT CHILD

Future planning notwithstanding, approximately 85% of persons with developmental disabilities live with their families (Seltzer & Krauss, 1994); many live at home for most of their lives (Fujiura & Braddock, 1992). As many as one-third of adults with mental illness live with (mostly elderly) parents (Lefly, 1987). Furthermore, a large study conducted by the Learning Disabilities Association of America (1966) found that approximately 32% of their respondents (adults with learning disabilities) continued to live at home.

Although family-based care is not new, changing demographics have introduced important differences in the past few decades. In contrast to previous generations, children with disabilities now generally outlive their parents (Seltzer & Krauss, 1994).

The ratio between potential caregivers and care recipients is also changing. Parents of children with mental retardation, in contrast to those of previous generations, are more likely to have simultaneous responsibility for caring for their own parents due to longer life spans in general (Seltzer & Krauss, 1994). Furthermore, with relatively smaller families, there are fewer siblings to share increased caretaking responsibilities. The impact of these demographic changes is that caretakers are stretched even more thinly.

LIVING OUTSIDE THE SOCIAL SERVICE SYSTEM

A surprisingly large number of families with adult children who have developmental disabilities are described as living outside of the system. Jacobson, Sutton, and Janicki (1985) estimated that only 25% of older families with sons or daughters with mental retardation used formal services. Smith, Fullmer, and Tobin (1994) suggested that this may be a result of purposeful avoidance of the formal service system rather than a lack of knowledge of available services. This observation is supported by their finding that more than 80% of families studied indicated knowledge of service availability. A distancing from the service delivery system appears most pronounced in older families.

Smith et al. (1994) suggested that prior painful experiences with professionals is one factor for this distancing. Taking matters into their own hands, many families were compelled to develop coping skills and now may feel it is "inconceivable that the young professionals in mental retardation agencies could possess the same level of patience, understanding and competence that took them so many years to achieve with their son or daughter with mental retardation" (Smith et al., 1994, p. 31). Older families may be responding to widespread stigmatization in earlier interactions with professionals as well as current perceptions of ageism in the service delivery system (Smith et al., 1994). Smith et al. (1994) also noted that older mothers reported feeling they will be viewed as inadequate by younger and "better educated" professionals: "Thus older parents may feel reluctant to seek help from a service system which they feel stigmatizes both their offspring with mental retardation and themselves" (p. 32).

EMOTIONAL ASPECTS OF CORESIDENCE

It is not our intent to minimize the degree of distress some families feel when they are not able to launch adult children according to typical developmental timelines. But it is important to note that coresidence of adult children with their parents, in general, is not as atypical as many parents believe. Aquilino (1990) reported that the National Survey of Families and Households (NSFH) found 45% of parents between the ages of 45 and 54 had an adult child living at home. As "self-sufficiency" has become increasingly hard to achieve, there has been an increased "elasticity" in parental roles (Seltzer & Krauss, 1994). Although it is often assumed that elderly parents are the recipients of help from grown children, the reverse is very often true. It is not unusual for parents to resume a parenting role with their adult children when the children are faced with life stresses such as unemployment and divorce (Greenberg & Becker, 1988).

Many assumptions about the impact of extended parenting of dependent adult children with disabilities were based on inferences about the effects of caretaking of elderly relatives. Such extrapolations did not prove to be accurate when applied to mothers of grown children with developmental disabilities. A study by Krauss and Seltzer (1993) of more than 400 older mothers who provided in-home care for an adult child with mental retardation underscored these differences. They found that these mothers (who had a mean age of 66) had significantly better morale than caregivers of elderly family members. Comparisons to parents of young children with mental retardation revealed comparatively less stress.

Heller and Factor (1993) identified commonly overlooked sources of caregiver satisfaction for parents of adult children with disabilities. There is often more of a sense of reciprocity than is apparent to the outsider. Heller and Factor (1993) reported that more than half of the older parents reported that their adult children with developmental disabilities prevented them from feeling lonely, more than one-third contributed financially (through SSI), and more than 20% performed chores for parents. Aquilino (1991) also detailed unexpected positive effects experienced by some older mothers when they found themselves unable to retire from an active parenting role. Much less is known about the effects of a prolonged caregiving role on fathers.

Research on factors that mediate caregiver satisfaction have produced interesting results. It is important to note that the extent to which a caregiver derives satisfaction appears to be independent from the extent to which they feel the level of care is burdensome (Heller & Factor, 1993). Actually, many mothers who reported higher caregiver burdens were also relatively more satisfied compared to other caregiving mothers. The researchers assumed that social support would be the primary factor in the mothers' well-being, but the family's social climate (relationships between members) was actually the strongest predictor of mothers' well-being. These mothers did well despite the fact that their social support network outside of the family was much smaller than average. Mothers' well-being also appears to be mediated by the relationship between their adult children. In fact, sibling relationships (including the sibling with mental retardation) was a stronger determinant of maternal well-being than was the mother's own involvement with her children (Seltzer, Begun, Seltzer, & Krauss, 1991).

ADULTS WITH PSYCHIATRIC DISABILITIES

Until now, we have focused on coresidence of adult children with a developmental disability. Many adult sons and daughters with psychiatric disorders live with their parents as well; this is one situation in which the type of disability does very much affect family dynamics. Often coresidence is established and maintained, despite often-overwhelming distress, because the alternatives are even worse. The experiences of one family (Ginny and Joe Talbot and their son Mark) illustrate the trajectory that may lead to coresidence with adult children with relatively more severe psychiatric disorders:

> The social worker at the hospital gave us very little help or assistance as we looked around for decent housing for our son. We did all the leg work ourselves. We went to the mental health center in our county and got names and addresses of group homes.
>
> When we started looking at these places, Mark didn't like any of them. Neither did I for that matter. For the most part, the homes were filthy, smelly, disgusting and degrading. They looked like the snake pits that deinstitutionalization was

supposed to eliminate. I was shocked. If my son had not become mentally ill I would never have known that we—in our country—could tolerate such places. (quoted in Backlar, 1995, pp. 48–49)

Backlar (1995) described how the Talbots finally found a relatively good group home:

That didn't work out either. It had looked OK to us at the beginning, but it turned out that the supervision wasn't very good. These mentally ill folk were a pushover for anyone selling drugs, so drugs were real prevalent and there was no one willing to do nothing about it—maybe it was impossible. (p. 49)

This unsuccessful placement was followed by Mark living on the streets. Backlar (1995) described the Talbots' decision to have their adult son live at home:

The excruciating torture of not knowing, not knowing where or how he was, was ceaseless. To keep their son at home and safe—to save themselves—the Talbots were willing to live very inconvenient lives. The unbearable pain of not knowing negates the charm of a comfortable life. For Ginny and Joe, burdens and benefits easily tilt the scales in favor of knowing and discomfort. "We do much better knowing that he has a place to sleep, knowing that he's been fed. Now we rest easy. We know he is being cared for. Ginny and I would rather put up with the problems of living with Mark than the much worse problem we had when we didn't know where the hell he was. When we didn't know if he was alive or dead." (p. 55)

BOUNDARIES IN CORESIDENCE

Boundaries, as discussed elsewhere in this book, naturally change in families as a child reaches adulthood. The establishment of healthy boundaries is often more problematic when there is coresidence and when grown children are independent in some regards and dependent in others. It may be especially difficult for fathers to learn to readjust boundaries in ways that promote adult status. Referring to the work of Birenbaum (1971), Fewell and Vadasy (1986) wrote, "This support throughout the adulthood of the handicapped individual will crystallize the relationship at a parent-child status rather than allowing the relationship to develop into a more mature form" (p. 55). Setting boundaries helps militate against overinvolvement, although this is often more difficult for single parents. Backlar (1995) addressed this problem in the context of describing parenting adult children with schizophrenia:

> In many situations such as this, there is mutual overinvolvement that often takes a highly negative form. When one person assumes the entire burden, the patient is often more likely to project hostility onto the helper and to blame him or her for everything that goes wrong. The long-term dependency needs are both frustrating and frightening to psychiatrically disabled young adults. Since they cannot fulfill an age-appropriate social role, they continue to be enmeshed in the dependency-independence conflicts of adolescence. Thus a twenty-eight-year-old may respond to his mother as he did at fifteen—with moodiness, anger and acting-out. (p. 102)

Other problems in boundary setting involve boundaries that exclude the grown child with a disability from being fully within the emotional circle of the family. They are often left out of discussion of "emotionally charged" material such as issues involving death or other losses. Consequently, the individual is left to grieve alone without the support of others. Blotzer (1995) noted, "The painful irony is that closing the door to emotionally laden material in the hopes of protection usually has the opposite effect. It leaves the person alone with his fears and fantasies and with no opportunity for feedback" (pp. 152–153). This collusion to protect the child from pain (through the setting of boundaries around emotional material) is particularly problematic at this point in the life cycle when mourning becomes a more common part of the life phase as parents and older relatives die.

OUT-OF-HOME PLACEMENTS

When placement outside the family's home seems beneficial or inevitable, one-half to two-thirds of families choose placement in a facility rather than with other family members, although family members are often considered as the first option (Heller & Factor, 1991). Under more ordinary circumstances, leaving the family home is generally associated with growth (such as when a child leaves for college) and this tempers the losses inherent in launching. In families where adult children enter a residential facility, the losses may be more pronounced. An adult sibling described the emotional impact of the residential placement of his brother, Marc, who has autism:

> Surely this was the best and probably the only possible move for everyone in our family, including Marc. After all, his needs are provided for, and my parents finally have some time to themselves after twenty-six years of raising him.

However, emotions always have a way of lagging behind logic. The feelings that accompany sending your full grown son to an adult home range from elation and relief to guilt and anguish. In practical terms, my parents' life has now become indefinitely easier, but the void they feel is also immense. Whenever my father sees Sesame Street, my brother's favorite show, he cries. Taking care of my brother occupied my parents' time and energy, it felt comfortable. A new shoe always feels uncomfortable at first. (Siegel & Silverstein, 1994, p. 6)

According to Cole (1986), professionals may overestimate the extent to which placement is viewed with a sense of finality. It is not unusual for families to continue to grapple with their decision for residential placement. There is clearly no easy standard for evaluating the appropriateness of non-family placement, but Cole (1986) provided one criterion that may be useful to some:

Is in-home placement good and out-of-home placement bad? Should interventions be aimed at prolonging in-home placement? These questions are based on a fundamental misconception. What is good is bonadaptation—family integrity, individual and family growth, personal freedom, and a sense of control. The family will decide upon in-home versus out-of-home placement in order to maximize these features. Consequently, interventions should focus upon these issues, not placement per se. (p. 234)

Although it is unclear whether family or out-of-home residence is best for adults with disabilities and their families, it is clear that placement in large institutions is not an optimal choice. Community residences provide for greater degrees of choice and control over life and large institutions are being increasingly closed.

Many families are initially apprehensive about the closing of institutions in favor of community residences. Larson and Lakin (1991), in a study of parental attitudes regarding deinstitutionalization, found that initially more than 90% of parents were at least somewhat satisfied with the institution and only about 20% supported community placement. The vast majority changed their mind after community placement took place, however. Subsequently, parents reported an 88% rate of satisfaction with community placement and a marked change in feelings toward prior institutional care.

Tia Nelis (1995–1996), a former resident of an institution, expressed her thoughts on institutionalization as follows:

From my experiences with institutions and with life "on the outside," there are some things that I know to be true:

- I've never met anyone who would choose to live in an institution once they have moved out.
- Putting people away because they have a disability is wrong, just like segregation is wrong. People should only be locked up if they are dangerous.
- People with disabilities want to be friends and neighbors and coworkers with lots of different kinds of people, not just other people with disabilities.
- People who have lived in institutions all of their lives don't know how to make choices because they are not given the opportunity. We need to teach people how to make decisions and allow them to fail too.
- Community living is not always easy, perfect or safe, but at least people who live in the community are free. Next time people start talking about closing institutions, make sure you're asking and listening to the right people—those who live there. They know the truth about these places. (Nelis, p.27)

PLACEMENTS IN NURSING HOMES VERSUS GROUP RESIDENCES OR IN-HOME CARE

Approximately one-third of the residents in nursing homes are below the age of 65 (Atlantis/American Disabled for Attendant Programs Today [ADAPT], 1992). There is no doubt that choice of residence is often dictated by factors far beyond the control of the family, including the politics of federal funding. In 1990, a bipartisan report mandated by Congress found that of the $53 billion dollars spent by the nation on long-term care, "only 18 percent went to home care—despite the fact that four out of five disabled and almost three out of five elderly disabled live at home" (Atlantis/ADAPT, 1992, p.7). Advocacy groups such as ADAPT are working hard to challenge the allocation of funding to ensure that funds are directed to programs that provide attendant care in the home rather than institutional settings. An example of their position follows:

> It was agreed that we would have the best impact by working to ensure that any health care proposal includes our goal of 25% Medicaid funds be redirected to community based attendant services. National health care plans need to address the redirection of dollars to long-term, user controlled attendant services. (p. 3)

The problem is not a matter of an increase in total funding. ADAPT's observation is that it is far more cost-effective for services to be provided in the home (approximately $13,000 per year) rather than a nursing home (on average about $30,000 per year) (Reeves, 1996). There is no doubt that many people enter residential facilities because the funds are not available to provide the discrete services that would enable them to retain more independence in their own or family residences. Recognition of this need has led to a supported living philosophy that is gradually affecting some programs for adults with developmental disabilities (funding has primarily been in the form of federally financed pilot programs). The central tenet of this philosophy is that people with disabilities can and should live lives "of their choosing regardless of the severity of disability" (Smull, 1995, p. 14).

The comments of Kevin Otley, a man who had lived in an institution, provide a clear illustration of the differences in quality of life for adults with disabilities in supported living environments rather than more traditional settings:

> When I lived at Lake Owasso state institution in Minnesota, you had to ask for everything: "Can you let me out?," "Can I have a can of pop?," "Can I stay up a little bit longer?" When I moved into a group home, I had to follow all of the rules. I had to go to bed at a certain time, and when I was in bed, I had to be asleep. That was that. I lived with two other guys. We were being watched all the time, 24 hours a day, seven days a week. Two years ago I got married. My wife and I moved into our own apartment. Now that I have my own place, I make the decisions. I have my own keys. I can let myself out, and let myself back in. Now I can come and go when I want. I can make my own food, and I can decide whether I want to have breakfast or lunch, or when I'm ready for a snack. We can invite friends to stay over. My wife and I decide when the staff come over. They help us with some things, but we make our own decisions. (Lakin & Smull, 1995, pp. 2–3)

In addition to the establishment of independent community residences, support services programs have been used to help adults with severe developmental disabilities to remain in the family home. These programs tend to be small model programs, however, and there remains a great need for policies and programs that provide support for older families of adults with disabilities living at home. Many family support initiatives focus on the needs of young versus "adult" children despite the fact that the financial needs do not necessarily diminish as the children grow up (Heller & Factor, 1994).

One model program provided families with a service allotment that could be used flexibly for a variety of services (at a cost of about $1,200 per month). The pilot study revealed that families who were provided with this option had a decreased need for out-of-home placements and an alleviation of caregiver burden for the elderly parents who participated (Heller & Factor, 1994).

POSTPLACEMENT FAMILY INVOLVEMENT

In addition to its intrinsic value, family involvement has been found to be instrumental in facilitating effective community adjustment (Blacher & Baker, 1992). Blacher and Baker (1992) observed that although placement outside of the home historically has meant placement outside of the family, this disturbing phenomenon is not inevitable. Blacher and Baker (1992) reported that despite the importance of family involvement, the present picture is characterized by a lack of family involvement in out-of-home placements for adults with mental retardation with regard to both visitation and involvement in decision making. They questioned, however, whether research findings regarding lack of family involvement indicate family detachment or, rather, "a lack of opportunities for involvement, driven, in part, by some care provider anti-family bias" (p. 36).

Blacher and Baker (1992) described the roots of some of these negative attitudes:

> Staff ambivalence may arise from negative cognitions about parents who have placed their sons and daughters in an institution years ago. Younger staff members who did not experience the past professional ideology that pressured parents to place the child may blame parents for this decision ("They gave him up. What right do they have now?"). Staff members who rigidly ascribe to normalization principles will be even more likely to have negative thoughts about parents who place their children today ("Children should always live at home; these are bad parents"). Conversely, these staff members may have negative thoughts about parents who want high involvement with their adult offspring ("Parents should let go. They are fostering dependency"). Thoughts such as these can enormously influence staff members' receptivity to parent involvement. Like many cognitions that influence our behavior, however, these may not be entirely conscious. (p. 39)

Blacher and Baker (1992) provided a useful resource for personnel of residential facilities who want to increase family involvement. Their recommendations include encouraging facility administrators to prepare a brochure that specifies a variety of concrete ways in which families may choose to be involved.

SIBLINGS IN ADULTHOOD

Adults who have siblings with disabilities have been described as an overlooked group with regard to their own needs. On reaching adulthood, they may find that they continue to experience issues related to their sibling's disability; these issues are most complex for those individuals who, during childhood, felt compelled to become "little adults." As noted in Chapter 3, these siblings often become parentified if they had caretaking responsibilities that were out of harmony with their own developmental needs. Parentified siblings became used to being asked to defer their own needs and feelings for attention to be paid to those of their sibling.

Because relationships with siblings often become prototypes for subsequent relationships later in life, adult siblings may find themselves habitually putting their needs second to those of others. Siegel and Silverstein (1994) noted that this can result in "an adult personality marked by altruism at best and a martyred attitude at worst" (p. 25). Disregard of personal needs and feelings also can result in problems with self-esteem and depression.

The experience of growing up as a sibling of a child with a disability may also have an impact on the adult's work life by moving these siblings into humanitarian endeavors, such as special education, social work, and child psychology (Siegel & Silverstein, 1994). Siegel and Silverstein (1994) noted that it is particularly important for adult siblings to scrutinize such career choices to make sure they are not just an automatic extension of their lifelong helping role in the family: "The question that should be asked when an adult sibling enters a 'helping' profession is: what is the motivation? Is it to receive additional praise? Is it guilt?" (p. 135). They noted that if career choice is motivated by these reasons, disappointment often follows. On the other hand, if a helping profession has been chosen freely, with consideration of other options, it becomes a source of gratification.

Siblings may grow up with an exaggerated need to please their parents; as noted in Chapter 3, this may take the form of superachieving and perfectionism. Siegel and Silverstein (1994) described the ramifications of this pattern:

> Superachieving children feel they have to do extra well; this is the only way they can get attention from their parents and other significant people in their life. And they do as well as they do, not only to grab the attention of their parents, but also to make the parents themselves feel good, to make them feel whole, and to make them not feel like failures for having a handicapped child. These goals can amount to quite a burden for a child. Established in childhood, this pattern can be set up for life; the child becomes a severely driven adult to whom any form of failure is devastating. (p. 172)

Irrespective of whether siblings felt burdened regarding superachievement or parentification, adult siblings are likely to face more generalized concerns about their own futures. First (and particularly if their sibling's disability was due to genetic factors), siblings are likely to face anxiety about their prospects of having a child with a disability. Second, adult siblings often face a future in which they will be expected to play an instrumental role in supporting or caring for a brother or a sister who has a developmental disability. Caretaking by siblings in adult life can involve the excruciating decisions that were once made by parents. Neugeboren (1997) described his thoughts following difficult situations that would challenge anyone's resources. His brother, Robert, has mental illness:

> I found myself going through litanies of familiar questions and doubts: Should I call the local police and have them take him to a hospital and deal with getting him back to New York City? Should I ask Robert where he was all night, and if he had been drinking and/or doing drugs, and if he thought he could get back to the city himself? Should I leave my children and try to drive Robert the two hundred miles back to Staten Island? Should I call the hospital on Staten Island? Should I call some local psychiatrists and social workers I knew? Should I stay with Robert, or leave him alone? And how should I respond to his outbursts of anger, his bizarre behavior, his accusations, his questions, his tears? (p. 7)

Over the years, families often rely on the adult sibling's instrumental and emotional support. For example, Seltzer, Begun, Seltzer, and Krauss (1991) reported that adult siblings make up approximately one-quarter of the informal social network of adults with disabilities living with their parents. They also reported that these siblings play a pivotal role in the functioning of older mothers.

For some siblings, the extended caretaking role can be experienced as a burden, but the extent to which it is felt to be onerous is often mediated by other factors, such emotional closeness with the brother or sister with a disability and the extent to which their own developmental needs were considered in their family. As discussed in preceding chapters, it is not the type or severity of a child's disability that is the final determinant of the adjustment of other family members; rather, it is the extent to which a home environment can be created that promotes the healthy development of all members.

EMOTIONAL IMPACT

The emotional impact of having a sibling with a disability varies greatly and often includes a complicated mixture of love, anger, desire for caretaking, resentment, and empathy. The benefits from having a brother or a sister with a disability are easily identifiable by some who cite (in addition, of course, to love) factors such as the learning of tolerance and lack of prejudice toward others. The losses felt by some may be less easily described. Some feel a loss of their own individuality and recognition within the family system; for example, one person we met with noted a virtual absence of photographs of himself in the family house—possibly because they pointed out the contrast between the two siblings. For different reasons, older sisters and younger brothers may be particularly subject to negative impact. Older sisters are the ones most likely to assume additional caretaking tasks; in addition, they have also been found to receive less feedback regarding their helpfulness than in more typical families (Siegel & Silverstein, 1994, p. 29). Sibling caretaking is a double-edged sword. Although it poses its own burden, it does sometimes provide additional time with parents. For example, Siegel and Silverstein (1994) suggested that younger brothers get even less parental attention because they are often excluded from such caretaking. He noted that it is important for adult siblings to come to terms with the fact that anger, love, and resentment can coexist.

In adulthood, many of these same siblings are placed in the situation of being relied on to continue to help meet the sibling's needs. Many of these siblings will be part of the first generation to be faced with caring for elderly parents at the same time they may be caring for a sibling with a disability (Seltzer et al., 1991). Furthermore, they often have to juggle their growing responsibilities and the needs of a spouse, children, a career, and themselves.

In contrast to more typical sibling relationships, siblings of adults with disabilities generally give more emotional support than they receive (Seltzer et al., 1991). Adults with mental retardation are often aware of the lack of balance in some of these relationships. Zetlin's (1986) study of adults with mental retardation and their siblings led to the following observation:

> In most cases, the notion of reciprocity was important to the retarded adults and, in return for siblings' attention and support, they offered their assistance in various ways (e.g., baby-sitting for nieces and nephews, lending money). Although not always able to manage an equivalent exchange, the retarded adults believed some offering was necessary and so, for example, one woman always scraped together enough money for birthday and Christmas gifts for her sisters, and one man made a regular habit for collecting packets of jam from restaurants that he then presented to his sister. (p. 224)

Until now, we have primarily focused on situations in which a high degree of sibling involvement may be necessary. We have had several experiences with families in which siblings were parentified at a young age; these children either helped care for a parent who was in turn parenting the sibling with a disability or the children provided an unusual amount of direct caretaking of the sibling themselves. As the child with the disability became more self-sufficient in adulthood, the brothers and sisters had a noticeably difficult time letting go. In some families familiar to one of us (L. M.), the siblings were often more intrusive or overprotective than the parents. For example, when one middle-aged woman with severe epilepsy finally won her parents over to her plan to live independently away from the family's rural home, her sisters remained the most staunchly opposed, calling the therapist (L. M.) to stop the process. There is sometimes a need for the parent or professional to help siblings learn to pay attention to boundaries and the need for self-determination.

Siblings may also struggle with other issues and feelings that are more traditionally shared by parents. For example, one older brother reported a sense of shame in public, fearing that others would think his brother was his son. He did not feel this sense of shame in settings where his role as brother was more clearly indicated.

The sibling relationship is typically the longest lasting in a family and complicated by conflicting feelings and obligations. In addition, there is often a strong desire to help while simultaneously facing social service limitations, societal obstacles, and other external problems. In response to many of these needs, a number of support groups for adult siblings have been developed in several cities.

The Seattle chapter of Adult Siblings of People With Disabilities (ASPD) provides a model similar to other groups. Their objectives fall into three broad categories: (a) support, (b) information, and (c) advocacy. Support includes the sharing of emotions related to personal experiences of growing up with a sibling who has a disability. In addition, support is available for siblings who presently are experiencing crises or problems in relationship to their siblings. The information component includes sharing of resources on residential, financial, recreational, and vocational matters. Issues pertaining to trusts, wills, medical insurance, and guardianship are also often discussed. The third component focuses on helping siblings acquire the skills to be effective advocates for their brothers and sisters. This includes sharing advocacy strategies and listening to guest speakers on topics pertaining to legislation that affects people with disabilities and their families (National Association of Sibling Programs, 1993).

EQUAL ACCESS TO ADULT LIFE

The remaining portions of this chapter focus beyond the family on domains that greatly impact the quality of adult life. Carol Gill, a psychologist with a disability, made the following points in testimony at a public hearing on the problems of persons with disabilities:

It's prejudice, plain and simple, that spoils the quality of life for many people with disabilities. Their central problem is a narrow punitive standard that tells them they don't deserve to work, to live in their own homes, to marry, or to have children unless they can do it in the traditional way. When efforts to enjoy life are consistently thwarted by a handicapping environment, life loses meaning. (*Disability Rag ReSource*, 1993, p. 3)

Prejudice toward persons with disabilities has a variety of etiologies. Some correlate with other prejudices such as racism (Wright, 1983) and some come from genuine ignorance about the abilities of persons with disabilities. Regardless of the specific source, the result is discrimination that leads to closing doors to equal opportunities. Most often this is done under the guise of judging someone as "not capable" of engaging in valued life roles. Practitioners and parents, like the general population, often are guided by an implicit premise that someone needs to be independent to pursue a valued activity or role. Cottone and Cottone (1992) rejected this notion: "There is no such thing as independence for humans—there are only degrees of interdependence. What appears to be an independent individual is actually a person linked by many relationships, rather than connected by only a few" (p. 20). This viewpoint is consistent with the argument that we need to think more about accepting and promoting the idea of interdependence rather than independence (Condeluci, 1995). It is important that families and professionals accept the concept of interdependence as a viable option and to support adult children in endeavors that may exceed their self-sufficiency.

Fay Waxman (1993) identified the "right to intimate association," which is blocked for many adults with disabilities through the attitudes of family, professionals, and governmental policies. In this context we will look at issues pertaining to friendships, love, and parenting.

FRIENDSHIP

As described by Perske (1993), friends fill a role in adult life that family members cannot duplicate no matter how dedicated they are in their love and support.

People do numerous things with friends that they would never want their parents, brothers and sisters to know about. This does not mean that these activities were shameful, only that friendships are private affairs. Friendships stand outside the limiting judgments and protections of relatives. With friends, people can hope, dream and dare afresh. With friends, people try new feats, fall flat and try again: People make attempts with friends that they may never make with their parents watching. (p. 3)

Family members and friends meet different aspects of social support needs. Many adults with disabilities have support networks comprising family members and community agencies but few or no friends. Krauss, Seltzer, and Goodman's (1992) study found that almost half of adults with developmental disabilities who live with their parents had no friends, in contrast to those in nonfamily residences. Hill, Rotegard, and Bruininks (1984) found that 42% of adults with developmental disabilities in community programs had no friends and 63% of those in institutional settings reported a virtual lack of friends even among residents and staff.

The ways in which practitioners and family members can help facilitate friendships are similar. First, there needs to be recognition that families cannot fill all roles for social support. Second, there needs to be an understanding that despite social stigma and many instances of rejection, friendships are indeed possible. Bogdan and Taylor (1987) noted that we have concentrated so much on the (very real) phenomenon of stigma and rejection that we have lost sight of the equally real sociology of acceptance:

> Perhaps one of the reasons sociologists have concentrated on rejection and stigma is they have mainly studied casual and impersonal interaction between typical and atypical people (Goffman, 1963). With more sustained relations, there is greater variety and complexity. Typical people may treat people who are different with sustained hostility as well as love them with intense affection. In developing a sociology of acceptance, we are only concerned with caring and affection and regular contact over a sustained period. (p. 36)

Bogdan and Taylor (1987) are not the only ones to describe the ongoing occurrence of relationships being established over time with persons who share characteristics that are generally stigmatizing and with persons who are more typical of the social norm. Others similarly remind us that rejection is not inevitable (Lutfiyya, 1990; O'Brien & O'Brien, 1993). These authors provide many examples of relationships that evolved into friendships over time. These relationships are possible but not probable and, for this reason, have been termed "unlikely alliances" by O'Brien and O'Brien (1993). The third issue, then, becomes one of how to increase the probability of these alliances. Families and professionals need to consider avenues that make it easier for adults with disabilities to get to places where friendships can happen. With regard to the problem of isolation among adults with developmental disabilities, Perske (1993) referred to the work of other researchers:

> These findings call for action, and the researchers who report them have sensible recommendations to offer: use smaller residential settings rather than large settings because the surveys show that smaller settings offer people more social contacts; increase people's involvement with neighbors (about two thirds of whom were described by staff informants in the study of older residents as either "warm and accepting or friendly"); increase people's use of ordinary community places such as shops, churches, libraries and parks; increase people's attention to leisure time opportunities; and concentrate staff attention on building up people's social contacts. (p. 16)

Out of a lack of belief in the feasibility of alternatives, opportunities for friendships often center on activities with others with disabilities. Hazel Neal, a woman with an intellectual disability, addressed this point in an interview:

> Sometimes people tell us to go to Special Olympics and that, even if we don't want to they say we have to. They think it's for real and it's posta just be for fun. And all of us from the shop went camping and I ask if I could work in the kitchen and they said no, I hadda be with the other handicapped people. I was really hurt by that. (quoted in Schwier, 1994, p. 139)

Approaches that may enhance the probability that friendships will grow out of involvement with community organizations that are not centered on persons with disabilities can be found in Reidy (1989). From a systems perspective, it must be underscored that strategies for the evolution and support of friendships are greatly affected by the existence (or lack) of accessible transportation.

Friendship possibilities need to be supported but are often trivialized or controlled in residential settings. Referring to adults with developmental disabilities, O'Brien and O'Brien (1993) reported,

> Most residential settings manage friends' access to one another. This control is sometimes explicit, as when friends must have their contacts approved by an interdisciplinary team, when friends without disabilities are required to undergo some form of training as a condition of spending time with their friend. ... Other times, control of access is less direct: people have no privacy, visits with friends are interrupted by program routines, messages get lost, or activities that require

some cooperation from program staff break down because someone did not pass along the right permission slip or the van was re-routed. (p. 29)

Furthermore, residential staff may exercise undue control through "the power of definition." O'Brien and O'Brien (1993) noted,

> Staff define whom the person with a developmental disability is and what is good for him or her. They assert the right to say how it really is for a client. Often this process of definition reflects a preoccupation with finding fault in the person. A staff member describes a person with a developmental disability to the person's friend as "manipulative," and cautions the friend against being "sucked into" or "feeding" the person's dependency. A staff member nods knowingly when a friend makes a positive comment about a person with a developmental disability and says sagely, "I thought that too when I first met her." . . . A staff member passes along comments about syndromes and symptoms. (p. 29)

The experience of friendships is often denied in residential settings and the losses that sometimes go with friendships due to death, relocation, and so forth are often ignored. One young adult with spina bifida that one of us (L. M.) worked with learned of her friend's death by overhearing staff members talking. As she wept in the hallway of the residential program, she was disregarded, and later her request to attend his funeral was denied by staff members for fear that it would be "too upsetting" to her.

LOVE, ROMANCE, PARTNERSHIP, AND MARRIAGE

Cognitive Impairments

Externally imposed obstacles abound when adults with disabilities want to enter love relationships and marriage. This is most apparent when the disability involves cognitive impairment. A "forced choice between safety and sexuality" was the phrase used by Seltzer (1993, p. 175) to describe the dilemma faced by family and other caregivers regarding the romantic life of adults with developmental disabilities. Seltzer (1993) reported, "The hope among many who care deeply for their loved ones is for persons with mental retardation to remain asexual beings" (p. 175). This same dilemma is often felt by families of adults with other types of disabilities; consequently, this area of adult development is often thwarted. In the manner of all bad self-fulfilling prophecies, many people are never prepared for these domains of life and their subsequent failures to cope with demands are used as evidence to justify further restrictions on romance.

As discussed earlier, inaccurate predictions are often made about the capabilities of many who have disabilities. The comments of one man illustrated this well: "I think people take one look at me and say in their minds: He won't ever have sex, so why talk about it and get his hopes up? This makes me angry . . . because they could be wrong" (quoted in Schwier, 1994, p. 10).

As described in Chapter 4, sometimes the discouragement of romantic partnerships takes the form of encouraging career pursuits rather than romantic ones for females. Desires for a loving partnership cannot be sublimated into a career; gratification is not easily exchangeable.

As discussed in Chapter 5, sexual abuse of persons with disabilities is widespread and horrific. Yet it is not prevented and is paradoxically fostered by attempts to prevent the individual's psychosexual development (such as through lack of sexual education).

Parental and professional fears about romantic partnerships often center around pregnancy. In part, parents may fear that should a pregnancy occur, they will be faced with "one more person to supervise" (Gardner, 1986, p. 54).

Fears of sexual abuse, romantic rejection, and pregnancy often become entangled in a manner that precludes problem solving and may result in parental discouragement of all forms of romantic interest and sexuality. These entwined fears and misperceptions need to be separated to make them more manageable.

With regard to marriage, Schwier (1994) observed:

> If a 50 percent divorce rate is any indication, half the population can't very well attest with any great certainty as to its wisdom on solid and lasting relationships. Domestic violence has never been more prevalent. Couples, for myriad reasons, drift apart, fall out of love or, equally as devastating, fall out of like with one another. Children are split as homes divide. Given our own track record, how many of us are in a position to knowingly predict the failings of a relationship between two persons with a disability? In short, who are we to judge? (p. 26)

Schwier (1994) continued by referring to couples with intellectual disabilities that she interviewed about their relationships: "They wanted someone to like them for themselves, not someone paid to be there: not someone who will disappear in the next wave of staff turnover, someone other than parents and family" (p. 26). The meaning of a love relationship was well illustrated by one man with a developmental disability describing his relationship: "Closing his eyes, Michael says softly, . . . 'She makes me very happy most often. I know she cares for me. Very much. My heart feels good from her. I touch her. My heart is happy. She gives me a glad heart'" (Schwier, 1994, p. 29).

Access to intimacy is often blocked by others; the presumptuousness of their actions is well expressed by one woman with an intellectual disability. She said,

> If people said somebody who's handicapped can't get married, I would say nuts to that. It's their life. Give 'em the chance to make a mistake if they make a mistake. It's just like me goin' up to someone who wasn't labeled and tell them if I think they can get married or not. It's none of my business. Nobody asks me if they can get married, so why should I hafta ask them? (quoted in Schwier, 1994, p. 33)

Some people with intellectual disabilities cope surprisingly well in marriage. From the perspective of the experience of one of us (L. M.) as a marital therapist, one man's comments as he described his creativity, desire, and discipline in coping with his in-laws were impressive: "You know that one show of the Flintstones where Fred keeps saying over and over, 'I love my mother-in-law.' 'I love my mother-in-law.' Well, be darned if it didn't work. That's one thing that the Flintstones taught me that actually works"(p. 87).

Interdependence is built into the concept of marriage. Common sense tells us that if people with disabilities do have more problems in functioning, it makes little sense to insist that they live without a loving supportive partner who can also help when needed. Haavik (1986) observed, "Many spouses seemed to function better as a unit than either would have alone. One partner's deficits were balanced by the other's strengths, making them better able to cope with everyday demands" (p. 74).

Physical Impairments

Turning to the situation of people with physical disabilities, external discouragement of romantic pursuits is often as pervasive but more subtle. When it comes to romantic partnerships, adult children with a physical disability are often given guidance that places them in an untenable position by those close to them. If they choose a partner without a disability, others doubt that partner's sincerity and assume there is an ulterior motive that accounts for the relationships—that is, "What would an able-bodied man or woman want with you?" On the other hand, parents and professionals discourage partnerships with others with disabilities—as if to say, "Why would you want his or her problems too?"

PARENTING

Perhaps no other adult life activity provokes as much disapproval as the desire or decision of adults with disabilities to become parents themselves. The extent of prejudice against adults with disabilities is illustrated in the case of Bill Earl and Leigh Campbell-Earl. Their situation is illustrative but by no means an isolated case. In brief, their daughter was born 5 years after they were married. Both parents had physical disabilities that precluded independence in child care so they contacted their state agency, which provides personal care assistants for persons with disabilities. The Campbells were informed that personal care assistants were not allowed to touch the child unless the child also had a disability. This is one example in which governmental policy has an incredible impact on the quality of life for adults with disabilities. For those without independent means, this restriction means access is blocked to an aspect of life that many consider more meaningful than anything else.

The comment of a public policy analyst in the disability field highlights the ludicrous aspects of policies regarding personal assistance services: "I find it fascinating that under nonpersonal activities of daily living, 'home maintenance and minor repairs, yard work' are allowable home help services, but assisting in parenting and child care are not covered services. Something is wrong!" (*Disability Rag ReSource*, 1993, p. 8). This raises many questions. First, why is yard work covered and not the physical aspects of child care? This is a critical question because policies on personal care services preclude parents with disabilities who are not wealthy from having children. Second, why is such value placed on the physical aspects of child care when these are not the essential components of raising a child? Third, why do we obstruct the use of support services and insist that the physical tasks be performed without assistance?

It is not unusual for children to be removed from the home due to parental physical disability. The experiences of Tiffany Callo, a mother with a disability, are a case in point. She summarized the basic facts of her ordeals in this testimony:

How many of you legislators are parents? How would you like it if someone legally kidnapped your little boy or little girl? Would you miss them? It's the same with us. We have the same needs to have children, but not the same rights to keep them. As the country celebrates the second anniversary of the Americans with Disabilities Act, why should parents with disabilities still be discriminated against in our basic rights to be parents?

On March 3, 1987, I gave birth to my first son, David, a 7-pound bouncing baby with no disability. The Department of Social Services [DSS] assumed I was "unfit" because of my disability and took David away. On January 15, 1988, I gave birth to my second son, Jesse, also non-disabled. Jesse was not even 48 hours old before they tried to separate us. They kicked me out of the hospital. Today, both of my sons, David and Jesse, have been legally adopted by different families and they live in different states. As a result, I only get to see them once a year for two-and-a-half hours. (*Disability Rag ReSource*, 1993, p. 9)

For readers who are not familiar with the facts of this case (which is well documented in Mathews, 1992), it is hard to believe the decision to remove the children from their biological mother was not based on evidence of neglect or abuse. It must be underscored that the babies were both taken away based on the assumption that Tiffany Callo would be unable to care for them, without regard for the fact that the prediction could be wrong. It is also important to point out that removal of these children was not a matter of protecting the public from undue social service expenses. Describing the reactions the lawyer Tiffany Callo hired to obtain her own children, Mathews (1992) reported:

It appalled him that DSS, like nearly every other child-protective agency in the country, paid more than five hundred dollars a month to keep a single child in a foster home but could not spend the same amount on an attendant to help a disabled mother raise her child in her own home. It offended him that Tiffany was in court only because her children were healthy and nondisabled. If they had been born disabled, they would have immediately qualified for attendant care and could have been raised by Tiffany. Of course, if they had been disabled, probably no one but their mother would have wanted them anyway. (p. 22)

The nonphysical aspects of parenting (such as providing love, guidance, and nurturance) are the core of parenting. Physical tasks such as changing a diaper or lifting a baby safely are essential but can be performed in more than one way. In addition to the use of attendants or adaptive equipment, some people may be able to perform child care tasks that others would not consider feasible. One woman wrote,

In the rehab hospital after my accident, I asked my doctor whether I could have children. He said, "We'll see." At sixteen, I felt sure that I could probably not have children. Even if I could, I wondered what kind of mother I could be if I couldn't carry or chase my babies. This led to a needless grieving period. At nineteen, despite an IUD, I found myself "with child."

She described how she learned to accommodate with little assistance:

> After returning home, I realized that carrying my baby was not going to be a simple procedure for me, but I soon learned to improvise. A stroller in the house was the simplest solution for me. The carriers with straps to put on your front or back soon became invaluable when we left the house. I preferred the front carry because I could better maintain my balance. I soon found that I needed to train myself to use one crutch instead of two because with my baby, purse and diaper bag, I did not have enough arms. By the time one of my crutches broke, I was ready to solo. Ten years later, I still use one crutch. Another would feel like an extra arm. I have learned of many devices and aids to help parents and children with disabilities. One of my biggest fears has been that my children will be taken away because some bureaucrats decided that my physical limitations make me an inadequate parent. (*Disability Rag ReSource*, 1993, p. 25)

We believe the policy implications are clear. There is a pressing need for Medicaid to be changed so that parenting can be considered an activity of daily living. Leigh Campbell-Earl described the ramifications of maintaining the status quo:

> One of the joys of life is having and raising a child. Most people think that if handicappers have personal assistance, they will be productive members of society. They can go to school. They can have jobs. They can have a life. We have to expect that handicappers will want to have every experience of life. And this includes having a family. If we draw a line as to how much of a life we can live, we all lose. (*Disability Rag Resource*, 1993, p. 10)

This is not to say that all adults with disabilities make adequate parents. Adults with mental retardation, on the whole, have been found to have problems meeting the demands of parenting. Decisions for an individual adult should never be based on the performance of a whole group. Decisions need to be made on an individual basis after serious, nonbiased assessment and with genuine consideration paid to extensive parental training and the provision of support services.

Most important, the needs and rights of children should not be overlooked in the name of parental rights. The complexities of these issues as they pertain to parents with mental retardation are particularly well addressed in a book by Whitman and Accardo (1990); we refer interested readers to this comprehensive resource.

Many programs have focused on providing extensive support services to parents with disabilities (Haavik, 1986). Through the Looking Glass is a nonprofit agency in Berkeley, California, notable for providing expertise and assistive technology that enable many persons with physical or cognitive disabilities to meet the demands of parenting.

CONCLUSION

In closing (as discussed earlier), adults with physical or developmental disabilities are often regarded as childlike, and it is commonplace to hear adults with developmental disabilities described as "perpetual children." We wish to underscore that adults with disabilities are simply not children no matter how severe their functional limitations appear to be. Sometimes failure to mature is related to lack of opportunity to assume adult roles to the best of one's abilities. No judgments regarding what is possible should be made on the basis of disability without first considering all available resources and the possibility that activities and roles that appear improbable of attainment may actually be possible with sufficient supports.

CHAPTER 7

Sons and Daughters
in Old Age

The final phase of the life cycle involves reaping the fruits from previous developmental phases and preparing for the last transition. Referring to the eighth stage of development (a state of integrity versus despair), Erikson (1980) reported,

> Only he who in some way has taken care of things and people and has adapted himself to the triumphs and disappointments of being, by necessity, the originator of others and the generator of things and ideas—only he may gradually grow the fruit of the seven stages. I know of no better word than *integrity*. Lacking a clear definition, I shall point to a few attributes of this state of mind. It is the acceptance of one's own and only life cycle . . . an acceptance of the fact that one's life is one's own responsibility. It is a sense of comradeship with men and women of distant times and of distant pursuits. (p. 104)

A state of integrity contrasts to a state of despair, which is "the feeling that the time is short, too short for the attempt to start another life and to try out alternate routes to integrity" (Erikson, 1980, p. 104). It is clear that achieving a state of integrity rather than despair is related to the opportunity to choose, create, connect with other people, and assume responsibility for one's life course.

The ability to progress with the developmental tasks of old age is built on the foundation of earlier developmental phases. For illustration, we touch on only a few of the many interconnections between earlier life stages and those that follow. For example, the opportunities to choose and create extend back into childhood; career development that affects adulthood begins as children play and are encouraged to fantasize about "what they want to be when they grow up." In adolescence we see that opportunities for intimate connections with others, sexual development, and self-determination become prominent. Whether or not these opportunities are accessible and strengthened has a bearing on adulthood and whether adults with disabilities form close friendships, marriages, or families or act on career interests. Baltes and Cartensen (1996) described the impact earlier developmental periods have on life satisfaction in old age. He noted that the need in adulthood is to "augment and enrich one's own reserve capacities and resources" and added that this "is of the utmost importance since these will also assist to successful mastery of developmental tasks in later life" (p. 405). People who have grown up with disabilities are generally lacking these "reserve capacities and resources" due to limited opportunities for their development.

Tibbits (1979) provided a useful delineation of the developmental needs of the older individual:

1. To render some socially useful service
2. To be considered a part of the community
3. To occupy increased leisure time in satisfying ways
4. To enjoy normal companionships
5. For recognition as an individual
6. For opportunities for self-expression
7. For health protection and care
8. For suitable mental stimulation
9. For living arrangements and family relationships
10. For spiritual satisfactions (quoted in Thurman, 1986, p. 95)

This chapter will focus on many of these developmental needs as related to life satisfaction for elderly persons with disabilities. In addition to a foundation established in earlier life stages and (at least) the basic needs just cited, successful adaptation to old age requires a combination of internal coping strategies and external supports. In many respects, elderly persons with disabilities may have relatively fewer problems than the general population with internal adaptation to aging. This is a manifestation of the skewed developmental timelines discussed earlier in this book. Elderly persons with disabilities do face a greater number of external barriers, however; this pattern contrasts with the overall experiences of the general population.

With regard to internal adaptation to aging, many people with disabilities have already come to terms with problems that pose major obstacles to elderly persons who have not previously lived with significant disability. Seale (1996) noted many older persons struggle with the "acceptance of and reconciliation with the loss of power endemic in old age" (p. 401). Addressing the social roots of this loss of power, Kimmel (1974) reported, "There is some degree of *age grading* in our social structure, so that status and power awarded to individuals is in part because of their age" (p. 65). In Western cultures, status and power decrease with age. It is ironic (but not surprising) that the stigmatization experienced by people with disabilities throughout the life cycle in many ways prepares them for this loss of power.

With the disabilities that often accompany old age, many in the general population now experience significant limitations in their ability to be independent. This results in a second hurdle, the difficulty of accepting help. For many elderly persons who are facing an unaccustomed need to rely on others, the need for assistance is inseparable from a loss of dignity (Seale, 1996). Many refuse needed help because it is very threatening to their self-sufficiency (Seale, 1996). This contrasts to many people who have lived for years with a disability and have learned to accept the need for help without "losing face." They are often ahead of their peers with respect to this critical internal adaptation to aging.

The literature on aging and disability focuses primarily on persons with developmental disabilities. Reflecting on this stage of the life course of many persons with developmental disabilities, Edgerton (1994) observed, "They are good at being old, better, in fact, than they were at being young" (p. 53). He added that it is sadly ironic that at this point in the life cycle when many adults with mental retardation achieve a greater sense of well-being, they are simultaneously at greatest risk for serious health problems that can deprive them of a long-awaited happiness.

HEATH PROTECTION AND CARE

Edgerton (1994) noted that elderly persons with mental retardation are less likely than others to engage in preventive health care. In addition, they often have difficulty recognizing the early warning symptoms of serious health problems. He added that these problems appear most pronounced in the large numbers of persons in independent residences. In addition to acquiring common physical infirmities related to old age, elderly persons with physical disabilities may experience a worsening of their initial disability. For example, persons with cerebral palsy may experience more severe problems with joints, skeletal structure, breathing, and mobility as their bodies age even though this disability is not technically considered to be progressive in nature.

Obtaining the necessary health care to ensure a good quality of life is often obstructed by communication impasses with health care providers. As described by Edgerton (1994),

> Because many lack an adequate vocabulary of medical terms for their symptoms, they may have difficulty explaining the nature of their complaint or understanding the questions posed by a receptionist or nurse. Most older individuals with mental retardation are functionally illiterate, so filling out medical history forms without help is a virtual impossibility. Confronted by such difficult and embarrassing problems, they are likely to act as if they understand something when in fact they do not or to agree with whatever may be said to avoid the embarrassment of asking for clarification. In fact, some are so intimidated by these challenges of communication that they avoid seeking medical help altogether. (p. 64)

Edgerton (1994) suggested several changes that may ease access to health care. These include posting lists of neighborhood health care providers who accept Medicare in places that are frequented by elderly persons with mental retardation (i.e., bus stops, pharmacies, grocery stores). He suggested the use of mobile health vans and specially trained receptionists to ease access. It is critical to the long-range welfare of persons with disabilities that strategies be developed to remove the barriers to appropriate health care.

COMMUNITY SUPPORTS AND FORMAL PROGRAMS

The vast majority of elderly persons receive help from informal sources to maintain community residences despite the disabilities that generally accompany old age. Studies of elderly persons in the general population who become frail in old age indicate that approximately 70% to 80% of the help they receive is from informal sources (Martinson & Stone, 1993; Tennstedt, Harrow, & Crawford, 1996). This support is from "uncompensated helpers" such as children, extended family members, neighbors, and members of religious organizations. Receiving such informal help is often a critical factor in whether a person can continue to live in a community setting or becomes institutionalized (Tennstedt et al., 1996).

Although the rate of disability grows in the general population to the extent that it is commonplace for elderly persons, important differences remain for persons who acquired disabilities much earlier in life. For example, marital rates are lower than in the general population and the likelihood of having children is lower still. Consequently, persons with lifelong disabilities generally have less opportunity to receive care from spouses or children. Furthermore, many sources of informal help from neighbors and nonfamily persons are based on a reciprocal pattern of social exchange established over the years (James, James, & Smith, 1984). Persons with disabilities generally are less likely to have access to such relationships.

As persons with lifelong disabilities reach this stage of the life cycle, their parents have often died and siblings may themselves have acquired significant disabilities. Without reserve capacities in the form of relationships built up over the years, reliance tends to be on members of the family of origin.

In addition to a collapse of the informal support system, many older persons with disabilities find they are faced with fewer formal supports. Access to the types of rehabilitation services that may have helped in the past is limited. There is often an inverse relationship between age and access to rehabilitative services, although the needs do not diminish with age (Blake, 1981). This shrinking of rehabilitative services affects a broad range of treatments and support. For example, Brody (1983) reported that older persons who lost limbs had for many years been largely rejected for prosthetic services on the assumption that they could not learn to use the prostheses properly. Brody (1983) noted that this policy was unrelated to any evidence to support this assumption. Vocational rehabilitation services are also often restricted due to assumptions about age. Although in 1973 the State-Federal Vocational Rehabilitation (VR) Program formally removed the restriction against services after age 64, unspoken restrictions remain (Holland & Falvo, 1990). Myers (1983) concluded that only 2.4% of persons served by the State-Federal VR system were age 65 or older. Some individuals who have been able to integrate into the workforce find they may need to retire sooner than they would choose if additional supports were available (Holland & Falvo, 1990). In addition to the lack of choice about this major aspect of older age, restricted rehabilitative services result in even more devastating effects. Many elderly persons with disabilities find they cannot remain independent in their own homes without rehabilitative services and may be forced into institutionalization (Holland & Falvo, 1990).

In addition to a paucity of rehabilitative programs, elderly persons with disabilities are seldom integrated into existing community programs that might meet their needs. Coelho and Dillon (1990) reported,

> Much of the literature on elderly persons with developmental disabilities asserts that the vast majority of these persons are capable of engaging in community-based activities with nonhandicapped elderly others with little assistance.

Whereas an array of day program alternatives was provided to the population studied, not one of the elderly persons was receiving day activity services in a program for persons without disabilities. (p. 13)

Similarly, Sutton, Sterns, and Park (1993) found that less than 9% of the elderly adults with developmental disabilities they studied used community-based adult day care services.

As illustrated in the preceding chapters, gaining equal access to opportunities that impart a better quality to one's life is often an ongoing struggle throughout the life cycle of persons with disabilities. A large part of this struggle has been due to stigmatization by the public and professionals. At this point in the life cycle it is evident that stigma now places the older person with a disability in a position that has been described by Benedict and Ganikos (1981) as *double jeopardy;* biases against the elderly *and* persons with disabilities jeopardize access to a good quality of life obtained over the years.

LIVING ARRANGEMENTS

One of the most disturbing ways in which stigma results in discriminatory practices for the older person with a disability is in terribly restricted choice of residences.

Kuehn and Imm-Thomas (1993) described the magnitude of this problem: "Despite efforts since 1980 to promote deinstitutionalization, the majority of older adults with developmental disabilities may still be located in nursing homes and residential facilities" (p. 333). Older persons with mental retardation are overlooked for placement in group homes even though they are relatively less likely than many younger persons with mental retardation to experience difficulties in community adjustment (Janicki & MacEachron, 1984).

As mentioned in the preceding chapter, there is often a rush to find a new residence for an adult son or daughter after the death of the family caregiver. In addition to the emotional problems caused by such abrupt relocation, the choice of residence is made in haste and generally is not optimal. Many end up in nursing homes or are placed in residences with people with dementia. In this manner, the previously cited need for mental stimulation is not met. The lack of opportunity for self-determination seen in larger institutions affects access to life opportunities that can bring pleasure in old age. For example, pet ownership has been found to be very life enhancing for many persons in old age but is often contingent on self-determination of residence (Smith, Seibert, Jackson, & Snell, 1992).

RETIREMENT

As briefly mentioned, there is often little opportunity for choice about the timing of retirement even though retirement is a critical transition in older age. Adjustment to retirement is affected by degree of choice in this major transition; involuntary retirement is associated with higher rates of adjustment problems and lower life satisfaction (Howard, Marshall, Rechnitzer, Cunningham, & Donner, 1982). Work is highly valued by many, not only for income considerations, but also for the daily structure and availability of social contact that it provides. Interviews of older persons with developmental disabilities revealed that more than 90% looked forward to their earnings and approximately 75% found pleasure in the camaraderie with peers in the workplace (Factor, 1993).

Set ages for retirement for persons with developmental disabilities vary by state but are often governed by policies. For example, in Ohio, age 55 is set as the marker for beginning retirement options (Sutton et al., 1993). This demarcation is reportedly based on the assumption that there is often an extensive age-related intellectual decline in persons with Down syndrome; interestingly, the evidence for this premature deterioration is not found in the majority of persons with developmental disabilities (Sutton et al., 1993).

In addition to the needs for choice regarding the timing of retirement and access to rehabilitation services that will support continued work, persons with developmental disabilities need preretirement planning. Emphasizing the importance of preretirement planning in general, Kimmel (1974) noted, "One of the most important implications of studies on retirement is the importance of pre-retirement planning—or anticipatory socialization for the new set of roles that one will occupy when the work roles are no longer present" (p. 260).

Persons with disabilities have little preparation for this major life transition (Heller & Factor, 1993), although a limited number of innovative programs are beginning to address this need. For example, one program used the widely known model of supported employment as the base of a supported retirement program for older persons with developmental disabilities. The program matched individuals with volunteer companions with similar interests. The volunteers then provided assistance to support involvement in community-based activities (Sutton et al., 1993). This is important in light of the previously mentioned lack of integration into community programs.

Financial security plays an important role in postretirement adjustment. It is important to note the financial problems of many persons with disabilities. Minorities fare even worse. Macken (1986) found that the annual family income of approximately 53% of elderly African Americans with functional impairments was between $3,000 and $7000. Research on factors that contribute to a good quality of life has indicated that finances play a greater role than disability itself (Cameron et al., 1973).

PSYCHOLOGICAL PEACE IN OLD AGE

Psychological peace is one developmental goal in the final life stage that is facilitated by a belief that one's life had (and continues to have) meaning. As discussed in Chapter 6, this often involves a sense of generativity—the sense that one is leaving something behind when one's life ends. In addition, it is often affected by spirituality, acceptance of mortality, and life satisfaction.

SPIRITUAL MEANING

Spiritual growth for some is an important way to imbue life with meaning, and religious belief and practice often grows in importance in older age (Kimmel, 1974). Persons with disabilities may find that their access to houses of worship is limited due to physical and nonphysical barriers.

Historically, persons with mental or physical disabilities have been regarded by religious institutions as objects of pity or recipients of divine punishment rather than as viable active congregants. Wright (1983) reported that this is reflected in past (and sometimes current) practice in all major religions. Across cultures and religions, there has been a pervasive association between disability and perceived punishment for transgressions as summed up in the expression "blemished body—blemished soul."

> To the ancient Hebrews, illness and physical defect marked the person as a sinner. Twelve blemishes are enumerated in the Bible that disqualified a priest from officiating. Among those mentioned are a "blind man, or a lame, or he that hath a flat nose, or anything superfluous, or a man that is brokenfooted, or brokenhanded, or crookbackt, or a dwarf, or that hath a blemish in his eye, or be scurvy, or scabbed, or hath his bones broken" (Hentig, 1948a., p. 16). . . . The Hindu theological concept of Dharma explains an existing personal condition as the inevitable result of past behavior in previous incarnations. (Hanks & Hanks, 1948, quoted in Wright, 1983, p. 66)

Wright (1983) also described the "special status" afforded to persons with disabilities in the context of religious practice:

> In religious practices, blind persons have been accorded privileged positions (Barker et al., 1953, p. 273). Modern Turkey regards persons without sight as indispensable assets to religious ceremonies and funerals (Maisel, 1953, p. 23). In Greek legend many clairvoyants were blind (Hentig, 1948b, p. 23). Among the Koreans it is believed that blind persons have acquired an inner vision and are therefore held in high esteem (Maisel, 1953). (Wright, 1983, p. 91)

These "special statuses" may appear positive at first glance but are essentially still negative stereotypes because they set people with disabilities apart from the rest of society and exaggerate the extent of their differences.

Congregations have often excluded persons with developmental disabilities with the argument that they are unable to "understand" communion and other rituals (Gaventa, 1986). Gaventa responds to this objection with a salient question: Does everyone else understand? (p. 215). Another objection to including persons with developmental disabilities in congregations includes the observation that many have difficulty sitting through long sermons. Gaventa (1986) responded,

> How does anyone listen to a long service? The answer has to do with giving adults the kind of training needed to understand what is deemed appropriate behavior. It has to do with more effective preaching skills. When clergy work hard on being concrete and simple as well as abstract and complex, the compliments will come from many others. (p. 215)

The importance of opening up congregations extends beyond direct worship. Being a member of a congregation provides an opportunity to help others. Gaventa observed, "Those adults have very few opportunities within service systems to give rather than to receive. They need the opportunity, like nondisabled persons, to contribute to the lives of others" (p. 195). He referred to a poignant statement made by a woman with cerebral palsy who spent much of her life in residential institutions: "The real question was not whether you can be nice to handicapped persons; it is whether or not you can let them be nice to you" (McDonald, 1977, quoted in Gaventa, 1986, p. 214).

The Religion and Disabilities Program of the National Organization of Disability (Washington, D.C.) is one program dedicated to making religious communities and congregations more welcoming to adults and children with disabilities. To this end, they host workshops and conferences and publish several practical guides to help congregations become genuinely accessible. The guides include discussion of overlooked strategies for including persons with a variety of disabilities including psychiatric disorders, sensory disabilities, learning disabilities, developmental disabilities, and chronic illnesses (National Organization on Disability, 1996a, 1996b).

ACCEPTANCE OF MORTALITY

In general, aging is accompanied by a better understanding of death and a lessened fear of death (Kalish, 1981). This aspect of development is accelerated in midlife as we often encounter the death of friends and family members. Lipe-Goodson and Goebel (1983) found that although intellectual ability mediated the extent to which adults with mental retardation understand concepts of their own mortality, aging itself also had an impact. Persons with mental retardation are not generally afforded the same opportunities as others to progress with the developmental aspects of accepting mortality, however. This is partly because the stereotype of them as "perpetual children" results in shielding them from grieving processes within families.

Family members with retardation are often excluded from family funerals and from a sharing of the emotion of the bereaved. In this manner, they are also excluded from the rituals that give death some meaning. Seltzer (1993) noted, "These restrictions may make the acceptance of mortality more difficult, particularly since these individuals are likely to need more exposure to death-related rituals in order to construct meaning from their experiences" (p. 176). Hollins (1995) reported,

> In fact strenuous efforts are often made to protect persons with developmental disabilities from life's losses and disappointments. The harsh reality of their own and their parents' mortality is a secret they will have been judged too vulnerable to be told. Their death education has often been nonexistent, so their bewilderment at the disappearance of a loved one should be no surprise. It is imperative that all people be able to access the supports given to understand death and loss. Protecting someone usually results in more problems in that grief and mourning will not be properly experienced, leading to more significant future difficulties. (p. 1)

Hollins (1995) advised professionals to advocate for persons with developmental disabilities to be included in grieving processes. She observed, "Developmental disabilities is a broad category which encompasses mild developmental difficulties to profound mental retardation with multiple disabilities. The greater the handicap, the less likely the individual's grief will be recognized" (p. 2).

LIFE SATISFACTION

One woman with a physical disability looked back on her life from the vantage point of her old age and wrote,

> If you are not a cripple, you cannot possibly imagine the way the world reduces you to that condition. For a woman, especially, normality, acceptability, and marriageability depend upon looking whole. I have been in leg and arm braces since I was three. Boys never considered me fair game for dating, even though they liked me a lot to pal around with. Teachers never thought it possible that I might accomplish what others could do.
>
> Firms that I interviewed with approached me with fear and loathing. I got through because I believed in my inner wholeness, even if my outside leaves a lot to be desired. But the world around me saw a woman without—without the use of her limbs, without womanliness, without a man, without children. My disease was the lead actor in my life. Everything else had a cameo role. (Simon, 1988, p. 220)

According to Simon (1988), "disabilities that afflict girls and young women, in sharp contrast to those that women encounter in old age for the first time, frequently dominate identity formation and become the primary determinants of social and economic prospects" (p. 219). An elderly woman with epilepsy commented,

> Being single has been the least of my troubles. It is epilepsy that has branded me for life. It is epilepsy that kept me from marrying, as I did not want to bring a child into the world with such a curse. It is epilepsy that kept me close to home when I really wanted to rove the world. It is epilepsy that caused me to keep for forty-one years a foolish job that a moron could have performed. I was afraid, you see, that no one else would employ me. Back in the dark ages, few would. ("A Never-Married Woman," Philadelphia, June 1984, quoted in Simon, 1988, p. 219)

CHANGING TRENDS IN OPPORTUNITIES AND SUPPORTS

The woman just quoted referred to the era in which she grew up as the "dark ages." It is critical to note that both this woman and the one cited earlier were born in the 1920s or earlier when the opportunities for children and adults with disabilities were very different.

In many ways life was very restricted for people with disabilities in that era. Social stigma was more punishing, less information was available regarding causation and treatment of disabilities, and there were very few opportunities for employment and independent living. In addition, many families were embarrassed by or fearful of publicly discussing sons and daughters with disabilities. Lack of knowledge and superstitious and religious explanations for disabilities only added to the stigma experienced by families and their children. But society was also less transient. Families tended to live close together or multigenerationally. This phenomenon, characteristic of earlier years, formed the basis of a closely woven support system that for many today has been replaced by multiple, fragmented, and sometimes-unresponsive service providers.

Older persons with disabilities who relied on family support earlier in life may now have support systems that have diminished because of societal changes in the workforce and family living patterns. Most families today include two adults who are employed full time and live at a distance from other family members. Frequent family moves are far more common; consequently, former methods of intergenerational family support are less available.

Other societal changes in attitudes, opportunities, and lifestyles of persons with disabilities can be observed through intergenerational interviews. Following are the comments of a niece and her daughter describing the life of an 80-year-old woman with epilepsy. The niece described her aunt as follows:

> Aunt B's seizures began after she was already in school. She was an honors student who wanted to go to nursing school. Despite her grades, the family wouldn't let her go on because of the epilepsy which was "hidden" then. It was not discussed. But she did end up being the only one of seven siblings to graduate from high school. She was the youngest of an old-fashioned family and the combination of factors meant that she wasn't allowed to do much outside of family functions. She did go to the prom and had a few friends but didn't know any boyfriends. She was overprotected by the family. She never had a job and lived with her brother for most of her adult life because she couldn't live by herself. Her other main source of support was an aunt who lived around the corner. She never even went grocery shopping. Her brother did that and when he was sick, I went. She would have felt more fulfilled if other things were available to her, although she's always been included in weddings, picnics, and family cookouts. Maybe if she'd had a job, she would have felt more satisfied. She had to sell the house because of SSI requirements and has been in a nursing

home. She wasn't allowed to go back home again. My husband and I worked all day and my daughter was in school. I just couldn't leave her alone all day. It is hard to do that to someone. I never felt burdened by her but I never had no peace of mind. (Anonymous, interview, 1997)

The niece's daughter, in her mid-20s, made the following observations about her great-aunt:

If she grew up today, she would have gone to college. If seizure free for a year, she would have been able to drive all these years. She reminisces about simple missed opportunities like being able to ride a bike or the fact that she could teach me Spanish but wasn't to continue on in school (past high school). There were no outside sources of support other than family then. I think she feels unfulfilled when she sees other family members who have full lives. The family always assumed she would be taken care of but she was never taken seriously when she wanted to go somewhere independently because of concerns for her safety. Even when she decided to quit smoking, it wasn't an independent decision. She had to get used to people making choices for her. (Anonymous, interview, 1977)

The observations of this young woman and her mother reflect the changing trends mentioned earlier. Generations ago, family support was primary for the reasons mentioned earlier and the fact that service providers and specialists were a rare commodity. People with disabilities were reliant on family support, which was secure but at the same time diminished choice making, self-determination, and independence. People who have lived for years with disabilities and are presently elderly have been thrust into a changed world of service providers rather than family. Although in many ways this is a significant loss, one of the benefits of change has been the development of an ideology and public policy that advocates inclusion. This includes the right to education, community involvement, and jobs. There has been a move to shift policy and funding to allow alternatives to nursing homes and institutions.

We conclude with the comments of the mother of an adolescent with a seizure disorder. Regarding her daughter's future, she wrote,

She wants to go to college and to work with young children. Although it would be very challenging and she would require supports, there are many programs for students with disabilities. We tried to treat her like everyone else as much as possible. She had responsibilities. We tried to be sure she had social opportunities. She is learning to drive. Our goal for her is not to be taken care of but to help her become independent, to have dreams and to work for them. She has faced many obstacles. We don't want her stopped by attitudes. I want to know that she will be okay when I am no longer here . . . that she will have a job, a friend and a life to live. (Anonymous, interview, 1977)

In all likelihood, when this young woman reaches older age, she will be able to look back on a life that had a greater measure of contentment than the older women cited in this chapter.

CHAPTER 8

Therapeutic Interventions for Families Coping with Disability

This chapter explores various approaches to working with families that reside with a person with a disability. The interventions that are examined are primarily designed to promote healthy family relationships, although some of the approaches used to achieve this goal are not necessarily family interventions per se. That is, individual, marital, or group counseling approaches can be employed while keeping the family system in mind. As discussed in Chapter 1, a systems approach is considered central to both theoretical and treatment aspects of families in that when disability occurs it affects all family members.

Therapeutic approaches include interventions that are designed to change families. As should be apparent from earlier chapters, our orientation is that not all families need to be changed or helped. Unfortunately, as noted in previous chapters, in the past and to some extent in the present, professionals in the helping professions have had a pathology orientation and assumed that the presence of a person with disabilities would necessarily result in pathology in a family's functioning. Some families do express a need for help, either directly or indirectly, however, and professionals must be able to recognize and meet that need when it arises.

This chapter presents an overview of psychosocial interventions along with references for further reading. Some of the strategies discussed require extensive knowledge and training. For professionals who are not trained in counseling or psychotherapy, this chapter provides help in recognizing problematic family issues that are beyond their expertise and may necessitate making appropriate referrals to psychological specialists. We discuss the referral process later in the chapter. First, we examine the sometimes-problematic relationship between families and professionals.

BARRIERS TO EFFECTIVE
FAMILY-PROFESSIONAL RELATIONSHIPS

The evidence to date regarding the quality of relationships families experience with professionals is discouraging (Darling, 1991; Darling & Peter, 1994). Telford and Sawrey (1977) reported that parents of persons with disabilities are almost universally dissatisfied in their experiences with professionals. The authors quoted a mother who characterized her contacts with professionals as "a masterful combination of dishonesty, condescension, misinformation and bad manners" (p. 143). Some parents are perceived as problems with which professionals need to contend whereas others are blamed for causing or at least not preventing their child's disability (Seligman, 1979). Parents are sometimes considered a nuisance rather than a resource and are frequently criticized, analyzed, or made to feel responsible for their child's disability (Seligman & Seligman, 1980). Furthermore, it is not unusual to hear of parents being called lazy and stupid, demanding, greedy, conniving, or angry and defensive (Rubin & Quinn-Curran, 1983). Holden and Lewine (reported in Bernheim & Lehman, 1985) found in their research that there are high levels of dissatisfaction with mental health services. There are also complaints about physicians who are abrupt or ill mannered or withhold information. In a survey of families in five different locales, families reported that professionals increased their feelings of guilt, confusion, and frustration. The net result was that 74% were dissatisfied with the services received and cited lack of information about diagnosis and treatment, vague and evasive responses, professional avoidance of labeling the illness (which increased their confusion), lack of support during critical periods, lack of help in locating community resources, and little or no advice about how to cope with their child's symptoms or problem behaviors. Although some believe that parent-professional relationships have improved in recent years (Darling & Peter, 1994; Marsh, 1992), the community is currently experiencing massive changes in the systems of service delivery that are affecting the quality of existing services. These changes, rooted in mandates to reduce medical and other service fees, is resulting in frustration for professionals. One might expect that as their frustration and stress increases, relationships between professionals and their patients will again become less satisfactory until efforts are made to combine cost containment with effective, high-quality services.

Condemning the Professional

Negative indicators of professional-family relationships should constitute a strong stimulus for professionals to reexamine how they relate to families where a disability exists (Bernheim & Lehman, 1985). Although professionals must be held responsible for much of the tension that sometimes exists between families and themselves, Gargiulo (1985) held that some of the blame for the tension falls on family members. Family members sometimes condemn professionals for not recognizing the disability sooner and occasionally accuse the professional of causing the disability. Gargiulo (1985) argued that some parents inhibit the growth of a healthy relationship with professionals by withdrawing or by prematurely judging professionals to be insensitive, offensive, and incapable of understanding their situation. Many professionals who are attempting to help may not realize that the very proliferation of specialists sometimes complicates rather than clarifies issues for families.

Failed Communication

Use of Jargon

Another reason for a family's lack of information or confusion may be the professional's use of jargon, which serves to confuse rather than enlighten. Professionals need to be concrete (yet not condescending) with their clients or patients and be sensitive to cues that suggest that they are not being understood. The use of professional jargon does not generate respect; it causes confusion and distance and implies aloofness and insensitivity.

Disregarding the Big Picture

There is a tendency to concentrate on specifics and disregard the whole picture: "All too often the physician will concentrate on the medical aspects, the therapist on rehabilitation, and the teacher on education—each carefully avoiding the problem of the family by focusing on the problem of the child" (Ross, 1964, p. 74). Such a view disdains the family systems view that we embrace in this book. In this type of situation no one acts to assume the role of coordinator of services to help eliminate redundancies, miscommunication, and service gaps.

Lack of Information

Family members may visit numerous professionals but remain poorly informed about the nature and implications of the disability. For many families this problem is not due to their resistance to facts but rather to the failure of the professional to inform the family adequately. Sometimes parents' lack of knowledge about a child's disability may be attributed to the professional's anxiety and withdrawal from the family or a lack of sensitivity and social skills.

While acknowledging that family members can contribute to tension between themselves and professionals (Gargiulo, 1985), we argue that professionals must shoulder most of the responsibility for failed communications. To avoid problems we believe that professionals should (a) have a thorough understanding of family systems and especially the dynamics of families with a person who has a disability, (b) be expert in effective interpersonal relationship skills, (c) acquire extensive experience working with families of persons who have disabilities, and (d) have insight into their own attitudes about noncurable illness and disability. A primary obstacle to good communication skills is graduate school education, where students may be exposed to poor role models. As the renowned psychiatrist Irvin Yalom (1975) observed, "Pipe-smoking therapists often beget pipe-smoking patients. Patients during psychotherapy may sit, walk, talk and even think like their therapists" (p. 17). Likewise, professional educators often discount the social-modeling effects they have on the people they train.

PROFESSIONAL CONCERNS

Anxiety

Another source of difficulty is to be found in the anxieties disabilities may arouse in the professional (Darling, 1979; Ross, 1964; Seligman & Seligman, 1980). Due to their discomfort, professionals may withdraw from certain families and rationalize that other professionals will help them. The difficulty is that other professionals may have similar anxieties so that in the end the family is not helped by anyone.

Burnout

Professionals in medical, educational, and social service occupations are often stressed due to the nature of their work and the demands placed on them. Professionals in stressful occupations often are so fatigued psychologically and physically that they are in a poor position to interact comfortably and productively with family members. If we wish to help promote healthier family-professional relationships, we must create less stressful job environments for professionals, who typically begin their careers with energy, high goals, and positive expectations and attitudes.

Preoccupation with Personal Concerns

Preoccupation with personal concerns is another barrier to effective helping. When a family member is speaking, novice professionals often "think ahead," thereby making it difficult to empathize with them. Preoccupation with personal problems tends to distract from careful listening. Since the lives of professionals resemble those of their clients and patients, it is not surprising that occasional personal concerns can interfere with one's effectiveness. Occasional preoccupation is not a serious problem but chronic distractions can result in communication impasses. When the latter occurs it is helpful to talk with a trustworthy colleague, supervisor, or psychotherapist.

Bias Toward Family Members

Strong feelings about the family member(s) one is working with can be a major barrier to effective listening and rapport building. Angry or anxious feelings toward someone we are trying to communicate with generally limit our ability to be helpful. In regard to physicians, Darling (1979) provided compelling evidence that some medical practitioners view families with at least some degree of personal discomfort. With reference to educational settings, Seligman (1979) addressed the negative attitudes teachers sometimes harbor toward parents of children with disabilities and toward holding parent meetings.

Distractions

Professionals sometimes allow themselves to be distracted by phone calls and interruptions from secretaries and other colleagues. Such behavior conveys a lack of concern and respect as well as inattentiveness to family members. Families should be given a predetermined, uninterrupted period of time with clinicians. A phone call or a colleague "just wanting a word" tends to interrupt and is often considered discourteous. We might reflect on how we feel when our conversations with other professionals are marked by a series of interruptions.

Differing Worldviews

In regard to family-professional relationships, Darling (1991) argued that a central reason for misunderstanding rests with the different worldview each holds. Primarily due to life experiences and consequent expectations, family members and professionals often approach each other from different perspectives. In this regard, Friedson (1965) noted, "The separate worlds of experience and reference of the layman and the professional worker are always in potential conflict with each other" (p. 175). For professionals, the primary shapers of their worldview are their socialization in a stigmatizing society and being trained in a clinical perspective (Darling, 1991). Professionals are exposed to the same social influences as others in society and therefore they often harbor the predominant negative social attitude toward those who are different (Goffman, 1963). Such negative attitudes can be counteracted by professional training, but in Darling's (1991) opinion, stigma may actually be reinforced in medical schools and in other professional training programs.

In addition to stigmatizing attitudes, professionals are exposed to the clinical perspective in their training. This perspective includes a tendency to blame the victim, belief in the medical model, and adherence to the notion of professional dominance. Although the professional worldview tends to negatively affect the family-professional relationship, it is important to note that not all professionals adopt a clinical perspective that leads to stigma, distance, and dominance.

In regard to disability, the parents' worldview of stigmatizing attitudes toward those who are "different" resemble those of professionals, but the experience of giving birth to a child with a disability has a profound effect on their values, beliefs, and attitudes (Seligman & Darling, 1997). Parents who may have held negative attitudes toward persons with disabilities before the birth of their child often espouse loving sentiments toward their child and sometimes toward others with disabilities after the birth. Some become advocates for disability causes.

Whereas the status of the professional is *achieved*, the status of the parent is *ascribed*. In other words, professionals choose their careers but parents and spouses have little choice in becoming caregivers. Furthermore, professionals are concerned with all cases of a particular type whereas parents and spouses are concerned only with their own family members. Thus, professionals may tend to treat all patients the same. According to Darling (1991), patients resent universalistic treatment because, in their view, their disabled family member is unique.

Professionals are cautioned about becoming emotionally involved with their clients/patients (affective neutrality). On the other hand, family members expect professionals to treat them with empathy and compassion, which imply a limited emotional involvement in the family situation. These different perspectives can lead to tension in the family-professional relationship.

Professional dominance or control can result in family member anomie, or giving up. Instead of feeling like partners or contributors, family members are led to believe that it is the patient's task to follow the advice of the professional. One parent complains that "professionals seem to talk 'down' to parents. They feel they are the experts and the parents should do what they tell them to. I feel the expert on the child is the parent. Parents should be respected as such and should be listened to when they speak" (quoted in Marsh, 1992, p. 39). Sometimes professionals fail to obtain from parents important information that can be helpful in forming treatment plans. For example, it is helpful for professionals to know whether families have adequate support or no support, whether they have the financial resources needed for medical procedures or equipment and learning activities, and whether they have access to mental health professionals if the family is coping poorly.

In general, the clash of perspectives tends to render the family-professional relationship an additional stressor. But once again, it is important to recognize that many professionals provide adequate information delivered in jargon-free language and can be warm and understanding of the families' circumstances.

Timing of Interventions

The timing of professional interventions is a key barometer of the success of relationships between professionals and families. Professionals need to be sensitive to a family's receptiveness to a particular intervention. For example, when family members need to sort out their feelings, professionals, threatened by affective disclosures, should not hide behind a laundry list of agencies and services and avoid discussing emotional responses. Conversely, when parents ask about community resources and help with practical matters, the professional should avoid inquiries about their emotional reactions. The timing of an intervention determines whether family members truly hear what is being said; it also affects their level of trust in the professional and their perception of the professional's expertise.

THE FAMILY'S NEED FOR COUNSELING

A New Zealand freelance writer who was also the mother of a child with mental retardation believed that "no need is more clearly or more frequently expressed when the parents of the retarded gather than the need to talk to, and be counseled by, an informed, accessible, mature and sympathetic person" (Max, 1985, p. 252). After reflecting on her experience with a psychologist, another mother made the following observation:

> I talked to a psychologist, one time, and he made me feel good. He was just
> marvelous. At that time I was so depressed. I told him I thought I was going

crazy. I felt good after I talked to him, but it didn't last. That was so long ago. I just remember feeling better for a while. I think I need somebody, anybody that I could talk to. I could say how I feel and they would understand. (quoted in Marsh, 1992, p. 197)

We have indicated the challenges families must contend with in the face of disability, although we want to acknowledge again that many families adapt remarkably well. We discussed in Chapter 1 how a major event happening to one family member reverberates throughout the family unit, leading us to emphasize the wisdom of a systems perspective. The family must come to terms with its destiny—that of frustrated expectations and thwarted life goals. Depending on the nature and severity of the family member's disability, that person's capacity to achieve or maintain independence may be limited and family members may not be allowed to live out a "normal" family life cycle.

EMOTIONAL DRAIN

Family members experience many and mixed feelings, such as love and hate, joy and sorrow, elation and depression. In addition, there is anger and frustration in dealing with a complex and difficult service delivery system (Upshur, 1991). There are concerns about the future—about a child or adolescent's educational and vocational endeavors as well as prospects for independence or an adult's ability to return to work or to regain his or her independence. In addition, families will need to confront the stigmatizing attitudes of others in a variety of contexts.

FINANCIAL BURDENS

As noted earlier, financial burdens may be the major problem for some families (Darling & Peter, 1994). Medication, special equipment, physical therapy, speech therapy, physician visits, and counseling sessions all reflect potential sources of financial drain. Severe financial problems can, in themselves, create great strain within the family system. But in terms of emotional reactions, Harris (1983) believed that accepting the diagnosis can pose a significant problem. Seeking second, third, and fourth opinions regarding a diagnosis is to be expected and sometimes encouraged, although it can be a frustrating and anxiety-provoking endeavor. When guilt, anxiety, and denial are present, however, there may be an endless round of useless visits to professionals.

Burnout

Burnout is another problem experienced by some families over time as gains may slow down or plateau (Harris, 1983). The hope for a cure or significant improvement may decline as families begin to accept the chronicity of their family member's disability. Not only do family members need to carry on with the usual tasks of daily living but they must also attend to the increasing needs of their disabled family member. When these tasks strain the family's resources, behaviors symptomatic of burnout begin to emerge and threaten the family's ability to cope.

Fatigue

Fatigue, according to Harris (1983), is related to burnout and derives from the many tasks family members must assume, such as feeding, toileting, and managing disruptive behavior. Fatigued and burned-out family members need assistance from professionals to help explore the environmental factors and family dynamics that have contributed to their situation. Professionals can also help families obtain needed services, such as respite care to help relieve stress and to provide them some private time. To help families locate the services and providers familiar with chronic illness or disability, professionals ought to have the names of competent service providers at hand to pass on to family members.

Depression

Some family members may become clinically depressed, whereas others may be occasionally dispirited. The professional can help parents accept the fact that their distress is a reasonable response to a difficult situation. For family members who are seriously depressed, however, psychotherapy (and perhaps even medication) may be indicated. Professionals need to be able to distinguish serious clinical depression from temporary and mild dysphoria and make appropriate referrals. Harris (1983) noted that feelings, such as guilt and anger, and other problems, such as marital dysfunction, need to be dealt with by the professional. In addition, professionals should be alert to problems that may develop in more peripherally involved family members, such as siblings or grandparents. Marsh (1992) listed a number of family problems that can be remediated in counseling or psychotherapy, such as an unresolved or pathological mourning process, entrenched patterns of denial, anger directed toward the ill family member or other family members, overprotectiveness that can interfere with healthy separation, use of ineffective coping methods such as substance abuse, and threat of family dissolution.

PREVENTIVE MEASURE

Rolland (1993) argued that all families facing disability or chronic illness should routinely have a family consultation as a preventive measure. Such a consultation demonstrates that a psychosocial consultant is a member of the health care team, it normalizes the expectation of psychosocial stress in a nonpejorative manner, it reduces feelings of helplessness, and it promotes open communication among professionals and family members. As noted, however, some families do not need or request help of this kind, and their wishes should be respected.

The remainder of this chapter will focus on interventions that can help reduce stress and depression, change behavior, and alter dysfunctional thinking.

TYPES OF COUNSELING

INDIVIDUAL COUNSELING

Laborde and Seligman (1991) proposed a model comprising three distinct counseling interventions: educative, personal advocacy, and facilitative.

Educative Counseling

Educative counseling is useful when families need information. This approach is based on the premise that families know little about disability until they are confronted by it in their own family. During the infancy of a child with disabilities, the family's need for information tends to be stronger than its need for support (Seligman & Darling, 1997). During this early stage, and particularly relevant to health care professionals, educative counseling can be used to inform parents, to lessen their sense of confusion and ambiguity, and to decrease the stress that is partially a result of not being informed or of being misinformed.

In addition to being informed about the particulars of the disability, its etiology, and its prognosis, family members may need to know about available services, reading materials germane to their situation, and specialized equipment. Family members should know about their legal rights for service or education, as well as about organizations, self-help groups, and local professionals who can help with problems of a more psychological nature.

Educative counseling is not just for family members of newborns. Concrete information and guidance is needed at all stages of development as the illness or disability stabilizes, worsens, or improves. After the initial hospital stay, professionals such as social workers, rehabilitation counselors, and psychologists are often in a position to help family members gain access to information and community resources. Ferhold and Solnit (1978) sounded a note of caution regarding a guidance-oriented educative approach, however, when they advised that

> the counselor is more a facilitator of learning and problem solving than a teacher of facts or an instructor in child-rearing effectiveness. The counselor [should] avoid too many specific directions, even when they appear to be helpful in the short run, because they dilute the process of enabling parents and child to be active on their own behalf—the counselor needs to have faith that parents will make sound choices, allowing for some mistakes along the way; when the counselor can no longer accept the parents' decisions, he should withdraw. (pp. 160–162)

Personal Advocacy Counseling

Ferhold and Solnit's (1978) warning brings us to the next element in Laborde and Seligman's (1991) model, personal advocacy counseling. We have already established that families need guidance in finding relevant information and in locating appropriate services. We concur with Ferhold and Solnit (1978) that parents should normally be their own case managers. Parents are the logical choice to serve as chief coordinators and evaluators of service with the assistance of a competent professional. We have indicated earlier that families often face a bewildering array of services. A coordinator of these services could eliminate problems endemic to coping with a host of services and service providers. To fill this guidance role adequately, the professional must become familiar with general referral procedures and must be knowledgeable about how the various local service agencies operate. The professional acts as a broker of services by assisting the family in formulating a clear idea of which needs they wish to have met and deciding where to receive services. With information on hand, the professional can help the family develop a plan of action for obtaining needed assistance. In essence both family members and a competent professional serve as coordinators of services—a true partnership.

The primary goal of personal advocacy counseling is to help family members experience a sense of control over events in their own lives and in the life of the family member who is disabled. By experiencing more control, families can act with greater confidence and purpose when confronted with various choices or situations. Personal advocacy counseling works for the family's welfare in a positive and assertive manner. Family members are encouraged to ask questions of their service providers, to question a provider's responses to inquiries, to seek out second opinions, and to request services they believe they need and are entitled to. In short, parents are given the support and "permission" to obtain the professional help they need without guilt or feeling that they do not have the right to ask questions. Family members are encouraged to seek out professionals who are knowledgeable and candid yet compassionate and to feel confident enough to dismiss professionals who do not meet these requirements.

Facilitative Counseling

The third and final component of Laborde and Seligman's (1991) model resembles relationship counseling, wherein a professional helps a family member accept or change distressing emotions or behaviors in the context of a trusting relationship. As noted previously, families experience a plethora of contradictory emotions when they first learn of a disability or illness in a family member. It is essential that the professional accept expected distressing feelings and not inadvertently encourage family members to deny or repress them. The family requires time to overcome its grief, and the most helpful professional behavior is to be accepting and available, yet not intrusive.

When family members are ready to move on, they can be helped to see that they can still live productive lives. It is important to encourage appropriate care for the family member who is disabled while encouraging family members to pursue their own interests and aspirations. There is a need to understand that the key to successful family functioning rests on both closeness *and* independence. The family is severely compromised if its only purpose is to be in the service of the family member with a disability.

There may be a wish to "make up" for supposed past indiscretions by overprotecting the family member with disabilities. Professionals need to help family members explore the guilt that may be implicated in overprotective behavior and understand its negative effect. The professional needs to understand that as overprotectiveness increases between a disabled and nondisabled family member, others who do not share this bond may feel excluded.

There is generally affection experienced toward the family member with the disability, but some family members may find some aspects of the condition difficult to accept. Also, feelings of rejection, like other emotions, are cyclical— they come and go. It is important for professionals to help family members realize that feelings of anger and occasional or limited rejection are normal and that their expression is acceptable.

It is helpful if professionals can assist family members to consider strategies that facilitate involvement in activities that they may have withdrawn from

(Marshak & Seligman, 1993). Family members can be helped by calculating the actual risks involved in certain activities, learning cognitive techniques that help to correct inaccurate perceptions, learning social skills, and developing strategies to help reduce stress. Where social embarrassment and uncomfortable social situations lead to withdrawal, family members can learn "stigma management" or "impression management" skills that will help ease their social relations with others (Marshak & Seligman, 1993).

Problems can emerge when one family member begins to realize the implications of the disability or illness while the others continue to firmly deny it. To intervene successfully, the professional needs to know about family interactional patterns, especially issues of power and control. A disability can serve as a handy vehicle for the acting out of dysfunctional family patterns, and the member with a disability can be wrongly identified as the cause of family problems.

As a child with disabilities grows into adolescence and young adulthood, parents may have a difficult time giving up their son or daughter to a residential treatment setting or to independent living (see Chapter 4). For a number of reasons family members may be so invested in the family member who is disabled that they may find it exceedingly difficult to let go. Letting go is especially difficult for overprotective or enmeshed families who view change and independence with apprehension.

Ross (1964) argued that professionals who work with families need to have an appreciation for the existence of ambivalence. We may find it difficult to understand the existence of positive and negative emotions at the same time. Instances of ambivalence can often be seen in working with families. For example, families may want help but are unable to ask for it; they may request advice but not follow through on it when it is given; they may agree to certain plans but fail to carry them out.

A family's ambivalent behavior can be puzzling and even annoying, but a deeper appreciation of this behavior along with a greater tolerance of it can be developed by understanding the unconscious motivation that lies behind it. What family members verbalize may be what they believe on a conscious level, but what they do is often motivated by unconscious needs that become expressed in ambivalent behavior. It is the professional's task, then, to help family members understand their contradictory behavior, which, incidentally, may be as enigmatic to them as it is to the professional.

GROUP APPROACHES

Wright (1983) observed that it helps in coping when one can release deep feelings in the context of an accepting, supportive group of peers. Shared pain can be converted to understanding and perspective. By listening to the opinions and perceptions of others, one can achieve fresh insights that give hope and build esteem.

A group provides opportunities for insight, which is often followed by behavioral and cognitive change. Hornby (1995) listed the following as benefits of group approaches:

1. Family members realize that they are not alone in feeling burdened, guilty, and occasionally depressed.
2. Uncomfortable emotions can more easily be expressed in a group than in other social contexts, even the family.
3. There is a feeling of mutual support.
4. Group members learn communication skills (to listen better and to express themselves effectively).
5. Group members can be positively influenced by other group members. Family members are more apt to listen and consider another point of view or action in the context of peers whom they respect and with whom they can identify.
6. Modeling and role playing of difficult interpersonal encounters can easily be integrated into group work.

A central question in the area of group counseling is, "What is it about group approaches that is therapeutic or helpful for its members?" This question is perhaps best addressed by discussing the therapeutic factors noted by Yalom (1995). Some of these factors, which are the lifeblood of all therapeutically oriented groups, are briefly discussed below:

1. *Imparting of Information.* The communication of information may take several forms. Clients may be of help to other participants by revealing where certain services are available or where relevant job opportunities exist. Didactic instruction may be used by the leader to inform group members of illness- and disability-related information. Experts on illness and disability issues can be invited to speak at group meetings, often followed by a brief question-and-answer period and a time for discussion. Leaders can also educate and provide information on a variety of health issues and help participants understand issues related to identity concerns, anger, and the grieving process (Jacobs, Harvill, & Masson, 1988). Furthermore, information may be imparted to inform group members of the process and goals of the group. The uncertainty and anxiety of functioning in a group is alleviated to some extent by informing prospective participants about group functioning, group goals, expectations, and responsibilities of group members and of the leader.

2. *Instillation of Hope.* In seeing the progress of others in the group, a member may feel encouraged that positive changes can occur and that there is hope no matter what one's circumstances are. To see improvement in others who have overcome adversity is a particularly hopeful sign to members of a group. It is reassuring when a member's progress is noted and affirmed in the group.

3. *Universality.* To discover that others live and cope with a particular life circumstance lessens some negative aspects of one's own situation. Knowing that one does not struggle alone or that others have similar problems is a powerful source of relief and support for group participants. One mother acknowledged universality by remarking that

> meeting other mothers with similar experiences was wonderful. As much as we love our handicapped children, it was such an eye-opener to learn that other mothers had intense feelings at times of guilt, anger toward the child, resentment toward an abnormal lifestyle, and other negative feelings. I thought I was the only one that still feels this way after so many years. I left the meetings uplifted that my feelings are quite typical and really normal considering what our family has gone through. (quoted in Marsh, 1992, p. 195)

4. *Altruism.* Altruism refers to being useful to others, even during periods of stress and depression. One has ample opportunity to engage in altruistic behavior in groups. To be able to contribute to another's well-being can be an important source of self-esteem. Since many people who are members of counseling groups suffer from low self-esteem or depression, the process of helping others can be an ego-strengthening experience.

5. *Corrective Recapitulation of the Primary Family Group.* Because therapeutic groups resemble families in many respects, the opportunity is available for members to achieve insight and work on unresolved familial conflicts.

6. *Development of Socializing Techniques.* The development of socializing techniques may take the form of role simulations of constructive interpersonal behaviors that are learned in the group. Interpersonal styles that are problematic can be extinguished by feedback from others and by practicing useful ways of relating in the nonthreatening environment of the group. Socializing strategies can be especially useful in learning how to deal effectively with professionals or with a "difficult" family member.

7. *Corrective Emotional Experience.* Corrective emotional experience alludes to the insight gained and the perceptual change that takes place as one recognizes and realigns reactions one has had to significant others in the past. For example, in a sibling group, participants may learn that their parents often enlisted their assistance with a sibling who had a disability because they

felt so burdened by other family problems and because they saw the participant as their most capable child. The assumption that one had been picked on because one was the family's unloved child can be corrected in group. In essence, the corrective emotional experience forces group members to reality-test prior assumptions.

8. *The Group as a Social Microcosm.* In time, members reveal themselves to each other in the group as they relate to friends, relatives, spouses, and coworkers outside the group. Maladaptive behavioral patterns employed with others are, sooner or later, manifested in the group. Thus, the group elicits important "out-of-group" behaviors, thereby generating a condensed version of a member's larger social reality in the group.

9. *Cohesion.* When a group experiences cohesion, a sense of we-ness develops. When this happens members are more apt to contribute, take risks, and generally be more open. Members who are not threatened in the group generally feel a sense of belonging and acceptance and therefore relate more productively, are more tolerant of conflict, and attend regularly. Groups lacking cohesiveness generally cause members to exhibit a lack of trust, to feel threatened that their comments or observations will be criticized or rejected, to believe that the group's goals do not match theirs, and to generally experience a sense of danger.

Different Types of Groups

Irrespective of one's theoretical orientation, there are several different types of groups that presently exist:

1. *Counseling/Psychotherapy Groups.* Some professionals make a distinction between counseling and psychotherapy, in that therapy groups are considered more long-term, more in-depth, and more psychodynamically oriented than counseling groups. In some settings this is an accurate distinction but in others it is misleading. Therapy-oriented groups are face-to-face interactions of group members who may or may not share a particular condition or life situation. Therapeutic groups can have a variety of different purposes but, generally speaking, they are designed to help persons explore dysfunctional behavior patterns or to help people cope with social skill deficits and interpersonal problems.

2. *Support/Self-Help Groups.* Support groups are often homogeneous assemblages of people who come together to talk about their circumstances with others. In support or self-help groups members give and receive advice and practical help; learn or become educated about a particular condition (e.g., arthritis or multiple sclerosis); and advocate for social programs and

fund-raising. Support groups usually have leaders who emerge from the membership, but a minority of such groups are led by professionals.

These groups do not engage in in-depth exploration or even encourage behavior change. They are primarily driven by the human need for affiliation and interpersonal support in overcoming or coping with acute (e.g., bereaved parents) or chronic (siblings of persons with cystic fibrosis) conditions.

3. *Educational Groups.* Educational groups can be large gatherings of persons who share a problem but are not expected to interact with each other. The group members mainly listen and ask questions of the presenter or leader. One of the founders of group therapy, Joseph Pratt (1907), conducted educational/inspirational groups for dispirited persons with tuberculosis. Both therapeutic and support groups can have an educational component, but it is much more likely, in fact, quite common, for this to occur in support or self-help groups. In support groups, information is often integrated with discussion.

4. *Multiple-Family Groups.* In the area of disability, multiple-family groups are generally composed of more than one family that shares a common circumstance. An example would be family members of persons who have a mental illness. Some of these groups have two or three families whereas others are more sizable. The leader must exercise a fair amount of control so that the interaction is manageable and so that all families are given the opportunity to contribute. Support and information are commonly a part of these group experiences.

5. *Inpatient/Outpatient Groups.* Inpatient groups are conducted in an institutional setting (e.g., a hospital or rehabilitation clinic) whereas outpatient groups can be offered in a variety of places (e.g., mental health clinic, private practice). Both inpatient and outpatient groups can lean in the direction of support or therapy. It is not unusual for inpatient group members to join an outpatient group to consolidate changes made while in an institution. Outpatient groups can provide a source of support during the transition from the institutional setting to one's natural surroundings.

Organizational Issues in Group Formation

Before forming a group, the leader should consider a number of practical issues. Some preliminary thought and planning may make the difference between a productive or unproductive experience.

1. *Pregroup Interview.* Group members are less anxious and better prepared if they meet with the group leader before the group convenes. This allows the leader to become acquainted with the prospective group member and determine whether he or she is suitable for the group and whether the group

meets the needs of the participant. Remember that most clients are suitable group candidates but may not be appropriate for a particular group.

2. *Group Purpose.* It is essential to give some thought to the focus of the group. A focus or goal provides group members with a purpose and something to attempt to achieve during the life of the group. Setting group goals is important because they provide concrete bench marks and a sense of achievement for members and the leader alike.

3. *Selection of Group Members.* In selecting group members, client characteristics such as age, disability, sex, and so on can be considered. The question of what to look for in prospective group members is a subject of considerable controversy (Yalom, 1995). Experimentation and experience in group composition would appear to be the most helpful guide. It is our view that it is better to be more inclusive than exclusive, especially in support groups.

If time is seriously circumscribed, a leader may wish to consider bringing together people dealing with a similar disability or concern so that identification, mutual understanding, and support can occur rather quickly. There is some speculation that clients who share a common problem (e.g., parents of children with mental retardation or adults who themselves have physical disabilities) get down to business more quickly (Furst, 1960; Yalom, 1995). Groups that are more heterogeneous generally take longer to get going but may deal with their problems in more depth. Support and self-help groups are examples of homogeneous groups. Groups in private practice and in certain other clinical settings that serve people with a variety of problems exemplify heterogeneous group composition. There seems to be a trend toward support-oriented groups that share a particular problem or condition (Lieberman, 1990).

4. *Group Size.* Although there is some variation in opinion, the minimum number of group participants is 6 or 7, with a maximum of 12. Group size should, in part, be a function of the nature and purpose of the group. A group formed for didactic experience can be considerably larger than a group where personal and in-depth interaction is expected.

In considering group size for therapeutic groups, one should keep in mind that as size increases so do the possibilities for factionalism (subgrouping), diluted group interaction, and a greater expectation that the leader assume a strong leadership role. Moreover, in larger groups, the quieter and more withdrawn individuals tend to get "lost in the crowd." In contrast, as size decreases, greater pressure exists for those in the group to maintain the interaction (some mild, usually productive group pressure) and if the group becomes too small there is a constriction of new perceptions and ideas.

5. *Frequency of Meetings.* Another organizational variable that is considered prior to the first group meeting is how often should the group meet. For some groups, organizational or agency constraints may determine the frequency of meetings. For others, the leader may wish to hold sessions less often. Group goals, client characteristics, logistics, and convenience should help to determine the frequency of meetings.

6. *Duration of Group.* Duration refers to how long a group meets over time. A leader may wish to engage group members in a discussion of how long they should meet given the goals of the group. This could be done initially but may be more helpful to discuss after the group members have achieved minimal cohesiveness and have developed common goals. On the other hand, the leader may want to suggest how long the group will meet, based on experience. There are some peer or support groups that meet less often but continue for years. At any rate, some thinking through of the duration of the group as it relates to some of the issues discussed previously should prove advantageous.

7. *Length of Sessions.* Some of the same considerations discussed above apply here. Whether a meeting should last 1 hour or 3 hours should depend on the purpose of the group. Although session length has not been a major issue in the professional literature, an often-used and seemingly reasonable time period is 1 $\frac{1}{2}$ hours. A shorter period seriously restricts full participation, but on the other hand, meeting much longer may impinge on agency constraints or on other aspects of the rehabilitation process.

This section reviewed some concepts basic to the understanding of therapeutic groups. These as well as other generic group issues are addressed in depth in numerous books on group counseling and group psychotherapy (Friedman, 1989; Gladding, 1995; Lieberman, 1991; Seligman & Marshak, 1990; Yalom, 1995). Before undertaking group work, the leader should first be proficient in individual approaches and then schooled in the theory and practice of group practices.

MARITAL AND FAMILY COUNSELING

Marital Counseling

Marital counseling may be indicated when parents or spouses experience difficulties as a consequence of illness or disability in the family. As noted elsewhere in this volume, it is important to keep in mind that illness or disability can contribute to marital problems. In families where there is a member with a disability, the problems may be more related to clashing personalities, different interpersonal styles, disparate hopes, and dreams, and the like than to the disability, however.

Marital counseling offers the parents of a child with a disability an opportunity to explore conflicting roles, expectations, and the like in the context of a professional relationship. It can help with issues that pertain to their children, such as parenting concerns, or it can assist with problems related to extended family conflicts or to concerns that are attributable to the husband-wife interaction. Some couples or families express conflicts over more than one of these issues.

Medical Family Counseling Model

In the Medical Family Counseling (MCC) model, the focus of the intervention is the family member who has an illness or disability and systemic changes are generally achieved through that individual (Pollin, 1995). Alternative approaches may more readily include other family members than the MCC model, which focuses on the client (Elman, 1991; Rolland, 1994).

According to Pollin (1995), adjustment issues tend to fall into four central areas: interpersonal relations, practical tasks, emotional concerns, and cognitive work. Interpersonal relations refer to the struggle to maintain intimacy and mutual support in the face of illness or disability. Counseling would take the form of strengthening communication and coping skills for upcoming challenges and work toward reconciling the different coping styles and developmental needs and aspirations of all family members.

Practical tasks include the reallocation of roles, time and resource management, and future planning. Family members are encouraged to assess their needs and gather additional support outside of the family to help prepare for the long haul. Important under the practical task rubric is the need to gather relevant information about the disability and available resources.

In the area of emotional concerns, family members may need to process grief and loss and comprehend and come to terms with the anger and guilt that the disability arouses. While coping with mental stress and physical exhaustion, the family must remain flexible in the face of change and unpredictability. Family members may need help in expressing emotionally charged topics to avoid feelings of isolation from those to whom they are closest. "Above all, the family's challenge is to sustain hope and stay emotionally involved with one another, including the ill member" (Pollin, 1995, p. 123).

Closely related to emotional tasks is the cognitive work that family members are encouraged to consider. Under the stress some families endure, each member should clarify his or her values and reexamine priorities. Family members are encouraged to cultivate more positive values about their circumstances.

Family Therapy

According to the family therapist Elman (1991), the question of whom to include in the family sessions is determined, in part, by the therapist's therapeutic orientation and the availability and willingness of family members to participate. Most family therapists begin to work with those who are willing to come, with the goal that other members may join later. By their absence, reluctant family members are sending a message that it is not their problem, that they believe that they cannot help with the situation, or that talking about the disability arouses unbearable emotions. Elman (1991) believed that key issues in families where there is a family member with a disability include family roles, boundary issues, and helping the family normalize and reframe its experience of disability.

Family roles can be functional and flexible or they can be rigid, limiting, polarized, and dysfunctional. In well-functioning families, roles are appropriate to the circumstances of the family and they are capable of being modified as circumstances change. When a disability or illness is introduced into a family that is functioning well, role changes are easily negotiated and family members are not angry or threatened by role alterations, although these changes require time and patience as the family reacts to this intrusion into its life. According to Elman (1991), major polarized roles in dysfunctional families with a member who has a disability involve the caretaking parent or spouse and the indifferent or withdrawn family member. This situation often involves over- and underfunctioning family members. In therapy the overfunctioning adult is often instructed to do less, allowing the other one to do more.

Boundary issues refer to overinvolved and underinvolved family members, usually in relation to the family member who has a disability. The enmeshment of one family member (e.g., a mother is excessively close to her daughter who has a physical disability) may motivate the hurt and "neglected" father to withdraw. In this instance, the mother needs to understand that her daughter, despite the disability, can most likely function more independently than she thinks. She also needs to understand that her husband will react to the relationship between her and their daughter by withdrawing. On the other hand, the father needs to understand that his withdrawal intensifies the enmeshment between his daughter and wife, leaving him out "in the cold." His joining and supportive behavior can help reduce the intensity of the enmeshment, allowing for improved relationships between the parents and between the parents and their daughter.

Family members may be depressed about their situation, perhaps caused by feelings of guilt and anger. Normalizing mild forms of depression can help families understand that, in the context of the situation, their struggles are normal and expected. Normalization can help reduce feelings of stigma and isolation associated with disability.

Reframing involves reinterpreting a circumstance and putting it into a new context, or "frame." For example, a reframe of a mother's behavior from intrusive to caring and concerned alters the perception of and meaning attributed to the following situation:

> If a mother is defined as overinvolved and intrusive, the family therapist can respond empathetically to how much she cares for her disabled child and how hard she has tried to find ways to help the child to grow as successfully as possible. (Elman, 1991, p. 394)

In this situation the mother feels more understood than in the past and the other family members also view the mother in a different, more positive way. Reframing can also help the family adapt to its view of the disabling condition as illustrated by the following:

> Perhaps the most important reframe a family can make is to shift from a view of the disabled or ill child as being overly helpless to one in which the child's capacities that are not affected by the disability are highlighted. Families that are able to see those strengths in the child are less likely to be frozen in dysfunctional, overinvolved patterns that are detrimental to the growth of the child and other members of the family. (Elman, 1991, p. 395)

Other key topics in family counseling include communications, triangulation, control issues, and sexual functioning. In childhood, adolescent, and adult disability it is important to keep avenues of communication open (Rolland, 1994). Keeping secrets tends to heighten anxiety about the illness or disability. The ambiguity of silence creates tension, suspiciousness, and isolation—a deadly combination. The professional can help family members speak to each other. This task is made easier when it is understood that openness enriches family life whereas silence stagnates and depresses it.

Triangulation is in effect when person A is angry at or frightened of the reaction of person B. Instead of speaking with B, A approaches C to tell him how angry or fearful she is of B. This triangulation makes it difficult for A and B to have a relationship because A continues to be angry at B, and because B senses A's withdrawal. Triangulated families tend to be dysfunctional ones. Family members avoid talking directly to one another, culminating in misunderstandings that fuel discord. In addition to the triangulation of persons, an illness or disability can also become a source of triangulation. For example, a conflicted couple, who find it difficult to confront their problems with each other, instead focus on their daughter's disability as the main source of their conflict. This external focus reduces their tension and enhances the fiction that their relationship is conflict free.

People who have powerful control needs tend to overfunction and resent the "interference" of others. By the same token, the controlling overfunctioner usually resents the fact that others are not contributing. Overfunctioners fail to see that their overcontrolling behavior leaves little room for others to contribute. An illustration of overly controlling behavior is when a mother feels that only she can care for her infant with a disability. As a result she discourages other family members from contributing, thereby causing a rift between family members. The mother feels that she is taken for granted and others withdraw from the intense mother-child dyad.

Behavioral Parent Training

Behavioral parent training (BPT) has been used extensively (Harris, 1983; Kaiser & Fox, 1986) and has been the subject of numerous studies (Marsh, 1992). BPT has specific applications and tends to be used and recommended by professionals with a strong behavioral bent.

For some families the presenting behavioral problems of their children or adolescents are so severe and disruptive that parent training is a particularly useful intervention. Focusing on the disruptive behavior of children with mental retardation, Kaiser and Fox (1986) reported that parents have been trained successfully to modify diverse behavioral problems and to teach such adaptive abilities as chewing and feeding skills, motor imitation, self-help skills, appropriate play behaviors and social interaction with parents, articulation and vocabulary skills, and compliance behavior. One author described a program designed to train parents in groups as behavior modifiers of their children (Rose, 1974). This program involved becoming familiar with behavioral principles, learning about behavioral assessment, monitoring behaviors weekly, and developing treatment plans. An evaluation of this program showed that parents who varied in education level and social class were able to acquire the skills needed to modify their children's behavior.

Baker's (1989) model, Parents as Teachers, includes such goals as reducing problem behaviors, increasing the child's involvement in activities, and building basic self-help skills as well as teaching play, speech, and language skills. The program consisted of 10 training sessions where these skills were taught and applied. The sessions employed minilectures, small group problem-solving sessions, focused discussion, role-playing demonstrations, and other activities. Baker (1989) evaluated the program and found that the parents and children benefited from it.

In his book *Special Children, Challenged Parents,* Naseef (1997) discussed the trials, tribulations, and rewards of parenting youth with special needs. Naseef devoted a chapter to exploring patterns of misbehavior and how parents of youth with disabilities can help reduce problematic behaviors. Naseef also discussed such relevant topics as using time-outs, implementing natural and logical consequences, giving choices, structuring the environment, and the like.

Effective BPT can decrease some of the stress that parents of children and adolescents with disabilities experience (Kaiser & Fox, 1986; Naseef, 1997). With this in mind, we believe that it is important for professionals either to be trained in BPT or to be able to make an appropriate referral to someone who specializes in working with disruptive behavior in children. It is beyond the scope of this chapter to elaborate further on the BPT model; two excellent resources for professionals who wish to learn more about individual and group models of BPT are Harris's (1983) *Families of the Developmentally Disabled: A Guide to Behavioral Intervention* and Baker and Brightman's (1989) *Steps to Independence: A Skills Training Guide for Parents and Teachers of Children with Special Needs.*

A major problem with the BPT model is that some families fail to acquire or maintain newly learned skills. Rose (1974) indicated that some parents "never completed contracts but were either changing the responses to be observed or ineffectively implementing unauthorized procedures" (pp. 138–139). Reasons for parental noncompliance include parents' lack of time to do the training, lack of spouse support, limited materials for teaching, and lack of confidence. Another possible reason for parental noncompliance may be the presence of severely disruptive life events, such as death, divorce, illness in the family, or substance abuse. Some parents may not believe that the program is necessary or that they can actually influence their child's behavior after years of trying and failing. Other limitations include the assumption that all parents want or need BPT, that BPT may limit other forms of parental involvement, and that such training may fail to address other parent needs (Lyon & Lyon, 1991). Others caution that parent training can be a narrow approach to facilitating family adaptation in that it fails to embrace the whole family and the intricate dynamics that characterize family functioning (Marsh, 1992). Furthermore, in some cultural groups, the parent as teacher role is not an appropriate model. Many parents of lower socioeconomic status are so preoccupied by survival activities that they do not have time to be their children's teachers or therapists.

Caution must be exercised in asking parents to engage in "homework" or to act as their child's therapist. Consider the situation of parents who must follow the prescriptions of the special education teacher, the speech therapist, and the doctor. Max (1985) noted that the pendulum of fashion might be swinging too far, so that parents' onerous burden of impotence has been replaced by an equally heavy one of great expectations. She noted, "You feel that you have to do it all and it is so exhausting. But if you don't do everything they tell you to do, you feel that you're letting down all these highly qualified people who are giving up their good time to help your child" (p. 255).

REFERRALS

There are times when a professional needs to make a referral to another practitioner who may have specialized knowledge and expertise. The first task is to be sure a referral is indicated. A referral is appropriate when a specialist in another area of expertise is needed or when the referrer believes that another professional can offer a second opinion. Referrals should be timely in that it should be the opinion of the referrer and the family that another professional's involvement would be helpful at that time. Also, early, appropriate referrals are essential in instances where a delay may be harmful. Delays, for example, for early intervention can be costly to a child's progress.

As noted earlier in the book, professionals should be knowledgeable about referral sources or know where to get information about services. In Pittsburgh, for example, the United Way–sponsored book *Where to Turn* lists community agencies, their phone numbers and addresses, and information relative to what each has to offer. Most communities have similar resources. Generally speaking, professionals should be knowledgeable about medical, psychosocial, educational, and specialized community resources as well as information about support groups. It is helpful to be aware of ethical, well-informed, and respected professionals. It is useful too to be aware of professionals and specialized community services for persons having specific and rare disorders. Referrals to professionals who exhibit empathy, good communication skills, and specialized knowledge is appreciated by the family.

It is critical for the referrer to be clear about the reasons for the referral. It is also incumbent on the referrer to communicate why a referral is being made now. A lack of clarity on the these issues serves to confuse the family about why a referral is being made. Once one is certain about the motivation for a referral, it is equally important to communicate the reasons to the family using clear and jargon-free language. Referrals are accepted more readily when the recipient has a sound understanding of why a referral is being made and is in agreement with the recommendation.

Perhaps the most difficult referral to make is one to a mental health professional. Families may feel that a referral to a psychologist means that there may be mental illness in the family or that there are major dysfunctions that need repair. It is more likely that the family is attempting to cope with recently encountered new stresses or emotions related to the changes, tasks, and role changes that disability creates for family members. Marsh (1992) stated,

> Psychotherapy offers many potential benefits, including opportunities for family members to improve relationships within the family, to develop more effective coping skills, to achieve a greater sense of mastery and competence, to improve their self-esteem, and to replenish their energy for meeting the challenges that confront them. (p. 207)

Due to their anxiety or because they feel their defenses are threatened, families may initially resist a mental health referral. Being anxious, family members may not accurately hear the reasons for the referral (Pollin, 1995). Therefore, such referrals may need to be repeated or communicated in a different or clearer fashion.

An illustration of a poorly communicated referral is when a professional says, "I believe that you need to see a psychologist because you are not coping well with David's disability." A better way to communicate the need for counseling is illustrated by the referrer in this way: "You've been talking about how distressed you are about David's disability and what it means for your future and David's. You indicated that you have been crying a lot and finding it difficult to get a good night's sleep. It may be helpful to see a psychologist to have an opportunity to discuss some of your concerns. I know of a psychologist that works with family disability. I would be happy to give you her phone number, if you wish."

As recipients of referrals, professionals prefer to have the reasons for the referral articulated in a succinct manner. The professional may want to note why the referral is made at this time—that is, whether there is a precipitating event that led to the referral. The professional to whom the family is referred might also want to know whether the referrer would like a status report at some future time or a written report. Any information that is passed on from one professional to another requires the written permission of the client or patient.

CONCLUSION

In this chapter we have reviewed individual, group, and family approaches to help family members increase their coping abilities. We acknowledge that not all families need help from such resources, but for some families coping with disability, help may be sought out at different periods of the family and child's developmental life cycle. Although some family members need little help at the birth of a child with disabilities, they may experience a need for assistance when the child is an adolescent, when independence issues are paramount, or when parents are elderly and begin to have acute concerns about the future of their adult child. This chapter has also addressed issues that emerge in the parent-professional relationship.

References

Affleck, G., & Tennen, H. (1993). Cognitive adaptation to adversity: Insights from parents of medically fragile children. In A. P. Turnbull, J. M. Patterson, S. K. Behr, D. L. Murphy, J. G. Marquis, & M. J. Blue-Banning (Eds.), *Cognitive coping, families and disability* (pp. 135–150). Baltimore: Paul H. Brookes.

Allen, T., & Sligar, S. (1994). The assessment of deaf individuals in the context of rehabilitation. In R. Nowell & L. Marshak (Eds.), *Understanding deafness and the rehabilitation process* (pp. 113–137). Boston: Allyn and Bacon, 1994.

Alper, S., Schloss, P. J., & Schloss, C. N. (1994). *Families of students with disabilities: Consultation and advocacy.* Boston: Allyn & Bacon.

Alper, S., Schloss, P. J., & Schloss, C. N. (1995). Families of children with disabilities in elementary and middle school: Advocacy models and strategies. *Exceptional Children, 62,* 261–270.

Amado, A. N. (1993). *Friendships and community connections between people with and without developmental disabilities.* Baltimore: Paul H. Brookes.

Americans With Disabilities Act of 1990, 42 U.S.C.A. § 12101 et seq. (Pub. L. No. 101–336).

Anspach, R. R. (1979). From stigma to identity politics: Political activism among the physically disabled and former mental patients. *Social Science and Medicine, 13A,* 765–773.

Antonovsky, A. (1993). The implications of salutogenesis. In A. P. Turnbull, J. M. Patterson, S. K. Behr, D. L. Murphy, J. G. Marquis, & M. J. Blue-Banning (Eds.), *Cognitive coping, families & disability* (pp. 111–122). Baltimore: Paul H. Brookes.

Aquilino, W. (1990). The likelihood of parent-adult child coresidence: Effects of family structure and parental characteristics, *Journal of Marriage and the Family, 52,* 405–419.

Aquilino, W. (1991). Parent and child relations and parent's satisfaction with living arrangements when adult children live at home. *Journal of Marriage and the Family, 53,* 13–27.

Atlantis/American Disabled for Attendant Programs Today. (1992, March 1–15). *Incitement* [newsletter], *8,* 1.

Backlar, P. (1995). *The family face of schizophrenia.* New York: Putnam.

Bailey, D. B., & Wolery, W. R. (1984). *Teaching infants and preschoolers with handicaps.* Columbus, OH: Merrill.

Baker, B. L. (1989). *Parent training and developmental disabilities.* Washington, DC: American Association on Mental Retardation.

Baker, B. L., & Brightman, A. J. (1989). *Steps to independence.* Baltimore: Brooks.

Balser, R. M., Harvey, B. M., & Hornby, H. C. (1993). Putting youth with disabilities to work: A business education partnership. *OSERS News in Print, 6*(1), 13–17.

Baltes, M., & Cartensen, L. (1996). The process of successful aging. *Aging and Society, 16,* 397–421.

Bandura, A. (1977). *Social learning theory.* Englewood Cliffs, NJ: Prentice Hall.

Bandura, A., & Schunk, D. H. (1981). Cultivating competence, self-efficacy, and intrinsic interest through proximal self-motivation. *Journal of Personality and Social Psychology, 41,* 586–598.

Baroff, G. (1991). *Developmental disabilities: Psychosocial aspects.* Austin, TX: Pro-Ed.

Beardslee, M. D., & Podorefsky, M. A. (1988). Resilient adolescents whose parents have serious affective and other psychiatric disorders: Importance of self-understanding and relationships. *American Journal of Psychiatry, 145,* 63–69.

Beckman, P. J. (1983). Influence of selected child characteristics on stress in families of handicapped infants. *American Journal of Mental Deficiency, 88,* 150–156.

Beckman, P. J., & Pokorni, J. L. (1988). A longitudinal study of families of preterm infants: Change in stress and support over the first two years. *Journal of Special Education, 22,* 65–66.

Begleiter, M. L., Barry, Y. F., & Harris, D. J. (1976). Prevalence of divorce among parents of children with cystic fibrosis and chronic diseases. *Social Biology, 23,* 260–264.

Bender, W. N., & Wall, M. E. (1994). Social-emotional development of students with learning disabilities. *Learning Disabilities Quarterly, 17,* 323–341.

Benedict, R. C., & Ganikos, P. L. (1981). Coming to terms with ageism in rehabilitation. *Journal of Rehabilitation, 47,* 10–18.

Benz, M. R., Yovanoff, P., & Doren, B. (1997). School-to-work components that predict postschool success for students with and without disabilities. *Exceptional Children, 63,* 151–165.

Bernard, A. W. (1974). A comparative study of marital integration and sibling role tension differences between families who have a severely mentally retarded child and families of non-handicapped (Doctoral dissertation, University of Cincinnati, 1974). *Dissertation Abstracts International, 35A*(5), 2800–2801.

Bernheim, K. F., & Lehman, A. (1985). *Working with families of the mentally ill.* New York: Norton.

Birenbaum, A. (1971). The mentally retarded child in the home and family life cycle. *Journal of Health and Social Behavior, 12,* 55–65.

Blacher, J. (1984). Sequential stages of parental adjustment to the birth of a child with handicaps: Fact or artifact? *Mental Retardation, 22,* 55–68.

Blacher, J., & Baker, B. (1992). Toward meaningful family involvement in out-of-home placement settings. *Mental Retardation, 30*(1), 35–43.

Blake, R. (1981). Disabled older persons: A demographic analysis. *Journal of Rehabilitation, 47,* 19–27.

Blalock, G. (1988). Transitions across the life-span. In B. Ludlow, A. Turnbull, & R. Luckasson (Eds.), *Transitions to adult life for people with mental retardation: Principles and practices* (pp. 3–19). Baltimore: Paul H. Brookes.

Blatt, B. (1987). The community imperative and human values. In R. F. Antonak & J. A. Mulick (Eds.), *Transition in mental retardation: The community imperative revisited* (pp. 236–247). Norwood, NJ: Ablex.

Blotzer, M. (1995). Glimpses of lives: Stories of brief treatment. In M. A. Blotzer & R. Ruth (Eds.), *Sometimes you just want to feel like a human being* (pp. 15–162). Baltimore: Paul H. Brookes.

Blum, R. (1984). Sexual health needs of physically and intellectually impaired adolescents. In R. Blum (Ed.), *Chronic illness and disabilities in childhood and adolescence* (pp. 127–143). Orlando, FL: Grune & Stratton.

Bodieri, J. E., Sotolongo, M., & Wilson, M. (1983). Physical attractiveness and attributions for disability. *Rehabilitation Psychology, 28*(4), 207–215.

Bogdan, R., & Taylor, S. (1987, Fall). Toward a sociology of acceptance: The other side of the study of deviance. *Social Policy,* pp. 34–39.

Bos, C. S., & Fletcher, T. V. (1997). Sociocultural considerations in learning disabilities inclusion research: Knowledge gaps and future directions. *Learning Disabilities Research and Practice, 12*(2), 92–99.

Bowlby, J. (1951). *Maternal care and mental health.* Geneva: World Health Organization.

Boyce, G. C., Behl, D. Mortensen, & Akers, J. (1991). Child characteristics, family demographics and family processes: Their effects on the stress experienced by families of children with disabilities. *Counseling Psychology Quarterly, 4,* 273–288.

Brightman, A. (1984). Impressions. In A. Brightman (Ed.), *Ordinary moments: The disabled experience* (pp. 141–148). Baltimore: University Park Press.

Brinthaupt, G. (1991). The family of a child with cystic fibrosis. In M. Seligman (Ed.), *The family with a handicapped child* (2nd ed., pp. 295–336). Needham Heights, MA: Allyn & Bacon.

Bristol, M. M. (1984). Family resources and successful adaptation to autistic children. In E. Schopler & G. B. Mesibov (Eds.), *The effects of autism on the family* (pp. 289–310). New York: Plenum.

Bristol, M. M. (1987). The home care of children with developmental disabilities: Empirical support for a model of successful family coping with stress. In S. Landesman, P. M. Vietze, & M. J. Begab, (Eds.), *Living environments and mental retardation.* NICHD-Mental retardation research series (pp. 401–422). Washington, DC: American Association on Mental Retardation.

Brody, S. J. (1983). Rehabilitation of the aged. *Aging Newsletter, 1*(5), 1–12.

Bronfenbrenner, U. (1979). *The ecology of human development.* Cambridge: Harvard University Press.

Brooks, R. B. (1994a). Children at risk: Fostering resilience and hope. *American Journal of Orthopsychiatry, 64*, 545–553.

Brooks, R. B. (1994b). Children with ADD: Portraits of hope, courage and resilience. *Proceedings of the C.H.A.D.D. 1994 Annual Conference* (pp. 327–342). Fairfax, VA: Caset Associates.

Brotherson, M. J., Backus, L. H., Summers, J. A., & Turnbull, A. P. (1986). Transition to adulthood. In J. A. Summers (Eds.), *The right to grow up* (pp. 175–180). Baltimore: Brooks.

Brotherson, M. J., Turnbull, A. P., Bronicki, G. J., Houghton, J., Roeder-Gordon, C., Summers, J. A. & Turnbull, H. R. (1988). Transition into adulthood: Parental planning for sons and daughters with disabilities. *Education and Training in Mental Retardation, 23*, 165–174.

Cameron, P., Titus, D. G., Kostin, J., & Kostin, M. (1973). The life satisfaction of non-normal persons. *Journal of Consulting and Clinical Psychology, 41*, 207–214.

Cantwell, D. P., & Baker, L. (1984). Research concerning families of children with autism. In E. Schopler & G. B. Mesilbov (Eds.), *The effects of autism on the family* (pp. 41–63). New York: Plenum.

Carl Perkins Vocational and Applied Technology Act, Pub. L. No. 101–392.

Carter, B., & McGoldrick, M. (1989). Overview of the changing family life cycle: A framework for family therapy. In B. Carter & M. McGoldrick (Eds.), *The changing family life cycle: A framework for family therapy* (2nd ed., pp. 3–28). Boston: Allyn & Bacon.

Chadsey-Rusch, J., & Heal, L. W. (1995). Building consensus from transition experts on social integration outcomes and intervention. *Exceptional Child, 62*, 165–187.

Chadsey-Rusch, J., Rusch, F. R., & O'Reilly, M. (1991). Transition from school to integrated communities. *Remedial and Special Education, 12*(6), 23–33.

Chesler, M. A., & Barbarin, G. A. (1987). *Childhood cancer and the family*. New York: Brunner/Mazel.

Chigier, E. (1972). *Down's syndrome*. Lexington, MA: Heath.

Chilman, C. S. (1990). Promoting adolescent sexuality. *Family Relations, 39*, 123–131.

Cobb, S. (1976). Social support as a moderator of life stress. *Psychosomatic Medicine, 38*, 300–314.

Coelho, R., & Dillon, N. (1990, Spring). A survey of elderly persons with developmental disabilities. *Journal of Applied Rehabilitation Counseling, 21*(1), 9–15.

Cole, P. (1986). Out-of-home child placement and family adaptation: A theoretical framework. *American Journal of Mental Deficiency, 90*, 226–236.

Cole, S. S. (1986). Facing the challenges of sexual abuse in persons with disabilities. *Sexuality and Disability, 7*, 71–88.

Cole, S. S. (1991). Facing the challenges of sexual abuse in persons with disabilities. In R. P. Marinelli & A. E. Dell Orto (Eds.), *The psychological and social impact of disability* (3rd ed., pp. 223–235). New York: Springer.

Collins-Moore, M. S. (1984). Birth and diagnosis: A family crisis. In M. G. Eisenberg, L. C. Sutkin, & M. A. Johnsen (Eds.), *Chronic illness and disability through the life span* (pp. 39–46). New York: Springer.

Colwell, S. (1984). The adolescent with developmental disorders. In R. Blum (Ed.), *Chronic illness and disabilities in childhood and adolescence* (pp. 327–346). Orlando, FL: Grune & Stratton.

Condeluci, A. (1995). *Interdependence: The route to community.* Winter Park, FL: G R Press.

Cottone, L. P., & Cottone, R. R. (1992). Women with disabilities: On the paradox of empowerment and the need for a trans-systemic and feminist perspective. *Journal of Applied Rehabilitation Counseling, 23,* 20–25.

Covert, S. (1992). Supporting families. J. Nisbet (Ed.), *Natural supports in school, at work and in the community for people with severe disabilities* (pp. 121–163). Baltimore: Paul H. Brookes.

Cox, T. (1981). *Stress.* Baltimore: University Park Press.

Crnic, K. A., Greenberg, M. T., Ragozin, A. S., Robinson, N. M., & Basham, R. B. (1983). Effects of stress and social support on mothers and premature and full-term infants. *Child Development, 54,* 209–217.

Damrosch, S. P., & Perry, L. A. (1989). Self-reported adjustment, chronic sorrow, and coping of parents of children with Down syndrome. *Nursing Research, 38,* 25–30.

Dane, E. (1990). *Painful passages: Working with children with learning disabilities.* Washington, DC: National Association of Social Work Press.

Darling, R. B. (1979). *Families against society: A study of reactions to children with birth defects.* Beverly Hills, CA: Sage.

Darling, R. B. (1991). Initial and continuing adaptation to the birth of a disabled child. In M. Seligman (Ed.), *The family with a handicapped child* (2nd ed., pp. 55–89). Boston: Allyn & Bacon.

Darling, R. B., & Baxter, C. (1996). *Families in focus: Sociological methods in early intervention.* Austin, TX: Pro-Ed.

Darling, R. B., & Darling, J. (1982). *Children who are different: Meeting the challenges of birth defects in society.* St. Louis: Mosby.

Darling, R. B., & Peter, M. I. (Eds.). (1994). *Families, physicians, and children with special health needs: Collaborative medical education models.* Westport, CT: Greenwood.

Davis, F. (1961). Deviance disavowal: The management of strained interaction by the visibly handicapped. *Social Problems, 9,* 120–132.

Dawes, R. M. (1994). *House of cards.* New York: Free Press.

Deci, E. L., Nezlek, J., & Sheinman, L. (1981). Characteristics of the rewarder and intrinsic motivation of the rewardee. *Journal of Personality and Social Psychology, 40,* 1–10.

Deci, E. L., & Ryan, R. M. (1985). *Intrinsic motivation and self determination in human behavior.* New York: Plenum.

Dembo, T., Leviton, G. L., & Wright, B. A. (1956). Adjustment to misfortune: A problem of social psychological rehabilitation. *Artificial Limbs, 3,* 4–62.

Diana v. State Board of Education, Civ. Act. No. 70–37 RFP (N.D. Cal. Jan. 7, 1970, and June 18, 1973).

Dion, K. K., Berscheid, E., & Walster, E. (1972). What is beautiful is good. *Journal of Personality and Social Psychology, 24,* 285–290.

Doering, S. G., Entwistte, D. R., & Quinlan, D. (1980). Modeling the quality of women's birth experience. *Journal of Health and Social Behavior, 21,* 12–21.

Doherty, W. J. (1985). Family intervention in health care. *Family Relations, 34,* 129–137.

Donovan, K. (1995). Sally: Recovery of our missing pieces. In M. A. Blotzer & R. Ruth (Eds.), *Sometimes you just want to feel like a human being* (pp. 183–190). Baltimore: Paul H. Brookes.

Dorner, S. (1973). Psychological and social problems of families of adolescent spina bifida patients: A preliminary report. *Developmental Medicine and Child Neurology, 29* (supp 1), 24–26.

Dorner, S. (1975). The relationship of physical handicap to stress in families with an adolescent with spina bifida. *Developmental Medicine and Child Neurology, 17,* 765–777.

Dowdy, C. A., Carter, J. K., Smith, E. C. (1990). Differences in transitional needs of high school students with and without learning disabilities. *Journal of Learning Disabilities, 23,* 343–348.

Drotar, D., Baskiewicz, A., Irvin, A., Kennel, J., & Klaus, M. (1975). The adaptation of parents to the birth of an infant with a congenital malformation: A hypothetical model. *Pediatrics, 56,* 710–717.

Duncan, D. (1977, May). *The impact of a handicapped child upon the family.* Paper presented at the Pennsylvania Training Model Sessions, Harrisburg, PA.

Dunst, C. J., Trivette, C. M., & Cross, A. H. (1986). Mediating influences of social support: Personal, family, and child outcomes. *American Journal of Mental Deficiency, 90,* 403–417.

Dushenko, T. (1981). Cystic fibrosis: Medical overview and critique of the psychological literature. *Social Science in Medicine, 15B,* 43–56.

Dyson, L. (1991). Families of young children with handicaps: Parental stress and family functioning. *American Journal on Mental Retardation, 95,* 623–629.

Dyson, L. (1996). The experiences of families of children with learning disabilities: Parental stress, family functioning, and sibling self concept. *Journal of Learning Disabilities, 29,* 280–285.

Edgerton, R. B. (1988). Aging in the community—A matter of choice. *American Journal of Mental Deficiency, 92,* 331–335.

Edgerton, R. B. (1994). Quality of life issues: Some people know how to be old. In M. M. Seltzer, M. W. Krauss, & M. P. Janicki (Eds.), *Life course perspectives in adulthood and old age* (pp. 53–66). Washington, DC: American Association on Mental Retardation.

Education for All Handicapped Children Act of 1975, Pub. L. No. 94–142.

Ellis, A. (1958). Rational psychotherapy. *Journal of General Psychology, 59,* 34–49.

Elman, N. (1991). Family therapy. In M. Seligman (Ed.), *The family with a handicapped child* (2nd ed., pp. 369–406). Boston: Allyn & Bacon.

Elovitz, G. P., & Salvia, J. (1982). Attractiveness as a biasing factor in the judgments of school psychologists. *Journal of School Psychology, 2*(4), 339–345.

Erickson, M. T. (1969). MMPI profiles of parents of young retarded children. *American Journal of Mental Deficiency, 73,* 728–732.

Erikson, E. H. (1980). *Identity and the life cycle*. New York: Norton.

Erikson, E. H. (1982). *The life cycle completed: A review*. New York: Norton.

Everson, J. M., & Moon, M. S. (1987). Transition services for young adults with severe disabilities: Defining professional and parental roles and responsibilities. *Journal of the Association for Persons with Severe Handicaps, 12*(2), 87–95.

Eyer, D. E. (1992). *Mother-infant bonding: A scientific fiction*. New Haven, CT: Yale University Press.

Factor, A. R. (1993). Translating policy into practice. In E. Sutton, A. Factor, B. Hawkins, T. Heller, & G. Seltzer (Eds.), *Older adults with developmental disabilities: Optimizing choice and change* (pp. 257–275). Baltimore: Paul H. Brookes.

Farber, B. (1959). Effects of a severely mentally retarded child on family integration. *Monographs of the Society for Research in Child Development, 24* (2, Serial No. 71).

Farber, B. (1975). Family adaptation to severely mentally retarded children. In M. J. Begab & S. A. Richardson (Eds.), *The mentally retarded child and society: A social science perspective* (pp. 247–266). Baltimore: University Park Press.

Farber, B., & Ryckman, D. B. (1965). Effects of a severely mentally retarded child on family relationships. *Mental Retardation Abstracts, 11*, 1–17.

Fargiulo, R. M. (1985). *Working with parents of exceptional children*. Boston: Houghton Mifflin.

Farran, D. C., Metzger, R., & Sparling, J. (1986). Immediate and continuing adaptations in parents of handicapped children. In J. J. Gallagher & P. M. Vietze (Eds.), *Families of handicapped persons* (pp. 143–163). Baltimore: Paul H. Brookes.

Featherstone, H. (1980). *A difference in the family: Life with a disabled child*. New York: Basic Books.

Feingold, A. (1982). Physical attractiveness and intelligence. *Journal of Social Psychology, 118*, 283–284.

Feldman, D., Gerstein, L. H., & Feldman, B. (1989). Teachers' beliefs about administrators and parents of handicapped and nonhandicapped students. *Journal of Experimental Education, 58*, 43–56.

Felson, R. B. (1981). Physical attractiveness and perceptions of deviance. *Journal of Social Psychology, 114*, 55–59.

Ferguson, P. (1997, April). *Researchers with family members with disabilities*. Panel presentation at the annual meeting of the Council for Exceptional Children, Salt Lake City, UT.

Ferguson, P., Ferguson, D., & Jones, D. (1988). Generations of hope: Parental perspectives on the transitions of their children with severe retardation from school to adult life. *Journal of the Association of Severe Handicaps, 13*, 177–187.

Ferhold, J. B., & Solnit, A. (1978). Counseling parents of mentally retarded and learning disordered children. In E. Arnold (Ed.), *Helping parents help their children* (pp. 157–173). New York: Brunner/Mazel.

Fewell, R. (1986). A handicapped child in the family. In R. Fewell & P. Vadasy (Eds.), *Families of handicapped children: Needs and supports across the life span* (pp. 3–34). Austin, TX: Pro-Ed.

Fewell, R. R. (1991). Parenting moderately handicapped persons. In M. Seligman (Ed.), *The family with a handicapped child* (2nd ed., pp. 203–232). Boston: Allyn & Bacon.

Fewell, R. R., & Vadasy, P. (Eds.). (1986). *Families of handicapped children: Needs and supports across the life span.* Austin, TX: Pro-Ed.

Fichten, C. S., Robillard, K., Judd, D., & Ansel, R. (1989). College students with physical disabilities: Myths and realities. *Rehabilitation Psychology, 34,* 243–257.

Firestein, S. K. (1989). Special features of grief reactions with reproductive catastrophe. *Loss, Grief, and Care, 3,* 37–45.

Fleishman, R., & Shmveli, M. (1984). Patterns of informal social support of the elderly: An international comparison, *The Gerontologist, 24*(3), 303–309.

Floyd, F. J., & Zmich, D. E. (1989, August). *Parenting partnership of mothers and fathers of mentally retarded children.* Paper presented at the meeting of the American Psychological Association, New Orleans.

Forest, M., & Pierpoint, J. (1992). Families, friends and circles. In J. Nisbet (Ed.), *Natural supports in school, at work, and in the community for people with severe disabilities* (pp. 65–85). Baltimore: Brooks.

Foster, H. L. (1997, June). Who should learn new behaviors? The students or the teachers? *CEC Today, 3,* 14.

Frank, K., Karst, R., & Boles, C. (1989). *After graduation: The quest for employment by disabled college graduates, 20,* 3–7.

Freidrich, W. N., & Freidrich, W. L. (1981). Psychosocial assets of parents of handicapped and nonhandicapped children. *American Journal of Mental Deficiency, 85,* 551–553.

Frey, K. S., Greenberg, M. T., & Fewell, R. R. (1989). Stress and coping among families of handicapped children: A multidimensional approach. *American Journal on Mental Retardation, 94,* 240–249.

Friedman, W. H. (1989). *Practical group therapy.* San Francisco: Jossey-Bass.

Friedson, E. (1965). Disability as social deviance. In M. B. Sussman (Ed.), *Sociology and rehabilitation* (pp. 71–99). Washington, DC: American Sociological Association.

Frodi, A. M. (1981). Contributions of infant characteristics to child abuse. *American Journal of Mental Deficiency, 85,* 341–349.

Fujiura, G. T., & Braddock, D. (1992). Fiscal and demographic trends in mental retardation services: The emergence of the family. In L. Rowitz (Ed.), *Mental retardation in the year 2000* (pp. 216–338). New York: Springer.

Fulton, S. A., & Sabournie, E. J. (1994). Evidence of employment inequality among females with disabilities. *Journal of Special Education, 28,* 149–165.

Furst, W. (1960). Homogeneous versus heterogeneous groups. *Topical Problems in Psychotherapy, 2,* 170–173.

Gabel, H., McDowell, J., & Cerreto, M. C. (1983). Family adaptation to the handicapped infant. In S. G. Garwood & R. R. Fewell (Eds.), *Educating handicapped infants* (pp. 455–493). Rockville, MD: Aspen.

Gardner, N. E. (1986). Sexuality. In J. A. Summers (Ed.), *The right to grow up* (pp. 45–61). Baltimore: Paul H. Brookes.

Gargiulo, R. M. (1985). *Working with parents of exceptional children.* Boston: Houghton Mifflin.

Garmezy, N., Masten, A. S., & Tellegen, A. (1984). The study of stress and competence in children: A building block for developmental psychopathology. *Child Development, 55,* 97–111.

Garwick, A. W., Kohrman, C. H., Titus, J. C., Wolman, C., Blum, W. R. (1997). *Variations in families' explanations of childhood chronic conditions: A cross-cultural perspective.* Minneapolis: University of Minnesota Hospital.

Gaventa, W., Jr. (1986). Religious ministries and services with adults with disabilities. In J. A. Summers (Ed.), *The right to grow up* (pp. 191–226). Baltimore: Paul H. Brookes.

Gerber, P. J., Schneiders, C. A., Paradise, L. V., Reiff, H. B., Ginsberg, R. J., & Popp, P. A. (1990). *Journal of Learning Disabilities, 23,* 570–573.

Gladding, S. T. (1995). *Group work: A counseling specialty.* Columbus, OH: Merrill.

Gliner, J. A., & Sample, P. (1993). Community life options for persons with developmental disabilities. *OSERS News in Print, 6(1),* 25–32.

Gloeckler, L. C. (1993). Systems change and transition services for secondary youth with disabilities. *OSERS News in Print, 6(1),* 6–12.

Goffman, E. (1963). *Stigma: Notes on the management of spoiled identity.* Englewood Cliffs, NJ: Prentice Hall.

Gold, M. (1978). *Try another way* [film]. Austin, TX: Marc Gold and Associates.

Gold, M., Dobrof, R., & Torian, L. (1987). *Parents of the adult developmentally disabled: Final report presented to the United Hospital Trust Fund.* New York: Brookdale Center on Aging.

Goodheart, C. D., & Lansing, M. H. (1997). *Treating people with chronic disease: A psychological guide.* Washington, DC: American Psychological Association.

Graffam, J., & Turner, J. L. (1984). Escape from boredom: The meaning of eventfulness in the lives of clients at a sheltered workshop. In E. B. Edgerton (Ed.), *Lives in process: Mildly retarded adults in a large city* (pp. 121–144). Washington, DC: American Association on Mental Deficiency.

Greenberg, J., & Becker, M. (1988). Aging parents as family resources. *The Gerontologist, 28(6),* 786–791.

Groce, N. E. (1985). *Everyone here spoke sign language: Hereditary deafness on Martha's Vineyard.* Cambridge, MA: Harvard University Press.

Grossman, F. K. (1972). *Brothers and sisters of retarded children.* Syracuse, NY: Syracuse University Press.

Grzesiak, R. C. (1986). Psychotherapy in rehabilitation medicine: Population, process and problems. *Psychotherapy Patient, 2,* 133–145.

Guerin, P. J. (1976). *Family therapy: Theory and practice.* New York: Gardner Press.

Gumz, E. J., & Gubrium, J. F. (1972). Comparative parental perspectives of a mentally retarded child. *American Journal of Mental Deficiency, 77,* 175–180.

Gundry, M. (1989, November/December). Wanted: A diagnosis for my son. *Exceptional parent,* pp. 22–24.

Gurman, A. S., & Kniskern, D. P. (Eds.). (1981). *Handbook of family therapy.* New York: Brunner/Mazel.

Haavik, S. (1986). Marriage and parenthood. In J. A. Summers (Ed.), *The right to grow up* (pp. 67–90). Baltimore: Paul H. Brookes.

Haavik, S., & Menninger, K. (1981). *Sexuality, law and the developmentally disabled person: Legal and clinical aspects of marriage, parenthood and sterilization.* Baltimore: Paul H. Brookes.

Halpern, A. S. (1985). Transition: A look at the foundations. *Exceptional Children, 51,* 479–486.

Halpern, A. S. (1990). A methodological review of follow-up and follow-along studies tracking school leavers from special education. *Career Development for Exceptional Individuals, 13*(1), 13–27.

Halpern, A. S. (1993). Quality of life as a conceptual framework for evaluating transition outcomes. *Exceptional Children, 59,* 486–498.

Hamre-Nietupski, S., Krajewski, L., Nietupski, J., Ostercamp, D., Sensor, K., & Opheim, B. (1988). *Journal of the Association for Persons With Severe Handicaps, 13,* 251–259.

Hanley-Maxwell, C., Rusch, F. R., Chadsey-Rusch, J., & Renzaglia, A. (1986). Reported factors contributing to job terminations of individuals with severe disabilities. *Journal of the Association for Persons With Severe Handicaps, 11,* 45–52.

Hanley-Maxwell, C., Whitney-Thomas, J., & Pogoloff, S. M. (1995). The second shock: A qualitative study of parents' perspectives and needs during their child's transition from school to adult life. *Journal of the Association for Persons With Severe Handicaps, 20*(1), 3–15.

Haring, K. A., & Lovett, D. L. (1990). A follow-up study of special education graduates. *Journal of Special Education, 23,* 463–477.

Harris, S. L. (1983). *Families of the developmentally disabled: A guide to behavioral intervention.* New York: Pergamon.

Harris, S. L. (1994). *Siblings of children with autism: A guide for families.* Rockville, MD: Woodbine House.

Harris, V. S., & McHale, S. M. (1989). Family life problems, daily caregiving activities, and the psychological well-being of mothers of mentally retarded children. *American Journal on Mental Retardation, 3,* 231–239.

Hartup, W. W. (1996). The company they keep: Friendships and their developmental significance. *Child Development, 67*(1), 1–13.

Hasazi, S. B., Collins, M., & Cobb, R. B. (1988). Implementing transition programs for productive employment. In B. Ludlow, A. Turnbull, & R. Luckasson (Eds.), *Transition to adult life for people with mental retardation: Principles and practices* (pp. 177–195). Baltimore: Paul H. Brookes.

Hasazi, S. B., Gordon, L. R., & Roe, C. A. (1985). Factors associated with the employment status of handicapped youth exiting high school from 1975 to 1983. *Exceptional Children, 51,* 455–469.

Hasazi, S. B., Gordon, L. R., Roe, C. A., Hull, M., Finck, K., & Salembier, G. (1985). A statewide follow-up on post high school employment and residential status of students labeled "mentally retarded." *Education and Training of the Mentally Retarded, 20,* 222–234.

Heller, T. (1993). Self-efficacy coping, active involvement and caregiver well-being throughout the life course among families of persons with mental retardation. In A. P. Turnbull, J. M. Patterson, S. K. Behr, D. L. Murphy, J. G. Marquis, & M. J. Blue-Banning (Eds.), *Cognitive coping, families and disability* (pp. 195–206). Baltimore: Paul H. Brookes.

Heller, T., & Factor, A. R. (1991). Permanency planning for adults with mental retardation living with family caregivers. *American Journal on Mental Retardation, 96,* 163–176.

Heller, T., & Factor, A. R. (1993). Support systems, well-being and placement decision-making among older parents and their adult children with developmental disabilities. In E. Sutton, A. Factor, B. Hawkins, T. Heller, & G. Seltzer (Eds.), *Older adults with developmental disabilities: Optimizing choice and change* (pp. 107–122). Baltimore: Paul H. Brookes.

Heller, T., & Factor, A. R. (1994). Facilitating future planning and transitions out of home. In M. Seltzer, M. Krauss, & M. Janicki (Eds.), *Life course perspectives on adulthood and old age* (pp. 39–50). Washington: American Association on Mental Retardation.

Helsel, E., & Helsel, B. (1978). The Helsels' story of Robin. In A. Turnbull & R. Turnbull (Eds.), *Parents speak out: Views from the other side of the two-way mirror* (pp. 94–115). Columbus, OH: Merrill.

Herrenkohl, R. C., Herrenkohl, E. C., & Egolf, B. (1983). Circumstances surrounding the occurrence of child maltreatment. *Journal of Consulting and Clinical Psychology, 51,* 424–431.

Hetherington, E. M., Stanley-Hagan, M., & Anderson, E. R. (1989). Marital transitions: A child's perspective. *American Psychologist, 44,* 303–312.

Hill, B., Rotegard, L., & Bruininks, R. (1984). Quality of life of mentally retarded people in residential care. *Social Work, 29,* 275–281.

Hill, R. (1949). *Families under stress.* New York: Harper & Row.

Hill, R. T. (1958). Sociology of marriage and family behavior, 1945–1956: A trend report and bibliography. *Current Sociology, 7,* 10–98.

Hobbs, N., Perrin, A., & Ireys, S. (1985). *Chronically ill children and their families.* San Francisco: Jossey-Bass.

Holland, B., & Falvo, D. (1990, April-May-June). Forgotten: Elderly persons with disabilities—A consequence of policy. *Journal of Rehabilitation,* pp. 32–35.

Hollins, S. (1995, May-June). Managing grief better: People with developmental disabilities. *The Habilitative Mental Healthcare Newsletter, 14* (3), 1–4.

Hornby, G. (1994). *Counseling in child disability: Skills for working with parents.* London: Chapman & Hall.

Hornby, G. (1995). *Working with parents of children with special needs.* London: Cassell.

Houser, R. (1987). *A comparison of stress and coping by fathers of mentally retarded and non-mentally retarded adolescents.* Unpublished doctoral dissertation, University of Pittsburgh.

Houser, R., & Seligman, M. (1991). A comparison of stress and coping by fathers of adolescents with mental retardation and fathers of adolescents without mental retardation. *Research in Developmental Disabilities, 12,* 251–260.

Howard, J. H., Marshall, J., Rechnitzer, P. A., Cunningham, P. A., & Donner, A. (1982). Adapting to retirement. *Journal of the American Geriatrics Society, 30*, 488–500.

Imber-Black, E. (1988). *Families and larger systems: A family therapist's guide through the labyrinth*. New York: Guilford.

Individualized Education Programs. (1990, February). *NICHCY News Digest*.

Individuals With Disabilities Education Act of 1990, 20 U.S.C. 33, [sections] 1400–1485 (Pub. L. No. 101–476).

Innocenti, M. S., Huh, K., & Boyce, G. C. (1992). Families of children with disabilities: Normative data and other considerations on parenting stress. *Topics in Early Childhood Special Education, 12*, 403–427.

Jacobs, E. E., Harvill, R. L., & Masson, R. L. (1988). *Group counseling: Strategies and skills*. Pacific Grove, CA: Brooks/Cole.

Jacobson, J. W., Sutton, M. S., & Janicki, M. P. (1985). Demography and characteristics of aging and aged mentally retarded persons. In M. D. Janicki & H. M. Wisniewski (Eds.), *Aging and developmental disabilities: Issues and approaches* (pp. 115–1420). Baltimore: Paul H. Brookes.

James, A., James, W., & Smith, H. (1984). Reciprocity as a coping strategy of the elderly: A rural Irish perspective. *The Gerontologist, 24*, 483–489.

Janicki, M. D., & MacEachron, A. E. (1984). Residential health and social service needs of elderly developmentally disabled persons. *The Gerontologist, 24*, 128–137.

Jessop, D. J., & Stein, R. E. (1985). Uncertainty and its relation to the psychological and social correlates of chronic illness in children. *Social Science and Medicine, 20*, 993–999.

Jones, W., Hansson, R., & and Phillips, A. (1978). Physical attractiveness and judgments of attractiveness. *Journal of Social Psychology, 105*, 79–84.

Kahana, G., & Kahana, E. (1970). Grandparenthood from the perspective of the developing grandchild. *Developmental Psychology, 3*, 98–105.

Kaiser, A. P., & Fox, J. J. (1986). Behavioral parent training research. In J. J. Gallagher & P. M. Vietze (Eds.), *Families of handicapped persons* (pp. 219–235). Baltimore: Brooks.

Kalins, I. (1983). Cross-illness comparisons of separation and divorce among parents having a child with a life-threatening illness. *Children's Health Care, 12*, 100–102.

Kalish, R. A. (1981). *Death, grief, and caring relationships*. Monterey, CA: Brooks/Cole.

Kappes, N. (1995). Matrix. In D. J. Meyer (Ed.), *Uncommon fathers: Reflections on raising a child with a disability* (pp. 13–28). Bethesda, MD: Woodbine House.

Kazak, A. E. (1987). Families with disabled children: Stress and social networks in three samples. *Journal of Abnormal Child Psychology, 15*, 137–146.

Kazak, A. E., & Marvin, R. S. (1984). Differences, difficulties, and adaptation: Stress and social networks in families with a handicapped child. *Family Relations, 33*, 67–77.

Kazak, A. E., & Wilcox, B. (1984). The structure and function of social support networks in families with handicapped children. *American Journal of Community Psychology, 12*, 645–661.

Kimmel, D. (1974). *Adulthood and aging: An interdisciplinary developmental view*. New York: John Wiley.

Koch, W. H. (1986). *Planning for an aging developmentally disabled population: Some considerations.* Unpublished manuscript, University of Wisconsin, Center for Adult Development.

Kohler, P. D. (1993). Best practices in transition: Substantiated or implied? *Career Development for Exceptional Individuals, 16,* 107–121.

Korn, S. J., Chess, S., & Fernandez, P. (1978). The impact of children's physical handicaps on marital quality and family interaction. In R. M. Lerner & G. B. Spanier (Eds.), *Child influences on marital and family interaction: A life-span perspective* (pp. 299–326). New York: Academic Press.

Krahn, G. L. (1993). Conceptualizing social support in families of children with special health needs. *Family Process, 32,* 235–248.

Krauss, M. W., & Seltzer, M. M. (1993). Current well-being and future plans for older caregiving mothers. *Irish Journal of Psychology, 14,* 47–64.

Krauss, M. W., Seltzer, M. M., & Goodman, S. (1992). Social support networks of adults with mental retardation who live at home. *American Journal on Mental Retardation, 96*(4), 432–441.

Kriegsman, K. H., & Hershenson, D. B. (1987). A comparison of able-bodied and disabled college students on Erikson's ego stages and Maslow's needs levels. *Journal of College Student Personnel, 28,* 48–53.

Kriegsman, K. H., Zaslow, E., & D'Zmura-Rechsteiner, J. (1992). *Taking charge: Teenagers talk about life and physical disabilities.* Bethesda, MD: Woodbine House.

Kübler-Ross, E. (1969). *On death and dying.* New York: Macmillan.

Kuehn, M., & Imm-Thomas (1993). A multicultural context. In E. Sutton, A. Factor, B. Hawkins, T. Heller, & G. Seltzer (Eds.), *Older adults with developmental disabilities: Optimizing choice and change* (pp. 327–343). Baltimore: Paul H. Brookes.

Kushner, H. (1981). *When bad things happen to good people.* New York: Avon.

Laborde, P. R., & Seligman, M. (1991). Counseling parents with children with disabilities. In M. Seligman (Ed.), *The family with a handicapped child* (2nd ed., pp. 337–369). Boston: Allyn & Bacon.

Ladd, G. W., Kochenderfer, B. J., & Coleman, C. C. (1996). Friendship quality as a predictor of young children's early school adjustment. *Child Development, 67,* 1103–1118.

Lakin, C., & Smull, M. (1995). Supported community living from "facilities" to "home." *Impact, 8* (4), 2–3.

Lamb, M. E., & Meyer, D. J. (1991). Fathers of children with special needs. In M. Seligman (Ed.), *The family with a handicapped child* (2nd ed., pp. 151–179). Boston: Allyn & Bacon.

LaRossa, R. (1977). *Conflict and power in marriage.* Beverly Hills, CA: Sage.

Larry P. v. Riles, preliminary injunction 343 F. Supp. 1306 (N.D. Cal. 1972), aff'd 502 F. 2nd 963 (9th Cir. 1974).

Larson, S. A., & Lakin, K. C. (1991). Parents' attitudes about residential placement before and after deinstitutionalization: A research synthesis. *Journal of the Association for Persons With Severe Handicaps, 16,* 25–38.

Lasher, E., & Marshak, L. (1995). Interviews with adolescents with spinal cord injuries and their parents [Unpublished raw data].

Learning Disabilities Association of America. (1996). *They speak for themselves*. Pittsburgh: Author.

Lechtenberg, R. (1984). *Epilepsy and the family*. Cambridge, MA: Harvard University Press.

Lederer, W. J., & Jackson, D. D. (1968). *The mirages of marriage*. New York: Norton.

Lefly, H. D. (1987). Aging parents as caregivers of mentally ill children: An emerging social problem. *Hospital and Community Psychiatry, 38*, 1063–1070.

Levinson, D. J. (1978). *The seasons of a man's life*. New York: Ballantine Books.

Lewin, K. (1935). *Dynamic theory of personality: Selected papers*. New York: McGraw-Hill.

Lian, M. J., & Aloia, G. F. (1994). Parental responses, roles and responsibilities. In S. K. Alper, P. J. Schloss, & C. N. Schloss (Eds.), *Families of students with disabilities: Consultation and advocacy* (pp. 51–93). Boston: Allyn & Bacon.

Lidz, T. (1983). *The person: His and her development throughout the life cycle*. New York: Basic Books.

Lieberman, M. A. (1990). A group therapist's perspective on self help groups. In M. Seligman & L. Marshak (Eds.), *Group psychotherapy: Interventions with special populations* (pp. 1–18). Boston: Allyn & Bacon.

Lillie, T. (1993). A harder thing than triumph: Roles of fathers of children with disabilities. *American Association on Mental Retardation, 31*, 438–443.

Lipe-Goodson, P. S., & Goebel, B. L. (1983). Perception of age and death in mentally retarded adults. *Mental Retardation, 21*, 68–75.

Lipsky, D. K. (1989). The roles of parents. In D. K. Lipsky & A. Gartner (Eds.), *Beyond separate education: Quality education for all* (pp. 159–179). Baltimore: Paul H. Brookes.

Lipsky, D. K., & Gartner, A. (Eds.). (1989). *Beyond separate education: Quality education for all*. Baltimore: Paul H. Brookes.

Lobato, D. J. (1990). *Brothers and sisters with special needs*. Baltimore: Paul H. Brookes.

Luterman, D. (1984). *Counseling the communicatively disordered and their families*. Boston: Little, Brown.

Lutfiyya, Z. (1990). *Affectionate bonds: What can you learn by listening to friends?* Syracuse, NY: Syracuse University, Center on Human Policy.

Lynch, E. W., & Stein, R. C. (1987). Parent participation by ethnicity: A comparison of Hispanic, black and Anglo families. *Exceptional Children, 54*, 105–111.

Lyon, S., & Lyon, G. (1991). Collaboration with families of persons with severe disabilities. In M. Seligman (Ed.), *The family with a handicapped child* (2nd ed., pp. 237–264). Boston: Allyn & Bacon.

Macgregor, F. C. (1951). Cleft lip and palate: A prediction of psychological disfigurement? *British Journal of Orthodontics, 8*, 83–88.

Macken, L. L. (1986). A profile of functionally impaired elderly persons living in the community. *Health Care Financing Review, 7*, 33–49.

MacMillan, D. L., & Turnbull, A. P. (1983). Parent involvement with special education: Respecting individual preferences. *Education and Training of the Mentally Retarded, 18*(1), 4–9.

MacMurchy, H. (1916). The relation of feeblemindedness to other social problems. *Journal of Psycho-aesthetics, 21,* 58–63.

Mallory, B. (1986). Interaction between community agencies and families over the life cycle. In R. Fewell & P. Vadasy (Eds.), *Families of handicapped children: Needs and supports across the life span* (pp. 317–356). Austin, TX: Pro-Ed.

Mangrum, C. T., & Strichart, S. S. (Eds.). (1994). *Colleges with programs for students with learning disabilities.* Princeton, NJ: Peterson's.

Marfisi, C. (1996, Summer). The facts of life and disability. *Change Exchange, 1*(4), 1–2.

Margalit, M., (1997, April). *Coherence model for understanding loneliness development of children with learning disorders.* Paper presented at the annual meeting of the Council for Exceptional Children, Salt Lake City, UT.

Marsh, D. T. (1992). *Families and mental retardation.* New York: Praeger.

Marsh, D. T. (1993). *Families and mental retardation.* New York: Praeger.

Marshak, L. E. (1982). Group therapy with adolescents. In M. Seligman (Ed.), *Group therapy and counseling with special populations* (pp. 185–213). Baltimore: University Park Press.

Marshak, L. E., Prezant, F., Cerrone, P., & Seligman, M. (1997). Responses to survey of families with children who have disabilities [Unpublished raw data].

Marshak, L. E., & Seligman, M. (1993). *Counseling persons with disabilities: Theoretical and clinical perspectives.* Austin, TX: Pro-Ed.

Martin, J. E., Marshall, L. H., & Maxson, L. L. (1993). Transition policy: Infusing self-determination and self advocacy into transition programs. *Career Development for Exceptional Individuals, 16,* 53–61.

Martin, P. (1975). Marital breakdown in families of patients with spina bifida cystica. *Developmental Medicine and Child Neurology, 17,* 757–764.

Martinson, M., & Stone, J. (1993). Federal legislation and long-term funding streams that support community living options. In E. Sutton, A. Factor, B. Hawkins, T. Heller, & G. Seltzer (Eds.), *Older adults with developmental disabilities: Optimizing choice and change* (pp. 192–222). Baltimore: Paul H. Brookes.

Mathews, J. (1992). *A mother's touch: The Tiffany Callo story.* New York: Henry Holt.

Mattie T. v. Holladay, C. A. No. 75–31–5 (N.D. Miss. July 28, 1977).

Max, L. (1985). Parents' views of provisions, services, and research. In N. N. Singh & K. M. Wilton (Eds.), *Mental retardation in New Zealand* (pp. 250–262). Christchurch, New Zealand: Whitcoulls.

McAnarney, E. (1985). Social maturation: A challenge for handicapped and chronically ill adolescents. *Journal of Adolescent Health Care, 6,* 90–101.

McCandless, B. (1970). *Adolescents: Behavior and development.* Hinsdale, IL: Dryden Press.

McClelland, D. (1973). Testing for competence rather than for intelligence. *American Psychologist, 28,* 1–14.

McCracken, M. J. (1984). Cystic fibrosis in adolescence. In R. W. Blum (Ed.), *Chronic illness and disabilities in childhood and adolescence* (pp. 397–411). Orlando, FL: Grune & Stratton.

McCubbin, H. I., & Patterson, J. M. (1981). *Systematic assessment of family stress, resources, and coping: Tools for research, education and clinical intervention*. St. Paul: University of Minnesota, Department of Family Social Science, Family Stress and Coping Project.

McCubbin, H. I., & Patterson, J. M. (1983). The family stress process: The double ABCX model of adjustment and adaptation. *Marriage and Family Review, 6,* 7–37.

McGoldrick, M. (1993). Ethnicity, cultural diversity and normality. In F. Walsh (Ed.), *Normal family processes* (2nd ed., pp. 331–360). New York: Guilford.

McGoldrick, M., & Gerson, R. (1985). *Genograms in family assessment.* New York: Norton.

McGoldrick, M., Pearce, J. K., & Giordano, J. (1982). *Ethnicity and family therapy.* New York: Guilford.

McHale, S. M., & Gamble, W. C. (1989). Sibling relationships of children with disabled and nondisabled brothers and sisters. *Developmental Psychology, 25,* 421–429.

Meehl, P. E. (1960). The cognitive activity of the clinician. *American Psychology, 15,* 19–27.

Mehan, H. (1991). *Sociological foundations supporting the study of cultural diversity* (Research Report No. 1). Santa Cruz, CA: University of Santa Cruz, The National Center for Research on Cultural Diversity and Second Language Learning.

Mest, G. M. (1988). With a little help from their friends: Use of social support systems by persons with retardation. *Journal of Social Issues, 44,* 117–125.

Meyen, E. L. (1996). *Exceptional children in today's schools* (3rd ed.). Denver, CO: Love.

Meyer, D. (1986). Fathers of handicapped children. In R. Fewell & P. Vadasy (Eds.), *Families of handicapped children: Needs and support across the life span* (pp. 35–74). Austin, TX: Pro-Ed.

Meyer, D. (Ed.). (1995). *Uncommon fathers: Reflections on raising a child with a disability.* Bethesda, MD: Woodbine House.

Meyer, D. J., & Vadasy, P. F. (1986). *Grandparent workshops: How to organize workshops for grandparents of children with handicaps.* Seattle: University of Washington Press.

Meyer, D. J., & Vadasy, P. F. (1994) *Sibshops: Workshops for siblings of children with special needs.* Seattle: University of Washington Press.

Meyer, D. J., Vadasy, P. F., Fewell, R. R., & Schell, G. (1985). *A handbook for the fathers program.* Seattle: University of Washington Press.

Meyerson, L. (1963). Somato psychology of physical disability. In W. M. Cruickshank (Ed.), *Psychology of exceptional children and youth* (2nd ed., pp. 1–52). Englewood Cliffs, NJ: Prentice Hall.

Minuchin, S. (1974). *Families and family therapy.* Cambridge, MA: Harvard University Press.

Misra, A. (1994). Partnership with multicultural families. In S. Alper, P. J. Schloss, & C. N. Schloss (Eds.), *Families of students with disabilities* (pp. 143–179). Boston: Allyn & Bacon.

Moglia, R. (1993, Fall). Sexual abuse and disability. *TBI Challenge!* p. 6.

Moorman, M. (1992, January-February). My sister's keeper. *Family Therapy Networker,* pp. 41–47.

Morgan, S. R. (1987). *Abuse and neglect of handicapped children.* Boston: Little, Brown.

Morningstar, M. E., Turnbull, A. P., & Turnbull, H. R. (1995). What do students with disabilities tell us about family involvement in the transition from school to adult life? *Exceptional Children, 62,* 249–260.

Mulcahey, M. (1992). Returning to school after a spinal cord injury: Perspectives from four adolescents. *American Journal of Occupational Therapy, 46*(3), 305–312.

Mullins, J. (1979). *A teacher's guide to management of physically handicapped students.* Springfield, IL: Thomas.

Mullins, J. (1997). *A teacher's guide to management of physically handicapped students.* Springfield, IL: Thomas.

Myers, J. E. (1983). Rehabilitation counseling for older disabled persons: The state of the art. *Journal of Applied Rehabilitation Counseling, 14*(3), 48–53.

Nagler, M. (Ed.). (1993). *Perspectives on disability.* Palo Alto, CA: Health Markets Research.

Naseef, R. A. (1997). *Special children, challenged parents: The struggles and rewards of raising a child with a disability.* Secaucus, NJ: Birch Lane Press.

National Association of Sibling Programs. (1993, Winter). *Newsletter,* no. 3. http://www.chml.or. . . /sibsupp/nasp3.htm.

National Information Center for Children and Youth With Disabilities. (1990, December). *Vocational Assessment: A Guide for Parents and Professionals* (IRA publication). Washington, DC: Author.

National Information Center for Children and Youth With Disabilities. (1993, March). *Transition services in the IEP* (IRA publication). Washington, DC: Author.

National Organization on Disability. (1994). *Harris Survey of Americans with disabilities.* Washington, DC: Author.

National Organization on Disability. (1996a). *From barriers to bridges: A community action guide for congregations and people with disabilities.* Washington: Nation Organization on Disability.

National Organization on Disability. (1996b). *That all may worship: An interfaith welcome to people with disabilities.* Washington: Nation Organization on Disability.

Neider, C. (Ed.). (1963). *The complete essays of Mark Twain.* New York: Doubleday.

Nelis, T. (1995-1996). The realities of institutions. *Impact, 9* (1), 1, 27.

Neugarten, B. (1976). Adaptations and the life cycle. *The Counseling Psychologist, 6* (1), 16–22.

Neugeboren, J. (1997). *Imagining Robert: My brother, madness, and survival: A memory.* New York: Morrow.

Newman, J. (1991). Handicapped persons and their families: Historical, legislature, and philosophical perspectives. In M. Seligman (Ed.), *The family with a handicapped child* (2nd ed., pp. 1–26). Boston: Allyn & Bacon.

Niagra Regional Police Services. (1996). *Abuse of the disabled: Violence against women with disabilities* [Internet article]. http://www.vaxine.com/nrpsweb/ disabled.htm, pp. 1–3.

Nihira, K., Meyers, C. E., & Mink, I. T. (1980). Home environment, family adjustment, and the development of mentally retarded children. *Applied Research in Mental Retardation, 1,* 5–24.

Nisbet, J., Covert, S., & Schuh, M. (1992). Family involvement in the transition from school to adult life. In F. R. Rusch, I. DeStefano, J. Chadsey-Rusch, L. A. Phelps, & E. Szymanski (Eds.), *Transition from school to adult life: Models, linkages and policy* (pp. 407–424). Sycamore, IL: Sycamore.

O'Brien, J., & O'Brien, C. (1993). Unlikely alliances: Friendships and people with developmental disabilities. In A. N. Amado (Ed.), *Friendships and community connections between people with and without developmental disabilities.* Baltimore: Paul H. Brookes.

O'Connor, W. A. (1967). *Patterns of interaction in families with high-adjusted, low-adjusted and retarded members.* Unpublished doctoral dissertation, University of Kansas.

Offer, D., Ostrov, E., & Howard, K. I. (1984). Body image, self-perception, and chronic illness in adolescence. In R. W. Blum (Ed.), *Chronic illness and disabilities in childhood and adolescence* (pp. 59–73). Orlando, FL: Grune & Stratton.

Okolo, C. M., & Sitlington, P. (1988). The role of special education in LD adolescents' transition from school to work. *Learning Disability Quarterly, 11,* 292–306.

Olkin, R. (1995). Matthew: Therapy with a teenager with a disability. In M. A. Blotzer & R. Ruth (Eds.). *Sometimes you just want to feel like a human being* (pp. 183–190). Baltimore: Paul H. Brookes.

Olshansky, S. (1962). Chronic sorrow: A response to having a mentally defective child. *Social Casework, 43,* 190–193.

Olson, D. H., McCubbin, H. I., Barnes, H., Larsen, A., Muren, M., & Wilson, M. (1984). *One thousand families: A national survey.* Beverly Hills, CA: Sage.

Olson, D. H., Russell, C. S., & Sprenkle, D. H. (1979). Circumflex Model of Marital and Family Systems: Cohesion and adaptability dimensions, family types, and clinical applications. *Family Process, 18,* 3–28.

Olson, D. H., Sprenkle, D. H., & Russell, C. S. (1980). Circumflex Model of Marital and Family Systems II: Empirical studies and clinical intervention. In J. P. Vincent (Ed.), *Advances in family intervention assessment and theory* (Vol. 1, pp. 129–179). Greenwich, CT: JAI.

Opirhory, G., & Peters, G. A. (1982). Counseling intervention strategies for families with the less than perfect newborn. *Personnel and Guidance Journal, 60,* 451–455.

Orenstein, D. (1989). *Cystic fibrosis: A guide for patient and family.* New York: Raven Press.

Ozer, E. M., & Bandura, A. (1990). Mechanisms governing empowerment effects: A self-efficacy analysis. *Journal of Personality and Social Psychology, 58,* 472–486.

PACER Center. (1993a). *Living your life: A handbook for teenagers by young people and adults with chronic illness or disabilities.* Minneapolis, MN: Author.

PACER Center. (1993b). *Speak up for health: A handbook for parents.* Minneapolis, MN: Author.

Parke, R. D. (1981). *Fathers.* Cambridge, MA: Harvard.

Parker, J. G., & Asher, S. R. (1987). Peer relations and later personal adjustment: Are low accepted children at risk? *Psychological Bulletin, 102,* 357–389.

Parker, J. G., & Asher, S. R. (1993). Friendship and friendship quality in middle childhood: Links with peer group acceptance and feelings of loneliness and social dissatisfaction. *Developmental Psychology, 29,* 611–621.

Patterson, J. M. (1985). Critical factors affecting family compliance with home treatment for children with cystic fibrosis. *Family Relations, 34,* 79–89.

Patterson, J. M. (1988). Chronic illness in children and the impact on families. In C. Chilman, E. Nunally, & E. Cox (Eds.), *Chronic illness and disability* (pp. 69–107). Beverly Hills, CA: Sage.

Patterson, J. (1991a). Family resilience to the challenge of a child's disability. *Pediatric Annals, 20,* 491–500.

Patterson, J. M. (1991b). A family systems perspective for working with youth with disability. *Pediatrician, 18,* 129–141.

Patton, J. R., & Browder, P. M. (1988). Transition into the future. In B. Ludlow, A. Turnbull, & R. Luckasson (Eds.), *Transition to adult life for people with mental retardation: Principles and practice* (pp. 293–311). Baltimore: Paul H. Brookes.

Patton, P. L., de la Garza, B., & Harmon, C. (1997). Employability skills + adult agency support + family support + on-the-job support = successful employment. *Teaching Exceptional Children, 29* (3), 4–10.

Pearpoint, J., Forest, M., & Snow, J. (1992). *The inclusion papers.* Toronto: Center for Integrated Education and Community.

Peck, J. R., & Stephens, W. B. (1960). A study of the relationship between the attitudes and behavior of parents and that of their mentally defective child. *American Journal of Mental Deficiency, 64,* 839–844.

Pennsylvania Association for Retarded Children v. Commonwealth of Pennsylvania, 334 F. Supp. 1257 (E.D. Pa, 1971).

Penn State University. (1995). The wild dream team [Film]. Available from Continuing and Distance Education. State College, PA: WPSX TV.

Peplau, L. A., & Perlman, D. (1982). Perspectives on loneliness. In L. A. Peplau & D. Perlman (Eds.), *Loneliness: A sourcebook of current theory, research and therapy.* New York: John Wiley.

Perrin, J. M., & MacLean, W. E. (1988). Biomedical and psychosocial dimensions of chronic illness in children. In P. Karoly (Ed.), *Handbook of child health assessment* (pp. 11–29). New York: John Wiley.

Perske, R. (1993). Introduction. In A. N. Amado (Ed.), *Friendships and community connection between people with and without developmental disabilities.* Baltimore: Paul H. Brookes.

Peters, A. (1985, Fall). Telethons. *The Disability Rag,* pp. 16–18.

Pettitt, G., & Pettitt, J. (1993). Family viewpoint. *Journal of Vocational Rehabilitation, 3*(2), 47–49.

Pieper, E. (1976, April). Grandparents can help. *Exceptional Parent,* pp. 7–9.

Pollin, I. (1995). *Medical crisis counseling.* New York: Norton.

Powell, T. H., & Gallagher, P. E. (1993). *Brothers and sisters: A special part of exceptional families* (2nd ed.). Baltimore: Paul H. Brookes.

Power, P. (1991). *A guide to vocational assessment.* Austin, TX: Pro-Ed.

Pratt, J. H. (1907). The class method of treating consumption in the homes of the poor. *Journal of the American Medical Association, 49,* 755–759.

Preto, N. G. (1989). Transformation of the family system in adolescence. In B. Carter & M. McGoldrick (Eds.), *The changing family life cycle: A framework for family therapy* (2nd ed., pp. 255–283). Boston: Allyn & Bacon.

Prezant, F. (1996, March). *Parent professional collaboration.* Presented at annual in-service of Riverview Intermediate Unit, Shippensburg, PA.

Prezant, F., Borman, N., & Walker, G. (1991, November). *Parent perceptions of interactions with professionals and educational services.* Paper presented at the annual meeting of the American Speech, Language and Hearing Association, Atlanta.

Prezant, F., & Filitske, L. (1994, November). *Diversity awareness as a vehicle for sensitization to disability issues.* Paper presented at the annual meeting of the American Speech, Language and Hearing Association. New Orleans.

Prezant, F., & Filitske, L. (1996, March). *Parent-professional collaboration strategies to facilitate transition for children with disabilities.* Paper presented at the annual Pennsylvania Speech Language Hearing Association, Pittsburgh, PA.

Prezant, F., & Marshak, L. (1997, April). *Facilitating futures: Specific professional actions viewed by families as helpful or obstructive.* Poster session presented at the annual meeting of the Council for Exceptional Children, Salt Lake City, UT.

Prezant, F., Marshak, L., Cerrone, P., & Seligman, M. (1997, April). *Facilitating futures: Specific professional actions viewed by families as helpful or obstructive.* Poster session presented at the annual meeting of the Council for Exceptional Children, Salt Lake City, UT.

Pruett, K. D. (1987). *The nurturing father.* New York: Warner.

Questions and answers about the IDEA. (1993, September). *NICHCY News Digest, 3,* 1–15.

Rak, C. F., & Patterson, L. E. (1996). Promoting resilience in at-risk children. *Journal of Counseling and Development, 74,* 368–373.

Reeves. F. (1996, June 13). Wheelchair protest gets capital notice. *Pittsburgh Post Gazette,* p. C5.

Rehabilitation Act of 1973 as amended in 1992, 29 U.S.C. [sections] 720 et seq. (P.L. 99–506).

Reidy, D. (1989). *Integrating people with disabilities into voluntary associations: The possibilities and limitations.* Unpublished manuscript, Education for Community Initiatives, Holyoke, MA.

Repetto, J. B., & Correa, V. I. (1996). Expanding views on transition. *Exceptional Children, 62,* 561–563.

Resnick, M. D. (1984). The social construction of disability. In R. W. Blum (Ed.), *Chronic illness and disabilities in childhood and adolescence* (pp. 29–46). Orlando, FL: Grune & Stratton.

Richey, L. S., & Ysseldyke, J. E. (1983). Teachers' expectations of the younger siblings of learning disabled students. *Journal of Learning Disabilities, 16,* 610–615.

Rigoni, H. C. (1977). Psychological coping in the patient with spinal cord injury. In D. S. Pierce & W. H. Nichel (Eds.), *The total care of spinal cord injuries* (pp. 229–307). Boston: Little, Brown.

Ritchie, K. (1981). Research note: Interaction in families of epileptic children. *Journal of Child Psychology, 22,* 65–71.

Rolland, J. S. (1989). Chronic illness and the family life cycle. In B. Carter & M. Mc-Goldrick (Eds.), *The changing family life cycle: A framework for family therapy.* (2nd ed., pp. 433–456). Boston: Allyn & Bacon.

Rolland, J. S. (1993). Mastering family challenges in serious illness and disability. In F. Walsh (Ed.), *Normal family processes* (pp. 444–473). New York: Guilford.

Rolland, J. S. (1994). *Families, illness and disability.* New York: Basic Books.

Rose, S. (1974). Training parents in groups as behavior modifiers of their mentally retarded children. *Journal of Behavior Therapy and Experimental Psychiatry, 5,* 135–140.

Rose, S. D. (1989). *Working with adults in groups.* San Francisco: Jossey-Bass.

Rosen, M. (1984). *Sexual exploitation: A community problem.* Walnut Creek, CA: Planned Parenthood Association of Contra Costa.

Rosenberg, R. R. (1994). The California Quality of Life Project: A project summary. In D. Goode (Ed.), *Quality of life for persons with disabilities: International perspectives and issues* (pp. 176–184). Cambridge, MA: Brookline Books.

Ross, A. O. (1964). *The exceptional child in the family.* New York: Grune & Stratton.

Ross, A. O. (1975). Family problems. In R. M. Smith & J. T. Neisworth (Eds.), *The exceptional child.* New York: McGraw-Hill.

Rousso, H. (1988). Daughters with disabilities: Defective women or minority women? In A. Fine & A. Asch (Eds.), *Women with disabilities* (pp. 139–172). Philadelphia: Temple University Press.

Rubin, S., & Quinn-Curran, N. (1983). Lost, then found: Parents' journey through the community service maze. In M. Seligman (Ed.), *The family with a handicapped child: Understanding and treatment* (pp. 63–94). Orlando, FL: Grune & Stratton.

Rutter, M. (1979). Protective factors in children's responses to stress and disadvantage. In M. W. Kent & J. E. Rolf (Eds.), *Primary prevention of psychopathology: Social competence in children* (Vol. 3, pp. 49–74). Hanover, NH: University Press of New England.

Sabbeth, B. F., & Leventhal, J. M. (1984). Marital adjustment to chronic childhood illness: A critique of the literature. *Pediatrics, 73,* 762–768.

Salisbury, C. L., Gallucci, C., Palumbaro, M. M., & Peck, C. A. (1995). Strategies that promote social relations among elementary students with and without severe disabilities in inclusive schools. *Exceptional Children, 62,* 125–137.

Sandler, A. L. (1976). The effects of patient's physical attractiveness on therapist's clinical judgement. *Dissertation Abstract International, 36,* 3624.

Schilling, R. F., Gilchrist, L. D., & Schinke, S. P. (1984). Coping and social support in families of developmentally disabled children. *Family Relations, 33,* 47–54.

Schloss, P., Alper, S., & Jayne, D. (1993). Self-determination for persons with disabilities: Choice, risk and dignity. *Exceptional Children, 60*(3), 215–225.

Schnorr, R. F. (1993). "Peter? He comes and goes. . . ": First graders' perspective on a part-time mainstream student. In M. Nagler (Ed.), *Perspectives on disability* (pp. 423–434). Palo Alto, CA: Health Markets Research.

Schopler, E., & Mesibov, G. B. (1984). *The effects of autism on the family.* New York: Plenum.

Schorr-Ribera, H. K. (1987). *Ethnicity and culture as relevant rehabilitation factors in families with children with disabilities.* Unpublished manuscript, University of Pittsburgh.

Schulz, J. B. (1987). *Parents and professionals in special education.* Boston: Allyn & Bacon.

Schunk, D. H. (1985). Participation in goal setting: Effects on self efficacy and skills of learning disabled children. *Journal of Special Education, 19,* 307–316.

Schwab, L. O. (1989). Strengths of families having a member with a disability. *Journal of the Multihandicapped Person, 2,* 105–117.

Schwier, K. (1994). *Couples with intellectual disabilities talk about living and loving.* Rockville, MD: Woodbine House.

Seale, C. (1996). Living alone towards the end of life. *Aging and Society, 16,* 75–91.

Seligman, M. (1979). *Strategies for helping parents of exceptional children: A guide for teachers.* New York: Free Press.

Seligman, M. (1991). Grandparents of disabled grandchildren: Hopes, fears, and adaptation. *Families in Society, 72,* 147–152.

Seligman, M. (1993). Group work with parents of children with disabilities. *Journal for Specialists in Group Work, 18,* 115–126.

Seligman, M. (1995). Confessions of a professional/father. In D. Meyer (Ed.), *Uncommon fathers: Reflections on raising a child with a disability* (pp. 169–183). Bethesda, MD: Woodbine House.

Seligman, M. (1996). Siblings of children with autism: Forgotten children. *Contemporary Psychology, 48,* 800.

Seligman, M., & Darling, R. B. (1989). *Ordinary families, special children: A systems approach to childhood disability.* New York: Guilford Press.

Seligman, M., & Darling, R. B. (1997). *Ordinary families, special children: A systems approach to childhood disability.* New York: Guilford.

Seligman, M., & Marshak, L. M. (1990). *Group psychotherapy: Interventions with special populations.* Boston: Allyn & Bacon.

Seligman, M., & Meyerson, R. (1982). Group approaches for parents of handicapped children. In M. Seligman (Ed.), *Group psychotherapy and counseling with special populations* (pp. 99–116). Baltimore: University Park Press.

Seligman, M., & Seligman, P. A. (1980, October). The professional's dilemma: Learning to work with parents. *Exceptional Parent, 10,* 511–513.

Seligman, M. E. (1975). *Helplessness: On depression, development and death.* San Francisco: Freeman.

Seltzer, G. B. (1993). Psychological adjustment in midlife for persons with mental retardation. In E. Sutton, A. Factor, B. Hawkins, T. Heller, & G. Seltzer (Eds.), *Older adults with developmental disabilities: Optimizing choice and change* (pp. 157–184). Baltimore: Paul H. Brookes.

Seltzer, G. B., Begun, A., Seltzer, M. M., & Krauss, M. W. (1991, July). Adults with mental retardation and their aging mothers: Impact of siblings. *Family Relations, 40,* 310–317.

Seltzer, M. M., & Krauss, M. W. (1994). Aging parents with coresident adult children: The impact of lifelong caring. In M. Seltzer, M. Krauss, & M. Janicki (Eds.), *Life course perspectives in adulthood and old age* (pp. 3–18). Washington, DC: American Association on Mental Retardation.

Seltzer, M. M., & Seltzer, G. B. (1985). The elderly mentally retarded: A group in need of service. *Journal of Gerontological Social Work, 8,* 99–119.

Shapiro, D. E., & Koocher, G. P. (1996). Goals and practical considerations in outpatient medical crisis intervention. *Professional Psychology: Research and Practice, 27,* 109–120.

Shontz, F. C. (1977). Six principles relating disability and psychological adjustment. *Rehabilitation Psychology, 24*(4), 207–210.

Siegel, B. (1996). *The world of the autistic child.* New York: Oxford.

Siegel, B., & Silverstein, S. (1994). *What about me? Growing up with a developmentally disabled sibling.* New York: Plenum.

Siller, J. (1976). Attitude towards disability. In H. Rusalem & D. Malikin (Eds.), *Contemporary vocational rehabilitation* (pp. 67–68). New York: Grune & Stratton.

Silver, L. B. (1984). *The misunderstood child: A guide for parents of learning disabled children.* Mount Vernon, NY: Consumers Union.

Simon, B. L. (1988). Never-married old women and disability: A majority experience. In M. Fine & A. Asch (Eds.), *Women with disabilities: Essays in psychology, culture, and politics* (pp. 215–225). Philadelphia: Temple University Press.

Simpson, R. L. (1990). *Conferencing parents of exceptional children.* Austin, TX: Pro-Ed.

Simpson, R. L. (1996). *Working with parents and families of exceptional children and youth* (2nd ed.). Austin, TX: Pro-Ed.

Singer, G., & Powers, L. E. (1993). *Families, disability, and empowerment: Active coping skills and strategies for family interventions.* Baltimore: Brooks.

Sitlington, P. L., & Frank, A. R. (1990). Are adolescents with learning disabilities successfully crossing the bridge into adult life? *Learning Disability Quarterly, 13,* 97–111.

Sloman, M. D., Springer, S., & Vachon, M. (1993). Disordered communication and grieving in deaf members' families. *Family Process, 32,* 171–181.

Smith, D., Seibert, C., Jackson, F., & Snell, J. (1992). Pet ownership by elderly people: Two new issues. *International Journal of Aging and Human Development, 34*(3), 175–184.

Smith, D. G. (1991). *Parent's guide to raising kids in a changing world.* New York: Prentice Hall.

Smith G., Fullmer, E., & Tobin, S. (1994). Living outside the system: An exploration of older families who do not use day programs. In M. Seltzer, M. Krauss, & M. Janicki (Eds.), *Life course perspectives in adulthood and old age* (pp. 19–37). Washington, DC: American Association on Mental Retardation.

Smith, G. C., & Tobin, S. S. (1989). Permanency planning among older parents of adults with lifelong disabilities. *Journal of Gerontological Social Work, 14,* 35–59.

Smith, K. (1981). The influence of the male sex role on discussion groups for fathers of exceptional children. *Michigan Personnel and Guidance Journal, 12,* 11–17.

Smith, S. L. (1991). *Succeeding against the odds: How the learning disabled can realize their promise.* New York: Putnam.

Smull, M. W. (1995). Moving from supported living to a supported life. *Impact, 8,* 14.

Solnit, A. J., & Stark, M. H. (1961). Mourning and the birth of a defective child. *Psychoanalytic Study of the Child, 16,* 523–537.

Sonnenschein, P. (1981). Parents and professionals: An uneasy relationship. *Teaching Exceptional Children, 14*(2), 62–65.

Sourkes, B. M. (1982). *The deepening shade.* Pittsburgh, PA: University of Pittsburgh Press.

Sourkes, B. M. (1987). Siblings of a child with a life-threatening illness. *Journal of Children in Contemporary Society, 19,* 159–184.

Sparrow, M. (1996, August). The wild dream team. *Enable Pennsylvanians Magazine,* pp. 14–15.

Spekman, N. J., Goldberg, R. J., & Herman, K. L. (1993). An exploration of risk and resilience in the lives of individuals with learning disabilities. *Learning Disabilities Research and Practice, 8* (1), 11–18.

Spruill, L. (1996, Summer). Don't tell the cripples about sex. *Change Exchange, 1* (4), 3.

Stein, R. E., & Jessop, D. J. (1984). General issues in the care of children with chronic physical conditions. *Pediatric Clinics of North America, 31,* 189–198.

Stensman, R. (1985). Severely mobility-disabled people assess the quality of their lives. *Scandinavian Journal of Rehabilitation Medicine, 17,* 87–99.

Stephens, T., & Brown, B. (1980). Measures of regular classroom teachers' attitudes toward handicapped children. *Exceptional Children, 46,* 292–294.

Stewart, T. D. (1977–1978). Coping behavior and the moratorium following spinal cord injury. *Paraplegia, 15,* 338–342.

Stoneman, Z., & Berman, P. W. (1993). *The effects of mental retardation, disability, and illness on sibling relationships.* Baltimore: Paul H. Brookes.

Strax, T. E. (1991). Psychological issues faced by adolescents and young adults with disabilities. *Pediatric Annals, 20* (9), 507–511.

Strong, M. (1988). *Mainstay.* Boston: Little, Brown.

Strully, J., & Strully, C. (1992). The struggle toward inclusion and the fulfillment of friendship. In J. Nisbet (Ed.), *Natural supports in school, at work and in the community for people with severe disabilities* (pp. 165–177). Baltimore: Paul H. Brookes.

Suelzle, M., & Keenan, V. (1981). Changes in family support networks over the life cycle of mentally retarded persons. *American Journal of Mental Deficiency, 86,* 267–274.

Summers, J. A. (Ed.). (1986). The right to grow up. Baltimore: Brooks.

Sutton, E., Sterns, H., & Park, L. (1993). Realities of retirement and pre-retirement planning. In E. Sutton, A. Factor, B. Hawkins, T. Heller, & G. Seltzer (Eds.), *Older adults with developmental disabilities: Optimizing choice and change* (pp. 95–106). Baltimore: Paul H. Brookes.

Szymanski, E. M. (1985). Rehabilitation counseling: A profession with a vision, an identity and a future. *Rehabilitation Counseling Bulletin, 29,* 2–5.

Szymanski, E. M. (1994). Transition: Life-span and life-space considerations for empowerment. *Exceptional Children, 60,* 402–410.

Szymanski, E. M., Hanley-Maxwell, C., & Asselin, S. B. (1992). Systems interface: Vocational rehabilitation, special education and vocation. In F. R. Rusch, L. DeStefano, J. Chadsey-Rusch, L. A. Phelps, & E. M. Szymanski (Eds.), *Transition from school to adult life: Models, linkages and policy* (pp. 153–168). Sycamore, IL: Sycamore.

Szymanski, E. M., Turner, K. D., & Hershenson, D. (1992). Career development of people with disabilities: Theoretical perspectives. In F. R. Rusch, L. DeStefano, J. Chadsey-Rusch, L. A. Phelps, & E. M. Szymanski (Eds.). *Transition from school to adult life: Models, linkages, and policy* (pp. 391–406). Sycamore, IL: Sycamore.

Szymanski, L. S., & Jansen, P. E. (1980). Assessment of sexuality and sexual vulnerability of retarded persons. In L. S. Szymanski & P. E. Tanguay (Eds.), *Emotional disorders of mentally retarded persons: Assessment, treatment and consultation* (pp. 173–194). Baltimore: University Park Press.

Tallman, I. (1965). Spousal role differentiation and the socialization of severely retarded children. *Journal of Marriage and the Family, 27,* 37–42.

Tartar, S. B. (1987). *Traumatic head injury: Parental stress, coping style and emotional adjustment.* Unpublished doctoral dissertation, University of Pittsburgh.

Telford, C. W., & Sawrey, J. M. (1977). *The exceptional individual* (3rd ed.). Englewood Cliffs, NJ: Prentice Hall.

Tennstedt, S., Harrow, B., & Crawford, S. (1996). Informal care vs. formal services: Changes in patterns of care over time. *Journal of Aging and Social Policy, 17*(3/4), 71–91.

Tharinger, D., Horton, C. B., & Millea, S. (1993). Sexual abuse and exploitation of children and adults with mental retardation and other handicaps. In M. Nagler (Ed.), *Perspectives on disability* (pp. 235–245). Palo Alto, CA: Health Market Research.

Tharp, R. (1989). Psychocultural variables and constants: Effects on teaching and learning in schools. *American Psychologist, 44,* 349–359.

Thompson, R. J., & Gustafson, K. E. (1996). *Adaptation to chronic childhood illness.* Washington, DC: American Psychological Association.

Thorin, E. J., & Irvin, L. (1992). Family stress associated with transition to adulthood of young people with severe disabilities. *Journal of the Association of Severe Handicaps, 17* (1), 31–39.

Thurman, E. (1986). Maintaining dignity in later years. In J. A. Summers (Ed.), *The right to grow up* (pp. 91–115). Baltimore: Paul H. Brookes.

Tibbits, C. (1979). Can we invalidate negative stereotypes of aging? *The Gerontologist, 19,* 10–20.

Tingey, C. (1988). Cutting the umbilical cord: Parental perspectives. In S. M. Pueschel (Ed.), *The young person with Down syndrome* (pp. 5–22). Baltimore: Paul H. Brookes.

Travis, C. (1976). *Chronic illness in children: Its impact on child and family*. Stanford, CA: Stanford University Press.

Turnbull, A. P., Patterson, J. M., Behr, S. K., Murphy, D. L., Marquis, J. G., & Blue-Banning, M. J. (1993). *Cognitive coping, families, and disability*. Baltimore: Paul H. Brookes.

Turnbull, A. P., Summers, J. A., & Brotherson, M. J. (1986). Family life cycle: Theoretical and empirical implications and future directions for families with mentally retarded members. In J. L. Gallagher & D. M. Vietze (Eds.), *Families of handicapped persons* (pp. 45–65). Baltimore: Brooks.

Turnbull, A. P., & Turnbull, H. R. (1985). Developing independence. *Journal of Adolescent Health Care, 6*, 108–119.

Turnbull, A. P., & Turnbull, H. R. (1988). Toward great expectations for vocational opportunities: Family-professional partnerships. *Mental Retardation, 28*, 337–342.

Turnbull, A. P., & Turnbull, H. R. (1990). *Families, professionals, and exceptionality*. (2nd ed.) Columbus, OH: Merrill.

Turnbull, A. P., & Turnbull, H. R. III, (1993). Participatory research on cognitive coping: From concepts to research planning. In A. P. Turnbull, J. M. Patterson, S. K. Behr, D. L. Murphy, J. M. Marquis, & M. J. Blue-Banning (Eds.), *Cognitive coping, families, & disability* (pp. 1–14). Baltimore: Brooks.

Turnbull, H. R. (1993). *Free appropriate public education: The law and children with disabilities* (4th ed.). Denver, CO: Love.

Turnbull, H. R., Turnbull, A. P., Bronicki, G., Summers, J., & Roedger-Gordon, C. (1989). *Disability and the family: A guide to decisions for adulthood*. Baltimore: Paul H. Brookes.

Questions and answers about the IDEA. (1993, September). *NICHCY News Digest, 3*, 1–15.

Upshur, C. C. (1991). Families and the community service maze. In M. Seligman (Ed.), *The family with a handicapped child* (2nd ed., pp. 91–118). Boston: Allyn & Bacon.

U.S. Commission on Civil Rights. (1983). *Accommodating the spectrum of individualized disabilities*. Washington, DC: Author.

U.S. Department of Education. (1993). *Fifteenth annual report to congress on the implementation of the Individuals With Disabilities Education Act*. Washington, DC: Author.

U.S. Department of Education. (1996). *To assure the free appropriate public education of all children with disabilities* (18th annual report to Congress on the implementation of the Individuals With Disabilities Education Act). Washington, DC: Author.

Vadasy, P. F. (1986). Single mothers: A social phenomenon and population in need. In R. R. Fewell & P. F. Vadasy (Eds.), *Families of handicapped children* (pp. 221–249). Austin, TX: Pro-Ed.

Vadasy, P. F., Fewell, R. R., Greenberg, M. T., Desmond, N. L., & Meyer, D. J. (1986). Follow-up evaluation of the effects of involvement in the fathers program. *Topics in Early Childhood Education, 6*, 16–31.

Van der Klift, E., & Kunc, N. (1994). Beyond benevolence: Friendship and the politics of help. In J. S. Thousand, R. A. Villa, & A. I. Nevin (Eds.), *Creativity and collaborative learning: A practical guide to empowering students and teachers* (pp. 391–401). Baltimore: Paul H. Brookes.

Varekamp, M. A., Suurmeijer, P., Rosendaal, F. R., DiJck, H., Uriends, A., & Briet, E. (1990). Family burden in families with a hemophilic child. *Family Systems Medicine, 8,* 291–301.

Varley, C. K. (1984). Schizophrenia form psychoses in mentally retarded girls following sexual assault. *American Journal of Psychiatry, 141,* 593–595.

Vash, C. L. (1981). *The psychology of disability.* New York: Springer.

Vash, C. L. (1992). The freedom-protection continuum: A personal perspective. *Journal of Applied Rehabilitation Counseling, 23*(4), 59–61.

Vaughn, S., Elbaum, B. E., & Schumm, J. S. (1996). The effects of inclusion on the social functioning of students with learning disabilities. *Journal of Learning Disabilities, 29,* 598–608.

Venter, M. (1980). *Chronic childhood illness and familial coping.* Unpublished doctoral dissertation, University of Minnesota.

Vermeij, G. (1997). *Privileged hands: A scientific life.* New York: W. H. Freeman.

Vincent, L. J., & Salisbury, C. L. (1988). Changing economic and social influences on family involvement. *Topics in Early Childhood Special Education, 12,* 48–59.

Visher, E., & Visher, J. (1988). *Old loyalties new ties: Therapeutic strategies with step families.* New York: Brunner/Mazel.

Von Bertalanffy, L. (1968). *General systems theory.* New York: Braziller.

Wagner, M. (1989). *The transition experiences of youth with disabilities: A report from the national longitudinal transition study.* Menlo Park, CA: SRI International.

Wagner, M. (1992). *Being female—A secondary disability? Gender differences in the transition experiences of young people with disabilities.* Menlo Park, CA: SRI International.

Walker, A., Walker, A., & Ryan, T. (1996). Older persons with learning difficulties leaving institutional care—A case of double jeopardy. *Aging and Society, 16,* 125–150.

Wallinga, C., Paquio, L., & Skeen, P. (1987). When a brother or sister is ill. *Psychology Today, 42,* 43.

Walsh, F. (1989). The family in later life. In B. Carter & M. McGoldrick (Eds.), *The changing family life cycle* (2nd ed., pp. 311–332). Needham Heights, MA: Allyn & Bacon.

Waxman, B. F. (1993, May/June). The testimony of Barbara Faye Waxman. *Disability Rag ReSource,* pp. 6–7.

Wehmeyer, M. L. (1992). Self-determination and the education of students with mental retardation. *Education and Training in Mental Retardation, 27,* 302–314.

Weinrach, S. G., & Thomas, K. R. (1996). The counseling profession's commitment to diversity-sensitive counseling: A critical reassessment. *Journal of Counseling and Development, 74,* 72–477.

Weisbren, S. E. (1980). Parents' reactions after the birth of a developmentally disabled child. *American Journal of Mental Deficiency, 84,* 345–351.

Weiss, G., & Hechtman, L. T. (1993). *Hyperactive children grown up: ADHD in children, adolescents and adults.* New York: Guilford.

Werner, E. E. (1984, November). Resilient children. *Young Children, 40,* 68–72.

Werner, E. E. (1986). The concept of risk from a developmental perspective. *Advances in Special Education, 5,* 1–23.

Werner, E. E., & Smith, R. S. (1982). *Vulnerable but not invincible: A longitudinal study of resilient children and youth.* New York: McGraw-Hill.

Werner, E. E., & Smith, R. S. (1992). *Overcoming the odds: High risk children from birth to adulthood.* New York: Cornell.

Werner-Beland, J. A. (1980). *Grief responses to long-term illness and disability.* Reston, VA: Reston.

White, S., & Tharp, R. G. (1988, April). *Questioning and wait time: A cross cultural analysis.* Paper presented at the annual meeting of the American Education Research Association, New Orleans.

Whitman, B. Y., & Accardo, P. J. (Eds.). (1990). *When a parent is mentally retarded.* Baltimore: Paul H. Brookes.

Wikler, L. (1981). Chronic stresses of families of mentally retarded children. *Family Relations, 30,* 281–288.

Wikler, L., Wasow, M., & Hatfield, E. (1981). Chronic sorrow revisited: Parents vs. professional depiction of the adjustment of parents of mentally retarded children. *American Journal of Orthopsychiatry, 51,* 63–70.

Will, M. (1984). *OSERS programming for the transition of youth with disabilities: Bridges from school to working life.* Washington, DC: U.S. Department of Education, Office of Special Education and Rehabilitative Services.

Woodwill, G., Renwick, R. M., Brown, I., & Phahael, D. (1994). Being, belonging, becoming: An approach to the quality of life of persons with developmental disabilities. In D. Goode (Ed.), *Quality of life for persons with disabilities: International perspectives and issues* (pp. 57–74). Cambridge, MA: Brookline Books.

Wortis, H. Z., & Margolies, J. A. (1955). Parents of children of cerebral palsy. *Medical Social Work, 4,* 110–120.

Wright, B. A. (1983). *Physical disability: A psychosocial approach.* New York: Harper & Row.

Yalom, I. D. (1975). *The theory and practice of group psychotherapy* (2nd ed.). New York: Basic Books.

Yalom, I. D. (1985). *The theory and practice of group psychotherapy* (3rd ed.). New York: Basic Books.

Yalom, I. D. (1995). *The theory and practice of group psychotherapy* (4th ed.). New York: Basic Books.

Zetlin, A. (1986). Mentally retarded adults and their siblings. *American Journal on Mental Retardation, 91,* 217–225.

Zetlin, A. G., & Turner, J. L. (1985). Transition from adolescence to adulthood perspectives of mentally retarded individuals and their families. *American Journal of Mental Deficiency, 89* (6), 570–579.

Zinn, M. B., & Eitzen, D. S. (1993). *Diversity in families.* New York: HarperCollins.

Zucman, E. (1982). *Childhood disability in the family.* World Rehabilitation Fund.

Index

Please remember that this is a library book,
and that it belongs only temporarily to each
person who uses it. Be considerate. Do
not write in this, or any, library book.